DAD'S WAR PHOTOS

Adventures in the South Pacific

Other Titles Published by Cypress Cove Publishing

Down-Home Cajun Cooking Favorites

Rice Cooker Meals: Fast Home Cooking for Busy People

Slow Cooker Meals: Easy Home Cooking for Busy People

Cajun Country Fun Coloring and Activity Book

A House for Eliza: The Real Story of the Cajuns

From Cradle to Grave: Journey of the Louisiana Orphan Train Riders

Praise for *Dad's War Photos*

You have done a wonderful job with the photos and it is a fine tribute to your father's photographic archive. You are to be commended for the presentation of the images and captioning them so well and also for sharing it all with the wider world. I am sure the book will bring back many memories for those veterans who are still with us, but perhaps more importantly it will allow the younger generations, especially those whose forefathers served in the Pacific, to see and understand more about the war that encompassed the world. Perhaps it will help many to appreciate a little more the sacrifices that were made and the forfeiture of youth given up by so many to preserve the Freedom we have today .... and the sacrifices still being made.

Ray Bowden
Dorset, England
www.usaaf-noseart.co.uk

I enjoyed reading the book. The photographs interspersed with notes from the official history help to describe the story of your father's unit.

Peter Dunn
Brisbane, Australia
Webmaster, "Australia @ War"
www.ozatwar.com

Author and Publisher Neal Bertrand brings the battles and the people to life in his World War II book, *Dad's War Photos: Adventures in the South Pacific*. Bertrand uses "Official Military Records" and his father's personal photographs to tell the story of World War II in the South Pacific. Descriptions of the battles and numerous photographs of the planes, natives, and countryside involve the reader in the war. In the first part of the book, Bertrand includes information from a monthly war column titled, "Elsewhere in the War." The column describes daily the locations of all the battles throughout the world, and gives the reader a chance to experience the immense size, destruction, and loss of life.

Constance Monies Gremillion, whose father was a Major in the South Pacific
Lafayette, LA
Author of *A House for Eliza*
www.AHouseForEliza.com

WWII for the United States lasted from December 7, 1941, until August 15, 1945. There have been numerous stories written about what happened during the war. Most of these are a textual account from a narrow perspective. These usually have a few photos, but I've never seen a book that covers so much of the war in a pictorial form.

Beginning with enlistment in early 1943, this book presents a month-by-month account in pictorial form of what it was like to serve in an engineering battalion in support of the fighting troops in the South Pacific. You will see photos from Australia, New Guinea, Biak, and the Philippines. The author has also included official accounts of the activities directly from the battalion history records.

I highly recommend this book to anyone interested in seeing WWII from a different view.

Hughes Glantzberg
President of the 461st Bombardment Group (H) Association, for which
his father was the Commanding Officer during WWII
www.461st.org

Neal Bertrand has done a marvelous job of telling the story of his dad's war experiences in *Dad's War Photos: Adventures in the South Pacific*.

As someone who has produced several family histories, I can absolutely appreciate the amount of work that went into this. It is obviously a labor of love and a fitting tribute to Charles Bertrand.

I thoroughly enjoyed this book! Not only has Neal included some wonderful family history, complete with photos of medals, maps, and military paperwork, he has done a great job of presenting and captioning the photos and organizing the entire effort so any reader can get a real taste of where his dad went and what he saw. I especially enjoyed the World War II nose art photos.

What a wonderful piece of history this is for not only the Bertrand family, but for others who are interested in this period of history.

Sheila Fredrickson
Fort Worth, TX
www.LookGreatInPrint.com

Many war veterans do not talk about their war experiences. Curtis Bertrand did just the opposite. Bertrand's war story recounts his journey from Mallet, Louisiana, to the exotic South Pacific in images of life that he saw as part of the 863rd Engineering Aviation Battalion from 1943 to 1945. Bertrand's story is still being told, but this time it is told in a pictorial history book compiled by his son.

The photographs, documented by his unit's Official Military Record, provide a compelling story of a young man seeing strange people, exotic lands, death, weapons of war, and the camaraderie of American soldiers. The photographs of New Guinea natives evoke images in National Geographic; pictures of Bilibid POW camp and natives plowing rice in the Philippine Islands are reminiscent of Life magazine.

This book is a testimony to a soldier who will not be forgotten, for his wartime pictures are remembered in this book.

Alma Brunson Reed
Eunice, LA
Author of *Images of America: Eunice; Legendary Locals of Eunice,* and *A Pictorial Directory of Acadia Parish Patriots*

This is not just a book containing unique, never seen before photos, it's much more than that. It is a journey of a generation as seen through the eyes of a young American during the Pacific War. They say a picture speaks a thousand words, and in this book it does more than that. Become immersed in the journey as you travel through time, seeing glimpses of what it must have been like to be a raw recruit thrown into remote jungles of New Guinea. Witness from a photographer's eye the living conditions, the humor, and tragedy of war.

See photos of Manila and the devastation caused by its liberation from Japanese forces and you can understand why we all owe so much to that generation.

This is a story passed from father to son and well worth the read.

Capt. Matthew Laird Acred, ATPL Pilot & Aviation Historian
Manila, Philippines and Brisbane, Australia
www.asisbiz.com

I don't know that your father's intent was to be a photojournalist but, in essence, his photos, remembrances, etc. has made him that, a photojournalist. You've done him proud with this book, him and all of the other 'grunts' who saw and experienced WWII from the trenches and airfields of that horrible war. Well done, my friend.

Al Orgeron
Airplane Aficionado and WWII Airplane 'Buff'
Opelousas, LA and Marysville, MO

This is a fascinating first-person view of an enlisted man's perspective of his years of service during World War II in the South Pacific. Curtis Bertrand, a 23-year-old farm boy from south Louisiana, documented his adventure to the other side of the world not with words, but with photographs. From his enlistment and boot camp in 1943 through the liberation and clean-up of Manila to his arrival at home in December 1945, you witness his part of the war through his eyes and camera lens. Assembled chronologically, Bertrand's photographs, accompanied by the official Battalion Military Record of the 863rd Engineer Aviation Battalion, offer a near day-to-day view of his life during wartime. This is a part of the war few have documented so thoroughly from such a unique perspective.

Fred Leger
A life-long student of WWII history
Baton Rouge, LA

I keep getting distracted while trying to write something about this book because every page is a new discovery. Unearthing the reality of a man's personal journey through the horror of war, side by side with the larger macro-cosmic view of Bertrand's "Elsewhere in the War" segments has the teacher in me excited over and over again. So many pictures of humanity and soul: a woman walking on a tightrope, taking a moment of respite from the chaos with bomb damage clearly viewed behind her. A photo of a group of men with the caption: After working non-stop for months cleaning up debris and rebuilding Manila, permission was given to start their own football team for recreation. From a 50-kilogram bomb believed to be a dud, to 14-foot pythons, and the POW camp Old Bilibid Prison, from where 800 military and 500 American and Allied civilian prisoners were liberated... this book is filled with teachable moments; stories of horror and heroism; discussions; lessons... a pictorial treasure trove of ideas for introspection, analysis and consideration of the human condition. The presentation of facts and detail is direct and to the point. The personality in the voice of Bertrand's father gives breath and heartbeat to the journey. The lessons about human nature that can be extracted here are endless – from the tiny details that bring us to life, to mankind's world-defining orchestration of global conflict. Like so many pilots who soared into the fire with their muses singing at their side – The Butcher's Daughter, Scarlet Night, Empty Saddle, Pop's Blue Ribbon – I am inspired to do bold things with this amazing piece of educational artillery. I want to bring this book to school tomorrow and use it all year long.

Matt Harman
Teacher, Principal
Lafayette, LA

DAD'S WAR PHOTOS

Adventures in the South Pacific

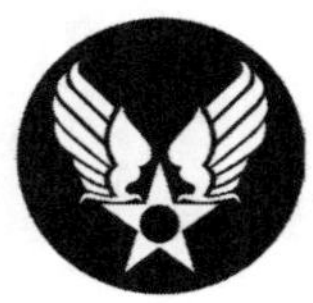

BY NEAL BERTRAND

FOREWORD BY JAMES J. BOLLICH

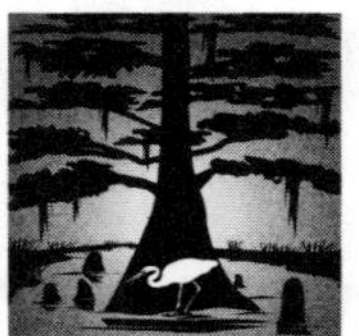

Cypress Cove Publishing

LAFAYETTE, LOUISIANA

Publisher's Cataloging-In-Publication Data
(Prepared by The Donohue Group, Inc.)

Bertrand, Neal.
Dad's war photos : adventures in the South Pacific / by Neal Bertrand ; foreword by James J. Bollich.

pages : illustrations, maps ; cm

Issued also as an ebook.
ISBN: 978-1-936707-24-9 (softcover)
ISBN: 978-1-936707-25-6 (hardcover)

1. Bertrand, Curtis, 1920-2000--Pictorial works. 2. World War, 1939-1945--Oceania--Pictorial works. 3. World War, 1939-1945--Oceania--Personal narratives. 4. United States. Army--Military life--History--20th century--Pictorial works. 5. Oceania--History--20th century--Pictorial works.
I. Bollich, James. II. Title.

D767.9 .B47 2015
940.54/26 2013912203

For information, contact Neal Bertrand at
neal@CypressCovePublishing.com

Visit our website at www.DadsWarPhotos.com

Library of Congress Control Number: 2013912203

Cypress Cove Publishing
P.O. Box 91195
Lafayette, LA 70509-1195
USA

Phone (888) 606-3257

EDITORS Sevie Zeller and Gail M. Kearns, To Press and Beyond
BOOK DESIGN AND PRODUCTION Elizabeth Bell, eBell Design and Jeremy Bertrand
MAP PRODUCTION Jiban Dahal

To the memory of my father, Charles Curtis Bertrand.
He is sorely missed by many, especially me. He would be proud of this book and how his war pictures are so prominently displayed.

Contents

FOREWORD

I am a veteran of World War II, and in my conversations with other veterans of that same period, I find that, much to the great disappointment of their families, many veterans have never recorded their military experiences either verbally or in writing. In many cases, it will never happen because the veteran is now deceased. It is unfortunate because every veteran has a story to tell, and they are all very different and deserving to be told.

In the case of Charles Curtis Bertrand, all was not lost after his passing because he had the opportunity to record his entire time in the service by way of hundreds of photographs taken with a small Kodak camera that he had in his possession. With these photographs and the official military record of the 863rd Engineer Aviation Battalion to which he was assigned, his son, Neal Bertrand, was able to accurately resurrect the story of his father's military career.

When Japan attacked Pearl Harbor on December 7, 1941, I was already in the Philippines, having arrived there only 18 days before with the 16th Bomb Squadron of the 27th Bomb Group. We had just completed maneuvers in Louisiana where we trained with dive-bombers when we received orders to pack up for overseas duty. Little did we know that we would be at war so soon after our arrival.

Just like Charles C. Bertrand, I also had a camera and took many pictures during the fighting. Unfortunately, mine were never developed and still lay buried in the jungles of Bataan where I hid them when we received word that we were being surrendered by our general. I was offered a chance to go look for them when the war ended and I was back in Manila on my way home. However, I had been in a prisoner-of-war camp for three and a half years and at the time going back to Bataan did not interest me at all.

Many years later, I wished that I had gone back looking for them. They would have gone well with a book that I wrote describing my experiences as a prisoner of the Japanese (instead of drawings that I eventually used).

I have read many books about the war in the Pacific during World War II, most being about the actions of the marines, infantry, or fighter pilots. This book is different because it describes in detail the actions of the engineers whose work was as vital as all the others in the final defeat of our enemy.

Neal Bertrand has put together a book about an important time in history. It is a book that would make his father feel proud of his efforts should he still be alive to see the results.

James J. Bollich
Bataan Death March Survivor
Author, *The Bataan Death March, A Soldier's Story*

AUTHOR'S NOTE

A comment on the "Official Military Record Entry," which appears throughout this book.

I was fortunate to obtain the official Military Record of my father's battalion. One could think of this document as a daily diary. The reader will observe throughout this book sections titled Official Military Record Entry, as well as Work Summary, and Historical Reports. The daily work progress and events were logged in by an officer. At the end of the month a summary of the work accomplished was noted and handed over to superior officers for evaluation and analysis, then kept for history's sake. I kept the 1940s wartime language of this diary record as I found it, including their use of the nicknames "Japs" and "Nips." These names were common then, but are considered to be derogatory now.

I have traced my father's steps through the South Pacific on a month-by-month basis. At the beginning of each month I included a section titled "Elsewhere in the War," so the reader will see at a glance the wartime battles that took place in various parts of the world during the respective months. Many of these events may be unfamiliar to some readers. An Internet search of these battles and skirmishes on Google or YouTube would be educational for those interested in learning more.

INTRODUCTION

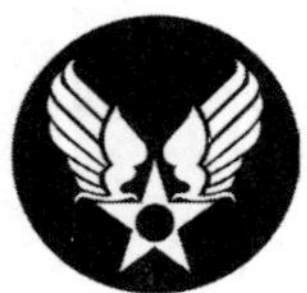

"Daddy, can I look at your war pictures?" I often asked this question as a young boy growing up because I liked to look at the old photos he took in World War II. They were unique images of people and places he witnessed firsthand.

We sat at the kitchen table and went through his photo albums. He reminisced about the various places where he had been stationed while I hung on to his every word. But some of those details did not stick in my mind because as a young boy I had no knowledge of world geography, and I did not know where New Guinea, Biak, and the Philippine Islands were.

He took many pictures of war planes with their often erotic nose art – bombers, fighter planes, cargo planes, gliders, and more. He photographed the native people in every country he was in. You will see the daily lives of New Guinea natives who stopped what they were doing to let him take their pictures. He was present when the natives on Biak had a huge party to celebrate their queen's birthday with a parade, dancing, and an outrigger canoe race.

Looking back, I regret not interviewing him and going over each photo, hearing what he had to say about each experience, and writing down some notes about it. I would love to have heard his account of approaching the Philippines, seeing our battleships blowing up enemy tanks on the beach, while the Japanese pilots were flying their planes into our ships. What was it like when the air raid sirens sounded and Japanese planes flew over their camp and dropped bombs? What was it like to photograph Bob Hope and experience his USO show? I did not hear any of these stories from him. I didn't know he experienced all of these adventures until I read the battalion's diary.

I'm thankful I remember most of the stories he told me. Some were hazy memories until I read the diary.

Come along! Be a virtual eyewitness to the experiences my country boy father had as he ventured away from his farm life and journeyed to the other side of the world, experiencing these adventures in the South Pacific.

CHAPTER 1

A Brief History of the Bertrand Family Ancestry

My family's farthest documented Bertrand relative came from Brittany, France, as a soldier in the French army and settled near Montreal, Canada, in the 1600s. Several decades later, Gilles Joseph Bertrand's farmlands and property were confiscated from them, their homes and barns were burned, and they were forcibly expelled – at gunpoint – to leave Canada. Why? They refused to change from their Roman Catholic religion and swear allegiance to the English monarch, King George II. That behavior on the part of government and military is now called ethnic cleansing.

Dad's ancestors arrived in south Louisiana as exiles around the 1760s. Some came from the Montreal area and others from an area of Nova Scotia, Canada, called Acadie, or Acadia. They were known as Acadians. Over time, the French pronunciation of Acadian was shortened to Cajun, and that today, many people of mixed French, Spanish, and German ancestry (among others, probably) identify as Cajun because they assimilated into the culture.

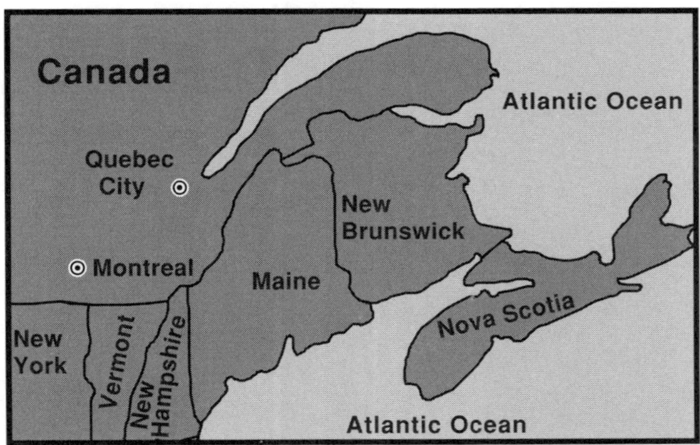

Our ancestors came from Nova Scotia and the Montreal, Canada area.

After arriving in St. Landry Parish, Louisiana, in the 1760s, Gilles Joseph's son, Amable Bertrand, joined the Opelousas Militia and was listed as a corporal in 1777. He fought in the Galvez Expedition when the militia marched to the Baton Rouge area and fought against British troops.

Since it can be proven we have a direct ancestral line to Amable fighting in the Galvez Expedition during the Revolutionary War, my father would have qualified for membership in the Sons of the American Revolution (SAR), as could I and my sons.

CHAPTER 2

Life Prior to World War II

Charles Curtis Bertrand was born on October 27, 1920, to Numa and Lenore Ledoux Bertrand. He was a country boy and grew up on a farm in the small community of Mallet, Louisiana. It is just north of U.S. Hwy 190, between Lawtell and Prairie Ronde, and between Opelousas and Eunice, located in St. Landry Parish. He spent 11 quality years with his father until he passed away in 1931.

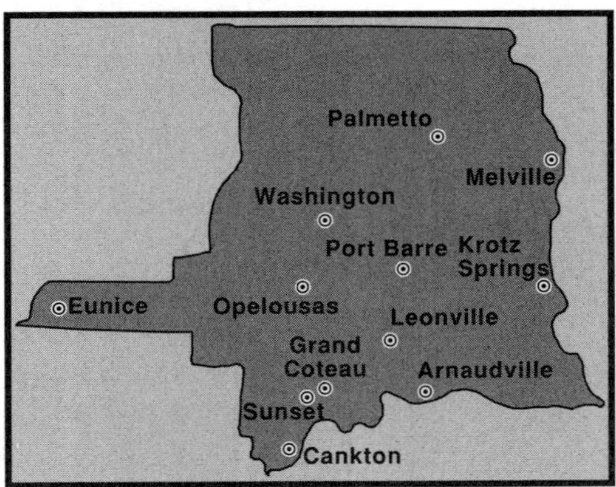

Map of St. Landry Parish, Louisiana.

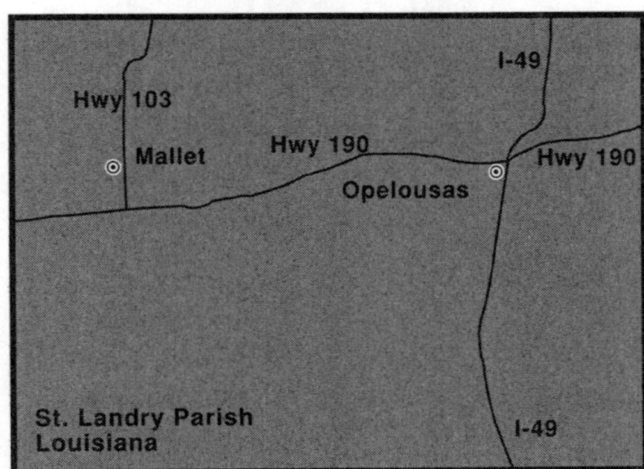

Dad lived in Mallet, six miles west of Opelousas.

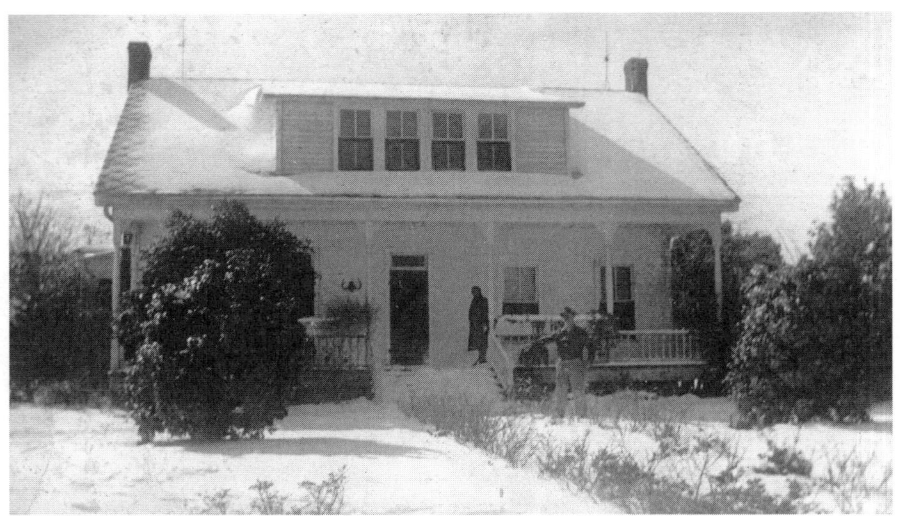

**A rare snowfall at the Numa Bertrand home in Mallet, LA.
The home was built around 1905.**

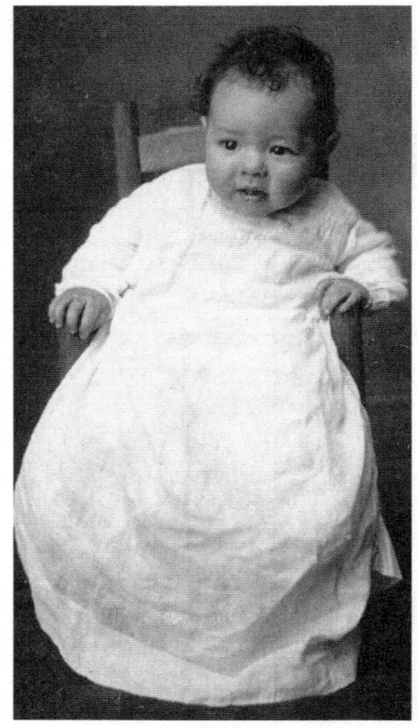

Curtis

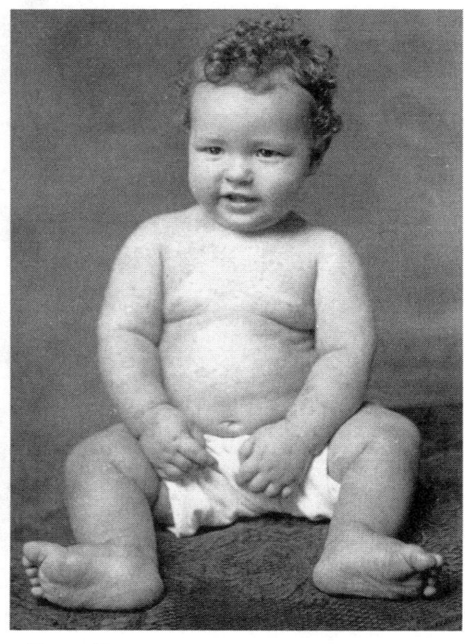

Curtis Bertrand at about one year of age.

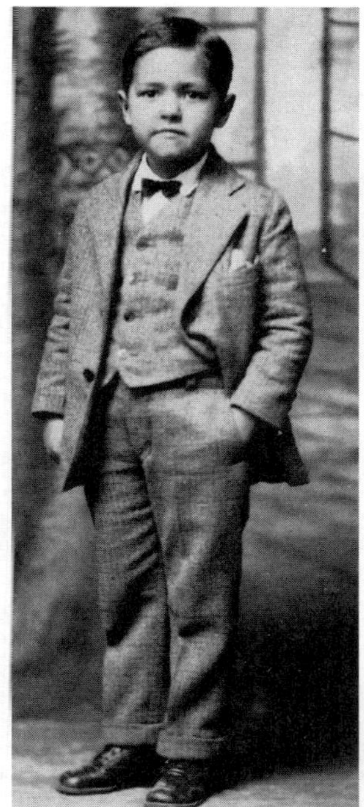

Curtis at about five years.

Dad first went to school in a one-room schoolhouse across the street from his home in the country. Later on he attended a Catholic school called the Academy of the Immaculate Conception in nearby Opelousas. After graduating high school he attended Louisiana State University in Baton Rouge for a while and was active in Army ROTC where he learned what was required to be a good soldier. After a few semesters he decided he preferred the farm life rather than textbooks, so he returned home.

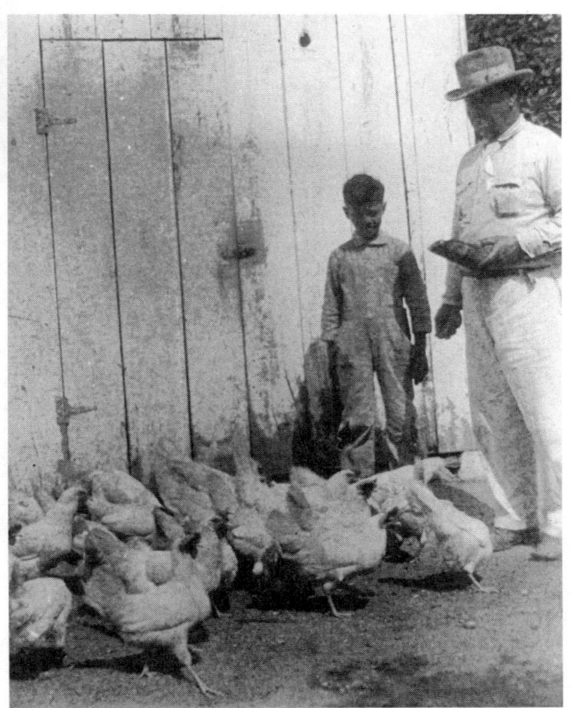

Curtis and his father feed chickens on the farm.

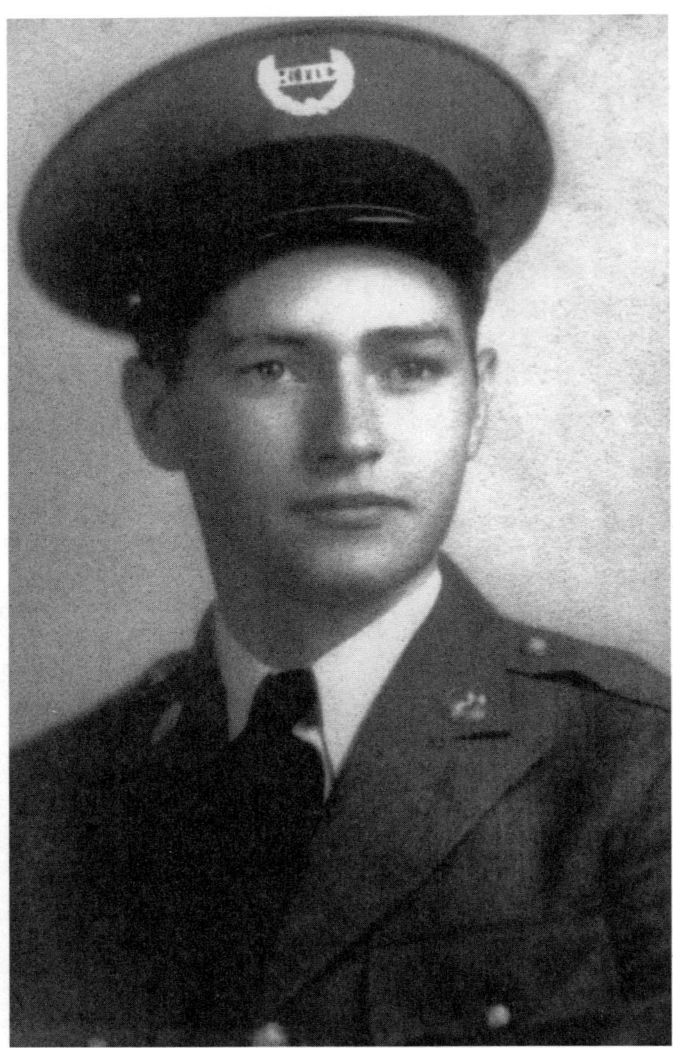

Dad's Army ROTC photo at Louisiana State University, circa 1938.

Chapter 3

Leaving Home

Dad stayed informed about the war in Europe and in the Pacific. He did not enlist but waited to be drafted. His cousins and friends were also going into the military.

When Dad left his home in the country in January of 1943, he went to boot camp at Fort Leonard Wood, Missouri.

Boot Camp

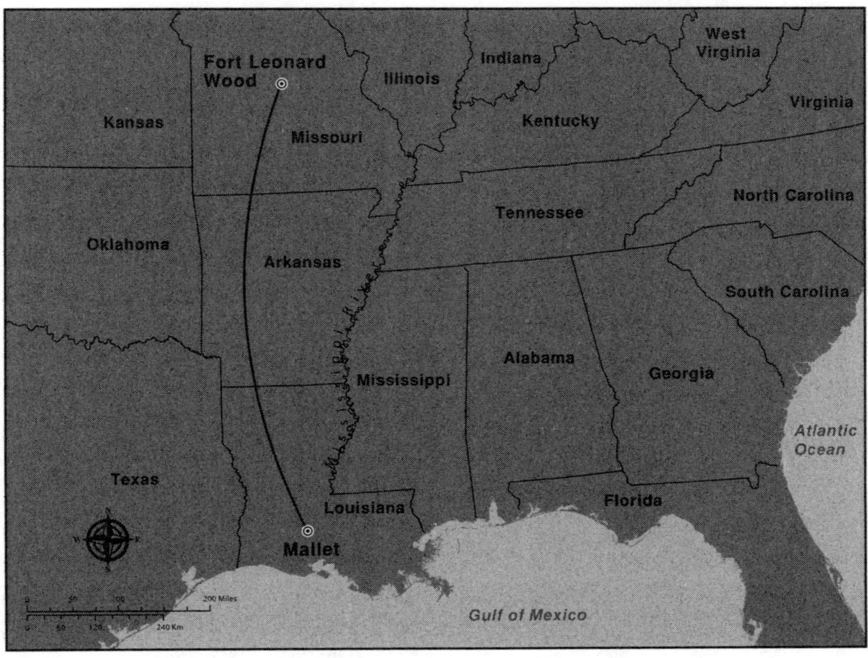

He left home and traveled from Mallet to Boot Camp in Fort Leonard Wood, Missouri.

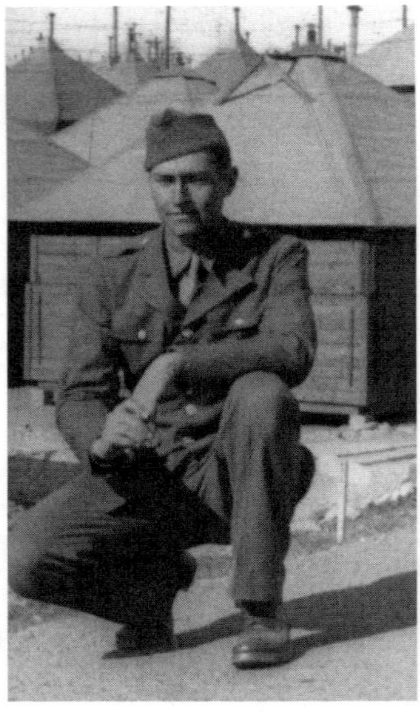

Dad in boot camp at Fort Leonard Wood, Missouri.

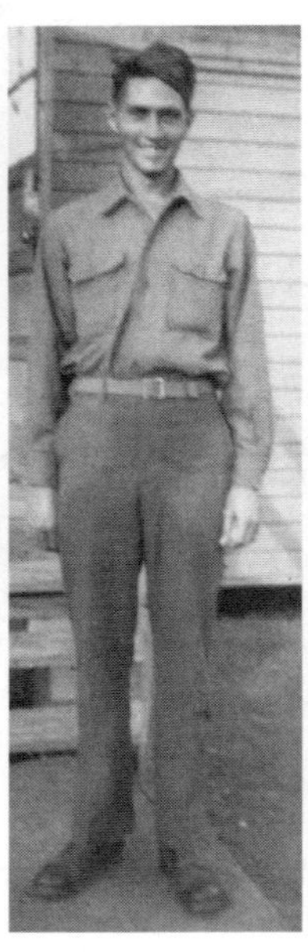

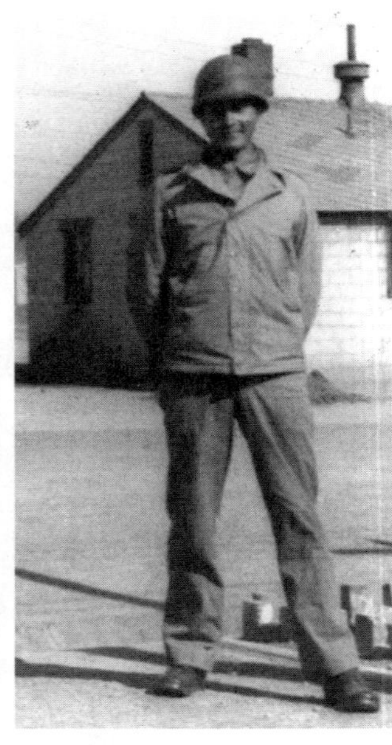

What two months of boot camp can do for a skinny man.

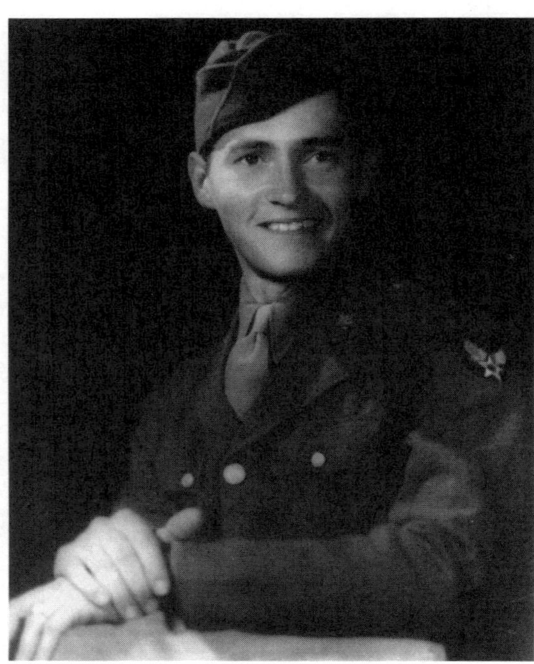

Boot camp portrait.

Geiger Field, Washington

When it came time to match him with a job specialty, the military asked what he did for a living and what he was good at. He told them he was a farmer and had experience maintaining tractors and other farm equipment. When he was given his Army job assignment, he found himself in familiar territory maintaining all the road and airstrip building equipment, such as trucks, bulldozers, and graders. He changed the motor and transmission oil, kept them greased, and did other associated tasks. When he wasn't busy with this, he helped out in other areas.

After he completed boot camp, he went for additional training in his specialty. He was stationed at the headquarters of the 863rd Engineer Aviation Battalion at Geiger Field in Spokane, Washington, where he endured cold and snowy conditions.

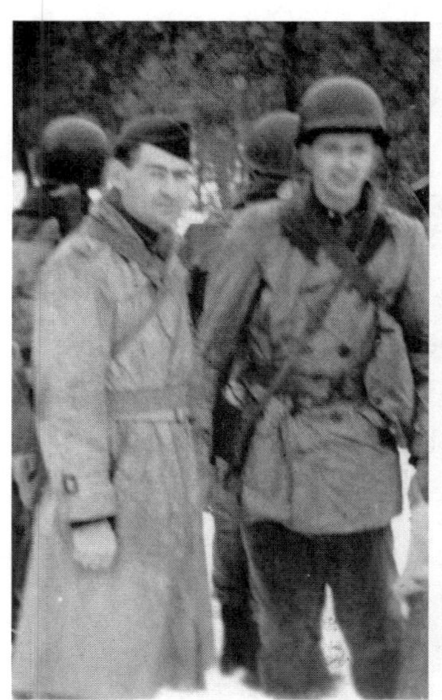

This battalion was activated on Aug. 1, 1942 at Geiger Field, Washington, as the 1st Battalion, 922nd Engineer Aviation Regiment. It was later redesignated on Feb. 1, 1942, as the 863rd Engineer Aviation Battalion.

This new wintertime location in the Pacific Northwest was quite a departure from the hot, humid subtropical climate of south Louisiana. He was assigned to Headquarters and Service Company, or H&S Company for short.

Major Harvey and Lt. Sitz in the snow at Geiger Field, Washington.

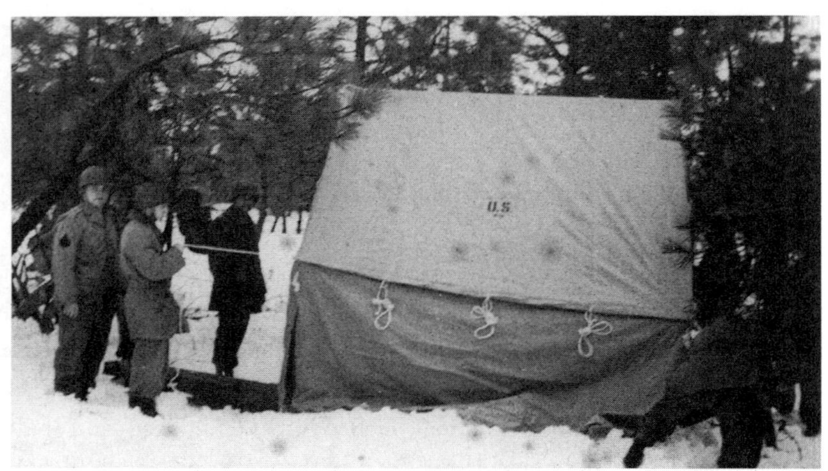

Winter has made its presence felt at Geiger Field.

When I asked Dad if he was ever in a combat situation where he was in danger or killed the enemy, he said he never killed anyone. He did, however, have some close calls with death in New Guinea and on the island of Biak.

On one occasion, he was running for cover because the enemy was firing on their position. After the firefight was over he discovered a bullet had passed through his lower pants leg near his ankle.

On another occasion, enemy planes were flying overhead at night and being shot at and hit by our anti-aircraft guns. A large piece of shrapnel came crashing through his tent and landed on the ground between him and his buddy.

Dad told me the following account one week before his death in September 2000. During a Japanese air raid on their camp and airfield, everyone scrambled for cover, including about 15-20 visiting Aussie soldiers who took cover in a bomb crater. A bomb landed in the crater and killed them all.

JANUARY 1943

ELSEWHERE IN THE WAR

Jan. 2: Japanese resistance ends at Buna, New Guinea.

Jan. 7: Japanese land more troops at Lae, New Guinea.

Jan. 10: Soviet troops launch an all-out offensive attack on Stalingrad; they also renew attacks in the north (Leningrad) and in the Caucasus.

Jan. 14: The Casablanca Conference of Allied leaders begins. Winston Churchill and Franklin D. Roosevelt discuss the eventual invasion of mainland Europe, the impending invasion of Sicily and Italy, and the wisdom of the principle of "unconditional surrender."

Jan. 18: The Warsaw Ghetto Uprising starts.

Jan. 20: USS Silversides attacks a Japanese convoy 286 miles from Truk, Caroline Islands, en route to the Solomon Islands, sinking transport Meiu Maru and damaging Surabaya Maru.

Jan. 21: Last airfield at Stalingrad is taken by Red Army forces; the Luftwaffe is unable to supply German troops.

Jan. 22: Allies liberate Sananada, New Guinea.

Jan. 23: British Eighth Army captures Tripoli, Libya.

Jan. 27: Fifty bombers mount the first all-American air raid against the large naval base at Wilhelmshaven, Germany.

Jan. 29: The naval Battle of Rennell Island, near Guadalcanal, begins. The Japanese beat the Americans, and the USS Chicago is lost.

Jan. 29: Battle of Wau, New Guinea.

Jan. 30: The last Japanese clear out of Guadalcanal undetected.

<> <> <> <> <>

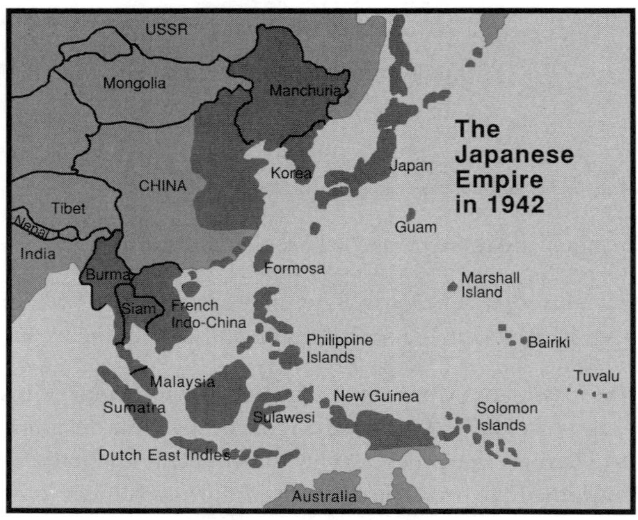

This map shows the expansion of the Japanese Empire in 1942. One of their intentions was to capture and occupy Australia. They attacked Darwin, Australia, but were driven back.

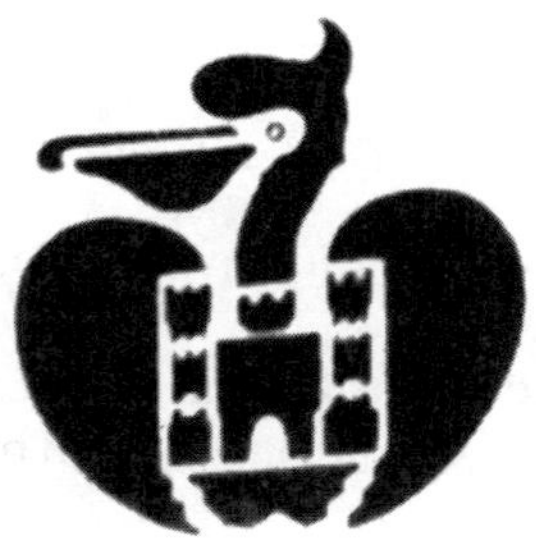

The logo of the 863rd Engineer Aviation Battalion.

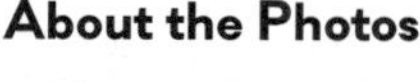

About the Photos

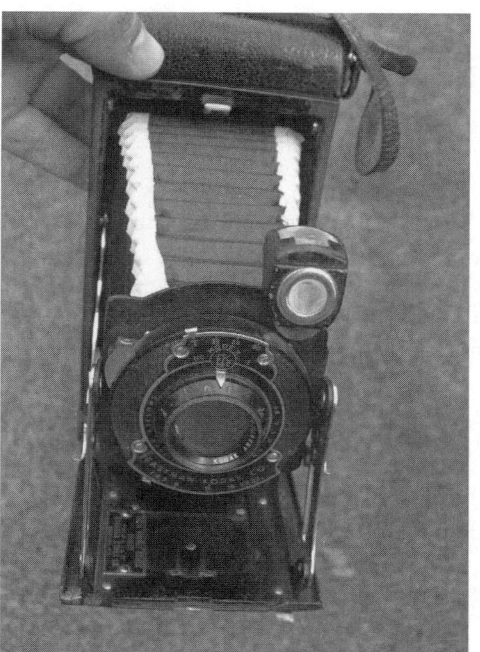

This is the camera my dad used to document his journey across the Pacific.

During the war, Dad took nearly 800 pictures with this camera shown here. The model name tag says it is a "No. 1A Pocket Kodak Junior" fold-up camera. It appears he had a leather carrying case made for it, which has a drawing of the South Pacific area on it.

According to my research, this model was manufactured between the years 1929-1932. It was most likely handed down to him by his parents. He took the pictures to show his family back home on the farm what he was experiencing in the war. (He never expected these pictures from his private collection to be made available and viewed by others outside of family and friends.)

This camera was already old when he took it with him to war. Then it endured extreme tropical heat of 130 degrees and humidity while in the South Pacific. It's indeed a blessing that these pictures came out as well as they did with this antique camera.

FEBRUARY 1943

ELSEWHERE IN THE WAR

Feb. 2: In the Soviet Union, the Battle of Stalingrad comes to an end with the official surrender of the German 6th Army.

Feb. 5: The Allies now have control of Libya. Allies and Nazis fight in Tunisia, North Africa.

Feb. 5: Essen, Germany, is bombed, marking the beginning of a four-month attack on the Ruhr industrial area.

Feb. 8: The Chindits, British Indian "special forces" begin an incursion into Burma.

Feb. 9: Guadalcanal is finally secured; it is the first major achievement of the American offensive in the Pacific during WWII.

Feb. 11: U.S. General Dwight D. Eisenhower is selected to command the Allied armies in Europe.

Feb. 28: The SS United Victory, the first Victory ship, is launched. This class of transport will prove to be crucial in hauling men and supplies across the oceans.

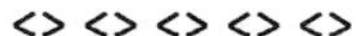

MARCH 1943

ELSEWHERE IN THE WAR

Mar. 2: Battle of the Bismarck Sea. United States and Australian naval forces, over the course of three days, sink eight Japanese troop transports near New Guinea, resulting in heavy loss of Japanese lives.

Mar. 6: Battle of Medenine in Tunisia. It is Rommel's last battle in Africa as he is forced to retreat.

Mar. 10: The U.S. 14th Air Force is formed in China, under General Claire Chennault, former head of the "Flying Tigers."

Mar. 13: German forces empty the Jewish ghetto in Kraków, Poland. Most Jews sent to labor or extermination camps; 2,000 were killed in the streets.

Mar. 18: General Patton leads his tanks of II Corps into Gafsa, Tunisia.

Mar. 26: In the Aleutian Islands region of Alaska, U.S. Navy forces intercept Japanese who were reinforcing a garrison at Kiska.

<> <> <> <> <>

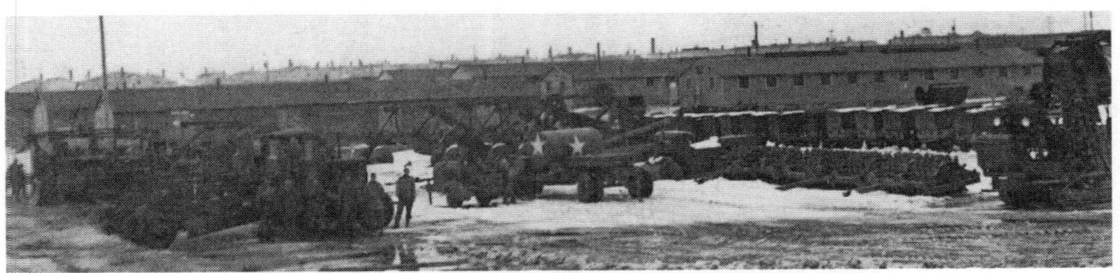

Snow on the ground at Geiger Field. My father's battalion is preparing for deployment overseas.

OFFICIAL MILITARY RECORD ENTRY:

Mar. 20: Prepare to leave Geiger Field; on Mar 26, 1943, battalion moved to Ft. George Wright nearby in preparation to move out to California.

APRIL 1943

ELSEWHERE IN THE WAR

Apr.12: The last units of the Afrika Korps surrender in the northern corner of Tunisia.

Apr. 22: Commence campaign to capture two major Japanese bases at Salamaua and Lae, New Guinea.

Apr. 18: Admiral Yamamoto, chief architect of Japanese naval strategy, is killed when his plane is shot down by American P38s over Bougainville Island.

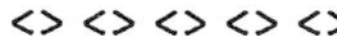

OFFICIAL MILITARY RECORD ENTRY:

Apr. 8 - Move out on trains from Washington headed to Camp Stoneman in Pittsburg, California, in the San Francisco Bay Area; arrived April 11.

Apr. 15-30 - Loading the ship for deployment overseas.

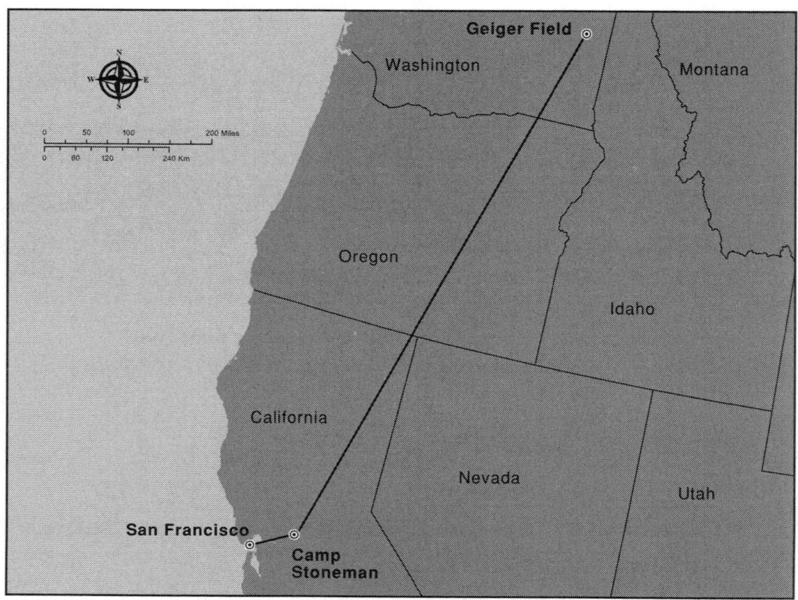

Dad traveled from Geiger Field in Washington to San Francisco.

MAY 1943

ELSEWHERE IN THE WAR

May 2: Japanese aircraft bomb Darwin, Australia.

May 11: The Japanese kill over 30,000 in the Changjiao, China, massacre.

May 11: American troops invade Attu Island in the Aleutian Islands in an attempt to expel occupying Japanese forces.

May 13: German Afrika Korps and Italian troops in North Africa surrender to Allied forces; Allies take over 250,000 prisoners.

May 15: The French form a resistance movement.

May 16: The Dambusters' raids by RAF 617 Squadron on two German dams, Mohne and Eder; the Ruhr war industries lose electrical power.

May 16: The Warsaw Ghetto Uprising ends. The ghetto is destroyed.

May 24: Admiral Karl Dönitz orders the majority of German U-boats to withdraw from the Atlantic because of heavy losses due to new Allied anti-sub tactics.

May 31: American B-17s bomb Naples.

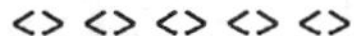

OFFICIAL MILITARY RECORD ENTRY:

May 1 – Arrangements are being made to set up 12 50-caliber machine guns on board the 33,000-ton Luxury Liner U.S.S. Mount Vernon, to be manned by our gun crews during the voyage. This vessel is a Navy Ship instead of the usual Army Transport used in the transportation of troops.

May 5 – Leave Camp Stoneman by truck en route to ship.

May 6– The battalion embarked aboard ship in an efficient and orderly manner. Thirty Officers and 774 enlisted men (EM) comprised the battalion. Ship under way at 0800 hours (8 a.m.), with air protection for the first three hours.

May 8 – EM in high spirits, and gambling going on all over the ship.

May 9 – Nearing equator.

May 11 – Crossed the equator. There is a centuries-old ceremony held aboard Navy ships when someone crosses the equator for the first time. It is called King Neptune holding court. This occurred on May 12, 1943.

The Officers went through initiation ceremonies that left them soaking wet and holding their sore backs. The EM went through a scalping process that left half the Battalion with the weirdest looking hairdos ever seen anywhere before. All Officers and EM that went through the initiation process received a certificate proclaiming them to be members in good standing of the Court of King Neptune.

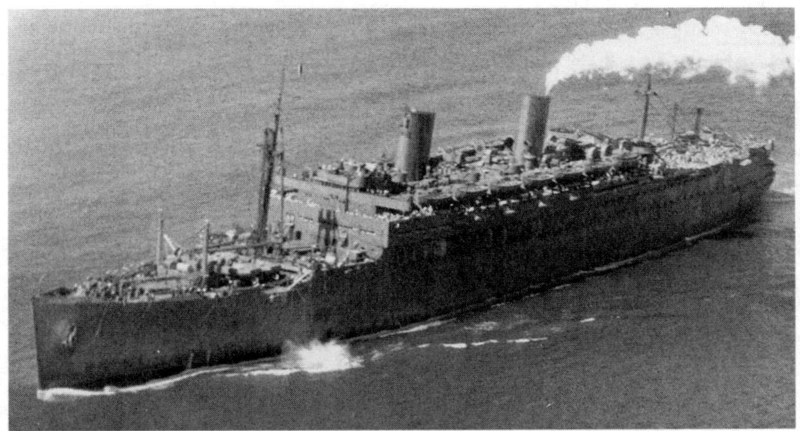

USS Mount Vernon (AP-22). Photo taken from an airship belonging to Lighter-than-Air Squadron (ZP-31) from NAS Santa Ana. Photo courtesy of www.shipscribe.com.

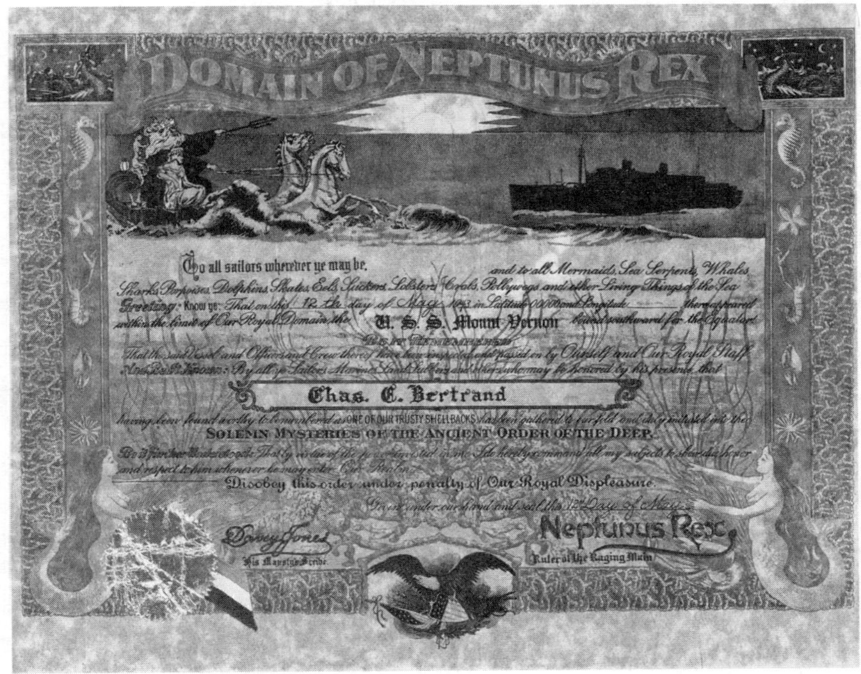

DOMAIN OF NEPTUNUS REX

To all sailors wherever ye may be, and to all Mermaids, Sea Serpents, Whales, Sharks, Porpoises, Dolphins, Skates, Eels, Suckers, Lobsters, Crabs, Pollywogs and other Living Things of the Sea

Greeting: Know ye: That on this 12 th day of May 1943 in Latitude 0000 and Longitude ______ there appeared within the limits of Our Royal Domain the U. S. S. Mount Vernon bound southward for the Equator.

That the said Vessel and Officers and Crew thereof have been inspected and passed on by Ourself and Our Royal Staff

And Be It Known: By all ye Sailors, Marines, Land Lubbers and others who may be honored by his presence that

Chas. E. Bertrand

having been found worthy to be numbered as ONE OF OUR TRUSTY SHELLBACKS has been gathered to our fold and duly initiated into the

SOLEMN MYSTERIES OF THE ANCIENT ORDER OF THE DEEP.

Be it further understood: That by virtue of the power invested in me I do hereby command all my subjects to show due honor and respect to him whenever he may enter Our Realm.

Disobey this order under penalty of Our Royal Displeasure.

Given under our hand and seal this 12th Day of May

Davey Jones
His Majesty's Scribe

Neptunus Rex
Ruler of the Raging Main

Court of King Neptune certificate Dad received when he crossed the equator.

OFFICIAL MILITARY RECORD ENTRY:

May 18 - Enemy submarines sighted by lookouts, necessitating wide detours and full speed.

May 20 - Picked up a U.S. Navy Destroyer that came out to convoy us into the port at Sydney, Australia. It was a welcome sight to everyone as it spelled the completion of a long and tedious trip.

So began Curtis Bertrand's adventure abroad, which sure beat his experience away from home at Louisiana State University in Baton Rouge. He was able to take in the sights and sounds of our great nation on the way to boot camp, heading west to the Pacific and then down the coast to San Francisco.

My father took a two-week boat ride to the other side of the world and was initiated in the King Neptune ceremony where he and his battalion received a college-worthy hazing. Friendships were solidified, and boys were made into men.

Yet that youthful exuberance would quickly fade as my father and his battalion looked toward a much more serious horizon. The first of three war-torn destinations in Australia lay ahead. They would soon come to know the Japanese aggression firsthand.

CHAPTER 4

A Visit to Australia

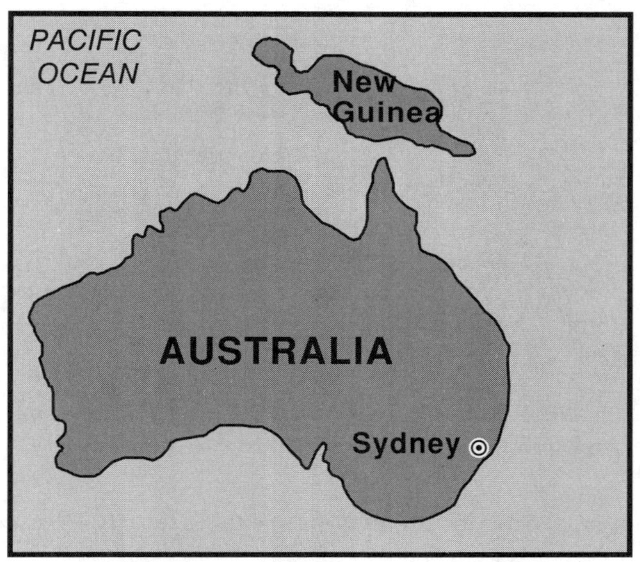

The South Pacific area of Australia and New Guinea.

OFFICIAL MILITARY RECORD ENTRY:

May 21 - Everyone is excited as the pilot ship came out and a pilot came aboard to take us into port with the aid of a tug boat. Disembarking started at 1900 hours (7 p.m.) as all units left details behind to help clean up and police the ship. The battalion was transported by bus to Camp Warwick where tents were ready for them to set up quarters.

May 22 - Necessary regulations governing passes into town were laid out and included possession of train tickets, rubbers (condoms), and copies of prophylactic stations in town, by all EM.

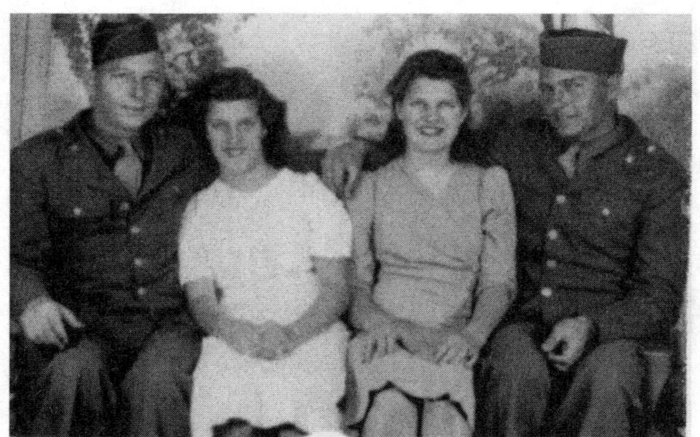

My father (right) with fellow soldier and their dates in Sydney.

After the troops settled in they were allowed to see the city. Here are some sights and souvenirs from Australia.

A coal-burining car.
Sydney, Australia, May 1943.

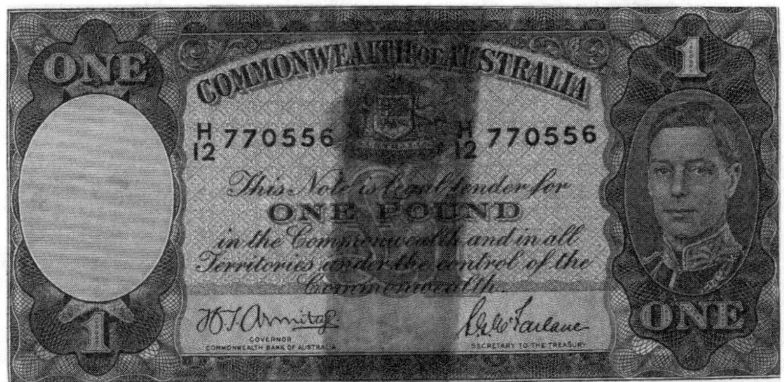

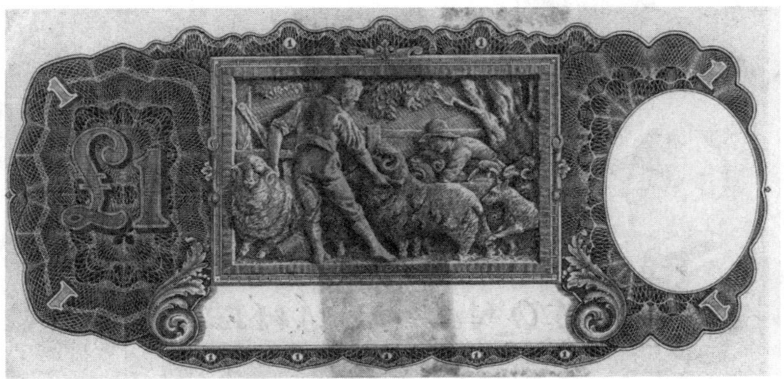

Australian one-pound note.
Dad put a strip of tape across the front to stick it in his photo album.

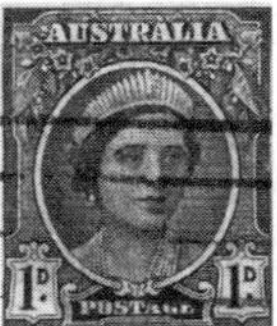

Australian postage stamp. Elizabeth Bowes-Lyon (August 4, 1900 - March 30, 2002) was the wife and queen consort of reigning King George VI from 1936 until her husband's death in 1952. After that she was known as Queen Elizabeth the queen mother, to avoid confusion with her daughter, Queen Elizabeth II.

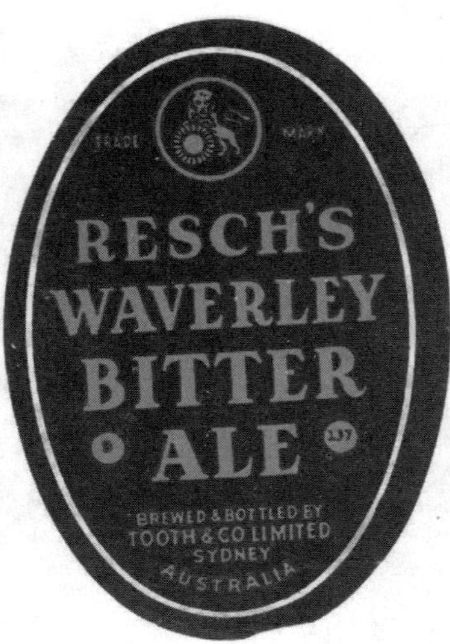

An Australian beer label Dad saved as a souvenir.

Curtis and his friends visited the Taronga Zoo in Sydney where they saw animals not seen in America, like the kangaroo.

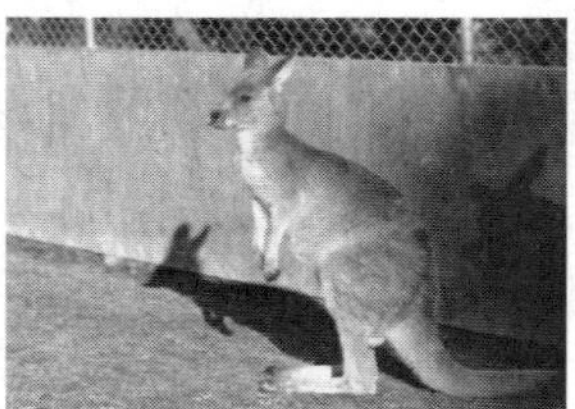

Kangaroo

OFFICIAL MILITARY RECORD ENTRY:

May 25 - Preparations being made for the battalion's next move to Brisbane.

JUNE 1943

ELSEWHERE IN THE WAR

June 8: Japanese forces abandon Kiska Island in the Aleutians, their last foothold in the Western Hemisphere.

June 17: Allies bomb Sicily and the Italian mainland as signs of a forthcoming invasion increases.

June 20: Operation Cartwheel opens with landings by the U.S. 4th Marine Raider Battalion at Segi Point on New Georgia in the Solomon Islands. It will not be secured until August.

June 23: American troops land in the Trobriand Islands, close to New Guinea. The American strategy of driving up the Southwest Pacific by "Island Hopping" continues.

June 24: Attacks continue against Germany's Ruhr industrial valley.

June 30: American troops land on Rendova Island, New Georgia, as a part of Operation Cartwheel.

<> <> <> <> <>

Due to Brisbane's proximity to the South West Pacific Area (SWPA) theater of World War II, the city played a prominent role in the defense of Australia. Brisbane became a temporary home to thousands of Australian and American servicemen. It was the Pacific headquarters of U.S. General Douglas MacArthur, Supreme Allied Commander, after he was forced out of the Philippines when the Japanese invaded those islands in December 1941. His headquarters were later moved to Hollandia, New Guinea, in August 1944.

OFFICIAL MILITARY RECORD ENTRY:

June 28 - Arrive in Brisbane, Queensland, Australia by train.

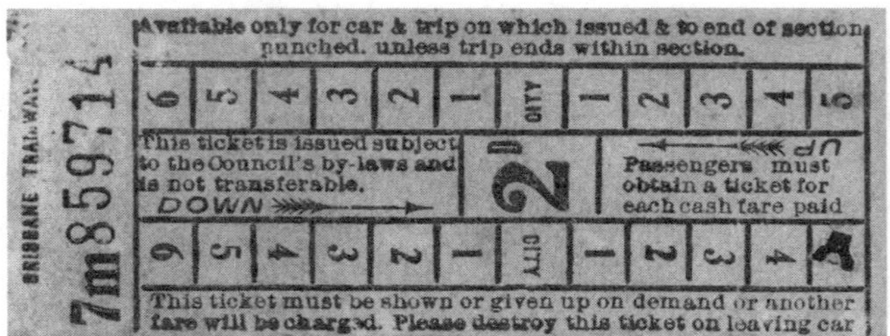

Brisbane tramway ticket.

My dad's battalion was stationed in three Australian cities during the summer of 1943. Each stop was necessary for the complex task of getting the numerous battalions organized, fully equipped, and putting the finishing touches on the engineering and battle planning strategy. This map shows these three cities. The battalion's first stop was in Sydney, where they were stationed for five weeks. They later boarded a train and arrived in Brisbane at the end of June, and stayed 12 days. Then they boarded the SS Howard Stansbury for Townsville and remained for two weeks. They later took that ship to Oro Bay, New Guinea.

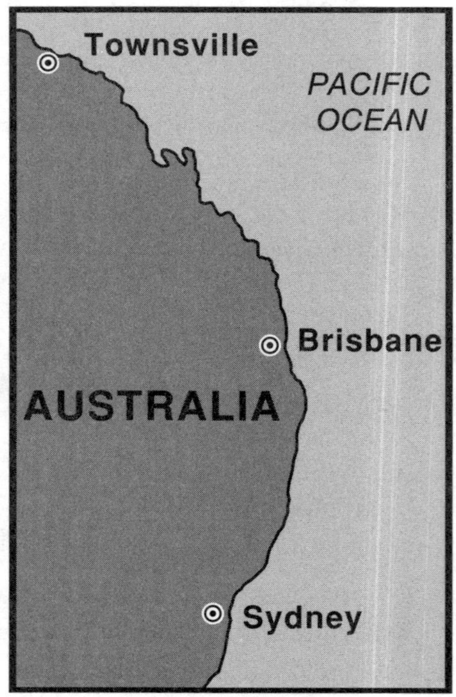

A map of the eastern coast of Australia.

JULY 1943

ELSEWHERE IN THE WAR

July 5: Germans launch an offensive attack on Kursk, Russia.

July 7: Rocket scientist Wernher von Braun briefs Hitler on the V-2 rocket; Hitler approves project as top priority.

July 10: Operation Husky is launched. The Allied invasion of Sicily to liberate Europe begins.

July 12: The Tank Battle of Prokhorovka, Russia, is the largest tank battle in human history and part of the Battle of Kursk.

July 19: The Allies bomb Rome for the first time.

July 21: The Operation Bellicose targeting of Friedrichshafen, Germany, is the first bombing of a V-2 rocket facility.

July 22: The fall of Palermo in the Allied invasion of Sicily inspired a revolt against fascism in Italy; Mussolini is overthrown.

July 23: The RAF bombs Kiel in the first major raid on a German city since April 1943 and the heaviest RAF raid of the war.

July 24: The Operation Gomorrah firestorm bombing of Hamburg, Germany, begins (the heaviest assault in the history of aerial warfare at the time).

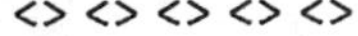

OFFICIAL MILITARY RECORD ENTRY:

July 10 – Leave Brisbane on SS Howard Stansbury headed north for Townsville.

July 14 – Arrive in Townsville, Queensland, Australia and stayed in a staging area called Armstrong Paddock.

July 15 – Set up battalion mess hall, and troops assigned to tents.

July 30 – Prepared to leave on the following day to continue our "boat ride."

July 31 – Troops embarked on SS Howard Stansbury. Took on 100 tons of drinking water, or 1/3 of water capacity of ship. Sailed at 1900 hours (7 p.m.).

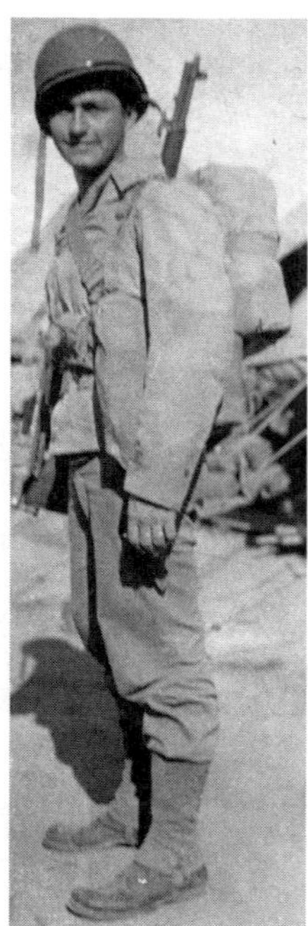

My dad with full pack is ready to get on the ship and move out to New Guinea. Photo taken in Townsville, Australia. Dad wrote on back of photo: "Gas mask on side; blankets, toilet articles, underwear and camera in my back pack. July 31, 1943."

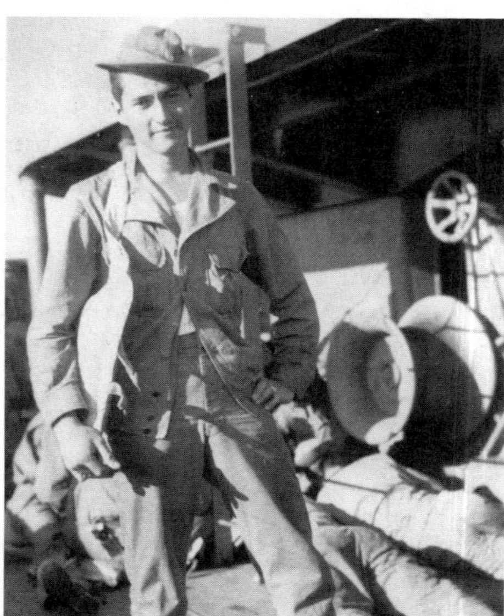

Curtis on board SS Howard Stansbury on the way to Oro Bay, New Guinea.

AUGUST 1943

ELSEWHERE IN THE WAR

Aug. 1: American daylight air raid on Romanian oilfields at Ploesti.

Aug. 2: John F. Kennedy's PT-109 is rammed, cut in two, and sunk off the Solomon Islands.

Aug. 6: The U.S. wins the Battle of Vella Gulf off Kolombangara Island in the Solomon Islands.

Aug. 7: The Allies win the Battle of New Georgia in the Solomon Islands.

Aug. 15-20: Allies destroy Japanese airfields in Lae, New Guinea.

Aug. 15: Battle of Vella Lavella Island. Allies vs. Japanese in another island hopping skirmish.

Aug. 17: Operation Husky completes the Allied invasion of Sicily.

Aug. 17: Germany V-2 rocket facility bombed at Peenemünde.

Aug. 24: U.S. troops declare Kiska Island secure, the Battle of the Aleutian Islands ended.

<> <> <> <> <>

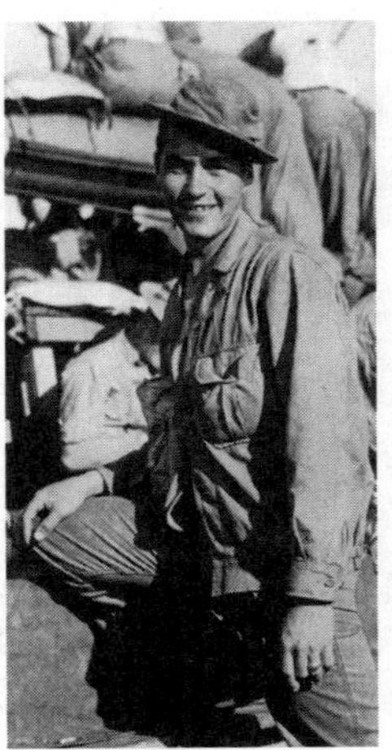

On board ship sailing to their first camp in New Guinea.

If only I could get inside my dad's head and hear what he was thinking as he was on this ship to New Guinea. I can only imagine.

He just spent three months in Australia, in three cities, seeing things he had never seen before. He saw kangaroos and other animals unique to this country, and a coal-burning steam engine car. I'm sure he couldn't wait to tell his brothers about this!

As the SS Howard Stansbury steams through the open seas, he hopes there are no enemy submarines in the area to sink the ship. That fear is lurking in his mind. As he looks around, some of the guys on deck are laughing and horsing around, gambling, playing cards and dice.

He could be thinking, what is the war like where I am going? How dangerous will it be? Oh sure, the officers at Geiger Field calmed our nerves telling us our infantry will face the enemy, that we will arrive only after all the Japanese have been killed in and around our camp area. In the event the enemy does attack, they are just an annoying inconvenience for a while, that's all – just like some mosquitos in my face. Well, that's a big relief! After all, I'm just a grease monkey, not a trained infantryman. Oh God, I don't want to die.

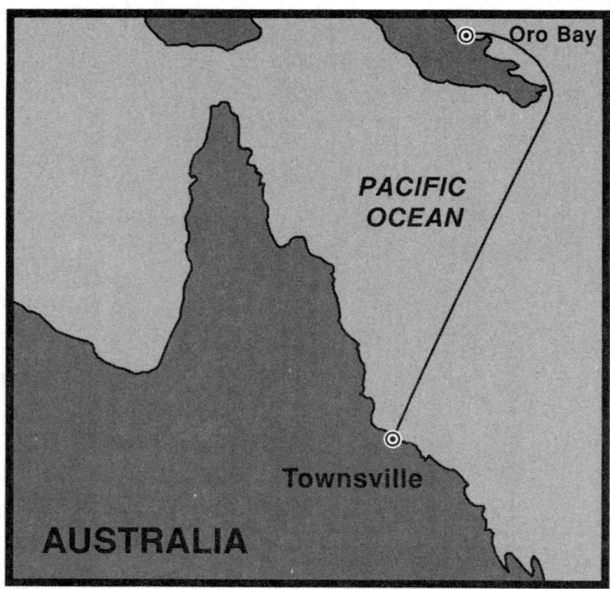

The battalion sailed from Townsville to Oro Bay, New Guinea.

CHAPTER 5

Dobodura: Their First Stop in New Guinea

After being on board the SS Howard Stansbury for five days the battalion arrived at Oro Bay, New Guinea, without incident. They disembarked in barges and drove in trucks to their campsite in Dobodura, about five miles away. They set up pup tents so they could have a place to sleep. Because there were no dock facilities constructed yet at Oro Bay, two jetties had to be built with heavy equipment to be able to unload the supply ships. Once that was accomplished they could proceed with their mission, namely, to construct the needed airport facilities and airstrips (called airdromes).

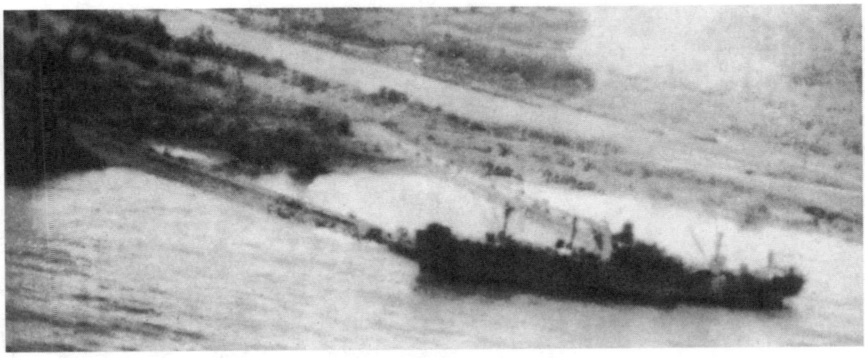

Two jetties had to be built by the battalion to reach the supply ship to unload it. Oro Bay, New Guinea.

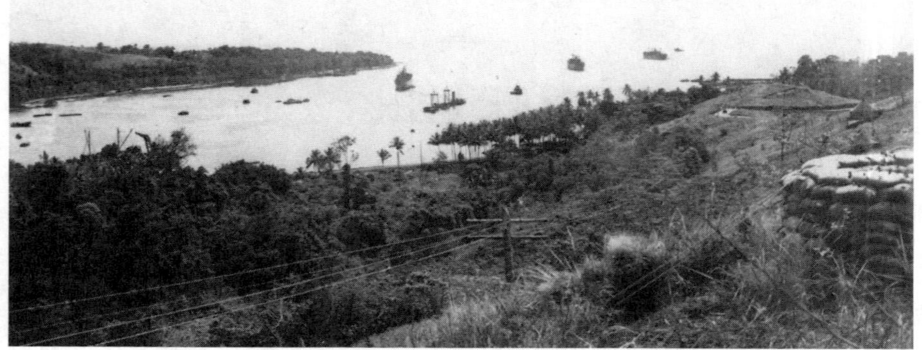

Ships can be seen in Oro Bay, New Guinea.
On the far right, there appears to be an anti-aircraft emplacement.

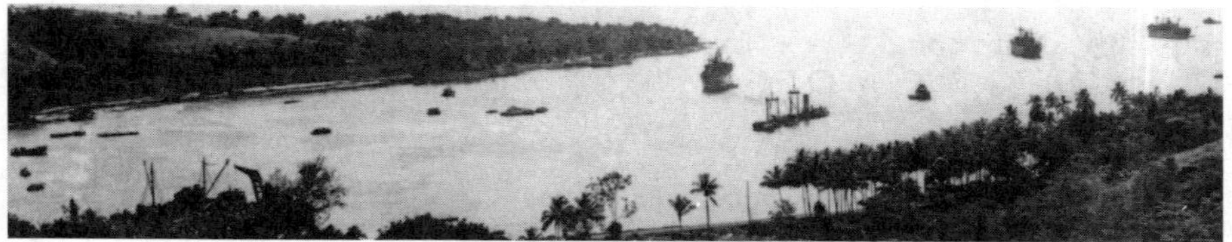

This is a zoomed-in shot of the ships in Oro Bay.

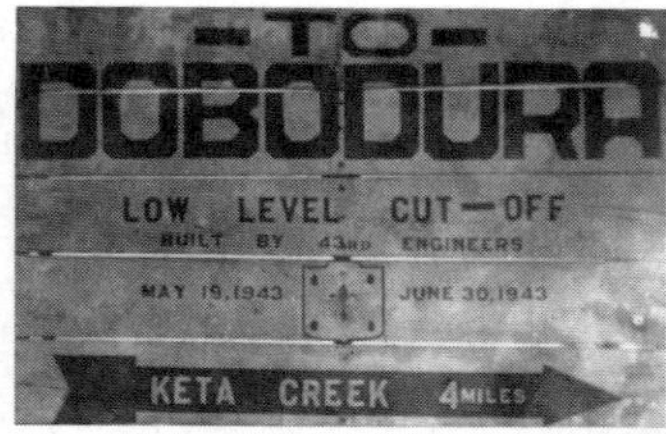

Dobodura sign.

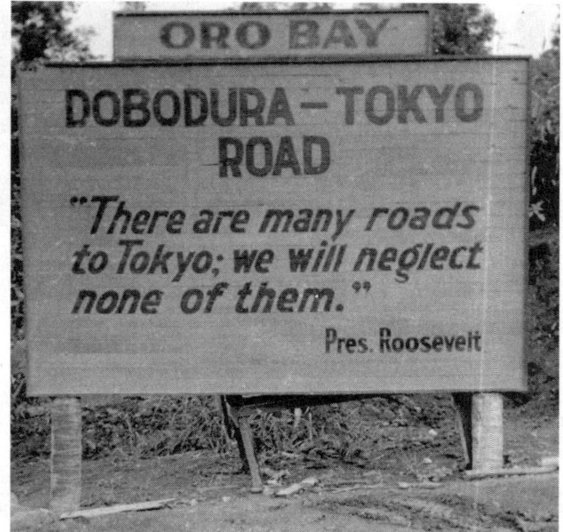

A morale-boosting sign to encourage the troops.

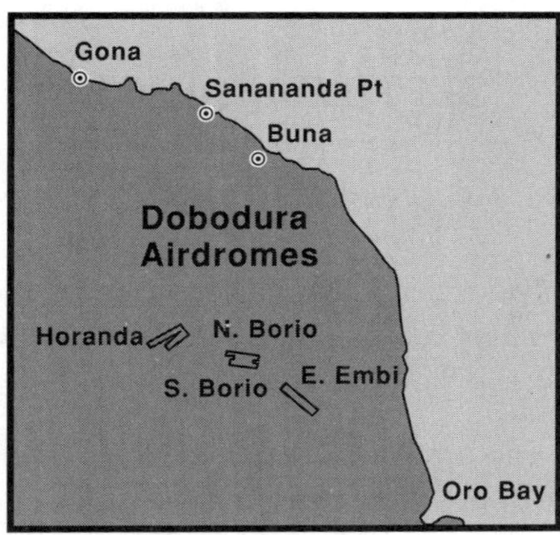

This is the area of New Guinea where Dad was stationed.

OFFICIAL MILITARY RECORD ENTRY:

Aug. 5, 1943 - Reached our destination, Oro Bay, New Guinea, just about five miles from Dobodura, with no enemy action during the entire trip. Disembarked in barges, trucked to campsite and set up pup tents temporarily. We got our first mail call in over a month. Morale is up 100 percent.

Aug. 12 - Pvt. Frank R. Cuarema of Co. C is seriously hurt by a fragment of shrapnel from a dud anti-aircraft shell picked up by T/5 Erven S. Studinski and explosion caused when tossed aside.

Aug. 14 - Lt. Jenkins appointed investigation officer in the coming general court martial of T/5 Studinski, in which he will be charged with manslaughter due to gross negligence.

Aug. 26 - Through the untiring efforts of our Chaplain, Lt. Earl D Burris, we were honored and entertained by a U.S.O. show consisting of Harry Ross, master of ceremonies, Al and Sid Reese, singers extraordinaire, and Al Gustafson, accordionist. The show was very good, and the entire battalion enjoyed it very much. We showed our appreciation of their efforts by treating them royally for the two days they rested here.

Aug. 30 - Since we drained the swamp, malaria is pretty well under control, with only five cases throughout the battalion. It goes to show that preventative measures are very important.

SEPTEMBER 1943

ELSEWHERE IN THE WAR

Sept. 3: Mainland Italy is invaded as Allied forces under Bernard L. Montgomery land at Reggio di Calabria. An Italian Armistice is signed, and Italy drops out of the war.

Sept. 4: U.S. troops occupy Nadzab and Lae, New Guinea. Australian troops take Salamau.

Sept. 9: Operation Avalanche, the Allied land invasion of Salerno, and Operation Slapstick, the British airborne invasion of Taranto, both in southern Italy, are launched.

Sept. 19: The Finisterre Range Campaign, an Allied offensive against the Japanese begins, eastern New Guinea.

Sept. 21: British midget submarines attack German battleship Tirpitz, crippling her for six months.

Sept. 22: Huon Peninsula Campaign begins; Allies begin ousting Japanese from eastern New Guinea.

<> <> <> <> <>

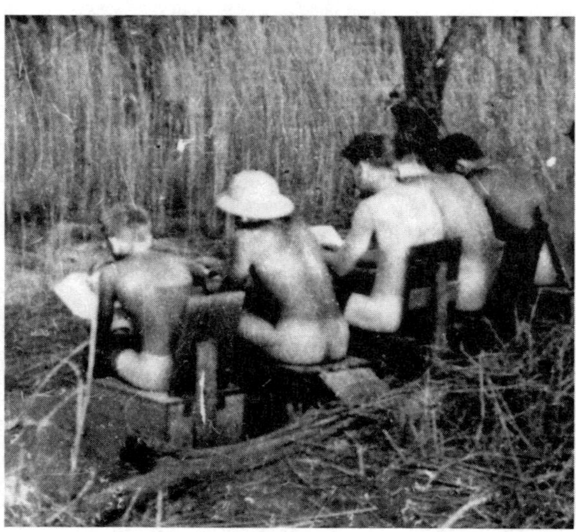

The latrine (outdoor toilet) area.

OFFICIAL MILITARY RECORD ENTRY:

Sept. 1 - The 475th Fighter Group commanded by Lt. Col. Prentise with Major Sehins as Executive Officer took over the completed strip #15 as their new permanent base. In appreciation for a good job well done, they informed us that they would put on a flying show for us upon their return from a mission today. 15 P-38s of the 431st Squadron circled the field three times, flying as low as twenty feet over the strip and zooming up to a higher altitude in almost a vertical line. Their ability as flyers was apparent, and the show gave us an idea of how it would feel to have planes sweep down to within strafing distance. The 432nd Squadron, also of the 475th Fighter Group, taxied to their respective hardstandings in the afternoon.

Note: (A hardstanding is a hard-surfaced area for parking aircraft.)

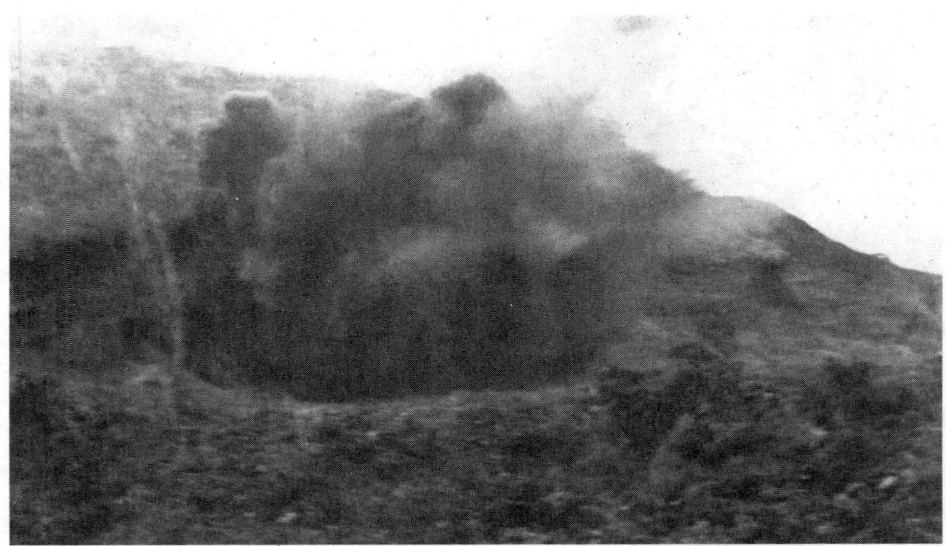

The engineers are blasting a hill to get rock and gravel to make the airdrome runways.

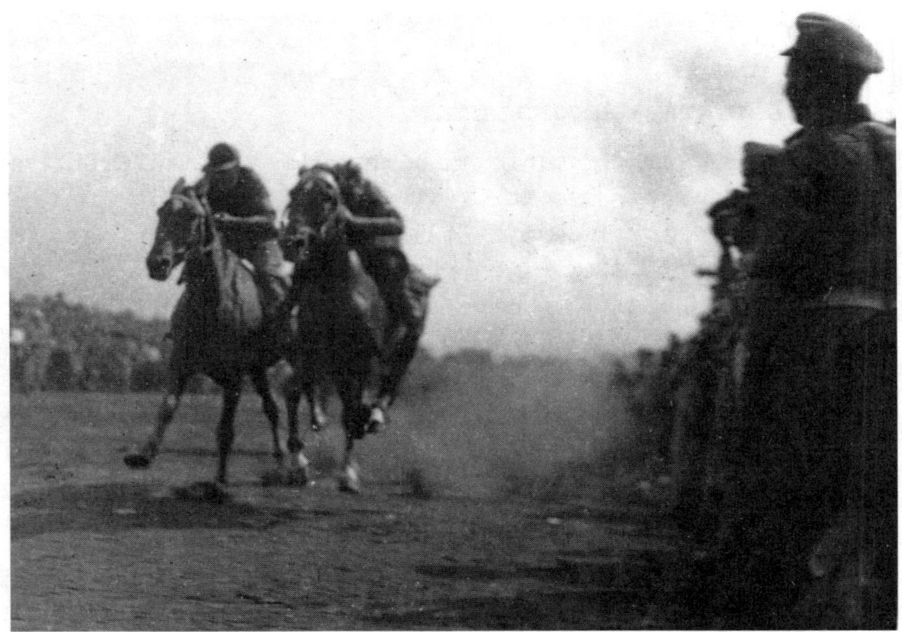

Enjoying a horse race in Soputa, New Guinea, which is northwest of Dobodura.

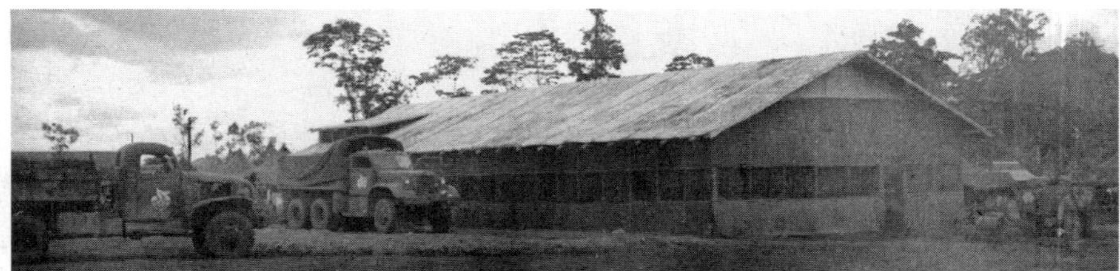

The mess hall.

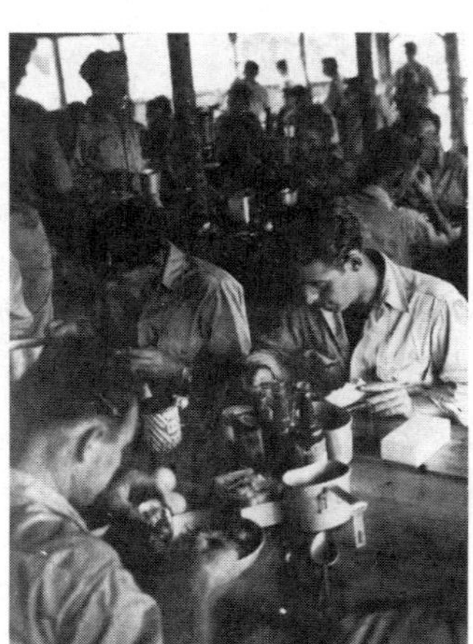

It's chow time inside the mess hall.

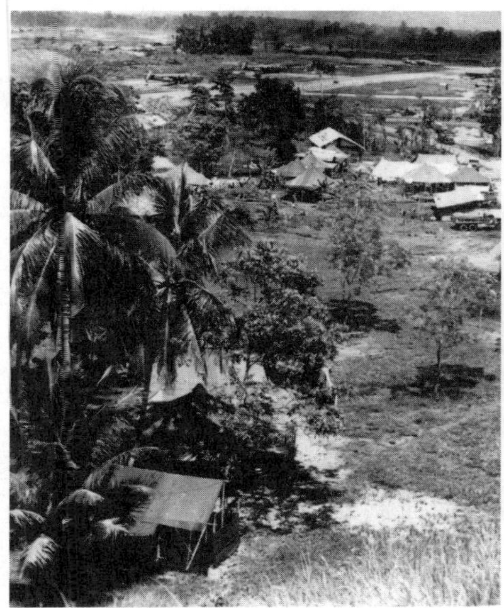

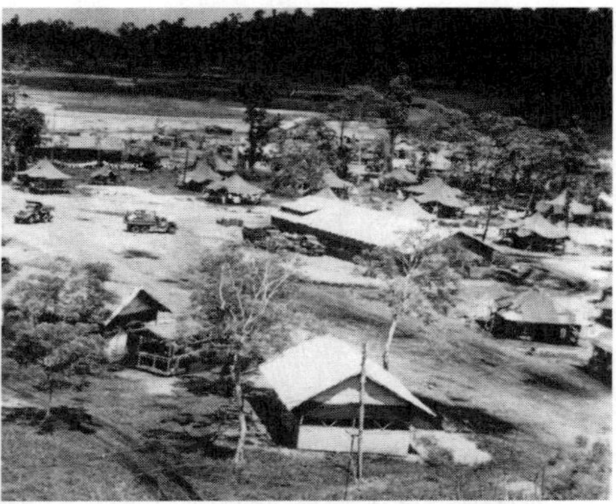

The first camp in New Guinea. My father was here from Aug 5, 1943, until Jan 5, 1944. Airplanes are in the background.

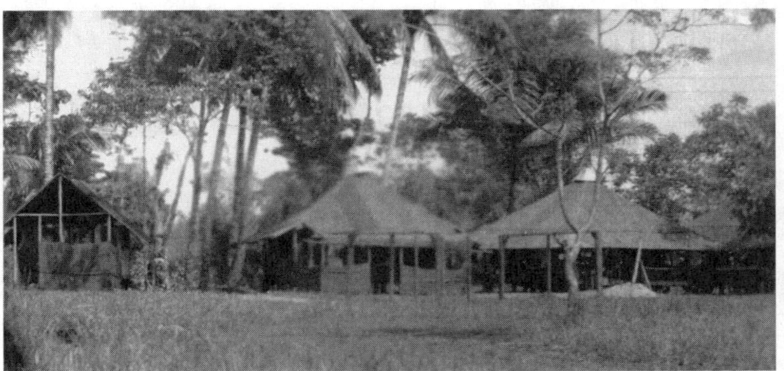

Officers' tents.

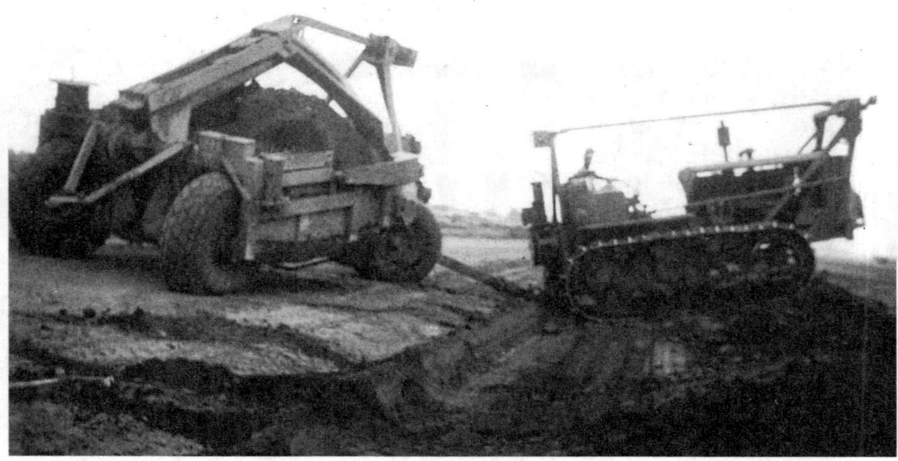

Eight-yard tow-behind dirt scraper pan (left) and D-8 Caterpillar bulldozer (right) building an airstrip.

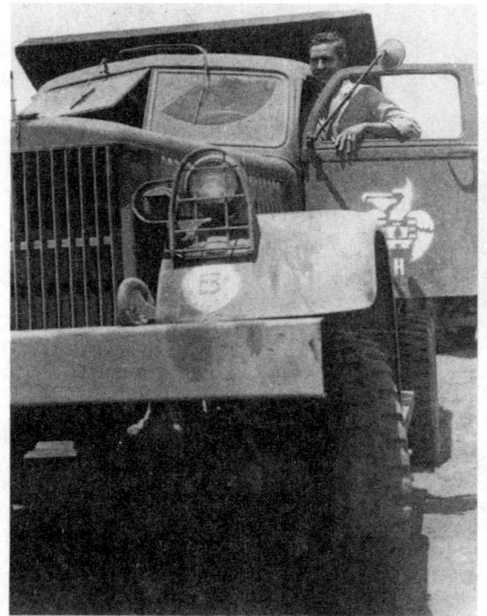

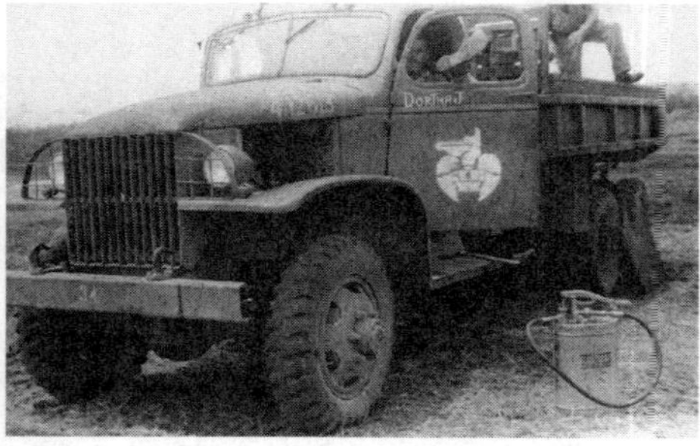

My father, Curtis Bertrand, and his four-ton dump truck (left). Fellow workers taking a break in the dump truck (right).

This M3 Stuart Tank (see next page), Hull #2017, belonged to the Australian Army, 2/6th Armoured Regiment, B Squadron, 5 Troop, according to *The Vital Factor: A History Of 2/6th Australian Armoured Regiment 1941-1946.* It was transported to Milne Bay in 1942 and then by barge to support infantry in the Battle of Buna in New Guinea. It was one of seven M3 Stuarts supporting troops of the 2/9th Infantry Battalion at Cape Endaiadere.

On Dec. 24, 1942, this tank suffered a hit to the assistant driver's hatch from one of the Japanese 76.2mm (3-inch) Type 3 Naval Guns emplaced at old strip at Buna Airfield. During this battle the naval guns, which were normally aimed skyward as anti-aircraft weapons, lowered their gun barrels horizontally to fire at the approaching Australian tanks and troops.

This tank and the naval gun were recovered from the Buna battlefield in mid-1973. They were exported to the National Museum of the Pacific War in Fredericksburg, Texas, where they are still on display.

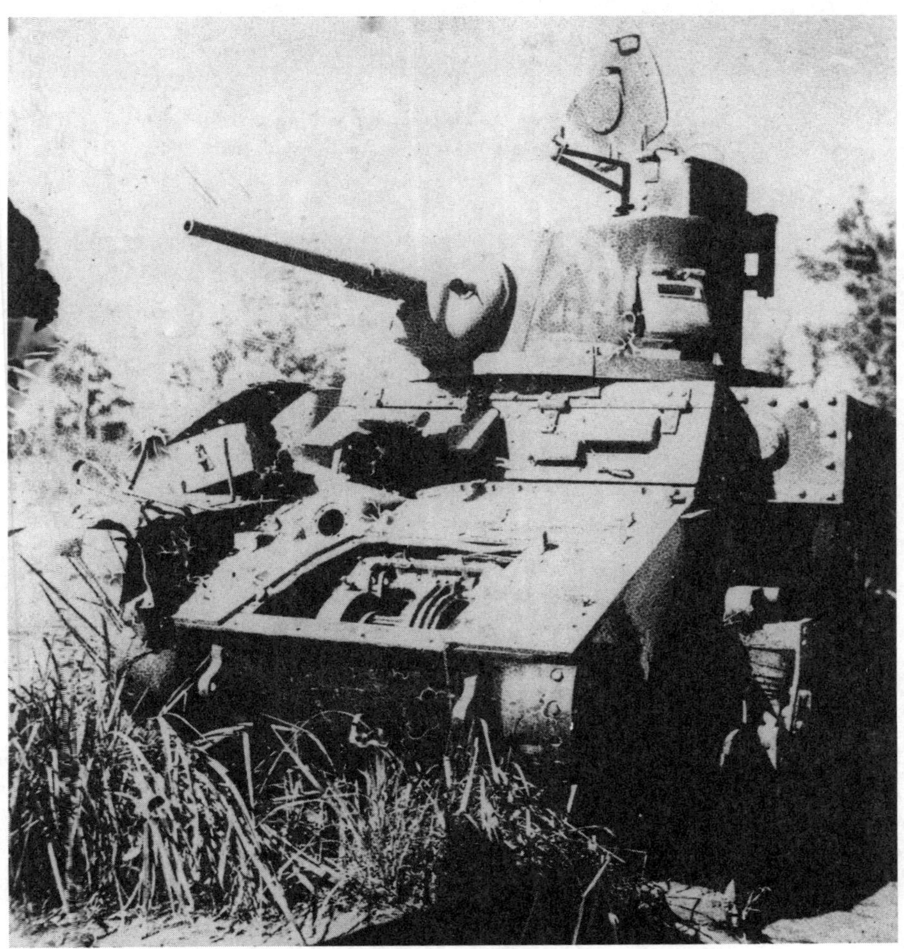

M3 Stuart tank disabled on the battlefield at Buna.

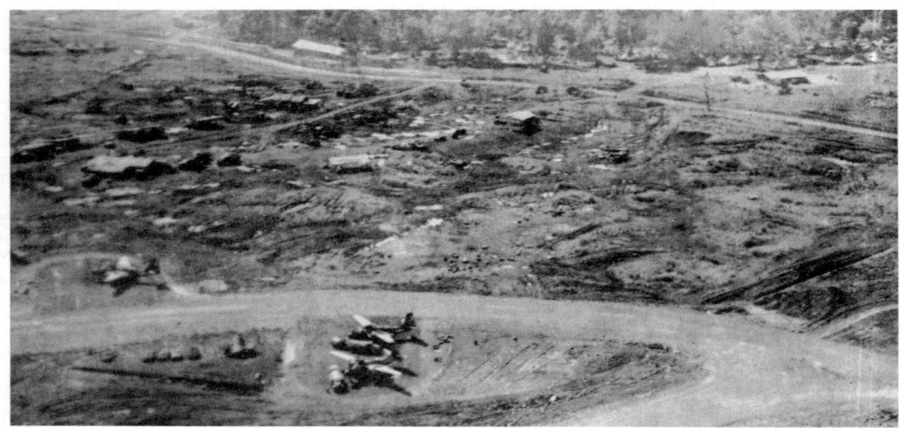

Aerial view of the work the battalion did making airstrips for U.S. bombers and fighter planes to land and refuel. (Left side)

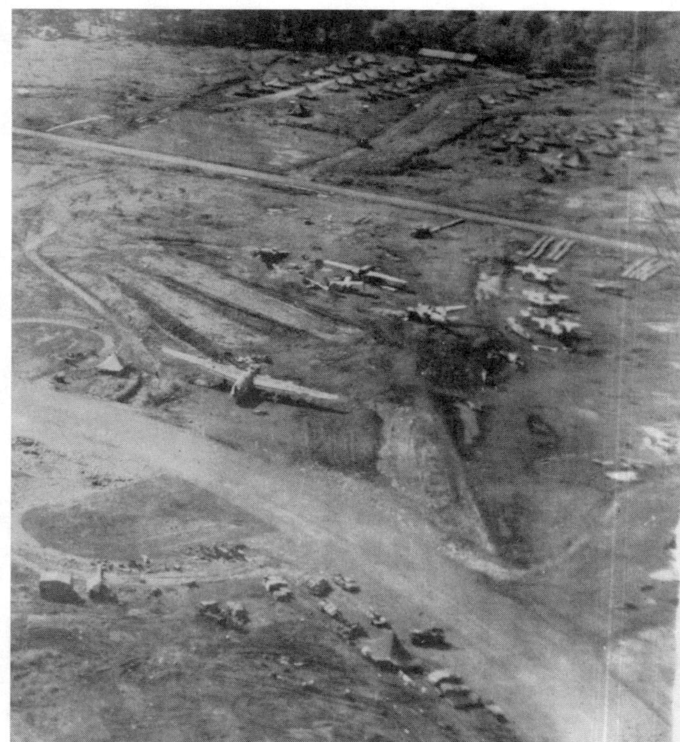

Right side of above scene.

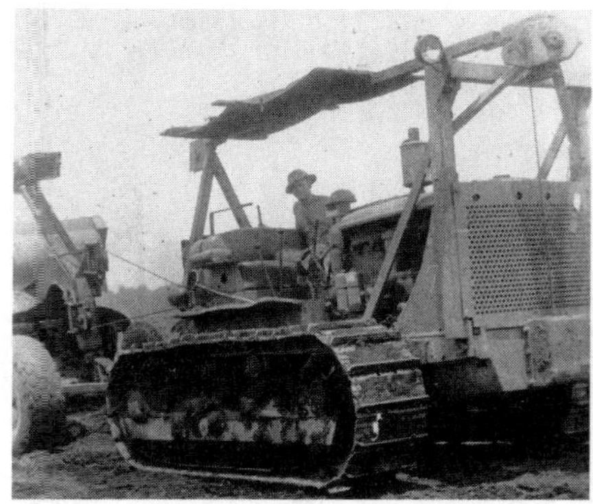

Bill Habetz, Dad's friend from Ragley, Louisiana, on his bulldozer.

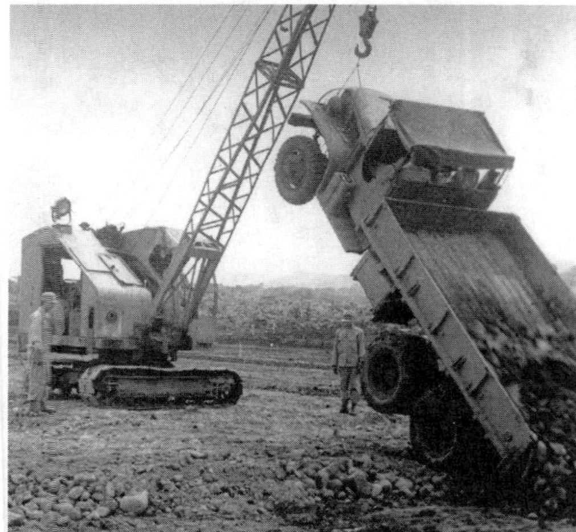

A crane lifts a dump truck to empty a load.

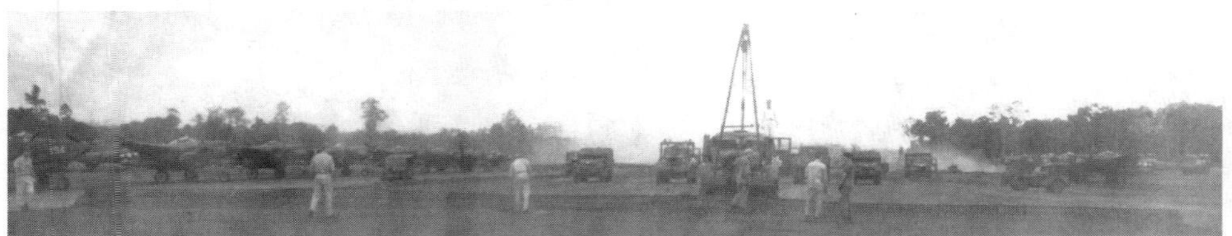

Strip 15 at Dobodura. The crane is lifting a long section of Pierced Steel Planking, also called Marston Matting. P-38s are parked on both sides of strip so the work can get done.

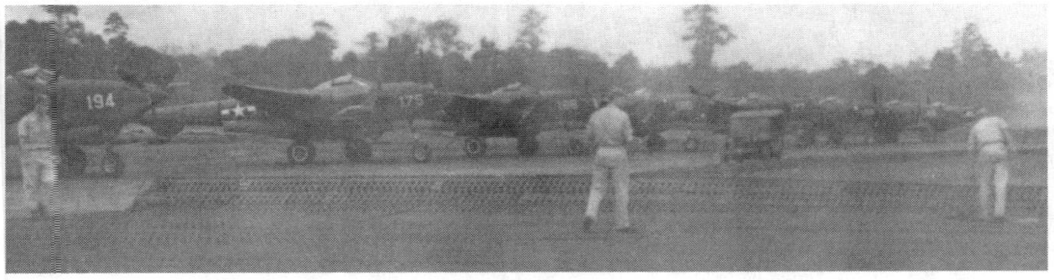

A zoomed-in section to show more detail of scene above.

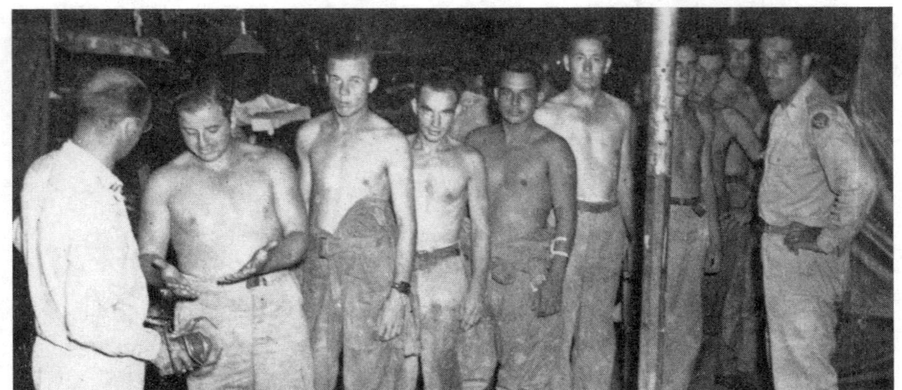

Capt. Mosey and Capt. Leona inspecting Company A cooks in New Guinea.

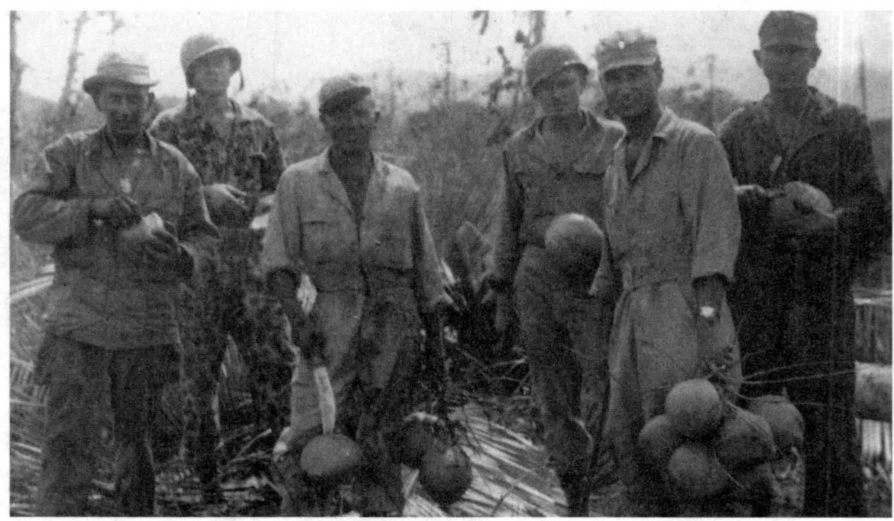

Collecting coconuts.

OFFICIAL MILITARY RECORD ENTRY:

Trucking detail for hauling sand: 18 to 20 trucks with two shifts of drivers plus necessary servicing and maintenance personnel from H&S Company 863rd Engineers working on this project.

Sept. 7 - A yellow alert at 2035 hours was changed to a red alert at 2040 hours with the all-clear being sounded at 2141 hours. This same group consisting of five flights of enemy planes returned and was checked to be about 28 miles from this area. The inconsiderate Nips executed this raid during our moving picture show, causing us to have two fairly long intermissions, but inasmuch as "The Show Must Go On," we completed the showing of the pictures by 2345 hours.

Sept. 18 - This is the fourth day without any alerts. Evidently our Lae campaign is keeping the Nips too busy to annoy us.

Sept. 22 - A red alert called in lasted 53 minutes, and the following information as to casualties was received from the Aussies: 1 Dutch freighter was hit, 4 men killed and 30 wounded, 3 trucks hit, 2 small harbor boats hit and damage of the wharf. This was all in the Buna area.

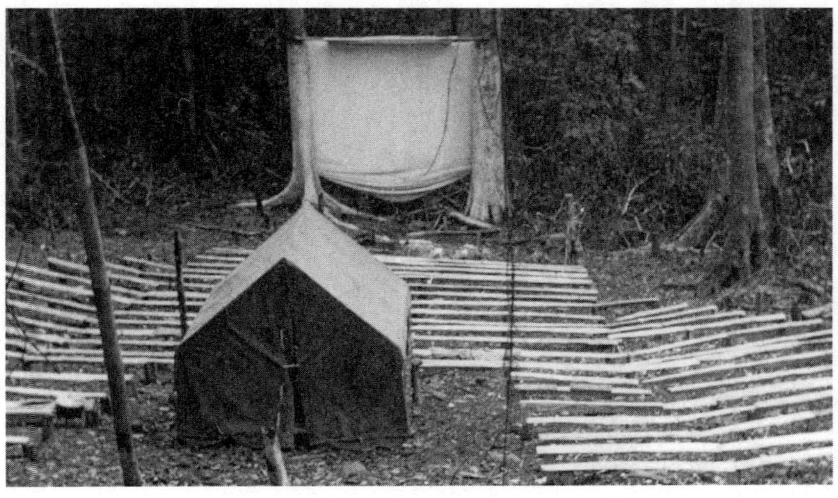

The movie theater in Dobodura.

OCTOBER 1943

ELSEWHERE IN THE WAR

Oct. 6: The naval Battle of Vella Lavella completes the second phase of Operation Cartwheel.

Oct. 12: Operation Cartwheel begins a bombing campaign against Rabaul, New Britain Island.

Oct. 13: One month after Italy surrendered to Allied forces, it declared war on Nazi Germany, its onetime Axis powers partner.

Oct. 27: Allies invade and win Battle of the Treasury Islands, Solomon Islands. Japanese are isolated further.

Oct. 28: U.S. Marines conduct raids on Choiseul, Solomon Islands. The battalion attempts to divert Japanese attention away from impending invasion of Bougainville area.

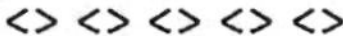

OFFICIAL MILITARY RECORD ENTRY:

Oct. 10 - Another red alert was called in at 2230 hours, and the all-clear was not sounded until 0005 hours. This alert was the "McCoy," as the Nips came over and our Ack Ack (anti-aircraft) batteries sent up a heavy barrage that kept the enemy at a very high altitude. As far as could be determined, the damage was one gasoline dump set afire in the Buna area, seven EM killed and 23 wounded from the 1913th Engineer Aviation Battalion, and about 30 wounded in the Marine group stationed near the 1913th Engineers.

Oct. 13 - A yellow alert was called in at 0345 hours and changed to a red at 0400 hours, with the all-clear sounding at 0445 hours. It was learned that the Nips were over but were intercepted by our Night Fighters before they could reach here.

Oct. 15 - A yellow alert was sounded at 0810 hours and changed to red at 0815 hours with the all-clear sounding at 0907 hours. The score as received was eight Jap dive bombers hit over Oro Bay and crashed into the sea, with five more shot down while flying away.

Oct. 16 - A yellow alert was sounded at 0945 hours and changed to a red at 0950 hours with the all-clear sounding at 1120 hours. Score for the day, 22 zeros downed and possible five more. Our losses were three fighters.

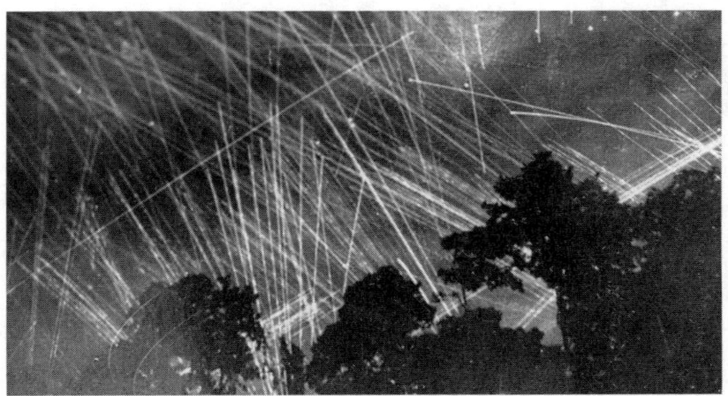

Anti-aircraft tracer fire.

NOVEMBER 1943

ELSEWHERE IN THE WAR

Nov. 1: Bombing of Rabaul, New Britain Island.

Nov. 1: Bougainville Campaign begins.

Nov. 6: Russian Army liberates the city of Kiev, Ukraine, from German army. Russia suffers loss of 700,000 casualties.

Nov. 20: Battle of Tarawa begins. U.S. Marines land on Tarawa and Makin atolls in the Gilbert Islands.

Battle of Makin Atoll, Gilbert Islands. A four-day battle to capture a tiny Japanese base resulted in the loss of an aircraft carrier and 763 U.S. men killed.

Nov. 24: Heavy bombing of Berlin continues.

Nov. 26: Battle of Cape St. George, North of Bougainville, ended Japanese resistance in the Solomon Islands. Allies achieve superiority in night combat using advanced radar.

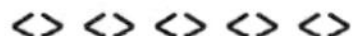

OFFICIAL MILITARY RECORD ENTRY:

Nov. 16 -

1. A dud believed to be a 50-kilogram bomb, dropped by the enemy the day before, landed in B Company area. The bomb disposal group from U.S. Advanced Base B dug about 12 feet for the bomb and struck water. It was decided to fill up the hole with rock and sand, rope off the area for a week to make sure there would be no casualties if it went off and left it at that. Four (4) 50-kilogram bombs landed in the dispersal area of strips #11 and #13 with no damage resulting.

2. Lt. Col. Harvey, the battalion commander, gave the EM of H&S Company a talk on the work of the battalion. He gave them a clear word picture of how priorities worked and changed with each change of the tactical situation. He commended them in person on the splendid job they were doing. By his marvelous command of words and being the forceful speaker that he is, the colonel had the men hanging on to his every word. At the close of the talk there was a spontaneous burst of applause from the men which brought a sort of blush of embarrassment to Harvey's face. Morale up 1000 percent.

DECEMBER 1943

- - - - - - - - - - -

ELSEWHERE IN THE WAR

Dec. 15: Battle of Arawe, New Britain Island. Part of Operation Cartwheel, the battle was considered of little value.

Dec. 24: U.S. General Dwight D. Eisenhower becomes the Supreme Allied Commander in Europe.

Dec. 26: Battle of Cape Gloucester, New Britain Island. Japanese airfield captured, Allied shipping routes secured.

<> <> <> <> <>

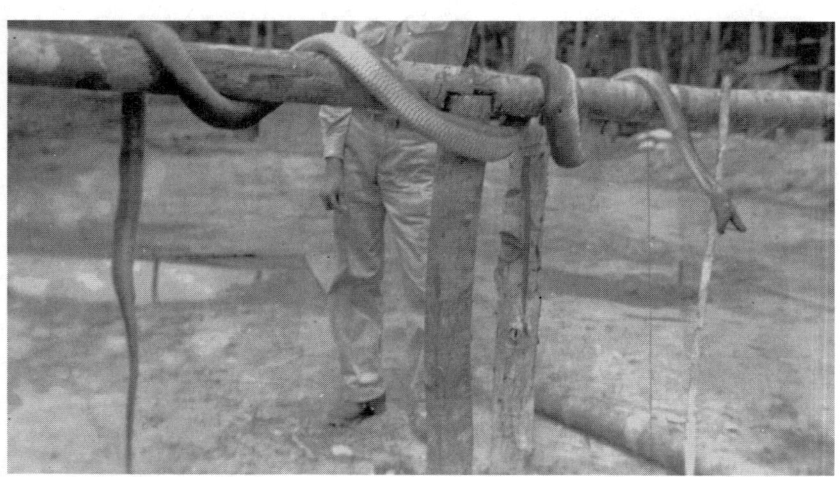

A 14-foot-long python – another one of the local hazards.

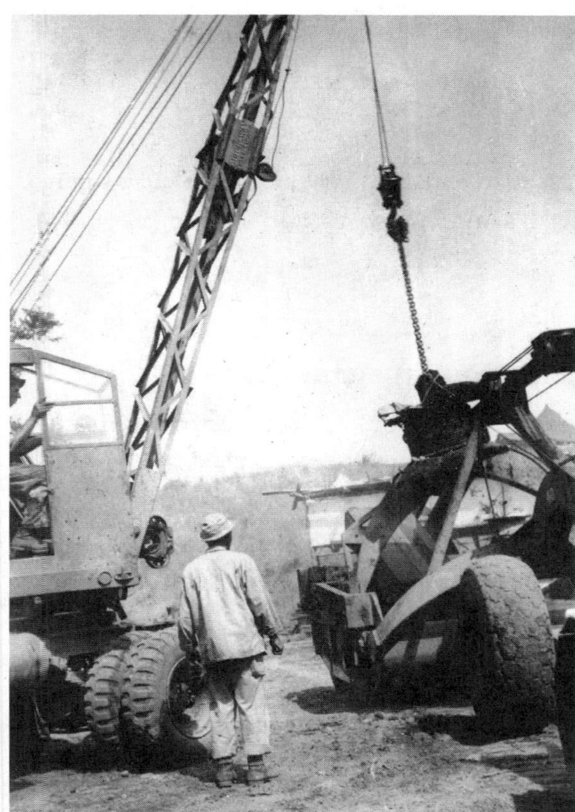

The Quick-Way Truck Shovel (on left) is loading a Carry-All for a move from Dobodura to Saidor. Jan. 4, 1944.

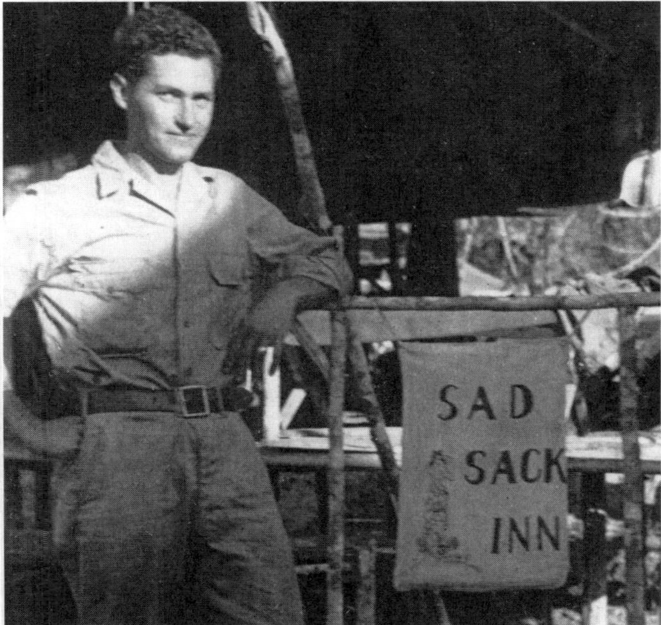

Curtis Bertrand in front of old Sad Sack Inn. This is the last day at this campsite. Battallion is preparing to leave camp in Dobodura, to move to Saidor, New Guinea. Jan. 5, 1944.

Routine work and maintenance continued through this month and is summed up below in the summary report of work done from Aug. 6, 1943 to Jan. 5, 1944.

OFFICIAL MILITARY RECORD - WORK SUMMARY ENTRY:

The summary of major construction work in the Borio and West Embi Drome Area, Dobodura, New Guinea, is as listed below. The work started Aug. 6, 1943:

A. The building of a two-lane all-weather road from the main Oro Bay Road to battalion camp area, four miles in length; Construction of access road for fighter group.

B. Thirteen miles of taxiways were completed, these being 75 feet wide from ditch to ditch. 170 Heavy Bomber-type hardstandings were built in this dispersal area.

C. A steel matted strip 6000 feet long and 100 feet wide, with 50-foot shoulders and four 100 x 700-foot alert areas at the ends, was completed. (Borio Strip #10).

D. A 7500 x 100-foot steel mat covering was laid on Borio Strip #15. The strip was originally constructed 6000 feet in length, but this battalion extended it to 7500 feet with 500-foot earth overruns at each end.

E. The major building construction consisted of a Quartermaster bakery, laundry, refrigeration, and a Red Cross recreation building; battalion infirmary; battalion headquarters; engineering office; battalion supply office; chapel and theatre; motor pool and heavy equipment supply and parts buildings, grease rack and filling station; PX building; Liberty Ship Dock; air transport building.

F. The Borio and West Embi dispersal areas were connected by a causeway 400-feet long.

G. A drainage program was carried out throughout the entire dispersal area as well as for the service roads. This necessitated the installation of approximately 30 barrel-type culverts.

H. Three large campsites were cleared, and three miles of all-weather access roads constructed.

I. An air freight loading dock 40x60-feet, truck height, was constructed.

J. A water point on the Zambogi River was installed for servicing the surrounding area. This necessitated the construction of a 12-foot tower and installing the two 1000 gallon tanks.

K. A bore sighting range 1400 feet long and 70 feet wide was completed; Battalion logging project - cutting and hauling logs four miles to Air Force sawmill; Built a campsite area for the 56th T.C. Squadron, 375th Group Operations, and for the 43rd Bomb Group.

L. Six months of work being completed in this area, the equipment was made ready to move Jan. 5, 1944.

CHAPTER 6

The Invasion of Saidor, New Guinea

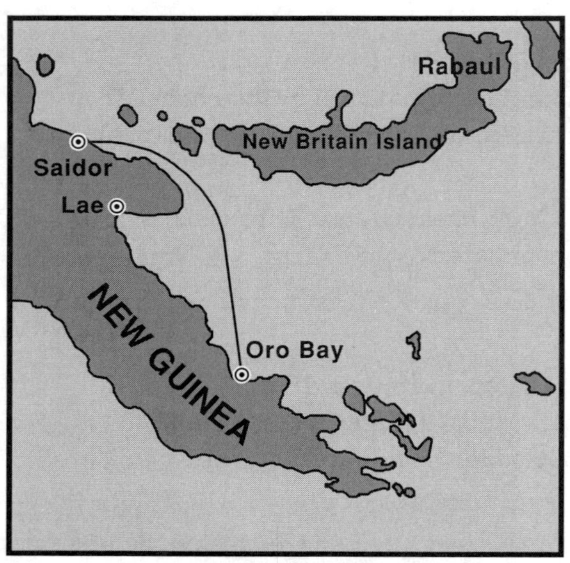

From Oro Bay to Saidor

One of the purposes of moving from the Dobodura area to Saidor was to cut off the escape of several thousand Japanese soldiers who were moving from east to west through the hills and mountains. Some were killed or captured, but many either escaped or died of starvation or exposure to the elements. It was also the continuing strategy of cutting off supplies and reinforcements to the Japanese bases in this area of the South Pacific called Operation Cartwheel. Rather than directly attacking their bases and stirring up a hornet's nest of enemy planes, it was decided by General MacArthur that the Allied Forces would blockade their bases, in effect laying siege to them and letting them wither away.

Everything was kept secret from the soldiers. Every time that they moved from one place to another, they were not told their destination until they were well under way. Their motto was "Loose Lips Sink Ships."

Here is the reproduction of a document from the official Military Record that explains the purpose of invading Saidor:

Saidor Campaign

S-E-C-R-E-T

HEADQUARTERS UNITED STATES FORCES

A.P.O. #321

Report of:

863rd Engineer Aviation Bn.

Michaelmas Operation

16 Dec., 1943 to 10 Feb. 1944

GENERAL

The seizure, occupation and defense of Saidor, New Guinea, and the subsequent control over that area to provide for the uninterrupted construction of airdrome facilities and light naval installations was conducted by the Commanding General, MICHAELMAS Task Force. The operation was referred to as MICHAELMAS, the secret code name for SAIDOR, and was directed in PO 7, Headquarters, ESCALATOR, the secret code name for ALAMO Force. The operation was initiated 2 January 1944, when elements of the Task Force under command of Brigadier General Clarence A. Martin, USA, made an amphibious landing on beaches between SAUI and WILWILAN, Northeast NEW GUINEA, and was terminated on 10 Feb. 44. This officially terminated the DEXTERITY operations, of which MICHAELMAS was a part.

MISSION

a. ESCALATOR PO 7, 22 Dec. 1943, directed that the MICHAELMAS Task Force would:

(1) By overwater operation, land assault elements in the MICHAELMAS area on D-Day and seize, occupy and defend that area.

(2) Establish control over such area adjacent to MICHAELMAS as would be required to insure uninterrupted operation of our air and light naval forces in that area; and initiate and expedite the establishment of airdrome facilities in the MICHAELMAS area to accommodate one group of fighters, with first priority given to the completion of an air transport landing strip.

(3) Assist in the establishment of air elements in the MICHAELMAS area as requested by the Commander, Allied Air Force.

(4) Assist in the establishment of Light Naval facilities in the MICHAELMAS area.

(5) Construct minimum port and base facilities, the development of which would contemplate use of barges and small boats for unloading of large ships rather than construction of piers.

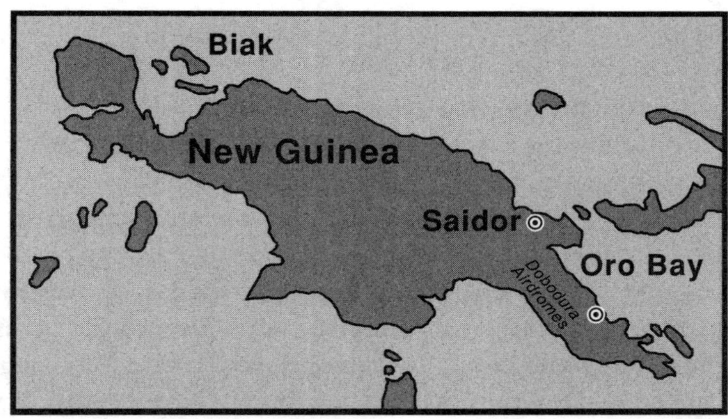

A map of New Guinea shown in relation to the northernmost tip of Australia. My father's battalion was stationed at the Oro Bay/Dobodura area first, then they later moved on to Saidor. From there, they would go to Biak.

HEADQUARTERS

863RD ENGINEER AVIATION BATTALION

APO 321

28 FEBRUARY, 1944

HISTORICAL REPORT

On December 24, 1943, the Commanding Officer was notified that the 863rd Engineer Aviation Battalion was attached to the Alamo Force for participation in the Michaelmas Task Force with the mission of constructing the Michaelmas Airdrome and Air Force facilities. Upon receipt of these orders, the unit was brought up to TBA (To Be Activated) strength as far as the equipment was available at APO 503. Movement to Saidor was accomplished by 4 LSTs (Landing Ship, Tank). Loading was started at 1430 hours 5 January, 1944, and all equipment was loaded by 1400 hours 6 January, 1944. The convoy arrived at Saidor Beachhead at 0700 hours, 8 January, 1944. Unloading and movement to campsite was completed on that date.

Defense plans of the Task Force called for B Company, this Battalion, to defend a section of beach immediately to the East of the mouth of the Nankina River. A and C Companies, supplemented by technicians from H&S Company, immediately started construction operations. A Company repaired the existing transport landing strip and erected a temporary control tower. C Company started the construction of roads; one to the beach and one from the gravel deposits near the Nankina River to the Airdrome site. Further Engineer operations were started in accordance with priorities and designs established by the Task Force Engineer.

Operations were hampered and progress was slow in the initial stages, due to local soil conditions, excessive rainfall, and inaccessibility of necessary materials. Construction of roads was seriously hampered by traffic during the preliminary stages of construction. As the quality and quantity of roads increased, construction proceeded more rapidly. Engineer operations were greatly facilitated by the locating of an ample supply of gravel for base and surface material.

During the operations, one H-10 steel Bailey bridge was constructed across the Nankina River, approximately five miles of hard surface roads were constructed, access roads to Task Force supply agencies were completed, and construction of dispersal areas started.

For the invasion, every battalion had a code name. The code name for the 863rd Engineers was BING. Dad arrived at Saidor on D-Day +6, which was January 8, 1944.

JANUARY 1944

- - - - - - - -

ELSEWHERE IN THE WAR

Jan. 2: Landing at Saidor, New Guinea, by Allied troops.

Jan. 19: Red Army troops push westward toward the Baltic countries.

Jan. 20: The Royal Air Force drops 2300 tons of bombs on Berlin.

Jan. 29: Battle of the Green Islands. Allied forces recaptured the islands from the Japanese. It became a forward base for the U.S, supplying material and mail to troops.

Jan. 31: Battle of Kwajalein Atoll, Marshall Islands. Allies capture this enemy base in its island-hopping march to Japan.

<> <> <> <> <>

The battalion is still in Dobodura, New Guinea, preparing to leave for Saidor.

OFFICIAL MILITARY RECORD ENTRY:

Jan. 3, 1944 - Our organization has been assigned to Michaelmas Task Force as per Verbal Order of Commanding Officer (VOCO).

Jan. 6 - Battalion strength is 29 officers and 777 EM (enlisted men). We are now departing from Oro Bay. The LSTs sailed at 1500 hours; in a convoy of nine LSTs and four destroyers and two corvettes. Company C's boat being the first to leave the beach, followed by H&S Company, B Co., with A Co. bringing up the rear due to slight trouble with one engine on the A Co. boat, which was soon repaired.

The ships anchored off Buna until the remainder of the convoy was formed, getting under way at 2330 hours. The lights on the shore at Buna resemble the lights of a small village.

Jan. 7 – Our destination was announced as Saidor, New Guinea. Finschafen was passed late in the afternoon.

Jan. 8 – Arrive at Saidor. The coast of Dekays Bay was sighted at dawn, and the LSTs beached at approximately 0800 hours, unloading commencing immediately. Our destroyers patrolled outside the Bay and were augmented by 10 P-47s and some PT boats. Made camp near shoreline and 400 yards from the Nankina River. It took four days to clear the dense jungle from our camp area.

This boat below looks similar to a Higgins boat, but it is actually a landing craft developed by the British independently from Higgins. It is based on the same idea, but has a different design. It is an LCA (Landing Craft, Assault), belonging to the Royal Australian Navy. Notice the initials R.A.N. and the Australian flag in the rear.

The Higgins Landing Crafts were built in New Orleans, Louisiana. They were used in every major American amphibious operation in the European and Pacific theaters, including D-Day in Normandy. Its military name was LCVP, which stands for Landing Craft, Vehicle, Personnel. The craft was designed by Andrew Higgins of Louisiana, United States, based on boats made for operating in swamps and marshes. More than 20,000 were built by Higgins Industries and licensees. Typically constructed from plywood, this shallow-draft, barge-like boat could ferry a platoon-sized complement of 36 men to shore at 9 knots (17 km/h). Men generally entered the boat by climbing down a cargo net hung from the side of their troop transport, and they exited by charging down the boat's bow ramp.

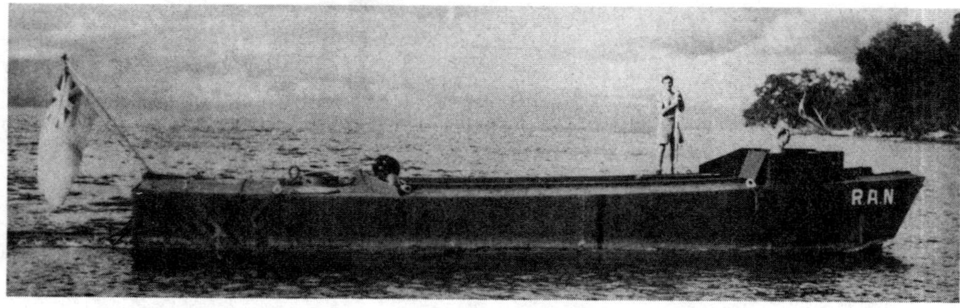

An LCA (Landing Craft, Assault) belonging to the Royal Australian Navy.

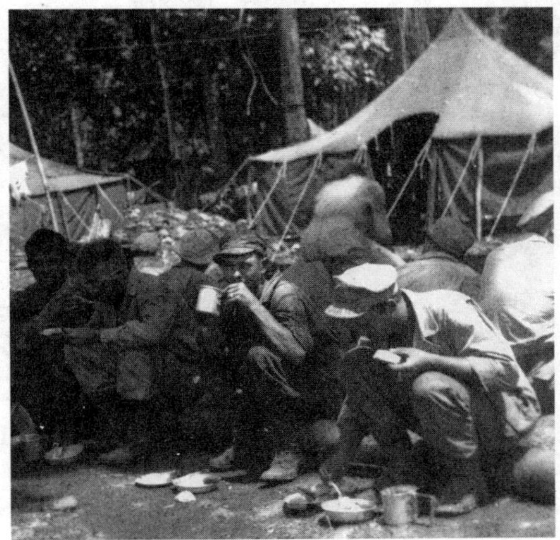

Upon arrival in Saidor, New Guinea.

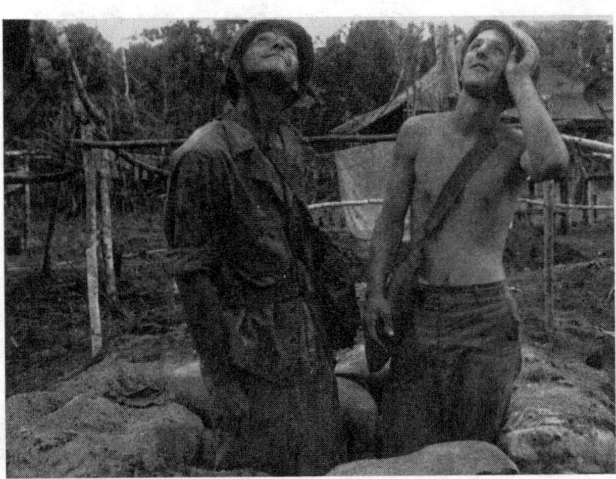

My dad and his good friend Clifford Wynne standing in a foxhole watching planes overhead.

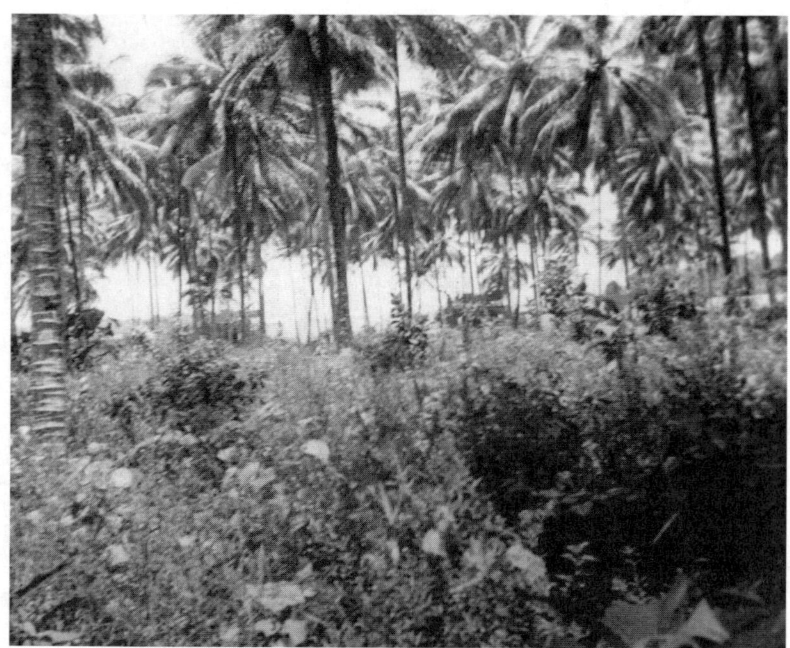

The camp area is near the beach. It took four days to clear all the weeds.

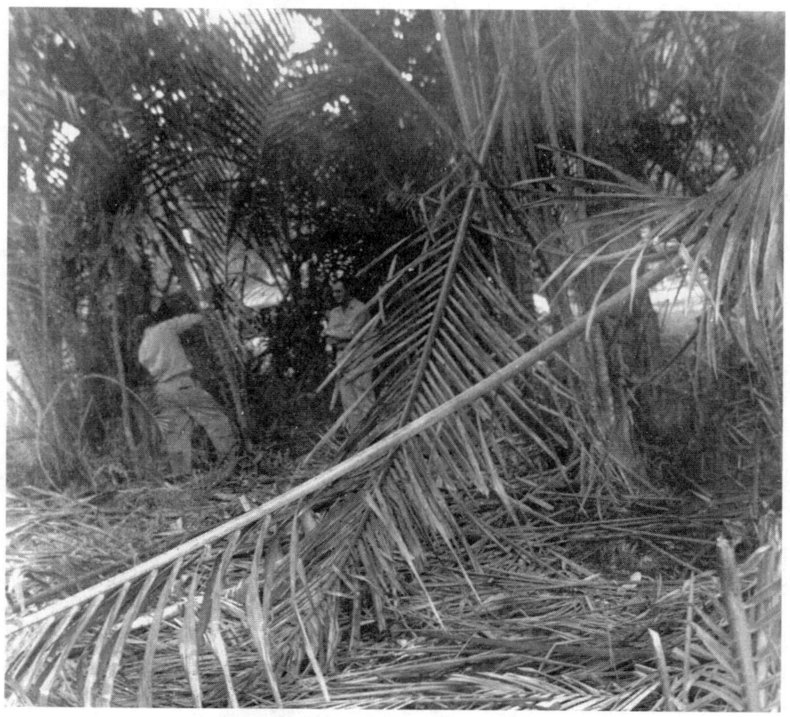

Almost done clearing the campsite area.

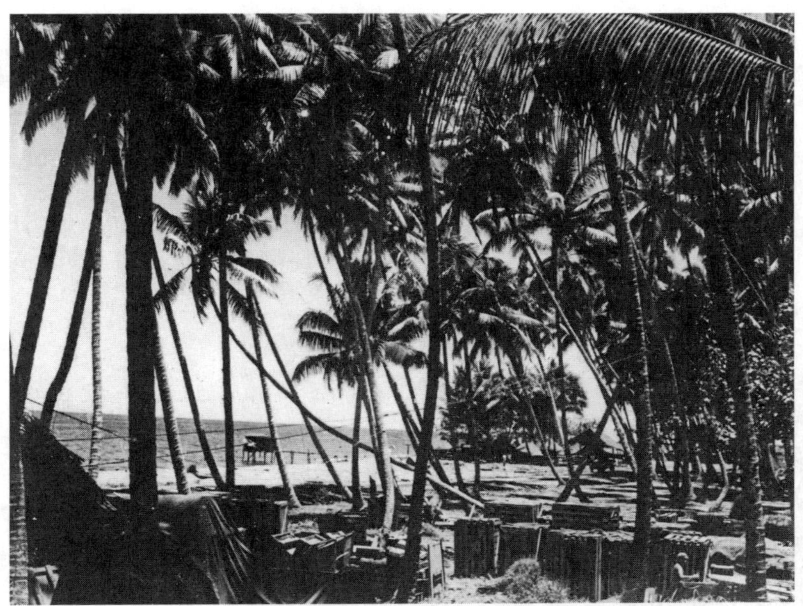

After the camp area was cleaned up.

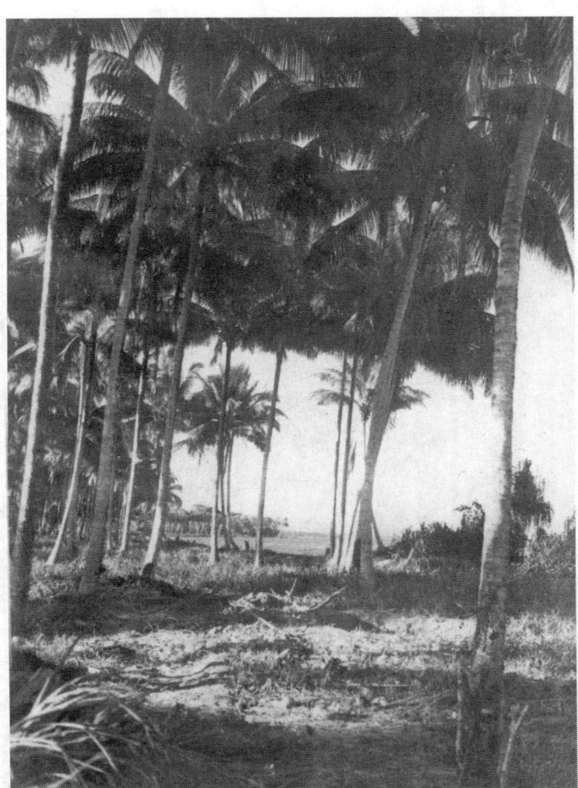

It cleaned up nice.

OFFICIAL MILITARY RECORD ENTRY:

Jan. 10 - The temporary strip for the C-47 Skytrain cargo planes, also known as Biscuit Bombers, has been sufficiently completed for the planes to land this morning, preceding by two days the scheduled completion date of 12 Jan.

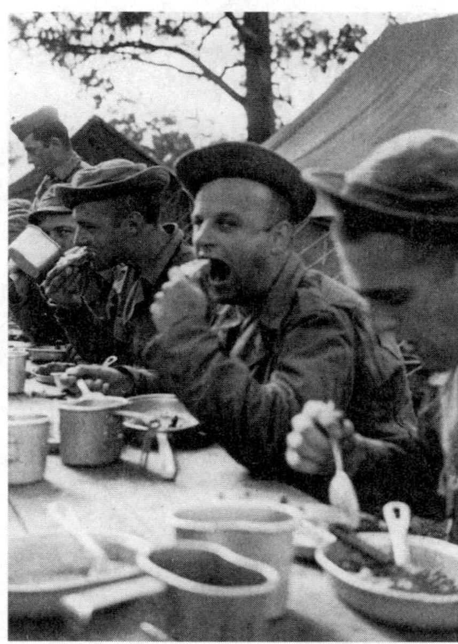

Chow time.

Curtis Bertrand, my dad, on right standing next to U.S. artillery piece.

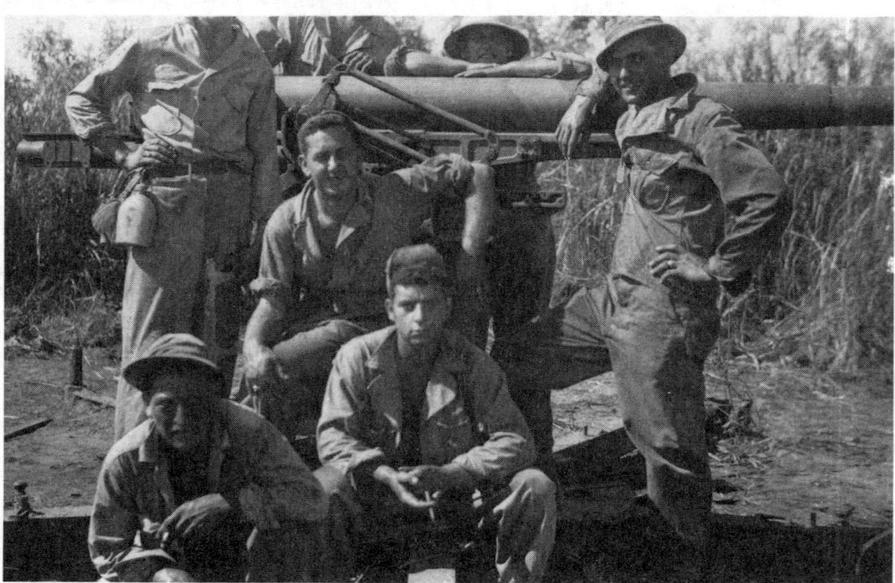

OFFICIAL MILITARY RECORD ENTRY:

Jan. 16 - 25 to 30 Jap planes attacked one of our LST convoys. Our fighters downed 18 enemy planes, and our destroyers sank a sub off the coast.

Jan. 17 - There were two red alerts at 0300 and 0420 hours. During the second alert, four planes were engaged as targets by the AA (anti-aircraft). No bombs were dropped. These are thought to be the ones that attempted to drop supply parachutes to enemy troops south of here. These parachutes fell behind our lines, indicating that the enemy has no idea of the location of their forces in that area.

Jan. 19 - We have had 14 1/2 inches rain from Jan. 12 - 18th.

Jan. 21 - 12 of our 2.5-ton dump trucks will be shipped to us before Feb. 1st. Nankina River is used for bathing and to wash clothes.

Jan. 22 - Biscuit Bombers have started bringing in supplies quite regularly. Weather has cleared, and road construction is on a 24-hour/day schedule.

Jan. 27 - 60 bags of mail and packages have arrived. Morale is way up.

Jan. 31 - Since Jan. 14 we've had 24 inches of rain.

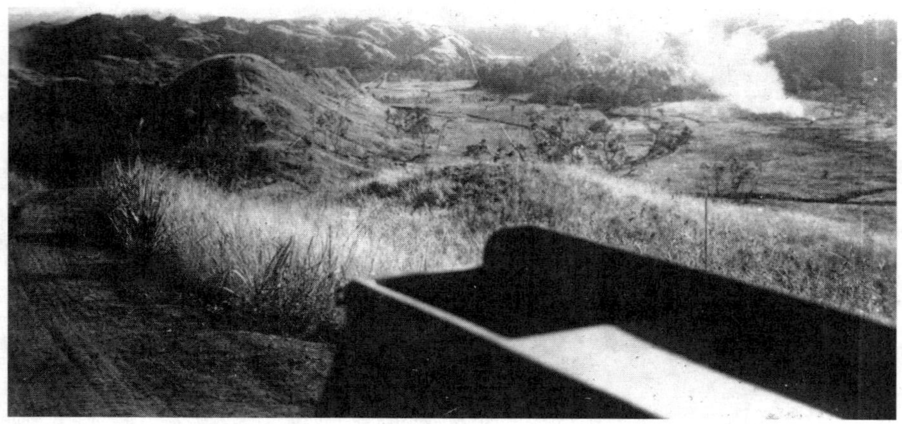

Our infantry men are firing mortar rounds on enemy position. Smoke visible on the right.

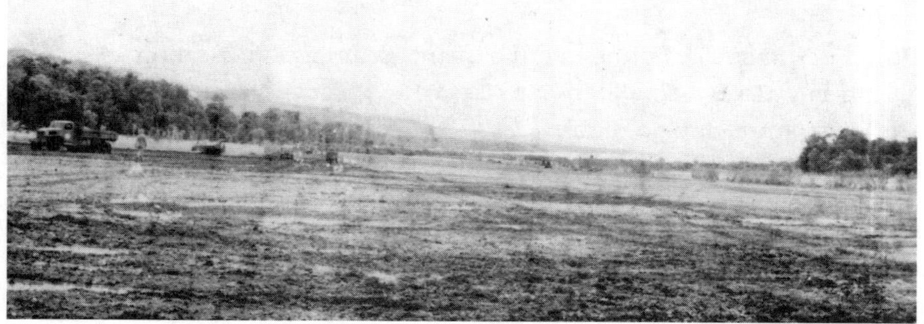

It is a mud field now, but an airstrip will be made out of this.

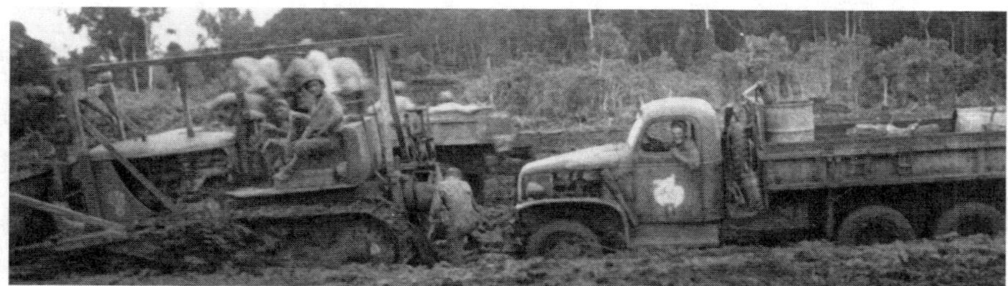

Bulldozer pulling out dump truck stuck in the mud. Dad's friend Mally Bass is doing the coupling. An additional 24 inches of rain would fall in the next two weeks! Jan. 15, 1944.

FEBRUARY 1944

ELSEWHERE IN THE WAR

Feb. 3: American planes bomb Eniwetok in the Marshall Islands, later to be a major B-29 base. After WWII more than 40 nuclear bombs would be detonated there.

Feb. 5: Battle of the Admin Box. Allied British, Indian, and Chinese troops thwart a Japanese counterattack in southern Burma.

Feb. 16-17: Operation Hailstone, a massive U.S. naval air and surface attack launched against the Japanese naval and air base at Truk in the Caroline Islands.

Feb. 17-23: Battle of Eniwetok, Marshall Islands, wrested an airfield and harbor from the Japanese to support attacks on the Mariana Islands to the northwest.

Feb. 19: Industrial city of Leipzig, Germany, is bombed for two straight nights; the P-51 Mustang fighter proves its worth.

Feb. 23: U.S. Navy planes attack the Mariana Islands of Saipan, Guam and Tinian.

Feb. 29-May 18: The Admiralty Islands campaign (Operation Brewer). U.S. air and sea superiority allowed the Allies to occupy the Japanese-held islands and completed the isolation of the major Japanese base at Rabaul.

<> <> <> <> <>

OFFICIAL MILITARY RECORD ENTRY:

Feb. 3 – Lt. Blay in hospital due to appendix.

Feb. 4 – B company assigned the Horseshoe gravel pit. We had a red alert at 0117 (1:17 a.m.). One plane coming in from the southwest dropped six bombs near the airstrip and nine small fragmentation bombs aimed at our searchlights. No casualties and no damage.

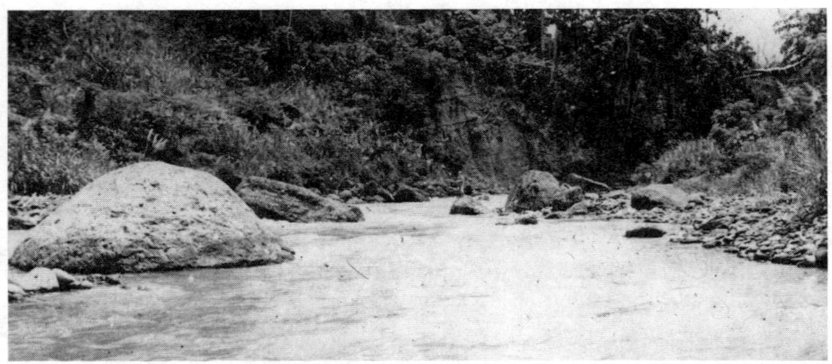

The calm, peaceful Nankina River before weeks of rainstorms and flooding.

Part of the job of an Engineer Aviation Battalion is to build the infrastructure of that area. In the case of primitive New Guinea, this meant constructing bridges over ravines and rivers, as well as building the roads to move the supplies where they were needed. Troops without food, water, guns, and ammunition cannot function properly, so the engineering team did what was required to achieve the goals.

Some bridges were built from native trees and cut into beams by the battalion sawmill. Some were Bailey bridges, a pre-fabricated bridge that came in a variety of sizes, widths, lengths, and load-bearing strengths.

To complete the tasks assigned them by the chief engineer in the quickest amount of time, it was necessary for work to be done on both sides of the Nankina River. To accomplish that, three bridges had to be built by separate engineer companies in the area: troops with the 863rd, the 808th, and the Australian Army each built one.

When one is in unfamiliar territory, it may be difficult to foresee what forces of nature are lurking nearby, and to determine the size and strength of the bridge and foundation substructure, or abutments, that are required. In this situation, there was a massive amount of rainfall in the area and in the nearby mountains, causing the river to rise. This rising water level causes logs, trees, and other debris to float downriver and act as a battering ram when it hits the bridge abutments.

In engineering terms, abutment refers to the substructure at both ends of a bridge span whereon the bridge's superstructure rests. Single-span bridges have abutments at each end which provide vertical and lateral support for the bridge, as well as acting as retaining walls to resist lateral movement of the earthen fill of the bridge approach. Multi-span bridges require piers to support ends of spans unsupported by abutments.

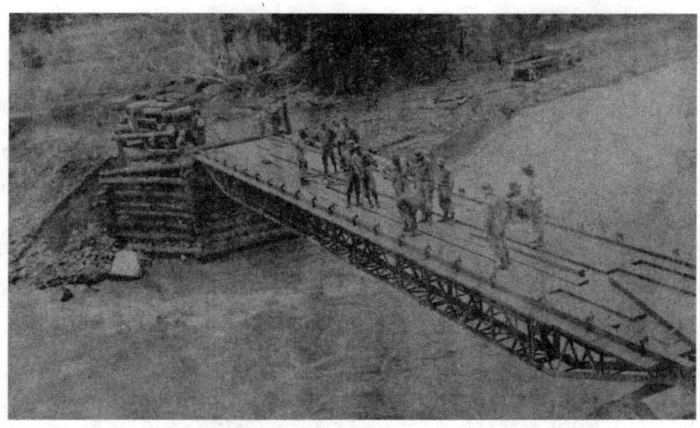

Company B of the 863rd is erecting a steel H-10 Bailey Bridge across the Nankina River.

In this scenario, there was an enormous amount of rainfall in a short amount of time so the peaceful Nankina River became a violent, raging torrent that destroyed the entire Australian bridge and washed away the abutments of the 808th bridge. The bridge that Company B, 863rd Engineer Aviation Battalion, built was not damaged.

On Jan. 20, the 863rd Engineers Company B was given the task of constructing abutments and approaches and erecting a steel H-10 Bailey Bridge across the Nankina River. H-10 means it can hold up to 10 tons of weight at one time. The job was completed on Feb. 10.

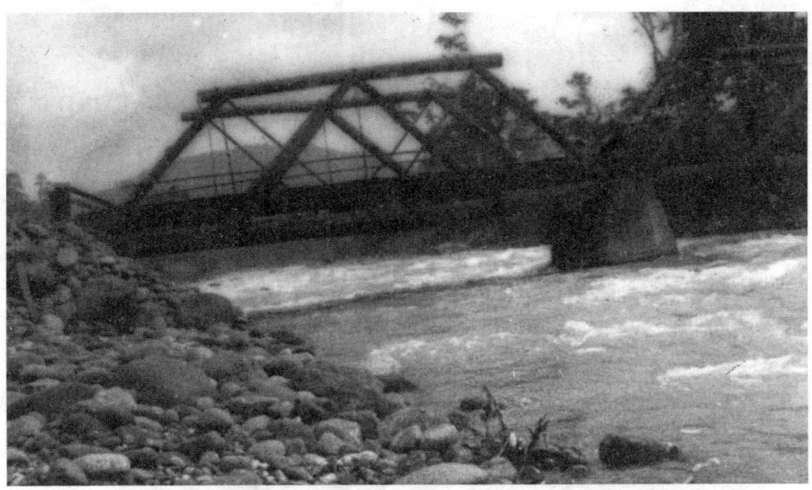

The 808th Engineers Aviation Battalion built this wooden bridge. The Nankina River is now a raging torrent after weeks of rain.

OFFICIAL MILITARY RECORD ENTRY:

Feb. 10 – The H-10 steel Bailey bridge over the Nankina River has been erected. The abutments for the bridge remained intact during the heavy rains that washed away the abutments of the 808th wooden bridge and the complete Australian bridge.

Feb. 17 – We attained a record of 1302 loads in one day from the Horseshoe gravel pit.

Feb. 18 – Dump trucks and heavy equipment arrive and four new refrigeration units, along with all of our crated battalion headquarter files. The administration section can now commence efficient operation.

Feb. 22 – Sawmill arrived on LST, to be in operation Mar. 5.

Feb. 23 – Tasked to build control tower for Strip 1, administration buildings and alert huts for strip 1; on Mar. 18 the control tower completed.

Feb. 29 – 218 Japs killed in action so far.

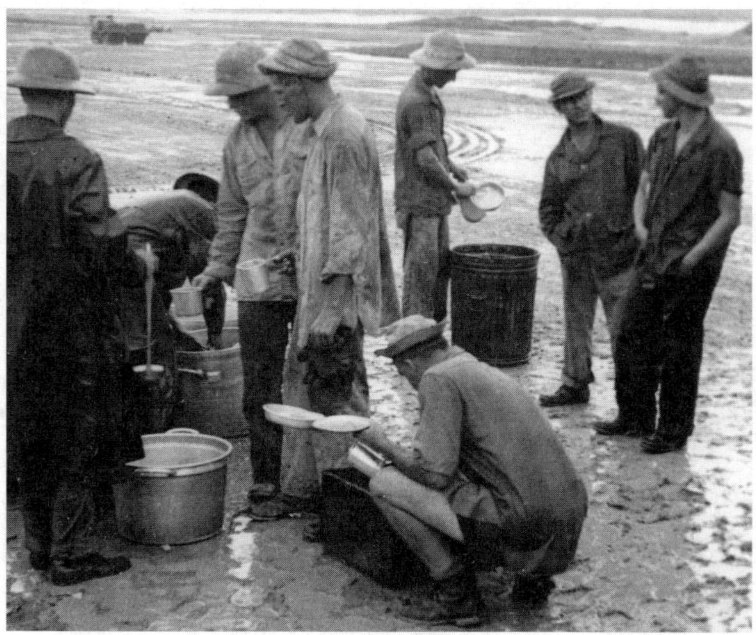

Chow time in the mud.

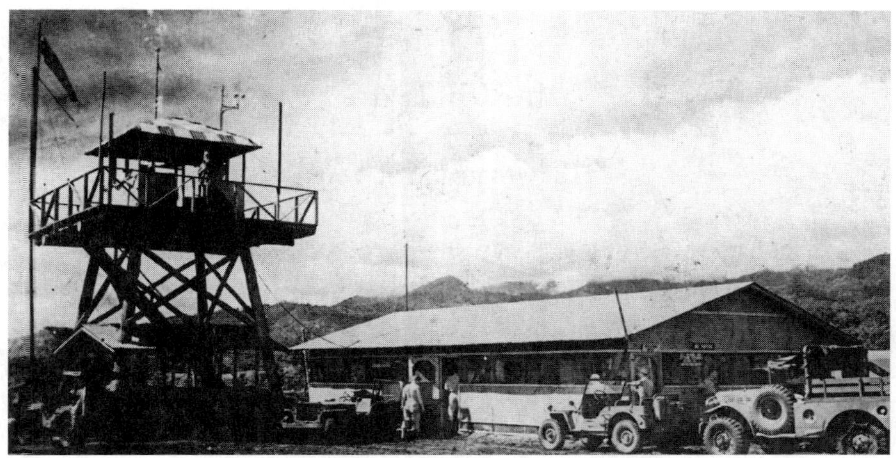

Control tower and operations building.

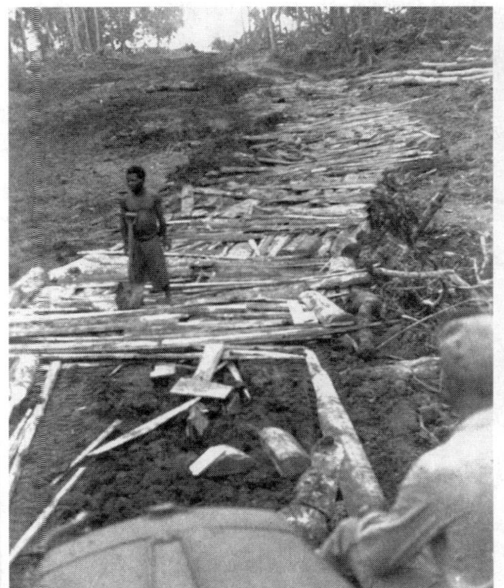

Native workers building a corduroy road so the vehicle can travel up and down the muddy terrain.

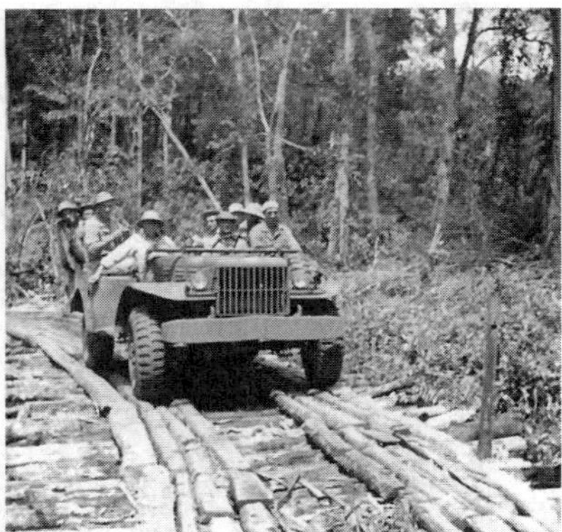

A personnel carrier coming down the completed corduroy road.

MARCH 1944

ELSEWHERE IN THE WAR

Mar. 6: Battle of Berlin. Daylight bombing raids start over Germany. Two thousand tons of bombs are dropped on vital industrial and military targets.

Mar. 7: Japanese begin an invasion attempt on India, starting a four-month battle around Imphal.

Mar. 8: American forces are attacked by Japanese troops on Hill 700 in Bougainville.

Mar. 8: Battle of Imphal, Manipur, India. Japanese armies attempt to invade India but were driven back into Burma with heavy losses.

Mar. 17: Heavy bombing of Vienna, Austria.

Mar. 20-26: Battle of Sangshak, Manipur, India. British Indian Army fight Japanese forces, allowing reinforcements to reach the vital position at Kohima before the Japanese.

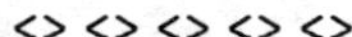

OFFICIAL MILITARY RECORD ENTRY:

Mar. 11 – Two Jap Mitsubishi G4M bombers, nicknamed Betty's flew overhead; one was engaged by our Ack Ack (anti-aircraft) fire and dropped no bombs. The other dropped four bombs that landed in the sea.

Mar. 15 – Dive bombers attack and start fire that destroys 2340 drums of 100 percent octane fuel. The plane approached over the mountains and was not detected until the bomb run was started. Only one of our ack ack guns fired with no results. Japs killed in action to date is 471.

Mar. 17 – Japs bomb base. Red alert #83 brought two twin-engine bombers, thought to be Betty's over the area at an altitude of 2300 yards, dove to 1500 to 2000 feet dropping four bombs on east end of strip due north of task force ammo dump. The planes returned on a second run dropping six bombs in the 860th Engineers Aviation Battalion area, wounding two men, destroying 16 tents and equipment, and damaging three vehicles.

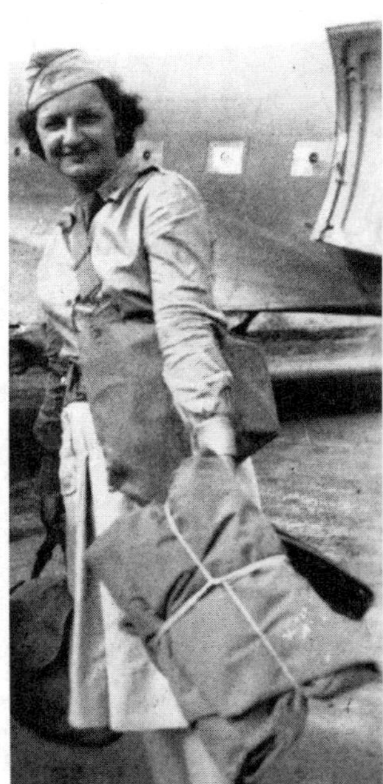
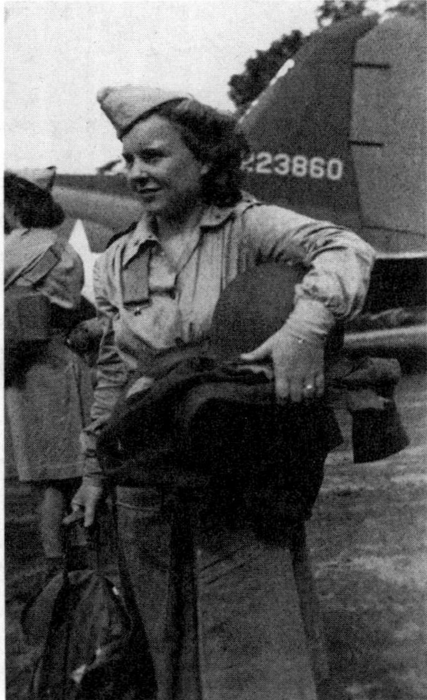

These servicewomen visiting the area are with the Women's Army Corps (WAC).

Dad and friends fooling around.

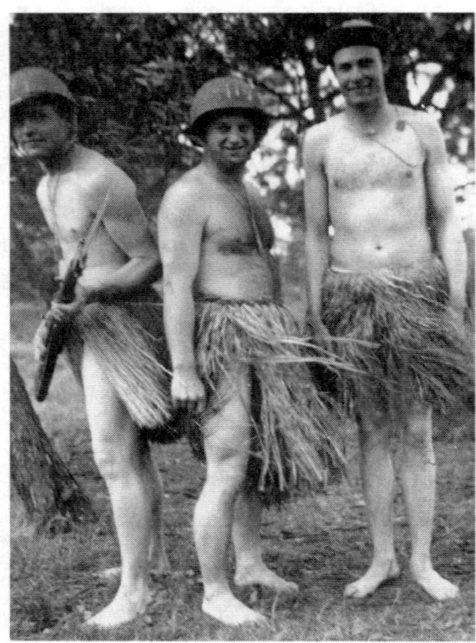

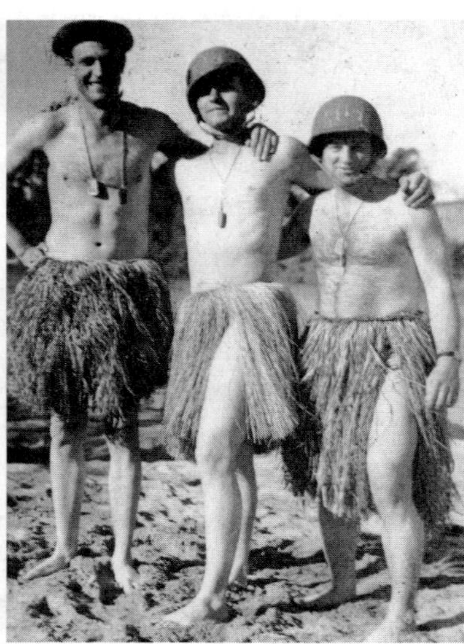

**My father (left), Ted Woodson, and Homer Fleming.
In the right photo are Homer Fleming, Curtis Bertrand, and Ted Woodson.**

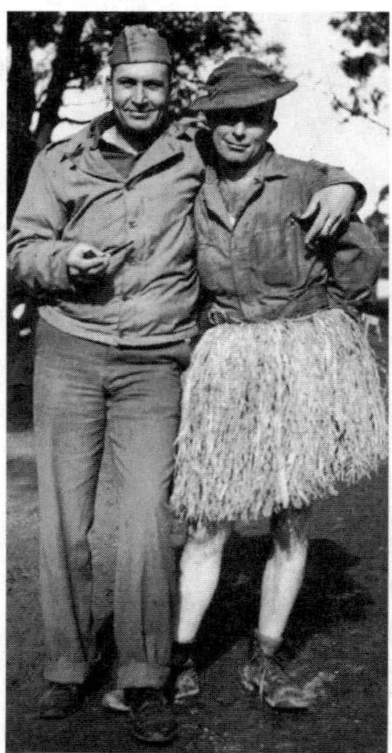

The cooks, Tex and Linscum, of my father's battalion.

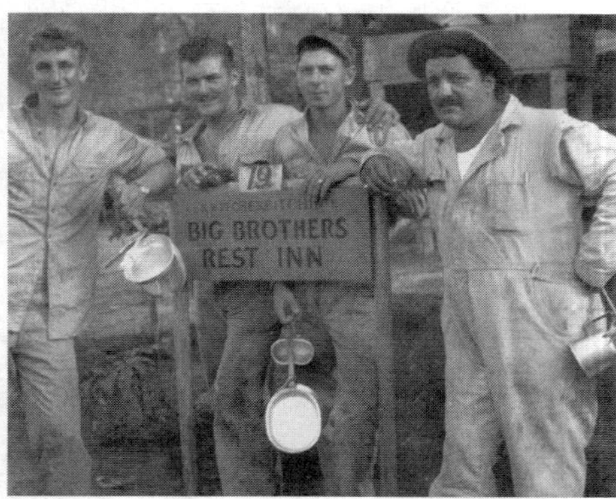

My father's friends, Wynne, Sandras, Bass, and Rose. The sign identifies the camp as "Kwitcherbitchin – Big Brothers Rest Inn."

APRIL 1944

ELSEWHERE IN THE WAR

Apr. 4: Battle of Kohima, Nagaland, India. Japanese attempted to capture Kohima ridge to cut off supplies to besieged British and Indian troops.

Apr. 14: Crimea and Odessa are liberated by Soviet forces.

Apr. 17: Americans land on Mindanao in the southern Philippines.

Apr. 22: U.S. troops land at Hollandia and Aitape in northern New Guinea cutting off Japanese forces.

Apr. 30: Vast preparations for D-Day are occurring in southern England.

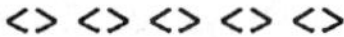

OFFICIAL MILITARY RECORD ENTRY:

Apr. 2 – Michaelmas Task Force dissolved. Battalion reattached to the 32nd Infantry Division as of Mar. 31.

Apr. 5 – Red Alert! A Helen bomber dropped three bombs in the 114th Engineers Bivouac Area.

Apr. 18 – Our PX (post exchange or store) is practically closed due to the fact that most of the merchandise has been sold in the four days it was open.

Apr. 20 – Telegram received by Task Force Engineer from Commanding General. Alamo Force requested status of Engineer Equipment and personnel for contemplated move on D plus 13 at the earliest. This will probably cancel all hopes of furloughs.

Apr. 21 – We will be inspected by the Task Force Engineer, accompanied by an inspection team from the Sixth Army, on 26 April. Schedule of the inspection will be submitted to the Task Force Engineer on 23 April, 1944.

Apr. 22 – Today is D-Day, so we should have approximately two weeks to prepare for our move. Liberty Dock now completed.

Apr. 28 – Inspection by Col. Bruce. Received a mark of excellence.

Apr. 29 – Started packing for next move; all construction stopped.

Apr. 30 – Motor pool is repairing all trucks and heavy equipment.

Our next move is delayed. Work continues by maintaining roads and bridge and hauling gravel.

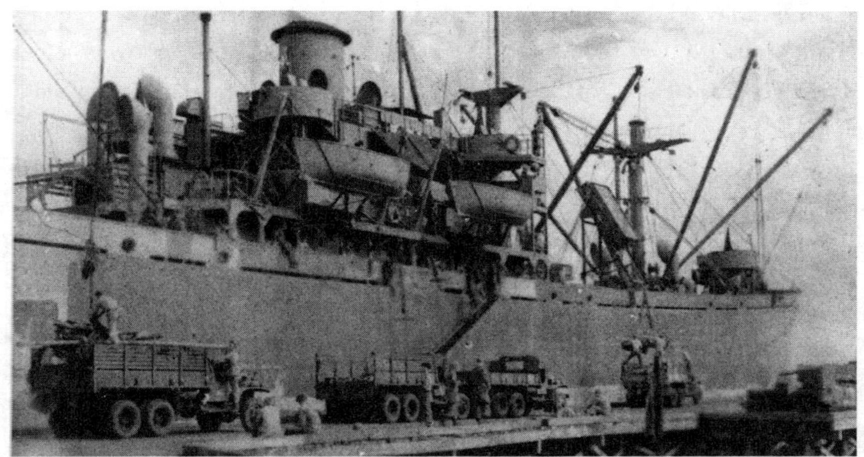

Unloading a Liberty ship at the new dock.

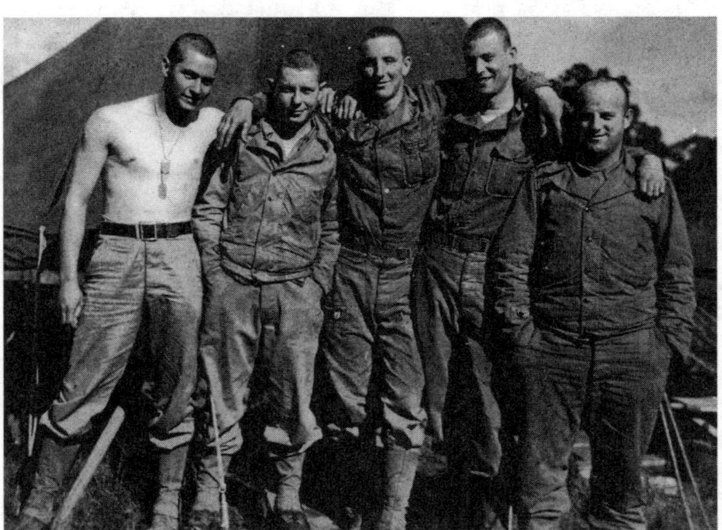

From left to right: Fresh haircuts on Curtis Bertrand, Mally Bass, Clifford Wynne, Homer Fleming, and Ted Woodson.

The Sawmill Operation

In order to build the needed structures for the war effort, lumber was required – and in a hurry. A control tower for the airdrome, as well as bridges over ravines and rivers, were just a few of the projects constructed that would keep the Pacific Campaign offensive moving forward.

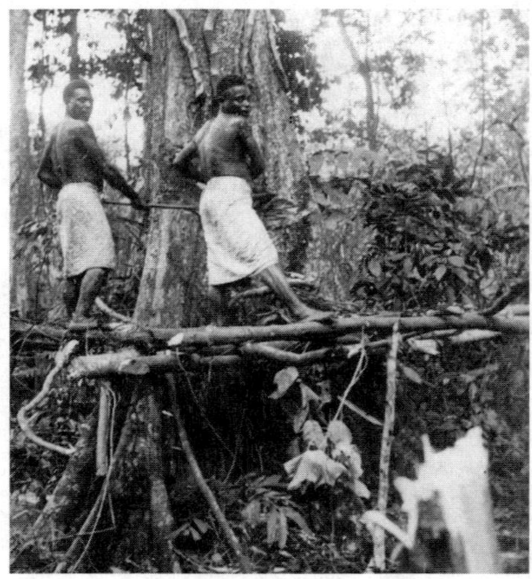

Native tree cutters.

The lumber for these projects was cut to order by the 863rd Engineer Aviation Battalion Company C sawmill. An officer and his men scouted for lumber in the jungle, selected and marked the trees they needed to cut, and sent teams of native New Guinea men to chop them down with axes. Sometimes a platform had to be built around the tree for the men to stand on and cut. It was dangerous and labor intensive, to say the least.

Once the trees were felled, the branches were cut off and the trees were transported by truck to the sawmill. After the lumber was cut to order, it was loaded onto another truck and delivered to the project site. Because of the constant threat of attack from the Japanese soldiers roaming in the nearby jungle, an armed U.S. soldier had to stand guard at all times to protect the laborers and equipment.

In this photo my father is holding a Thompson M1A submachine gun. It fired a 45 caliber round just like the Colt 45 911A1 caliber pistol. He wrote on the back of the picture, "Ain't I rugged, though?" The native men with him were the lumberjacks. They are proudly holding the axes they used to cut down trees for the sawmill.

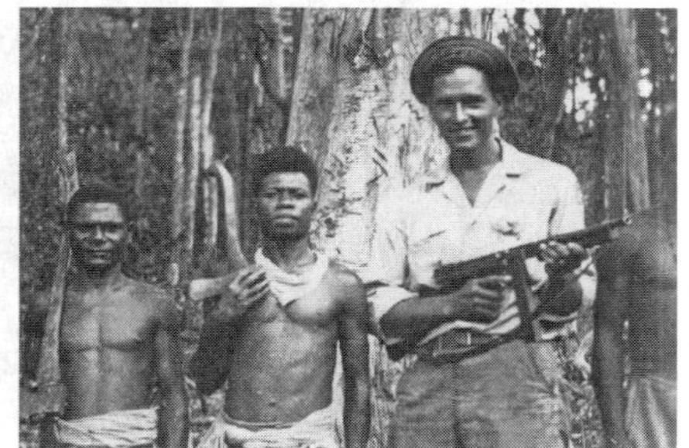

Dad standing guard with a Thompson submachine gun.

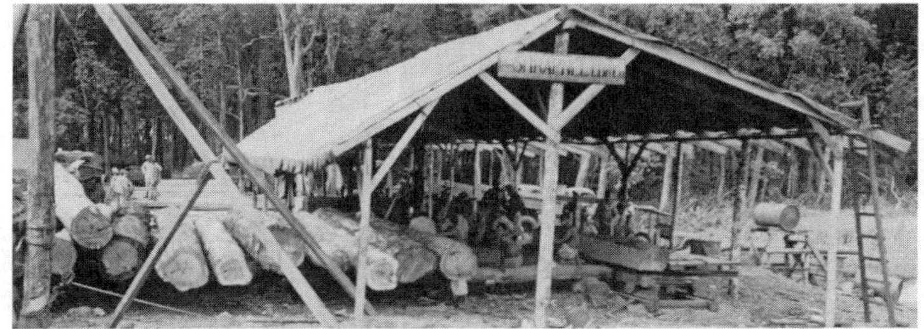

Logs were brought to the sawmill by truck and unloaded. They were rolled under the shed by laborers and positioned to be cut into planks or beams, whatever the work order called for. The cut lumber was loaded into another truck and hauled to the new job site.

This is the Company C sawmill that cut the lumber to make bridges, buildings, movie theater seating, and much more. The Company C men were out in the jungle with native laborers cutting down trees. The sign on the post reads "Shrapnel Labor Company."

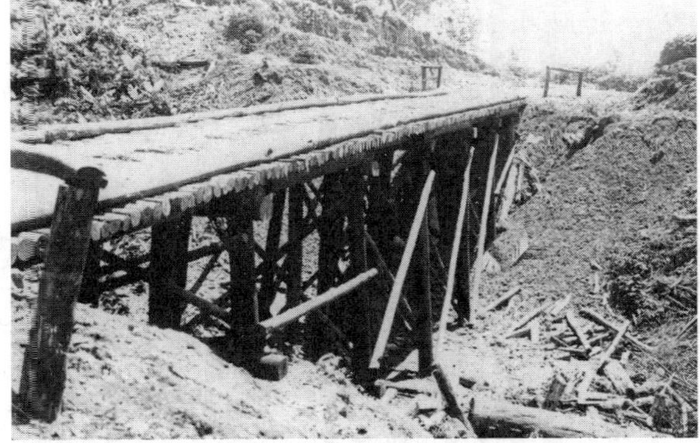

Bridge made from sawmill lumber.

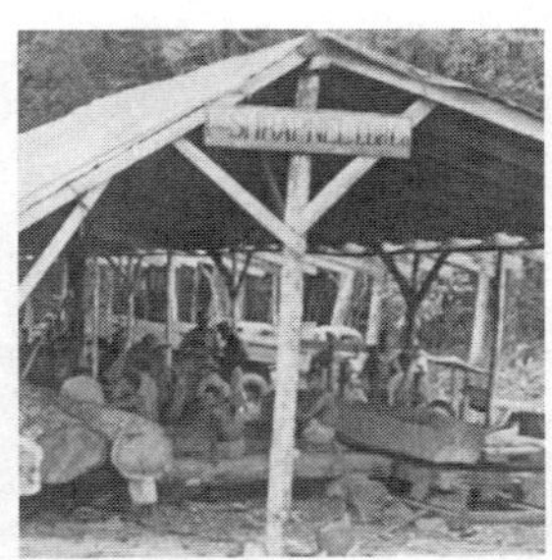

A closer look under the shed reveals laborers taking a break.

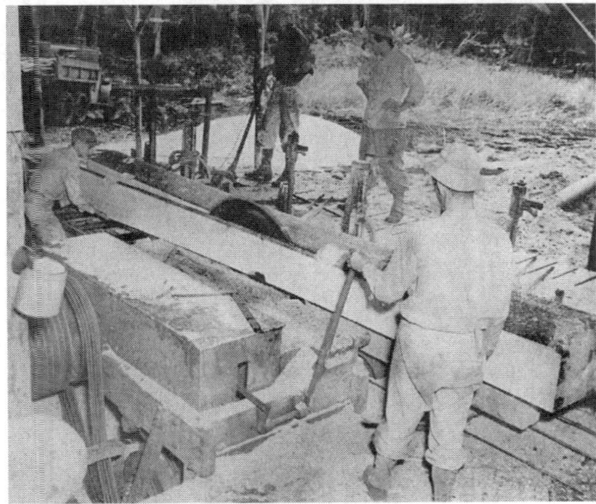

Cutting logs.

Company C sawmill produced 305,000 board feet of lumber while in Saidor. Man in foreground with his hand on the handle is controlling the power; the spinning saw blade is visible in the middle; the man at the back left is holding the cut plank. The two men at the top load the planks into the truck in background, left.

MAY 1944

ELSEWHERE IN THE WAR

May 15: Battle of Wakde Island, offshore New Guinea. A U.S. amphibious force landed and captured a Japanese airdrome after a three-day battle.

May 17: Operation Transom in Java. A major bombing raid on Japanese targets at Surabaya, Java, by American and British planes.

May 18: Battle of Monte Cassino near Rome ends with an Allied victory.

May 27: Operation Hurricane starts. Americans land on Biak, Dutch New Guinea, capturing three key Japanese air bases; stubborn resistance from enemy until August.

<> <> <> <> <>

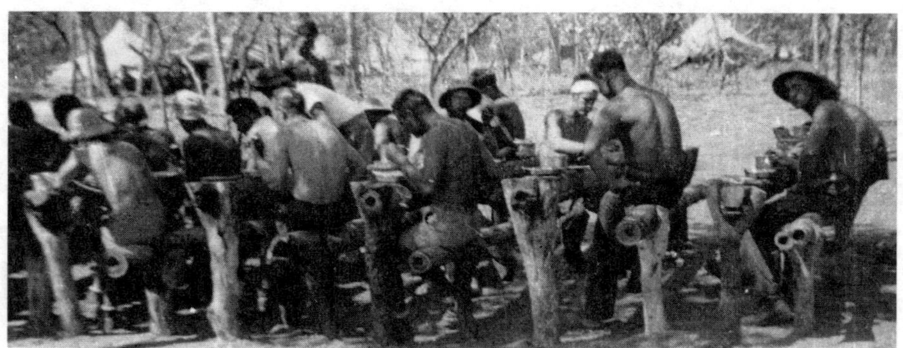

Temporary mess hall with homemade lunchroom seating.

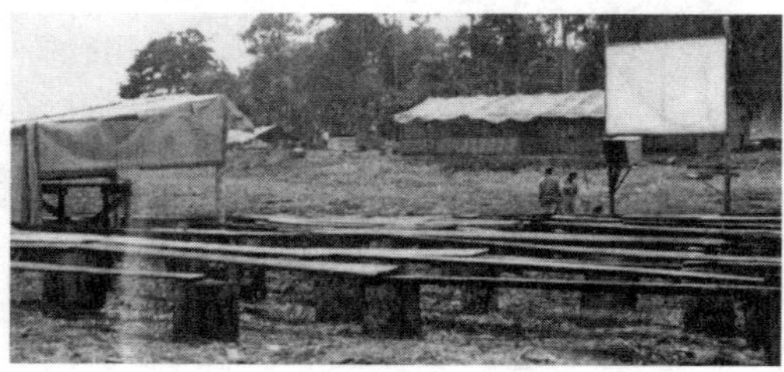

The 863rd Engineer Aviation Battalion movie theater in Saidor.

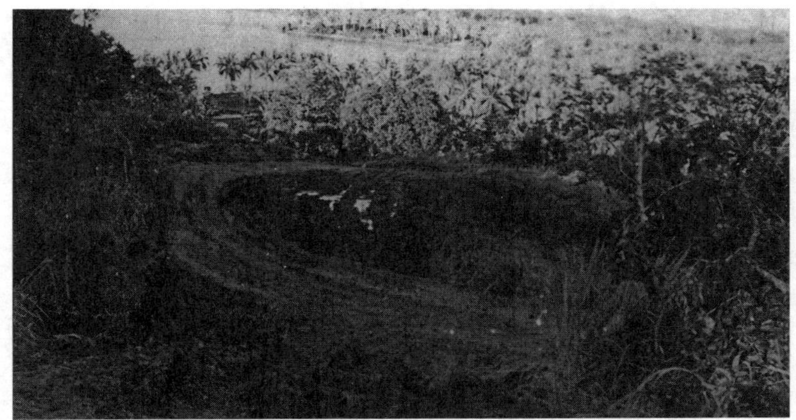

Horseshoe curve with bay in background.

The heavy machinery is building a revetment, a horseshoe-shaped barrier or levee to protect airplanes. One plane goes in each revetment, so they are not wingtip to wingtip on the airstrip which would make it too easy for the enemy to destroy the planes.

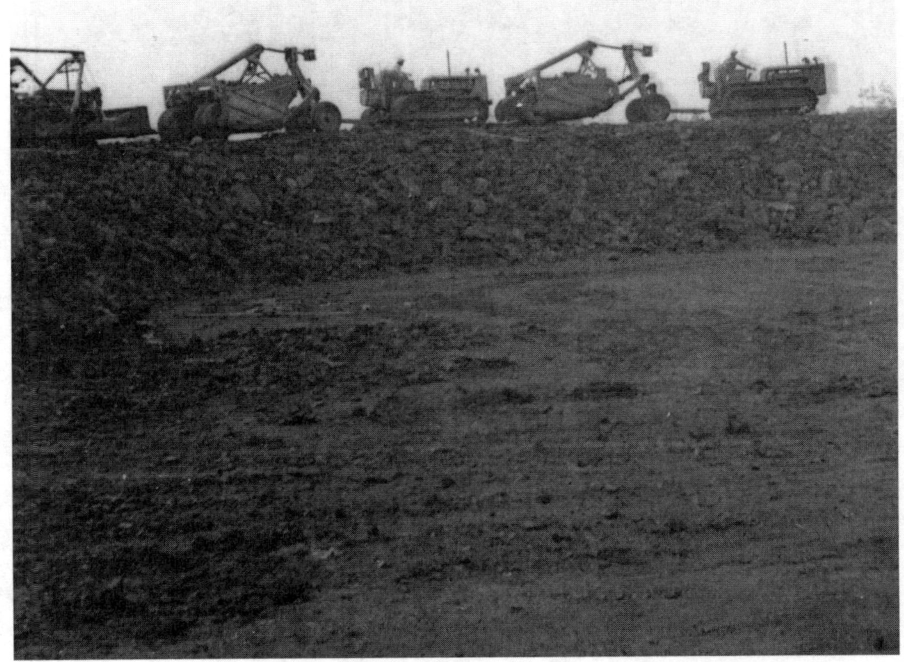

Building a revetment.

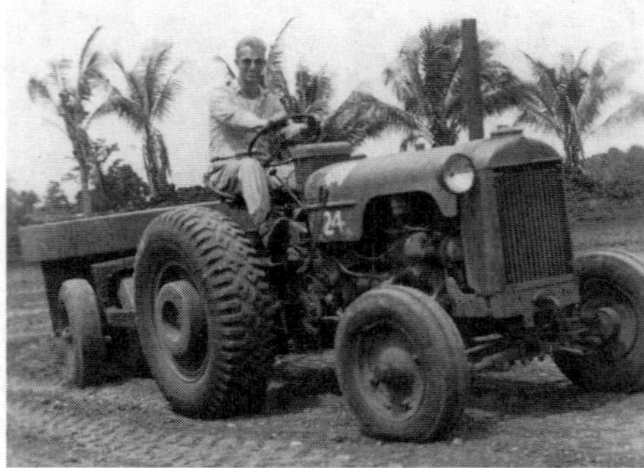

Lt. Betson is packing a hardstanding, which is a parking lot for a plane.

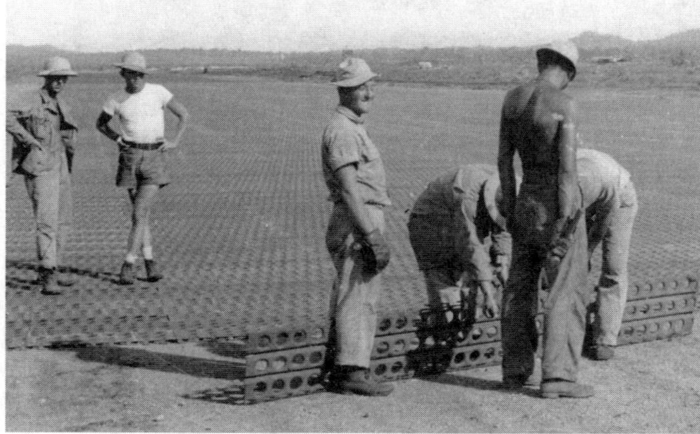

Laying the Pierced Steel Plank for the landing strip.

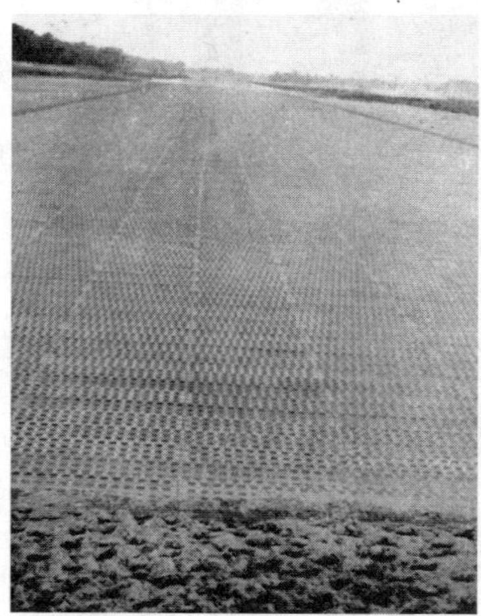

This finished airstrip in Saidor was 6000 feet long by 100 feet wide.

Laying the steel surface for the landing strip. The Pierced Steel Plank, or PSP Mat, also called Marston Matting, was developed by the U.S. Army Air Corps in anticipation of our involvement in World War II.

The Pierced Steel Planks are 10 feet long x 16 inches wide and made out of 10 gauge steel. The PSP mat was designed with holes to reduce the weight, improve aircraft traction and facilitate drainage. Flanging the holes kept the mat durable by compensating for the strength lost by removing a portion of the metal. The planks joined together by a locking mechanism consisting of alternating rows of slots on one side and sliding interlocking projection on the other. The use of spring clips lock the mats in place.

Getting Ready for the Next Move

The order came that it was time to move to another location. But before they moved, all of the troops and their equipment had to be officially inspected by the Colonel. After that, the troops had to brush up on their marksmanship skills. Therefore, a suitable location for a rifle range had to be selected and targets had to be made.

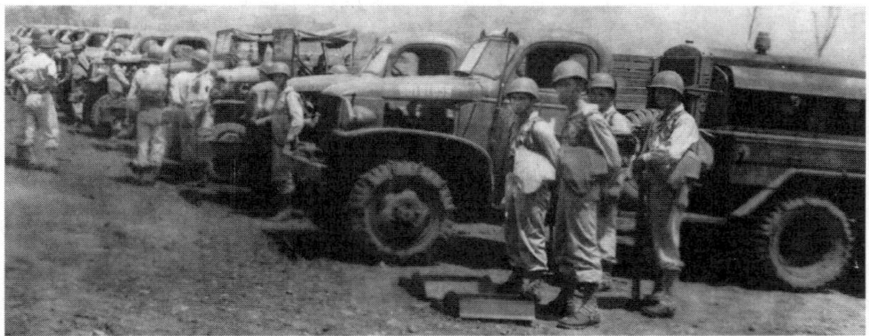

Truck inspection before leaving Saidor, New Guinea. May 5.

They are ordered to practice because the military brass knows what is happening at this moment at their next location.

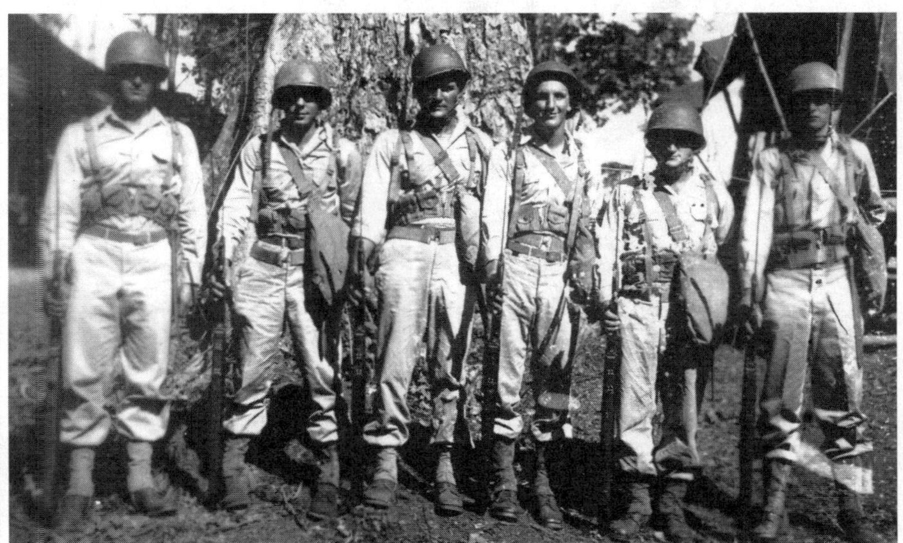

Inspection Day. (Left to right): Curtis Bertrand, Mally Bass, Philip Sandras, Clifford Wynne, Ted Woodson, and Homer Fleming.

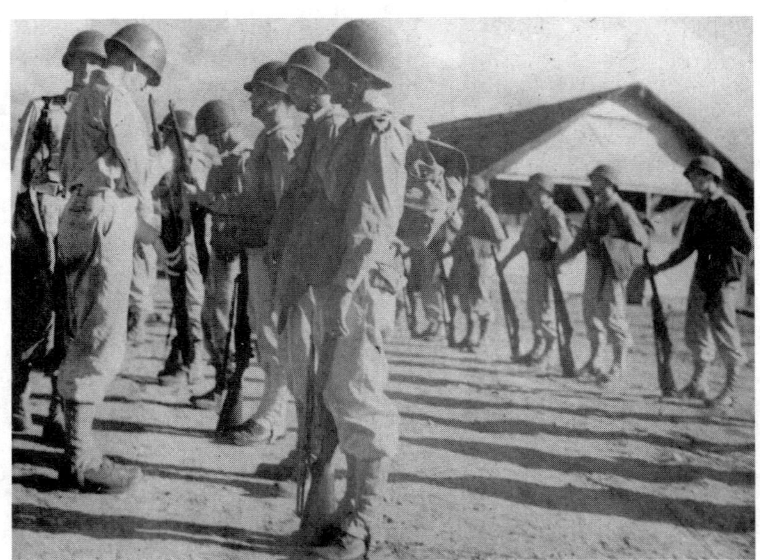

Inspection by Lt. Smith and Colonel Bruce.

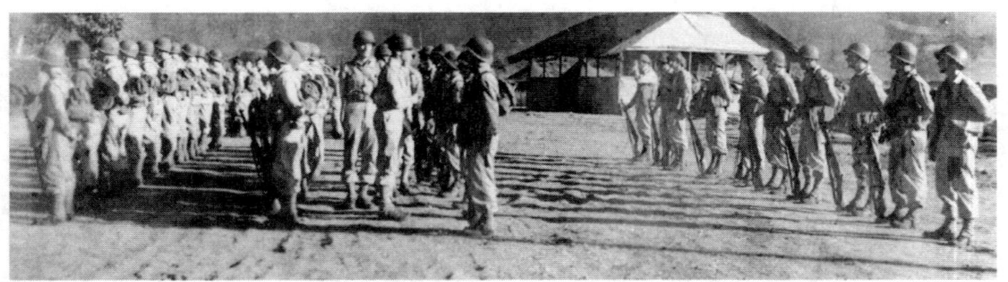

Troop Inspection.

OFFICIAL MILITARY RECORD ENTRY:

May 13 – Whole battalion has the day off for the first time in Saidor.

May 15 – Rifle range targets made; H&S Company shoots May 22.

May 25 – Telegram received from Commanding General of Alamo Force states that LSTs will arrive on June 2 for loading. Four LSTs will be made available for the battalion.

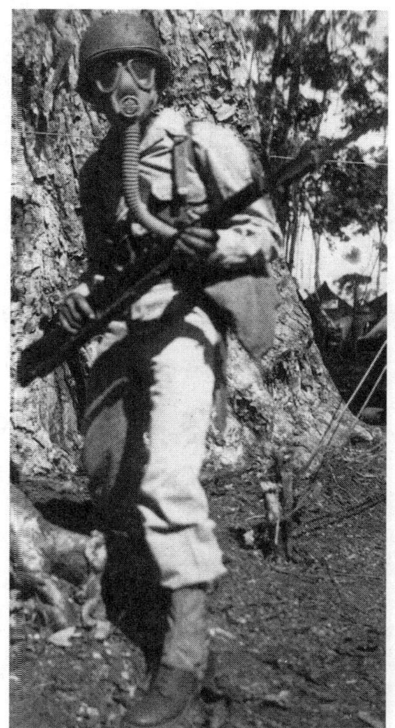

With gas mask on.

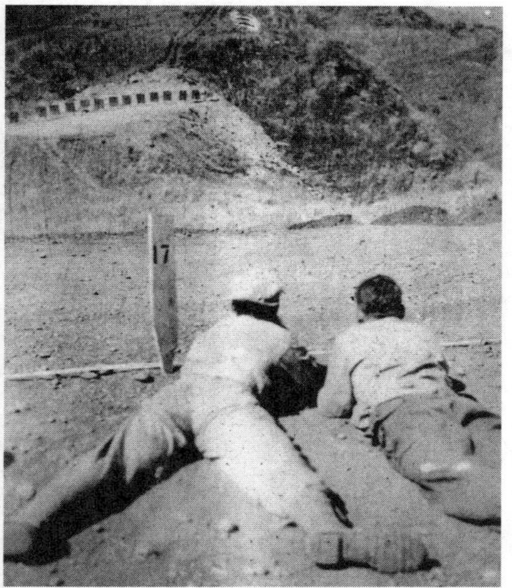

Dad is on the left. He wrote: "Shooting up a storm on firing range."

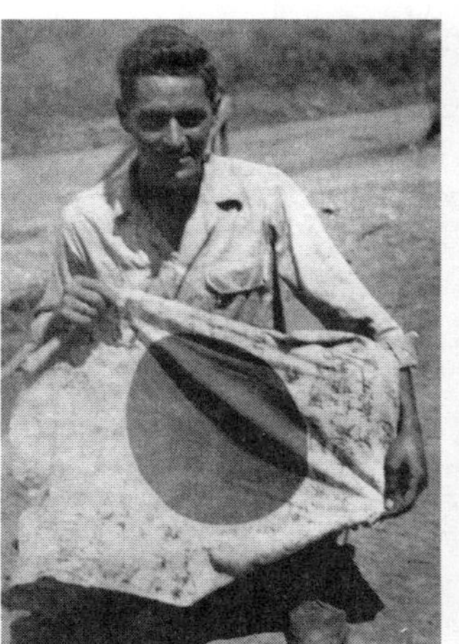

Dad, 23, holding a Japanese flag.

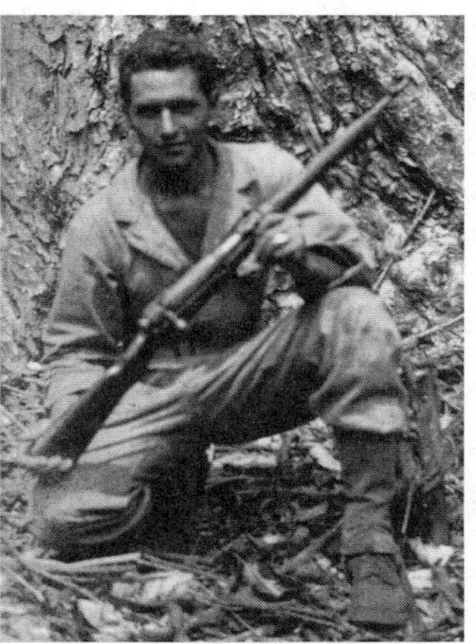

Dad holding a Japanese Arisaka rifle.

JUNE 1944

- - - - - - - -

ELSEWHERE IN THE WAR

June 2: The provisional French government is established.

June 3: There are daily bombings of the Cherbourg Peninsula and the Normandy area.

June 5: Rome falls to the Allies, becoming the first capital of an Axis nation to do so.

June 5: Operation Overlord commences when more than 1,000 British bombers drop 5,000 tons of bombs on German gun batteries on the Normandy coast in preparation for D-Day. Paratroopers land in Normandy and are scattered from Caen southward.

June 6: D-Day begins with the landing of 155,000 Allied troops on the beaches of Normandy in France. The allied soldiers quickly break through the Atlantic Wall and push inland in the largest amphibious military operation in history.

June 12: American aircraft carriers commence air strikes on the Mariana Islands east of the Philippines, including Saipan, preparing for invasion.

June 13: The U.S. Naval bombardment of Saipan begins. In response, Admiral Toyoda Soemu, commander-in-chief of the Japanese Navy, orders his fleet to attack U.S. Navy forces around Saipan.

June 15: U.S. Marine and Army forces invade the island of Saipan. U.S. submarines sight the Japanese fleet en route.

June 20: The Battle of the Philippine Sea ends with three Japanese carriers sunk and three more damaged, forcing the fleet to withdraw.

<> <> <> <> <>

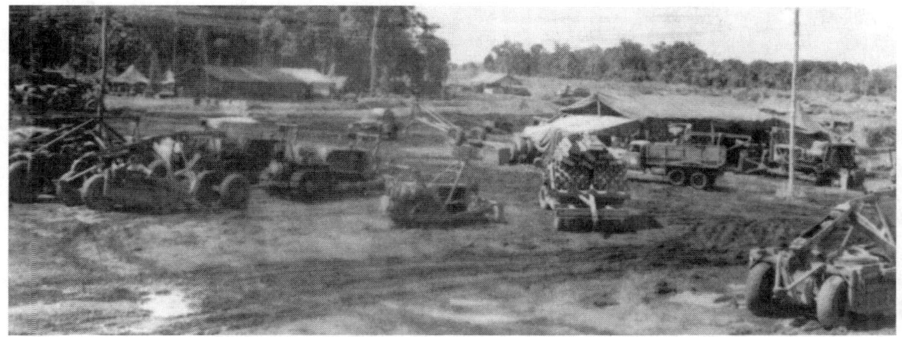

Getting equipment ready to move to next location.

OFFICIAL MILITARY RECORD ENTRY:

June 2 – Four LSTs arrive in morning. Loading of gasoline took four hours. Equipment loaded in afternoon.

June 3 – Loaded LST, and spent the night on it. Total battalion strength is 25 officers and 761 enlisted men (EM).

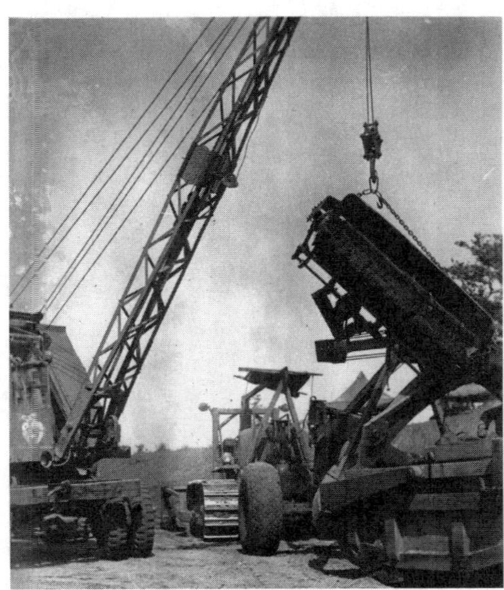

The Quick-Way Truck Shovel is loading equipment on a carryall.

My father's battalion left Saidor at 6:30 a.m. June 4. He, along with H&S Company, is on board a hospital ship with no sleeping accommodations. The remainder of the battalion is at sea aboard LSTs en route to Biak to join the 41st Infantry Division in a severe battle. Stand by to see what awaits them on Biak when they arrive June 7!

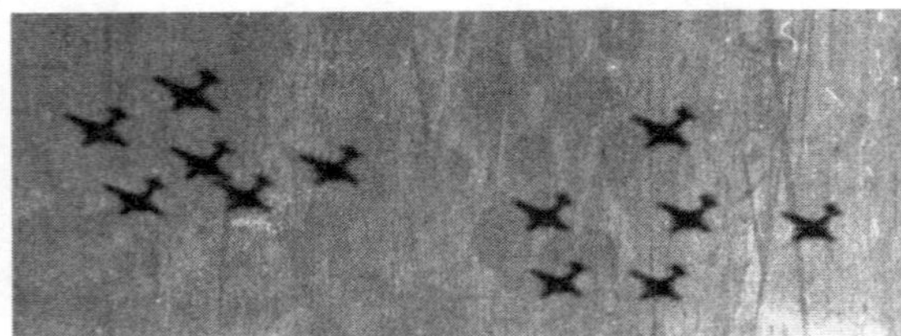

U.S. planes on the lookout for enemy planes, submarines and ships as they move from Saidor to Biak Island. Saidor, New Guinea.

OFFICIAL MILITARY RECORD - WORK SUMMARY ENTRY:

The summary of major construction work in the Saidor Area, New Guinea. The work having started Jan. 8 to May 31, 1944:

A. The construction of 12 miles of road was the first major project in this area.

B. The construction of 4 1/2 miles of taxiways 75 feet wide servicing 68 hardstandings.

C. The construction of abutments and approaches and the installation of a steel H-10 Bailey Bridge across the Nankina River.

D. The construction of a 200-foot x 800-foot loading area.

E. The major building construction included a Fighter Sector Building, an observation building, four alert huts, and the 309th Bomb Wing Headquarters.

F. An extensive drainage program was accomplished throughout this area.

G. The construction of a 320-foot standard 6th Army Liberty Dock with one connecting causeway.

H. The construction of a 900-foot-long bore sighting range.

I. Set up a sawmill which produced 305,000 board feet of lumber.

J. Having completed five months' work in this area, the equipment was made ready to move June 3, 1944.

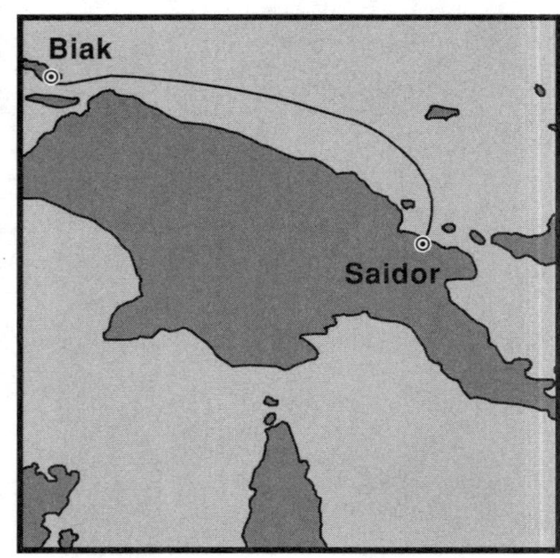

From Saidor to Biak.

CHAPTER 7

The Battle for Biak Island and the Capture of Mokmer Airdrome

The Japanese had taken the Pacific islands in giant strides and would not relinquish even the smallest of these without a bloody conflict. The Americans fought dot by dot on the ocean's map to drive back the invaders. The 863rd Engineer Aviation Battalion was ordered to move to continue the strategy of island hopping planned by General Douglas MacArthur, Supreme Commander of the Southwest Pacific Area.

This move was to a seemingly insignificant island called Biak. It was a part of the Schouten Island chain in the Netherland East Indies, previously held by the Dutch but under Japanese control for the past three years.

Given its size, Biak seemed irrelevant, but the Japanese built three airdromes there that MacArthur desperately needed. Those airdromes had to be captured leaving the airstrip, control tower and operations buildings intact. My father's battalion was responsible for capturing and keeping operational control of the airdrome near the native village of Mokmer.

There, the Japanese spent over a year building significant defensives, including large cannons and pillboxes of various sizes. These fortifications provided cover for the Japanese to post sentinels and shoot any approaching invader.

Pillboxes were usually constructed using reinforced concrete. When proper construction materials were in short supply, they were solidly constructed using coconut logs and covered with a thick dirt roof and camouflaged with tree branches to disguise their location from distant American cannons and approaching soldiers.

The U.S. Army Infantry staged a full-scale assault on southern Biak, including a gunnery duel and air attack, with mixed results. As my father's battalion approached by LST, they were hammered by deadly fire from Japanese coastal cannons on top of the ridge overlooking their landing zone.

For many young Americans, the shallows before the beach became a killing field. Coral reefs grounded LSTs a full five hundred yards from shore, forcing the soldiers to wade through cannon and machine gun fire in chest-high surf to the beach.

While the battalion was approaching Biak, the Japanese defenders were shooting their large cannons at them trying to sink their ships. One of the cannon shells landed in the shallow water near the ship and exploded, sending shrapnel flying everywhere. Two men in the battalion were wounded by this shrapnel as they were climbing down the landing net over the side of the ship. They later received the Purple Heart medal for their injuries.

Those who survived to the beach faced a terrain that sloped upward and changed elevation 50 to 200 hundred feet. The slope was pocked with caves where the Japanese had placed mortars and artillery. They had a bird's-eye view for miles around, enabling them to shoot at the U.S. troops and their machinery.

The Japanese defenders steadfastly held their positions, and on June 8, 1944, the American infantry had yet to dislodge the defenders. That was the day the LST carrying my father found its way onto the beachfront battlefield.

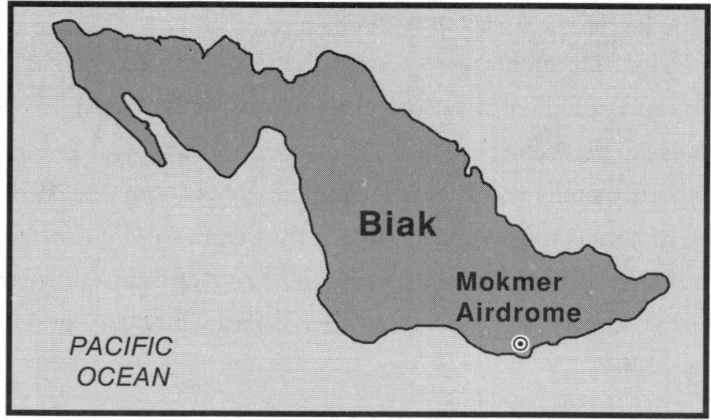

The island of Biak, showing the area where they landed.

OFFICIAL MILITARY RECORD ENTRY:

June 8 – The battalion (BN) was welcomed to Biak with an enemy bombing attack on our convoy. No hits were scored; two men on landing net hit by shrapnel. Landed at Bosnek at 1100 hours. Set up temporary camp west of the beachhead. Can't dig a slit trench – the island is coral.

June 9 – The Bn has the task of maintaining the present road along the shore, widening the road and making a 2-lane road up the hill (assigned to C Company).

DUKW 353

The DUKW 353, also known as Duck, is a six-wheel-drive amphibious truck manufactured by General Motors Co. (GMC) during World War II. It was mainly used for transporting goods and troops over land and water and for use approaching and crossing beaches in amphibious attacks.

A modification of the two-ton capacity deuce trucks, the Duck has a watertight hull and a propeller powered by a 270 cubic inch GMC straight-six engine. The DUKW weighed 6.5 tons empty and operated at 50 mph on land and 5.5 knots (6.3 mph) in water.

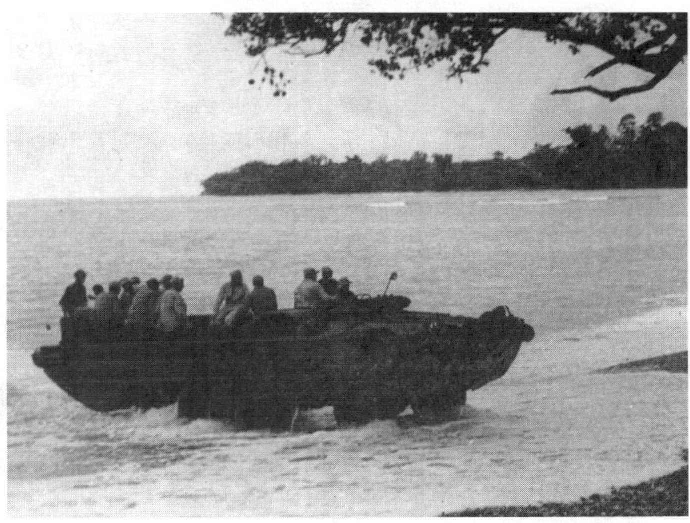

Troops coming ashore in a Duck.

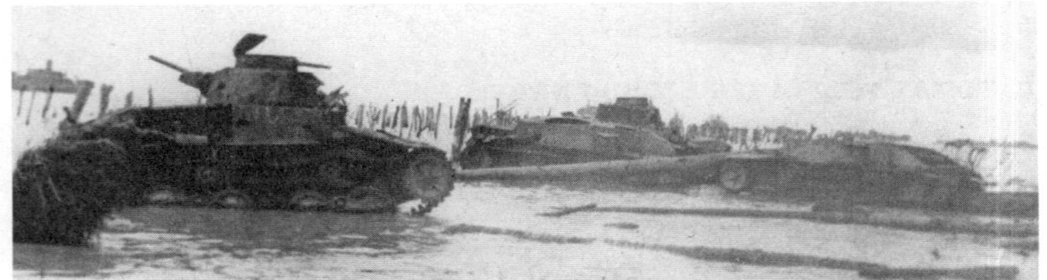

Three destroyed Japanese tanks.

Here is evidence of a tank battle that occurred just a few days before the 863rd landed on Biak. On the left is a Japanese Type 95 Ha-Go Light Tank. The tank in the middle is a Japanese Type 97 Chi-Ha Medium Tank with the gun turret shot off. As for the tank on the right, just the bottom chassis and tracks remain.

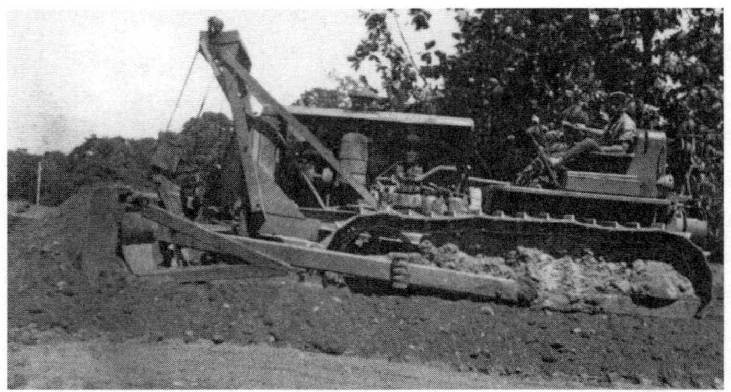

D-8 Caterpillar bulldozer.

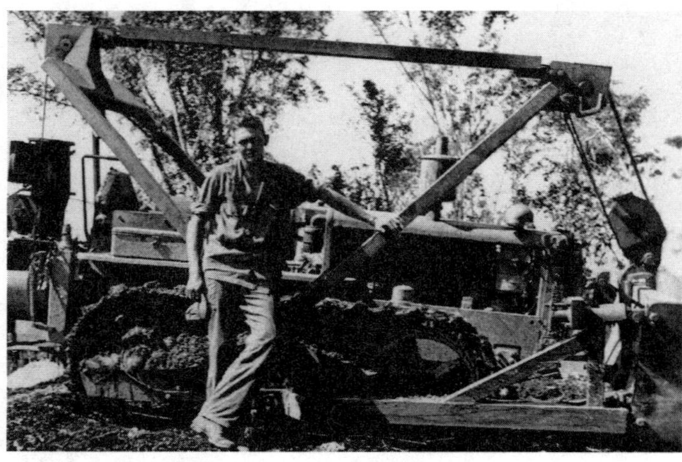

Morris "Tex" Moore and D-4 Cat Bulldozer.

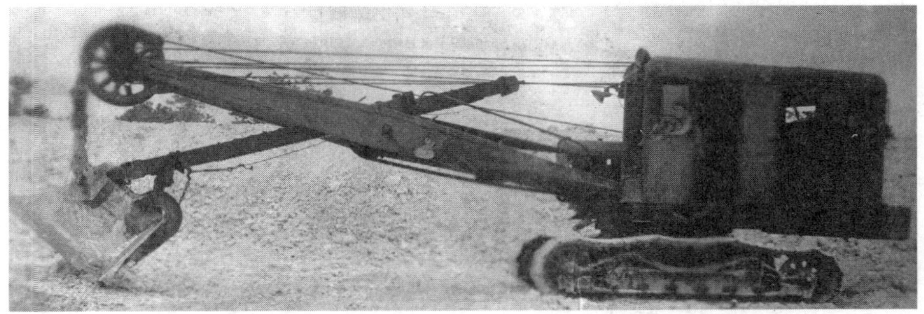

The two-yard shovel in the coral pit. The bucket holds two cubic yards of material.

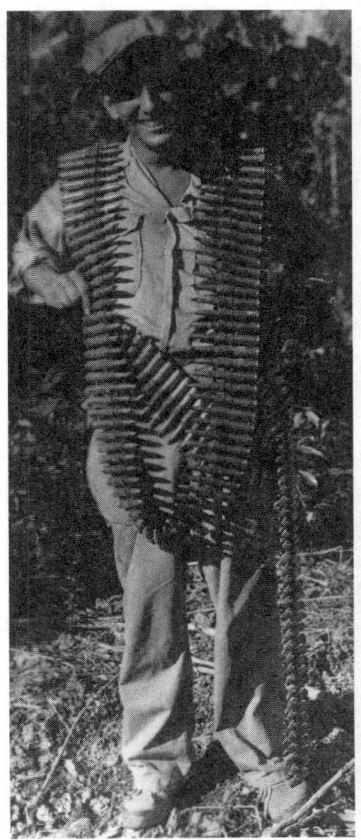

Darel Gipe passing 320 rounds of 50-caliber ammo.

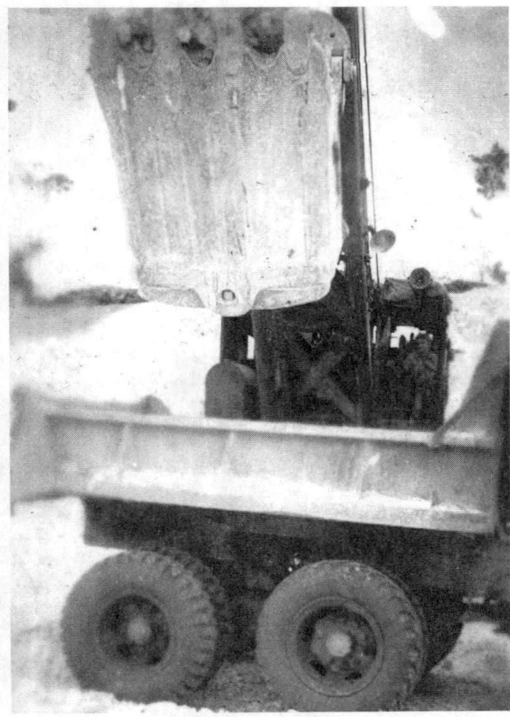

Darel Gipe from Boise, Idaho, is at the controls of this two-yard shovel. He is emptying a load into the dump truck.

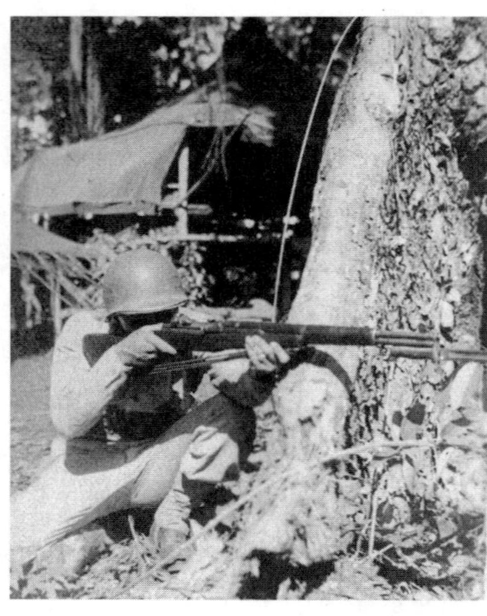

Company B was ordered to guard camp from Japanese filtering through the lines.

OFFICIAL MILITARY RECORD ENTRY:

June 9 – Company A plus 26 Enlisted Men (EM) from Headquarters & Service Company (H&S Co.) go to Mokmer Drome and get it in working order within 36 hours. 36 EM + 1 officer left behind to protect equipment.

June 10 – A Company landed at a village next to Mokmer Drome, going thru five-foot surf and 200 yards of coral reef. Equipment landed included tractors, graders, rollers, and trucks amid enemy artillery and mortar fire. Officers looking over Mokmer Drome were fired on by machine gun.

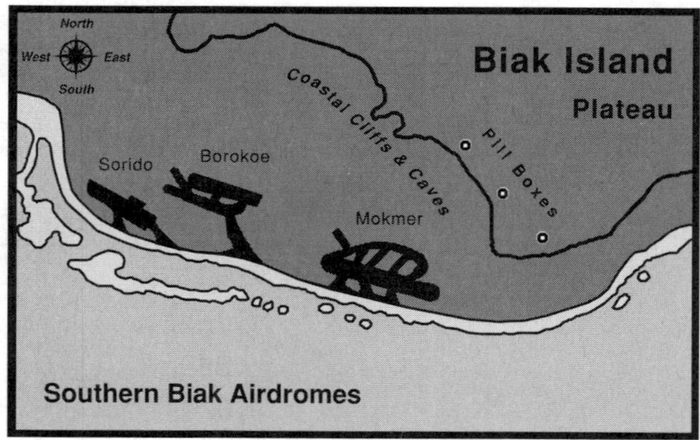

This map shows the three airdromes in the area. Other battalions were in charge of the Sorido and Borokoe airdromes. The area named "Plateau" is a high ridge with several pillboxes on top and caves from which the enemy was firing.

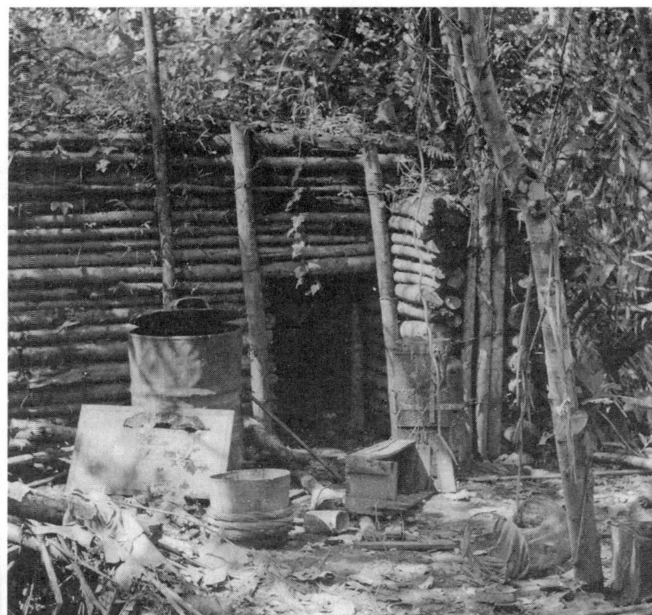

Enemy pillbox on top of the plateau.

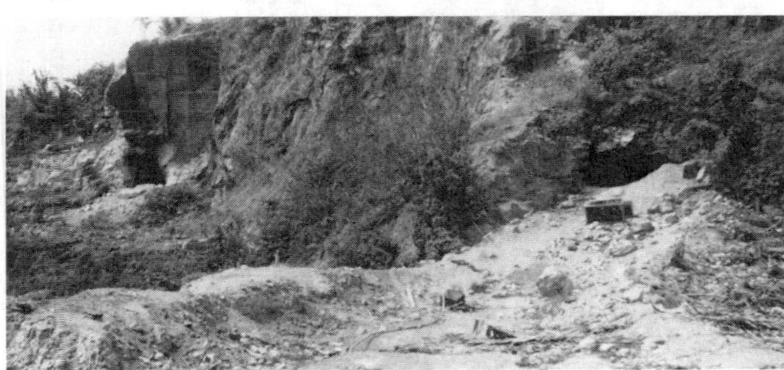

Some of the caves the enemy was shooting from.

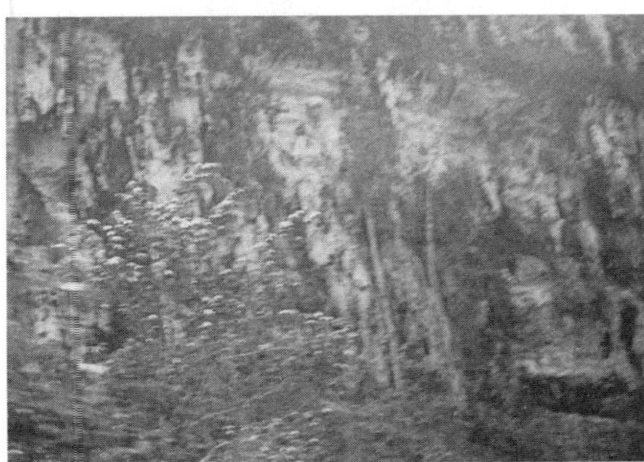

Coral cliffs of caverns.

Although this picture is blurry because it was taken from a moving truck, it shows the tall coral cliffs of caverns where the Japanese were hiding and shooting at troops working on the Mokmer Drome airstrip. Enemy pillboxes on top of the cliffs were overtaken and subsequently blown up by the infantry and engineers.

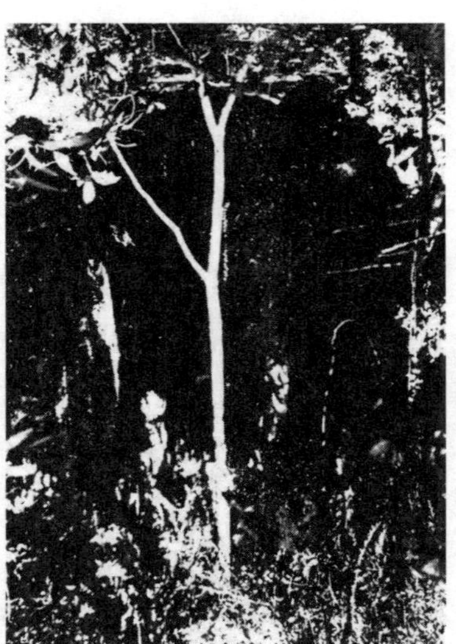

Another cave where the enemy was firing from.

OFFICIAL MILITARY RECORD ENTRY:

June 11 – B Company task: transport water to 163rd Infantry Regiment on front lines, and maintain road to that regiment. H&S and C Company will guard the Bn area.

The enemy-entrenched ridge overlooking Mokmer Drome is under heavy mortar and artillery fire from our guns. Our grader was driven off the strip by enemy machine gun fire.

Support work includes construction of roads to front lines, operation of a waterpoint, transportation of ammo, food, water to the front, and evac wounded to beachhead hospital.

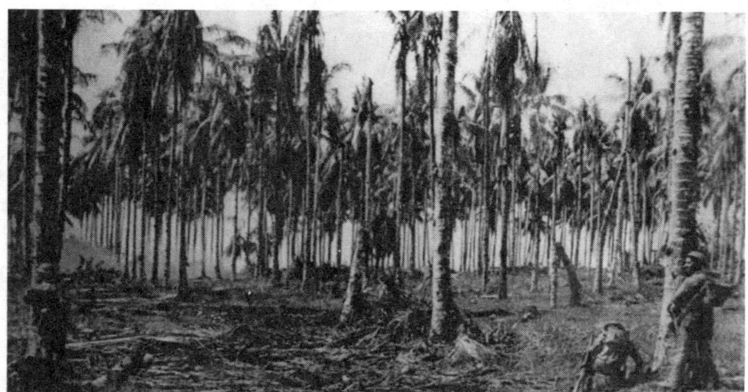

My dad wrote: "We are being fired on and trying to take cover behind trees. These trees have been through war. They're all shot up."

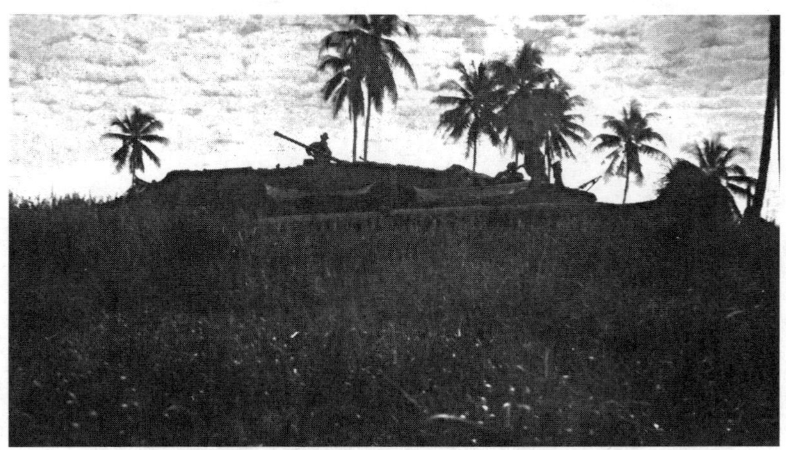

One of the gun emplacements. The gun on the hill is a 40mm Bofors. It was used primarily as an anti-aircraft gun.

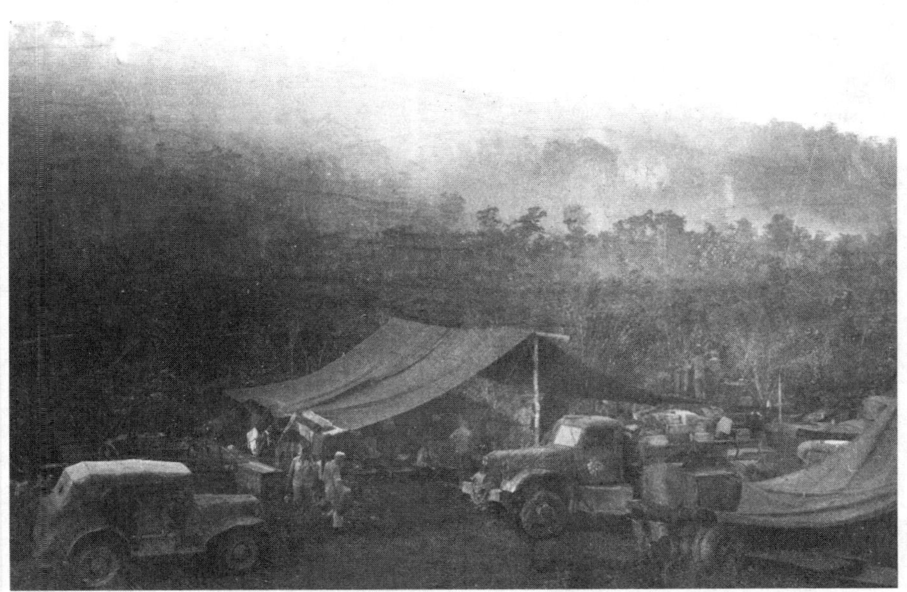

A smoky scene. The artillery and mortar fire pounds at caves on Woodpecker Ridge.

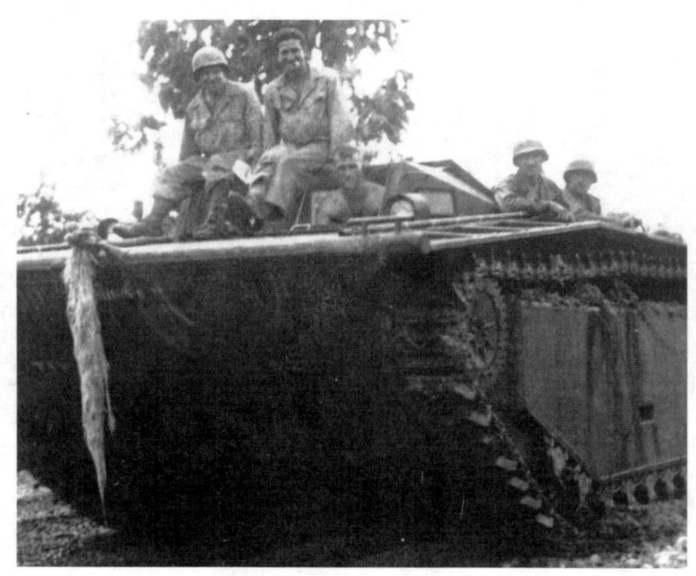

A tracked vehicle called a buffalo.

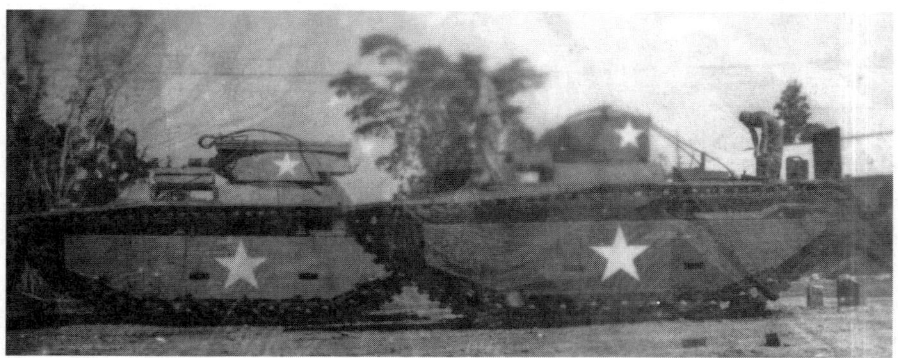

Two buffaloes being serviced.

OFFICIAL MILITARY RECORD ENTRY:

June 12 - Bombs dropped in the adjoining camp area during an enemy air raid early this morning caused three men from B Company who were on guard to be wounded. These are our first casualties as a result of enemy action.

A Company bivouacked on the Mokmer beachhead was attacked by the enemy resulting in one soldier being wounded in the leg and testicles. Enemy fire from the ridge overlooking Mokmer airdrome caused our work to stop for a while. Grading work on the strip commenced at 1000 hours (10:00 a.m.). Although operating under intermittent and sporadic enemy rifle fire, work continued until dark. By darkness, the Mokmer strip was in minimum operating condition for fighter planes. Four trucks were used to transport anti-aircraft artillery to the Mokmer drome. These trucks made two trips during the day, and one truck was incapacitated on its last trip by enemy mortar fire on the road. No casualties involved.

Our soldiers on the beachhead were re-supplied with ammo and grenades.

June 13 - Our graders were busy leveling the dirt on Mokmer Drome until another attack by enemy artillery, machine gun and rifle fire caused our work to stop.

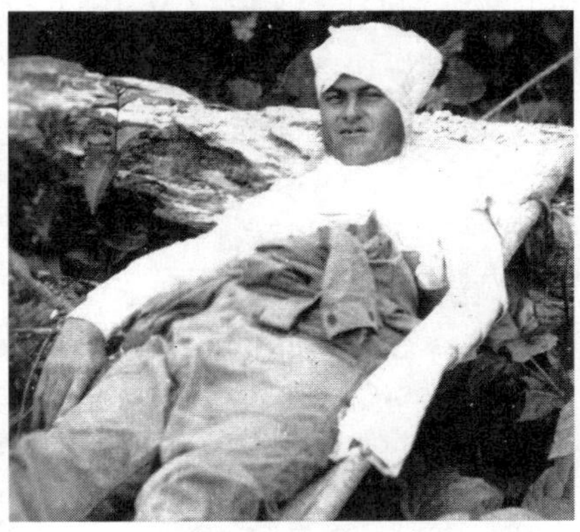

Wounded soldier on stretcher.

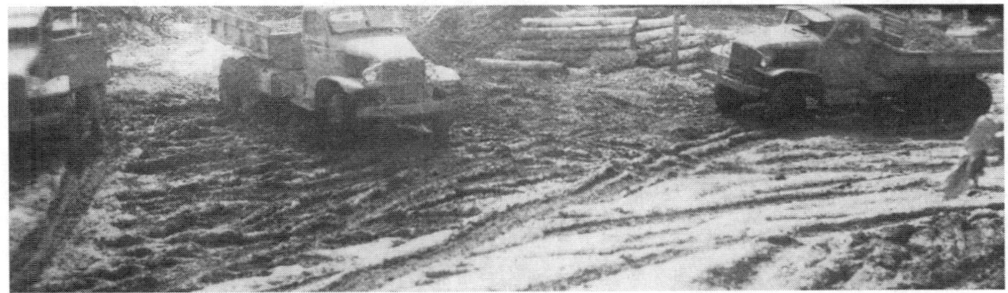

Working on Biak Island. Their job was to take over and repair Mokmer Airdrome.

OFFICIAL MILITARY RECORD ENTRY:

June 14 – An enemy counterattack was successfully broken up by our 180th Infantry. During this attack approximately 40 mortar shells landed within the A Company perimeter. Other than being severely shaken up, no casualties resulted.

B Company is working 18 hours/day on their job, which now requires that they construct a two-lane road out of the existing one-lane road from Bosnek Beachhead to the 163rd Infantry. Hauling of water to the infantry has stopped because the infantry has captured a Japanese water point.

June 16 – Destroyed Jap pillboxes. Infantry support operation today included a demolition mission against enemy pillboxes on the ridge overlooking Mokmer Drome. Lt. Chaisson and four men worked in front of the infantry with hand grenades and explosives and blew up several bothersome Jap pillboxes. This squad had one grenade thrown at them, which luckily did no damage, and claimed eight Japs as a result of this mission.

Work continued on the airstrip. Sniper fire resulted but work continued until dark.

A timber survey was done on nearby Auki Island, and the decision was made to set up our Company C sawmill there with Lt. Allan in charge.

There are two other airdromes near us. The Sorido drome is 4000 x 100 feet. The Borokoe drome is 5500 x 100 feet, and Mokmer Drome is the longest at 7000 x 100 feet.

The following pictures are the results of the battalion's successful attempts to stop the enemy from continuing to bother the 863rd Engineer Aviation Battalion. The Japanese were trying to kill them and hamper their progress. Every enemy soldier fought until the bitter end for their emperor and died an honorable death for their country. These photos were taken during their stay on Biak.

WARNING – GRAPHIC CONTENT

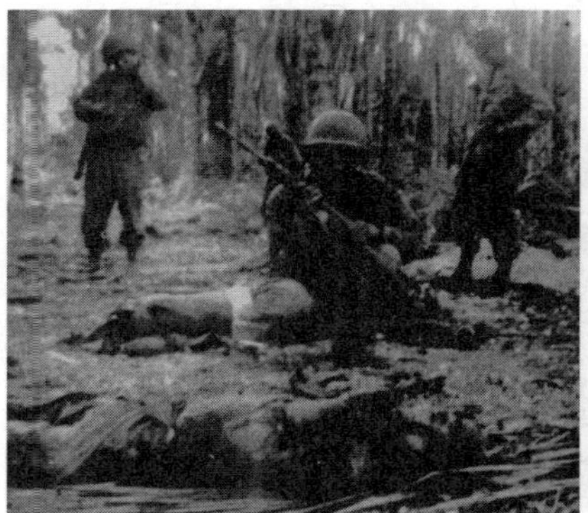

Checking out dead enemy with bayonets fixed.

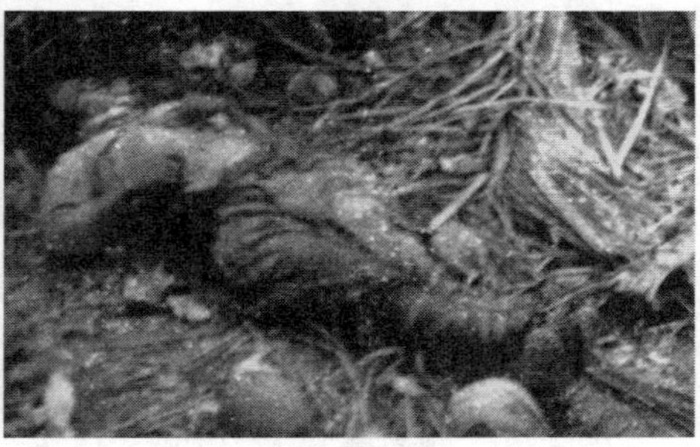

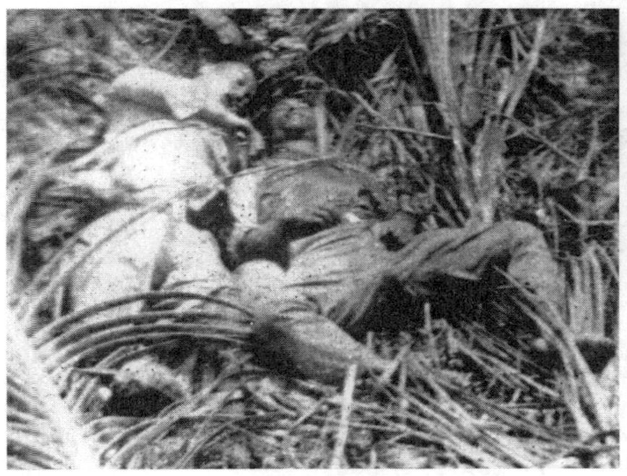

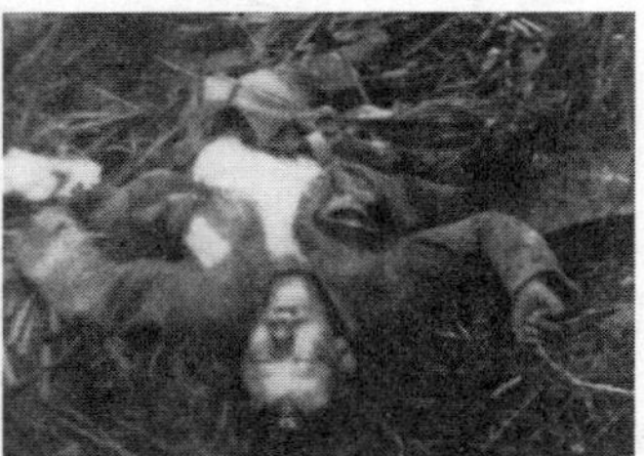

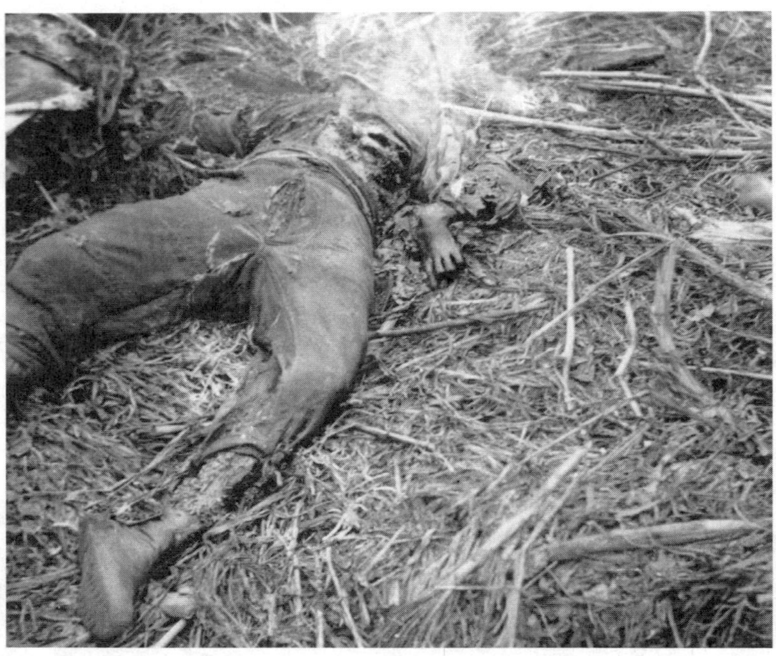

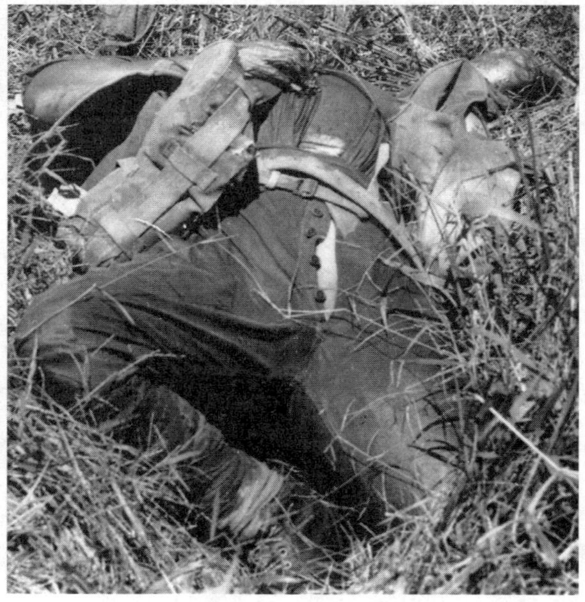

Enemy corspe in a state of decomposition.

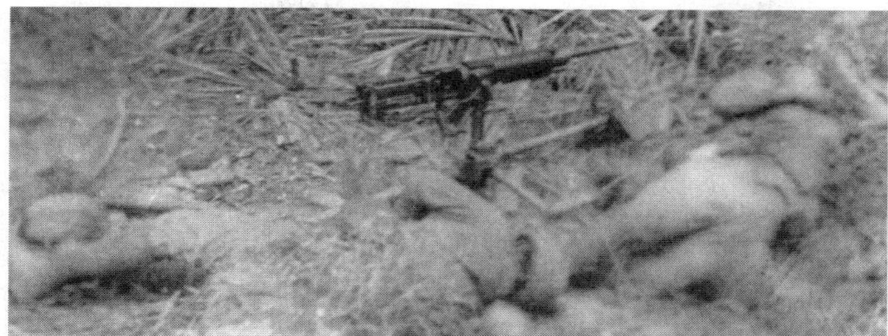

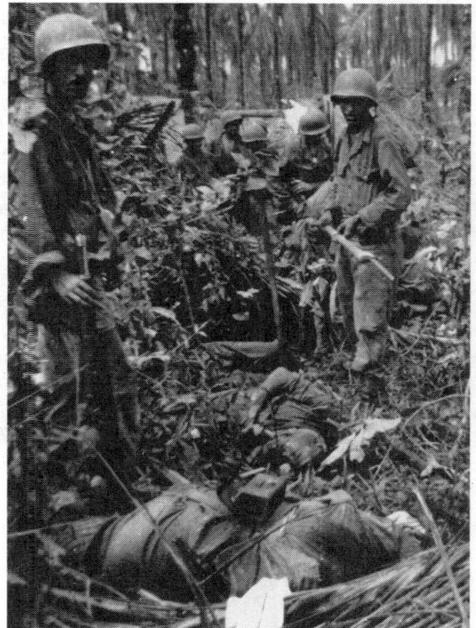

Dead enemy with machine gun. They were shooting at the heavy equipment operators on Mokmer Airdrome from on top the ridge.

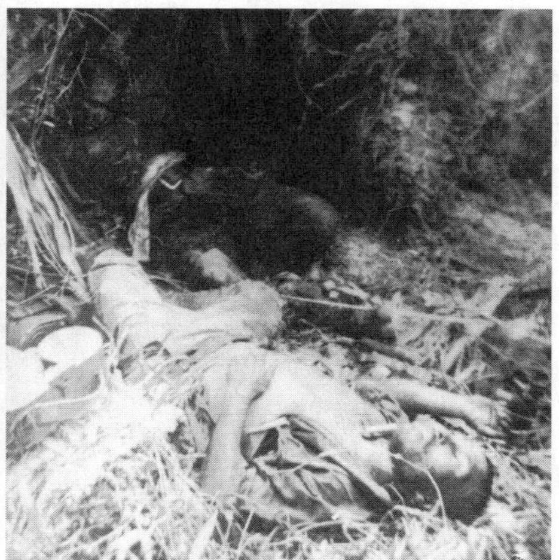

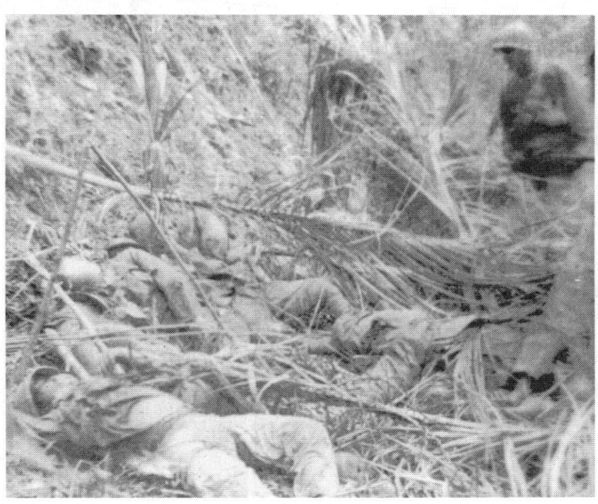

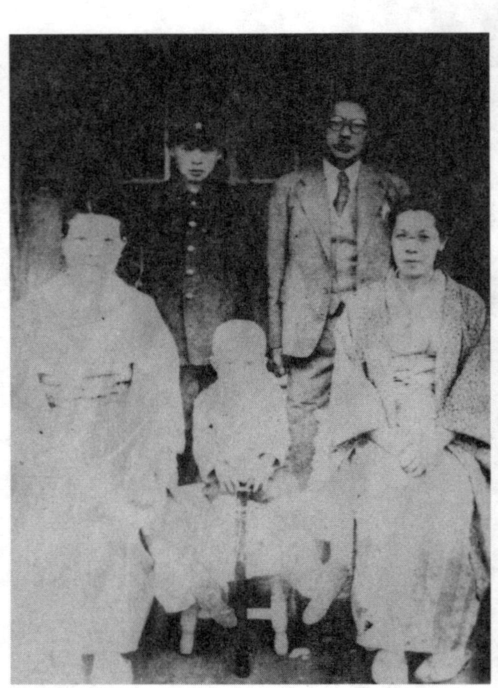

Photos from captured Japanese camera.

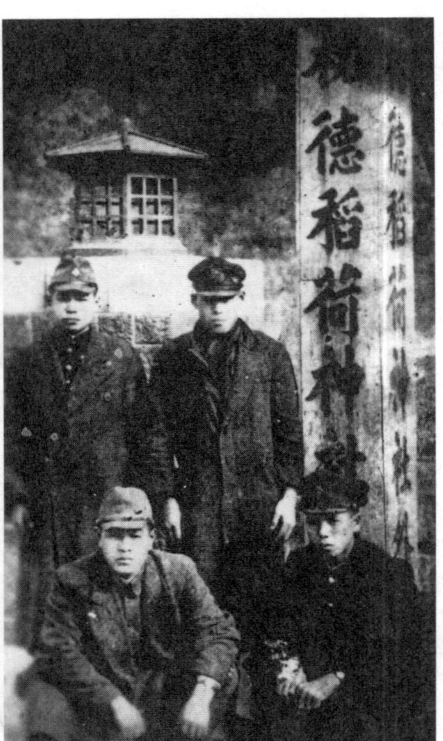

The sign written in Japanese reads "Temple of the Fox."

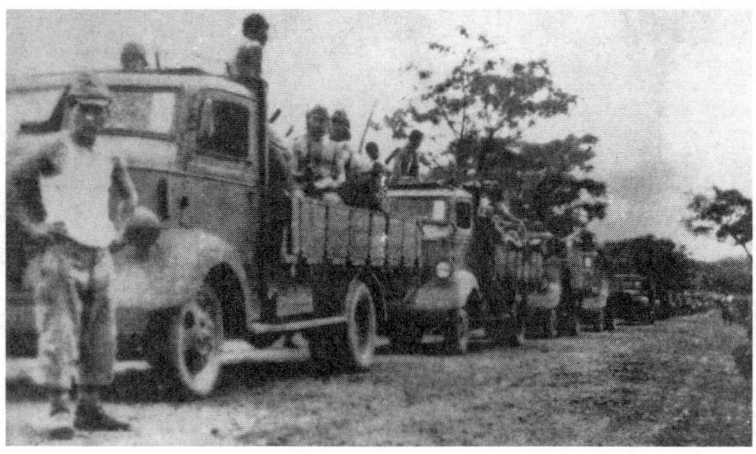

Enemy convoy.

OFFICIAL MILITARY RECORD ENTRY:

June 17 – Work continued on the Mokmer Strip with only occasional sniper fire throughout the day. The 100 x 4300-foot strip section is now in first class condition for fighter operation. Sufficient dispersal for a fighter group is available along the sides of the strip since the original Jap strip was 300 feet wide.

June 18 – A Company continued work on the Mokmer Drome, which has received no enemy fire for the last 48 hours. A 5000-foot strip, in excellent condition, is now available for fighters. Infantry support work continues with A Company continuing to hold the center of the perimeter and constructing roads to the front lines. A total of three tons of shrapnel has been policed from the strip to date.

– B Company continues work on the two-lane road from Bosnek to the front lines. This requires considerable blasting along a strip of the road that runs down a steep hill with nearly vertical embankments on both sides.

– C Company's job has now been enlarged to include extending a two-lane road to the bridge being constructed by the 116th Engineers at the foot of the cliff. This will require considerable blasting as the coral cannot be moved by bulldozer or grader.

– Enemy mortar shells fell about 200-yards up the road from our camp area at approximately 1800 hours (6 p.m.), and troops from that area have decided to sleep on the beach for the night.

– Lt. Allan of C Company with 30 EM left for Auki Island (about four miles away) where they will set up and operate a sawmill. They are the only troops on that island.

June 19 – A miniature war was conducted today by the enemy and our infantry about 75 yards from where C Company was working on their road job. This necessitated cessation of construction work as bullets flying in the vicinity made things slightly dangerous.

- A Company is working on a beach road from the stone jetty to bypass the area where the Japs have been dropping mortar shells on the road. This is fairly easy construction work as it is coral sand rather than rock and is much easier to move.

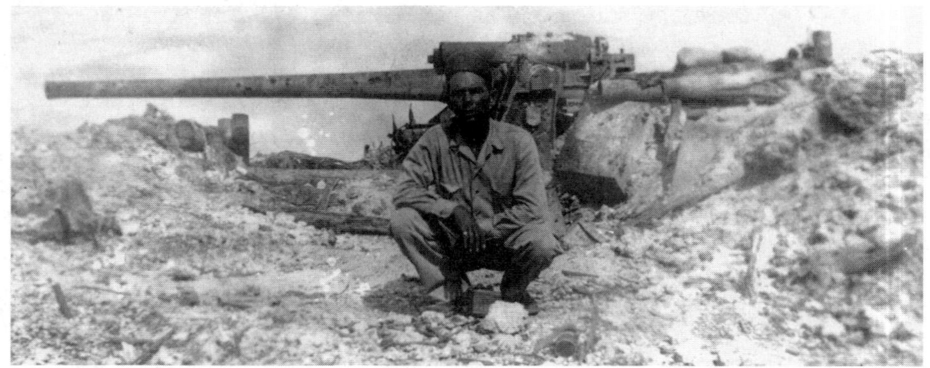

Ben Jones, a fellow soldier from Louisiana poses in front of a Japanese Type 10 120-mm dual purpose gun that has been disabled by U.S. infantry. This is one of the enemy guns that was firing on my father's battalion from on top of the ridge.

June 21 - We are in the process of moving our camp. H&S Company will be moving equipment first. Camp will be broken and personnel will move tomorrow.

- Battalion headquarters moved in the morning and was in operation at its new location near Mokmer at 1500 hours. This location is about 1200 yards from a Jap position on the ridge and a hole was placed through battalion headquarters tent by machine-gun fire not five minutes after it was erected.

June 22 - We have selected an area near Menoebaboe at the west end of Mokmer Drome. It seems to be a good area near the ocean and our "cats" are clearing it off so that we can move in on 23 June.

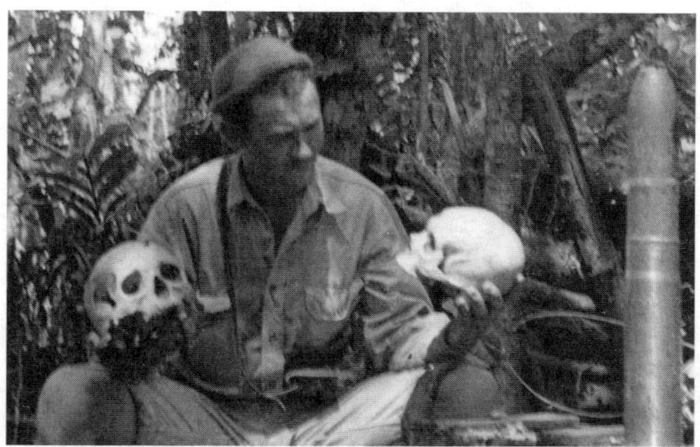

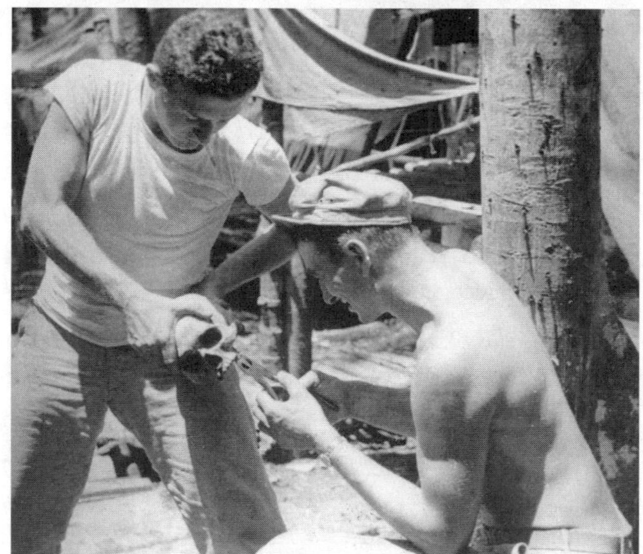

Pulling the gold teeth out of enemy skulls.

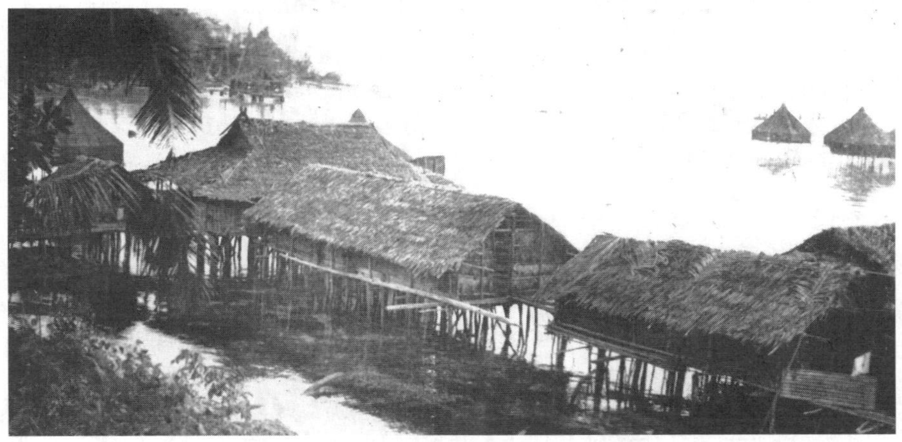

Native village.

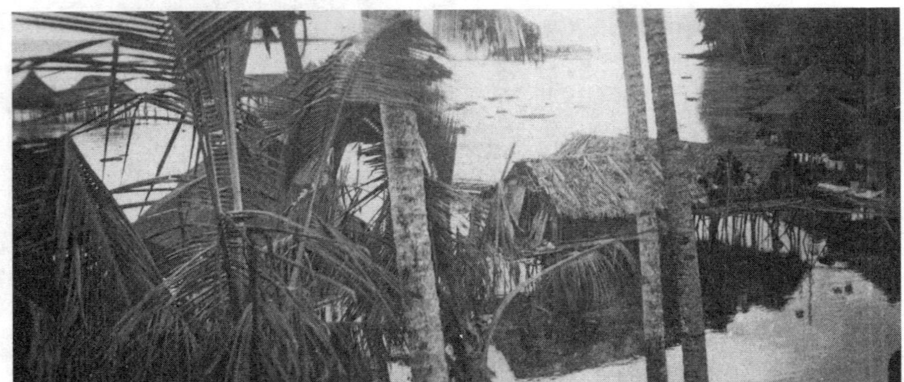

Huts built over the water.

OFFICIAL MILITARY RECORD ENTRY:

June 23 – The entire battalion moved into our new campsite and proceeded to erect tents and facilities and to clear the area in order to make it livable.

June 24 – Weekly progress report shows the Mokmer Airdrome in minimum operating condition for transports and fighters with 75 temporary hardstandings ready for fighter planes. These hardstandings were constructed in a day and a half by A Company.

– A Company continues work on the beach road from stone jetty to bypass the defile where the Japs have been dropping mortars.

– B Company has been assigned the job of widening the continuation of this road after it leaves the beach. This will require blasting as there are quite a few humps of solid coral which must be leveled.

– C Company is working with A Company on the airdrome, as well as operating the sawmill on Auki Island.

June 25 – We have acquired/captured Jap vehicles: one truck mounted water purification unit, one wrecker, one prime mover (with an air-cooled diesel engine) with wrecker attachments, one tank truck with four tank sections, a hydraulic bulldozer and an 8-ton roller now in use on Mokmer Airstrip.

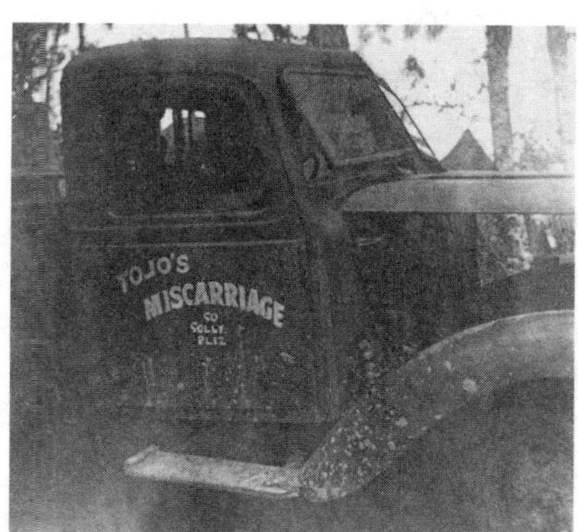

One of our guys painted this on the door of the captured truck: Tojo's Miscarrage. "So Solly Pliz" is written below.

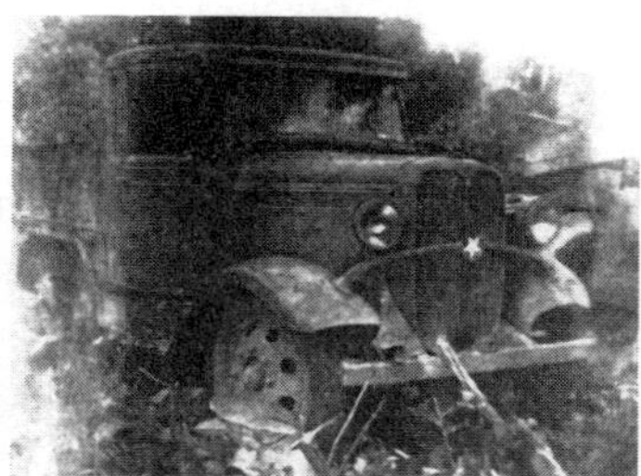

Captured Japanese truck.

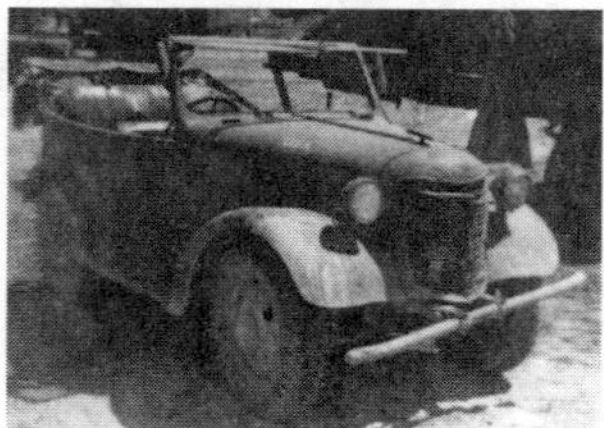

Captured car.

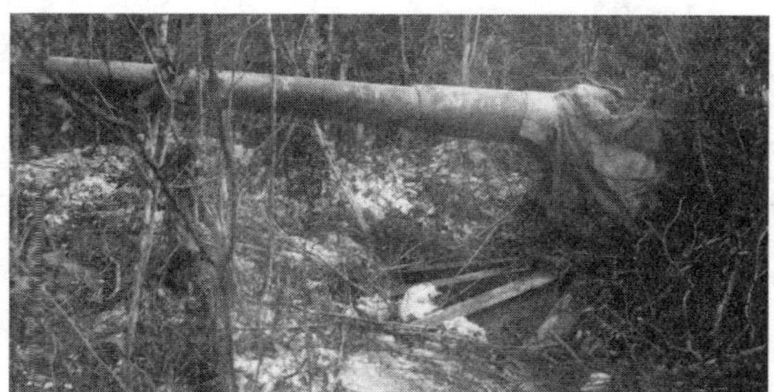

This big Japanese artillery cannon on the ridge above Mokmer Airdrome has been disrupted from killing any more of our troops.

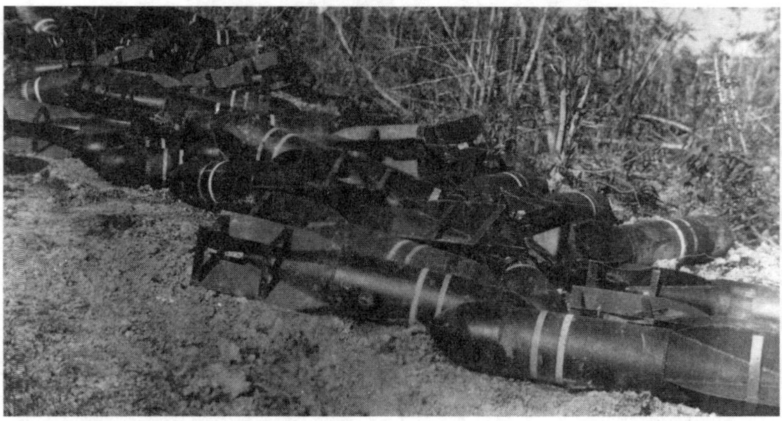

Captured Japanese bomb dump.

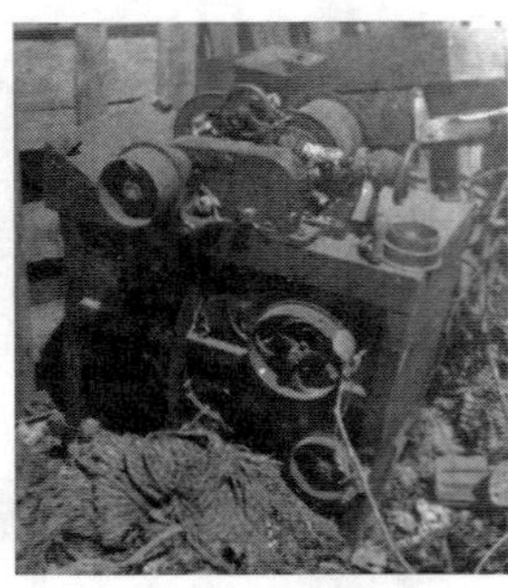
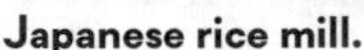

Japanese rice mill.

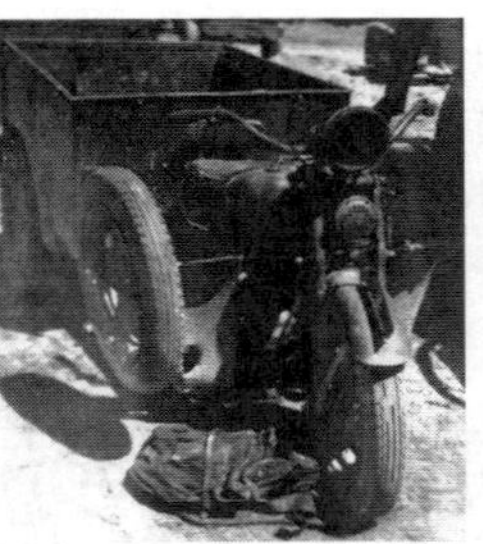

Captured motorcycle.

OFFICIAL MILITARY RECORD ENTRY:

June 26 – Occasional mortar and machine-gun fire continues to fall along the strip of road being constructed by B Company.

June 28 – More Jap equipment has been captured: several bulldozers, prime movers and two carryalls, which are almost identical to U.S.-made Le Tourneau brand.

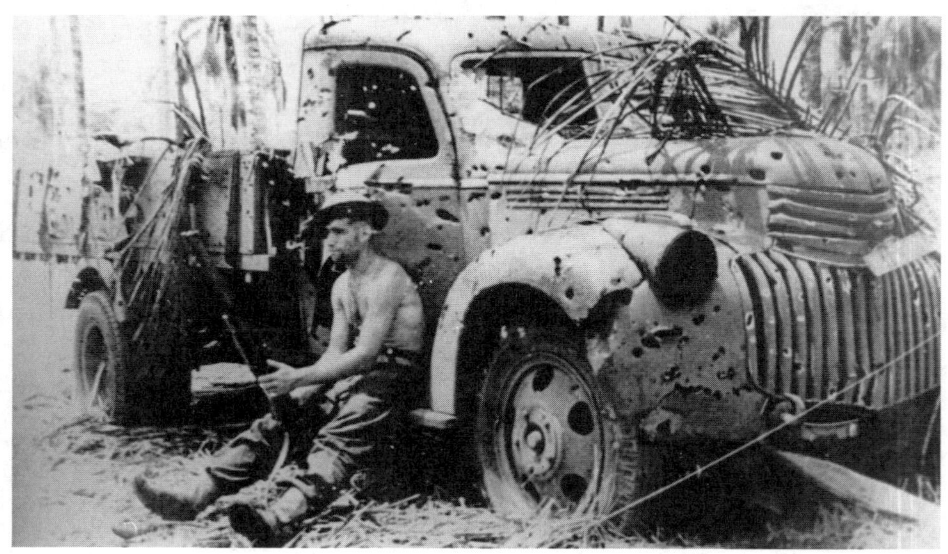

A soldier sitting on a bullet-riddled truck.

JULY 1944

ELSEWHERE IN THE WAR

July 2: U.S. battle Japanese on Noemfoor Island, located west of Biak.

July 3: The Allies in the Battle of the Hedgerows. They are stymied for two weeks by the agricultural hedges in western France, which intelligence had not properly evaluated.

July 6: Largest Banzai charge of the war; 4,300 Japanese troops killed on Saipan in a suicidal rush, killing 650 U.S. infantry.

July 9: Saipan is declared secure. The Japanese lost over 30,000 troops, and numerous civilians commit suicide.

July 9: Caen, France, falls to the British.

July 10: Battle of Driniumor River, New Guinea.

July 10: Tokyo is bombed for the first time since the Doolittle Raid of April 1942.

July 11: President Roosevelt announces that he will run for an unprecedented fourth term.

July 18: St. Lo, France, is taken.

July 18: General Hideki Tojo resigns as chief minister of the Japanese government.

July 21: Assassination attempt on Hitler fails (bomb explodes six feet away).

July 21: Second Battle of Guam.

July 24: Marines land on Tinian Island, the last of the Marianas (after Saipan and Guam); Tinian will eventually be a B-29 base, and the base from which the atomic bombers departed.

<> <> <> <> <>

OFFICIAL MILITARY RECORD ENTRY:

July 1 – Our first General Order of the year awarded Purple Hearts to T/3 Albert P. McGee of H&S Company and T/5 Dallas C. Cothan of C Company for wounds received from shrapnel.

July 4 – The permanent control tower for the strip which A Company has been working on has been completed today.

July 8 – Weekly progress report of this date shows the runway as 25 percent complete with 5000 feet usable and the taxiways 40 percent complete with 17000 feet usable and 75 usable hardstandings. Fighter Sector building 80 percent complete and construction of two fighter control buildings started.

July 14 – Memo sent to all companies ordering all personnel to put up mosquito bars for sleeping purposes. A rise in Dengue Fever made this necessary.

July 17 – Battalion given assignment to finish extension of strip and alert areas by July 24 as a heavy bomb group is expected on that day.

July 23 – Two plane accidents on strip today. Both were due to pilot's error in judgment on landing and not due to condition of strip.

July 25 – Our sawmill was moved here from Auki Island. It is set up and in operation.

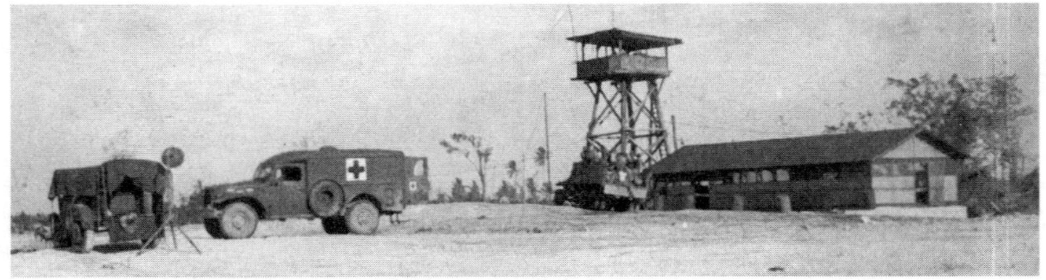

The operations building and control tower at Mokmer Drome on Biak.

AUGUST 1944

ELSEWHERE IN THE WAR

Aug. 4: Florence, Italy, is liberated by the Allies.

Aug. 10: Guam retaken; it was the first American base taken by the Japanese on Dec. 8, 1941, and was the first to be recovered.

Aug. 21: The Dumbarton Oaks Conference begins, setting up the basic structure of the United Nations.

Aug. 25: Paris is liberated by Allied forces. German military disobeys Hitler's order to burn the city.

Aug. 31: American forces turn over the government of France to Free French Forces.

Aug. 31: Verdun, France, falls to General George Patton's Third Army.

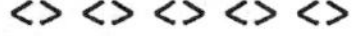

OFFICIAL MILITARY RECORD ENTRY:

Aug. 2 – We had movies in our area for the first time through the courtesy of the 808th Engineer Aviation Battalion who loaned us their projector and operator.

Aug. 5 – The area is clearing up nicely. Sawmill is in full operation.

Aug. 25 – Everyone possible, who could be spared from their work, was given off to allow them to see the Bob Hope Show. This was at Mokmer. Those that missed it in the afternoon caught it at Bosnek in the evening. It was a great show and a great morale builder.

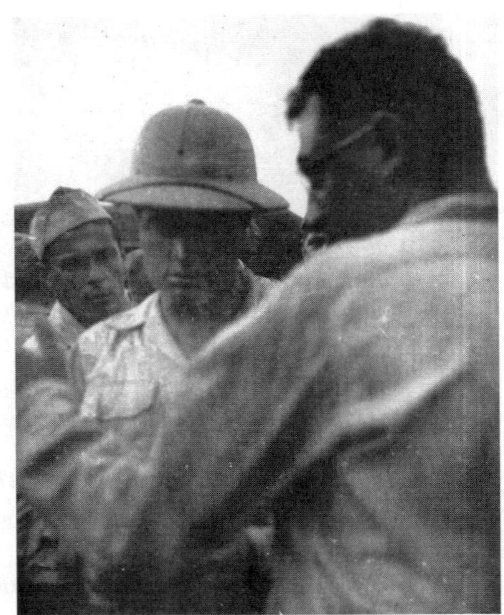

Bob Hope autographing.

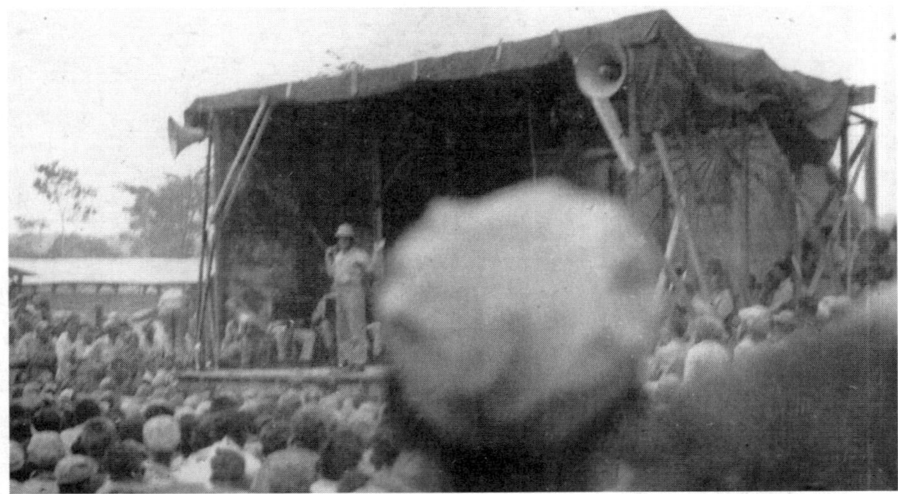

Bob Hope entertaining the troops at a USO show at Mokmer Drome, Biak.

OFFICIAL MILITARY RECORD ENTRY:

Aug. 28 - Sawmill crew reported signs of enemy activity in the vicinity of the mill. Field wire and tracks indicate the presence of an observation post. This is feasible as it overlooks the Mokmer Drome. Division headquarters deemed these signs important enough to warrant a combat patrol that will report to Lt. Allan in the morning.

Aug. 29 - Combat patrol investigated Jap tracks in sawmill area with no result. All caves and possible hideout places in the area were blown up. No enemy activity shown in area.

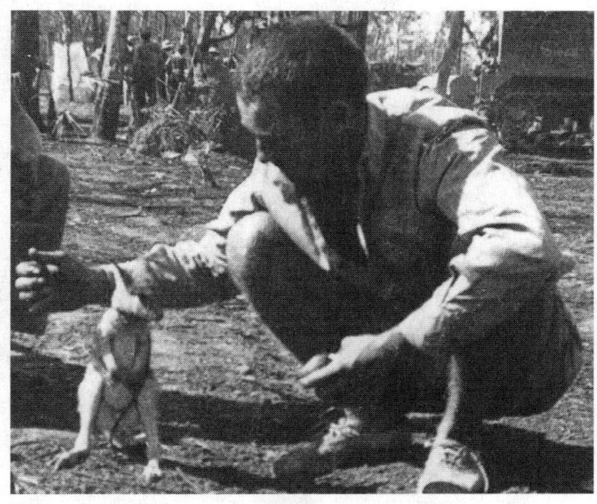

Feeding the little pet wallaby.

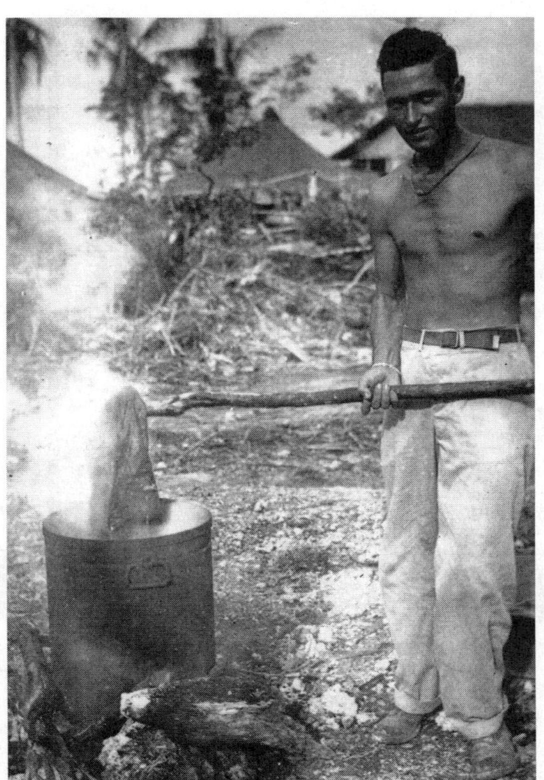

Wash day.

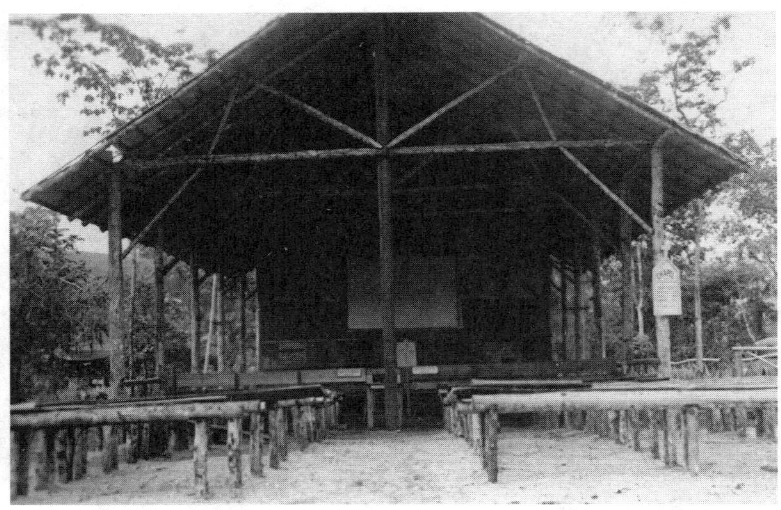

The Chapel.

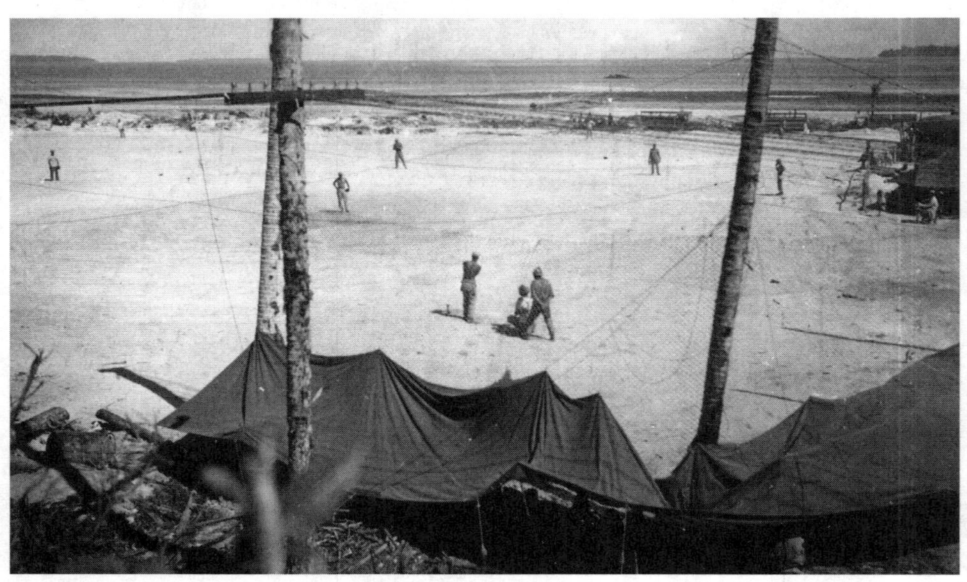

Baseball field. Two islands are visible in the distance. One of those, Auki Island, is where the sawmill was first set up, about five miles away. Notice the two utility poles in the foreground set up for phones and electricity.

SEPTEMBER 1944

ELSEWHERE IN THE WAR

Sept. 2: Allied troops enter Belgium.

Sept. 8: Admiral Halsey's Pacific Fleet sinks or damages 89 merchant vessels and 68 planes off Mindanao, Philippines.

Sept. 9: The first V-2 rocket lands on London.

Sept. 13: Destruction of Cebu harbor on Cebu Island, Philippines; U.S. Pacific Fleet attack Japanese in Philippines destroying 200 planes and several ships.

Sept. 15: American Marines land on Peleliu (present day Palau, east of Philippines) where a bloody battle would continue for two and a half months.

Sept. 18: Brest, France, an important English Channel port, falls to the Allies.

Sept. 18: The Second Dumbarton Oaks Conference begins, which will set guidelines for the United Nations.

Sept. 23: Americans take Ulithi atoll in the Carolina Islands for use as a naval base.

Sept. 25: British failure of Operation Market Garden in Holland results in 6,000 paratroopers captured.

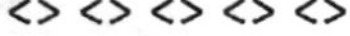

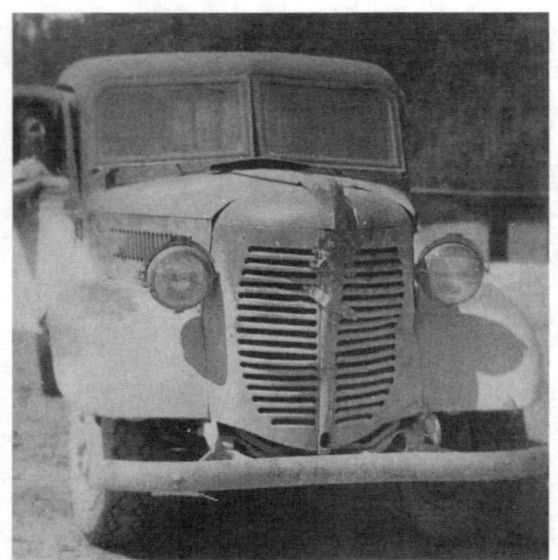

Clifford G. Wynne in Japanese truck.

Dad's good friend Clifford Wynne was loaned out to another battalion to drive a dump truck to haul ammunition. In the unloading process there was a huge explosion when a fragmentation bomb hit the ground. Wynne died instantly along with three men from the other battalion. My father took this very hard.

I remember asking my father if he had lost any good friends in the war. He responded with one name: "Wynne." I didn't press for details because I didn't want to risk seeing him get sad or with tears in his eyes. I had experienced the saddest days of my life when his brother Vernon died. I was in the sixth grade. It was the only time I saw my father cry, which broke my heart and made me cry like a baby.

My father's closest friends in the war were Wynne, Homer Fleming, Phillip Sandras, and Mally Bass. They all knew each other since training at Geiger Field, Washington. This picture of Wynne was taken just before he died on Biak. Sept. 25, 1944. R.I.P.

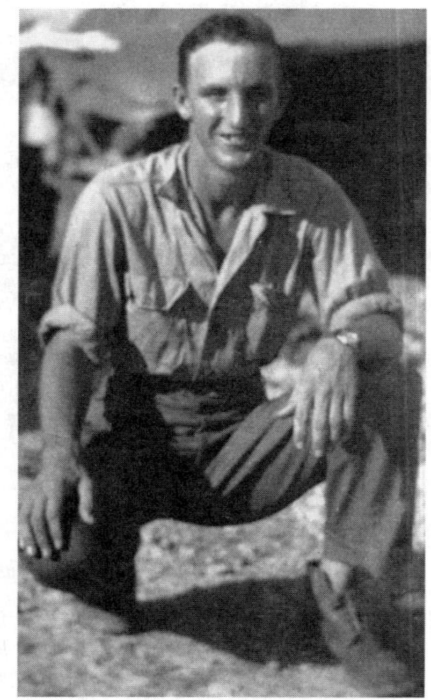

My dad's good friend Clifford G. Wynne, Jr.

OFFICIAL MILITARY RECORD ENTRY:

Sept. 2 – According to the control tower on Mokmer Drome, the temperature today is 135 degrees Fahrenheit.

Sept. 8 – An 81 mm mortar shell exploded in camp area when area dump was being burned. Shell was among debris piled up by bulldozer. Luckily no one seriously injured. Pvt. Lester was hit in ankle by a piece of flying shell casing causing it to swell slightly.

Sept. 25 – Pvt. Clifford G. Wynne, Jr., while on Detached Service (DS) to the 542nd Engineers, was detailed to drive his truck in the hauling of ammunition to Mokmer Dump #1. In the unloading process, a fragmentation bomb exploded, killing him and three other men working there. The battalion mourns the loss of a good and well-liked soldier. His funeral, held at Bosnek, was well attended by his host of friends in the battalion.

The summary of major construction work at the Mokmer Drome Area, Biak, Schouten Islands, work having started June 8, 1944.

A - A road from Bosnek to Mandom to accommodate the movement of incoming troops was constructed.

B - The construction in the drome area consisted of lengthening the existing strip, building taxiways and repairing existing ones. The strip was lengthened from 4000 feet to 7000 feet long with 500-foot overruns on the ends.

C - The construction of 1600-foot alert areas on each end of the strip.

D - Five miles of taxiways were constructed and continual maintenance of existing taxiways was necessary for operational purposes.

E - 130 hardstandings to accommodate heavy bombers were constructed.

F - The construction of a 900-foot bore sighting range. This necessitated the building of a 700-foot access taxiway and a firing table 130-feet in diameter.

G - A sawmill set up in operation.

H - The leveling and preparation of six tank sites and the construction of an AVGAS jetty.

I - The clearing of Gas Dump, Bomb Dump and Radar areas.

J - The major building construction in this area includes 3 anti-aircraft Command Post Buildings out of coconut logs, one being 18-foot x 18-foot and the other two 10-foot x 10-foot, a 40-foot x 100-foot Fighter Sector Building was erected, a 30-foot control tower and operations building were constructed at the strip, a building at the Engineer Dump, two Medical buildings and one Ordnance building.

K - Constructed revetments for our AA Artillery and ammunition positions.

L - At present (Aug 17, 1944) work is still progressing on taxiways and on the north shoulder of the strip. The taxiways and hardstandings are being resurfaced and widened.

Biak Historical Report from Aug 20 to Sept 24, 1944

The construction of the drome area continues in the form of widening existing taxiways and rebuilding hardstandings. A Company is assigned the construction, repair, and maintenance of the Mokmer Drome area. The task of erecting numerous warehouses and the construction of an AVGAS tank was assigned to B Company. The entire personnel of C Company are engaged in the logging and operation of a sawmill.

The construction in the drome area has been and remains hampered by the amount of heavy equipment waiting to be repaired due to lack of spare parts.

The lumber production is somewhat handicapped by the lack of good logging sites. Most of the logs in the Mokmer area are filled with shrapnel, and ideal areas are too remote for practical utilization.

The erection of buildings by B Company has seen little or no difficulty. The company has sufficient trained carpenters and is as a whole experienced in this type of work. Excellent results were obtained in using coral for the floors. This material when wetted and rolled takes on all the characteristics of concrete.

During this period 1600-feet of taxiway and 11 hardstandings were constructed. Twenty-four hardstandings were rebuilt to accommodate heavy bombers. Four new taxiways were constructed from the parallel taxiway to the strip, length approximately 1000 feet. North shoulder of Mokmer Strip, 7000-feet long, completed. Repair and maintenance continues in the drome area.

Construction of two prefabricated Ordnance buildings 47-foot x 108-foot, construction of a telephone exchange building 24-foot x 48-foot, and construction of a transportation building at the Liberty Dock 40-foot x 84-foot are the major building projects completed during this period.

The total lumber production for this period was 164,394 board feet.

Below is a copy of Mokmer Drome airplane dispersal area as of Sept 24, 1944. This is the official military map of Mokmer Drome showing the beach road at the very bottom and the main runway. The zig-zag zipper patterns are the taxiways with hardstandings, or parking lots for the planes. The large black blotches on each side are defects and were on the microfilm when it was converted to CD in the 1970s, thirty years after the war.

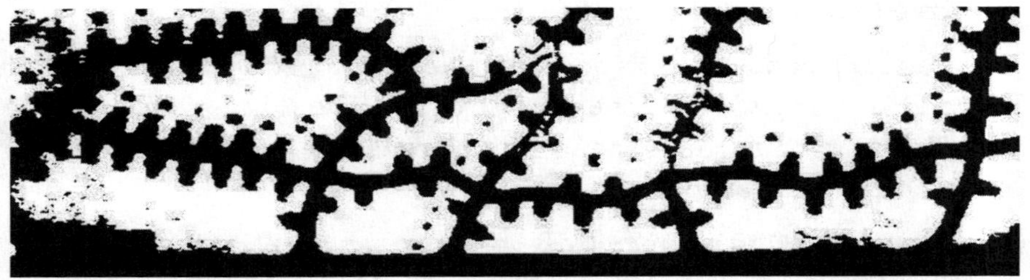

OCTOBER 1944

ELSEWHERE IN THE WAR

Oct. 1: Soviet troops enter Yugoslavia.

Oct. 1: Field Marshal Rommel, suspected in the failed bombing attempt on Hitler's life, commits suicide to save his family.

Oct. 4: British begin the liberation of Greece.

Oct. 9: Aircraft carrier planes strike Okinawa.

Oct. 14: Athens, Greece, liberated.

Oct. 20: Belgrade, Yugoslavia, is liberated from the Nazis.

Oct. 20: Battle of Leyte, the amphibious invasion of Leyte, Philippines.

Oct. 21: Battle of Leyte Gulf; 58 Japanese warships sunk or damaged; U.S. losses were negligible.

Oct. 21: Aachen is occupied by U.S. First Army. It is the first major German city to be captured.

Oct. 23: The battle of San Bernardino Strait. The Japanese attempt to stop MacArthur's landing on Leyte, Philippines.

Oct. 23: B-29s are now using Tinian Island, in the Mariana Islands, as a base for the systematic bombing of Japan.

Oct. 23: The Allies recognize General de Gaulle as the head of a provisional government of France.

Oct. 25: Battle of Samar, Philippines.

<> <> <> <> <>

OFFICIAL MILITARY RECORD ENTRY:

Oct. 2 – T/5 Irvin W. Behrends died this morning at the 41st Field Hospital from internal disorders. The funeral, held this afternoon, was attended by a host of his friends in the battalion. He was a good soldier and was well liked by the officers and enlisted men. He was a real loss to the battalion.

S-E-C-R-E-T

HEADQUARTERS
863RD ENGINEER AVIATION BATTALION

Historical Report

Period from Sept 25 to Oct 24, 1944

During this period, approximately three miles of road was constructed, an Aviation Gasoline (AVGAS) 10,000-barrel steel tank erected, a 90-foot x 120-foot loading platform constructed, a Bore Sighting Range constructed at Borokoe Drome and 45 bays constructed for Petroleum, Oils and Lubricants (POL) and AVGAS.

The major building projects erected during this period were:

- Transmitter and Receiver buildings for Radio Station
- Red Cross building and personnel quarters
- Tower for 8th Fighter Control
- Six buildings for RAAF Hospital
- APO warehouse buildings
- Operations building and Control Tower at Sorido Drome.
- Total lumber production for this period was 113,486 board feet.

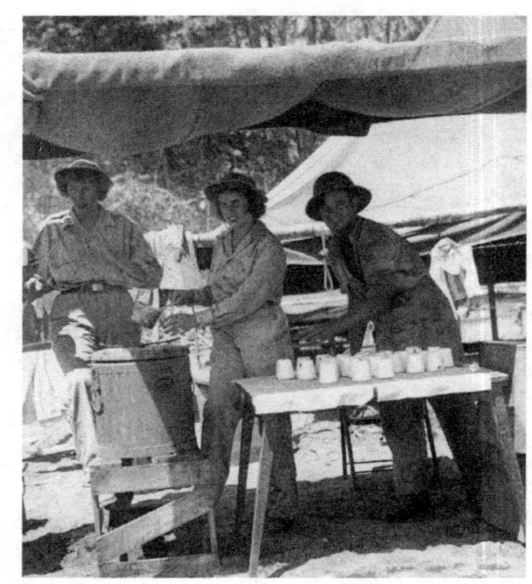

Red Cross women serving lemonade near the beach.

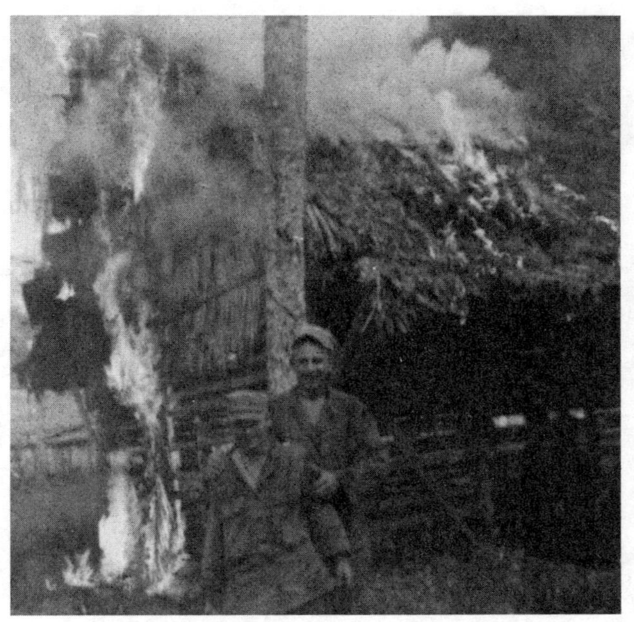

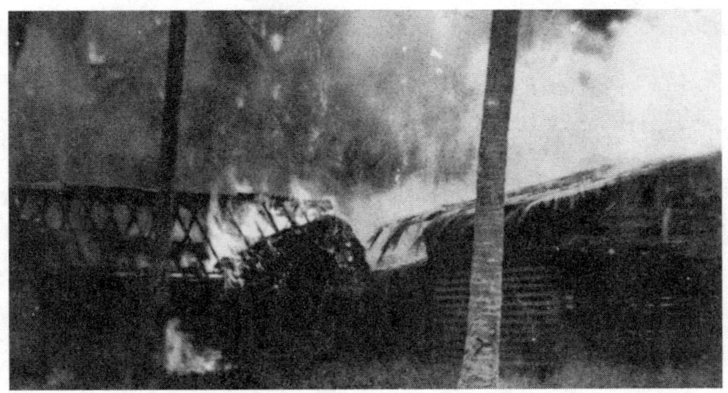

Burning buildings made from native materials before leaving Biak.

NOVEMBER 1944

ELSEWHERE IN THE WAR

Nov. 1: Aitape-Wewak Campaign, New Guinea.

Nov. 2: Belgium is now entirely liberated.

Nov. 5: U.S. planes bomb Singapore, which has been under Japanese control since 1942.

Nov. 6: Franklin Delano Roosevelt wins a fourth term.

Nov. 9: General Patton's troops and tanks cross the Moselle River and threaten the city of Metz.

Nov. 11: Battle of Ormoc Bay, Philippines.

Nov. 12: After numerous bombings while anchored in a fjord at Tromso, Norway, the German battleship Tirpitz is sunk.

Nov. 19: U.S. carrier-based planes destroy Japanese shipping in Manila harbor and destroy 118 planes.

Nov. 24: B-29 Superfortresses originating from Tinian bomb Tokyo in daylight raid.

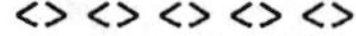

OFFICIAL MILITARY RECORD ENTRY:

Nov. 22 - Work on projects still continues. Unit will stop work to prepare for move on Nov. 25.

Historical Report

Period from Oct. 25 to Nov. 24, 1944

Routine work continues.

H&S Company's work included the administration, supply, operations section, and the furnishing of Heavy Equipment operators and truck drivers for the projects assigned to this Battalion.

Major work for A Company included the preparation of floors for 10 new buildings, grading and improving roads, and blasting coral mounds from west approach zone of Mokmer strip.

Major work for B Company included the erection of a water tower and latrine at Red Cross site; construct nine buildings; construct a Bailey Bridge for experimental and training purposes.

C Company's work consisted of operating sawmill and cutting and gathering logs. Lumber cut for this period was 131,200 board feet.

Unit schools and training consisted of practice of erecting of Bailey Bridge by Companies individually, Motor Maintenance course, which included weekly Command Motor Inspections, and Bazooka and Mortar instruction and practice firing under the tutelage of the 163rd Infantry.

DECEMBER 1944

ELSEWHERE IN THE WAR

Dec. 8: The softening up bombardment of Iwo Jima begins.

Dec. 15: General MacArthur lands American and Filipino troops at Mindoro, Philippines.

Dec. 16: Battle of the Bulge begins as German forces attempt a breakthrough in the Ardennes region of Luxembourg.

Dec. 17: A typhoon hits the Third Fleet of Admiral Halsey; three destroyers are capsized.

Dec. 26: The siege of Bastogne, Belgium is broken; the Ardennes offensive proves a failure.

<> <> <> <> <>

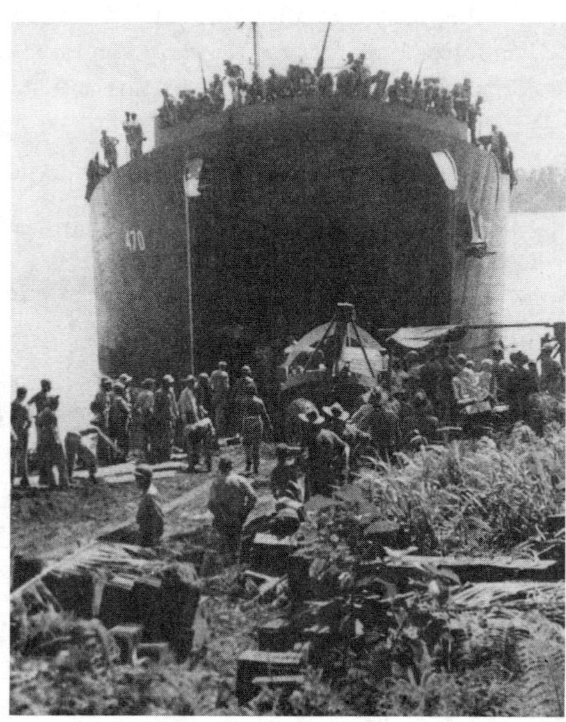

Loading up and leaving Biak Island on LST 470.

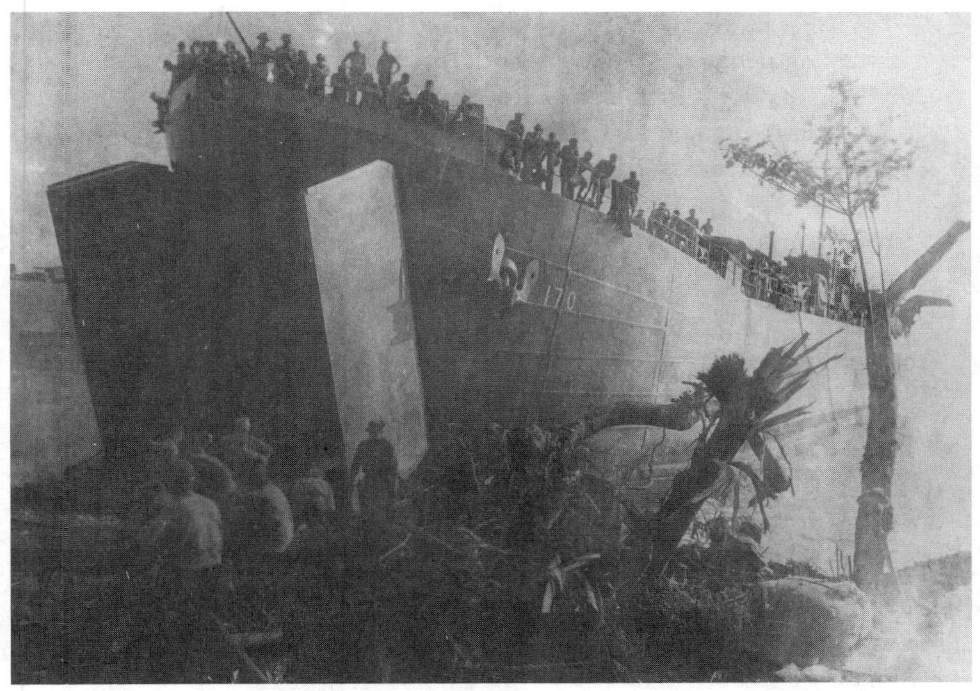

LST #170.

The Last Historical Report for Biak

Dec. 1 to Dec. 9

All jobs being completed, the battalion started putting equipment and vehicles in shape for the coming move. During this preparation period a training schedule was instituted, consisting of close order drills by Companies, Bailey Bridge construction, orientation and firing of bazookas, grenade launcher instruction, mine detector instruction, and mortar instruction, including firing.

A training program for the schooling of one radio operator per Company was inaugurated by our battalion radio operator. Completed first and second echelon maintenance of heavy equipment and motor vehicles bringing the condition of our equipment to tip-top shape. Equipment and motor vehicles waterproofed to ensure usability in emergency landings through surf.

Started loading on LSTs the morning of 9 December 1944 with all loading completed by midnight of that date.

OFFICIAL MILITARY RECORD ENTRY:

Dec. 7 - All preparations completed for move. Battalion is ready to move at an hour's notice.

Dec. 9 - Started taking down tents and loading same right after breakfast. The buildings erected from native materials were torn down and burned. Camp area thoroughly policed and left in excellent condition. A and B Companies loaded on LSTs in morning, followed by H&S and C Companies in the afternoon, with all loading completed by midnight.

Dec. 10 - Under way at 1300 hours at 11.2 knots per hour. Anchored at Woendi Island (a few miles southeast of Mokmer Drome) at 1459 hours.

Dec. 12 - Weighed anchor at 1200 hours with various speeds and courses to clear torpedo nets. Laid practice smoke screen. Anchored at south coast of Biak Island at 1550 hours. Under way again at 1613 hours.

Dec. 14 - Commenced zigzagging according to plan at 0740 hours. Ceased zigzagging at 0749 hours. Anchored in berth 24, Sorido Lagoon, Biak Island, at 1315 hours. Under way again at 1613 hours.

The battalion would be on the LST until their next stop at Calicoan Island, Philippine Islands, on December 21, 1944.

Closing Comments of Biak Story

Well, this was quite an experience for a country boy! He made some memories he would never forget. I have recounted some of the most memorable of these below.

The battalion was welcomed to the island with cannons shooting at them, wounding two of their troops with shrapnel as they climbed down the landing net.

The enemy was shooting at them, not only from the top of the ridge above their camp, but from the caves inside the coral cliffs.

The soldiers were exposed to enemy fire, but couldn't dig a foxhole to evade the bullets and bomb shrapnel whizzing by because the island is coral, which is as hard as rock.

But the work had to go on. So the grader and bulldozer operators got on their machines, despite the hazards of bullets hitting their equipment, in order to complete the restoration of Mokmer airdrome.

And then there was the memory of seeing all the dead bodies. And the smell! Oh, the gut-churning smell of human bodies decomposing in the hot sun was horrible and seared into his memory.

Since we had a farm and raised cattle, we experienced the unfortunate death of a cow now and then, only to find the dead carcass three days after it died and partially decomposed.

I asked my dad if a dead human smelled as bad as a dead cow, which to me is the worst smell in the world . . . well, my world. What he said surprised me. We were standing in front of his home when he told me, "A dead rat smells worse than a dead cow, and a dead human smells worse than a dead rat." To me this was mind-blowing. I hope to never experience that.

Unfortunately for the troops, they had to deal with the smell of death.

Now the time has come to continue on in this island-hopping campaign. Load 'em up and move 'em out. Our next destination awaits.

CHAPTER 8

The Philippines: The Battle of Manila and Its Reconstruction

From the time that my father's 863rd Engineer Aviation Battalion left the Biak area on Dec. 15 until Dec. 21 at noon, the battalion was on ships headed to the Philippine Islands. This section is about how my father's battalion helped to rebuild the infrastructure of Luzon, the northernmost island. But first, here is some back story.

Some Background and Introduction to the Philippines

The Philippines had been a U.S. protectorate and part of the American commonwealth since Spain ceded it at the close of the Spanish-American War in 1898. Spain agreed to sell the Philippines to the United States for the sum of $20 million.

In 1937 General MacArthur was called out of retirement and took command of 10,000 American Army troops, 12,000 Filipino enlisted men who fought as part of the U.S. Army, and 100,000 Filipino army soldiers, who were poorly trained and ill-prepared to fight.

The day of the Pearl Harbor bombing, Dec. 7, 1941, also saw the Japanese destruction of almost half of the American aircraft based in the Philippines.

The Japanese invaded the Philippines by amphibious assault, forcing General MacArthur and his U.S. and Filipino troops to evacuate to the Bataan Peninsula. Shortly thereafter he and his family and staff fled to the nearby island fortress of Corregidor.

A message from President Roosevelt arrived at Corregidor on Feb. 20, 1942, ordering MacArthur to leave immediately for Mindanao, then on to Melbourne, Australia, where he was to assume command of all United States troops. MacArthur balked at the idea of leaving but finally obeyed the president's order on March 11.

On the night of March 12, 1942, MacArthur and a select group that included his wife Jean and four-year-old son Arthur left Corregidor in four PT boats. After two days and nights of rough seas, MacArthur and his party reached Mindanao, where B-17s picked them up and flew them to Australia. His famous "I shall return" speech was first made in Terowie, a small town in South Australia, on March 20.

Bataan surrendered to the Japanese on April 9 and Corregidor on May 6.

On April 18, 1942, MacArthur was appointed Supreme Commander of Allied Forces in the Southwest Pacific Area (SWPA).

The staff of MacArthur's General Headquarters (GHQ) was built around the nucleus of officers who had escaped from the Philippines with him and who became known as the Bataan Gang.

MacArthur's GHQ moved to Brisbane – the northernmost city in Australia with the necessary communications facilities – in July 1942.

On Oct. 20, 1944, troops of Krueger's Sixth Army landed on Leyte, while MacArthur watched from the light cruiser USS Nashville. Later that afternoon he waded ashore with enemy snipers still active and shooting. MacArthur returned as he had promised.

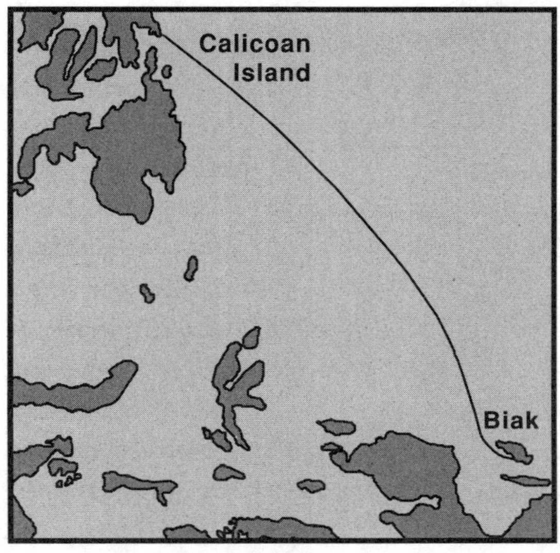

Their voyage from Biak to Calicoan Island in the Philippines.

Introduction to Calicoan Island

My father's battalion of 770 troops plus 50 or so officers left Biak at midnight on Dec. 9 aboard ships called LSTs, which stands for Landing Ship, Tank. It was a troop and equipment carrier. For security reasons, they were not told their destination until much later. On Dec. 21 at noon, Dad's H&S company, along with B company, landed without mishap at Calicoan Island in Eastern Samar Province, Philippines. They immediately started unloading the road building equipment. The bulldozers, two-yard shovel, rollers, graders, and trucks were the last to be loaded on the LST at Biak so that it could be unloaded first when they hit the beach at their new destination.

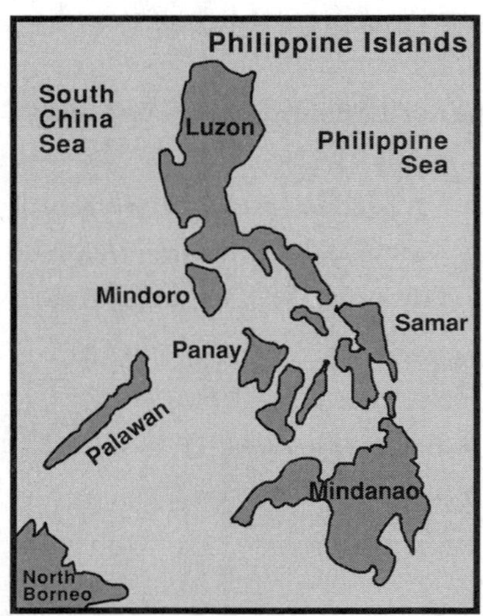

Map of Philippine Islands.

These two companies immediately went to work clearing and grading a beach road approximately 30 feet wide and 3/4 of a mile long along the campsite areas.

Unfortunately, both the C Company and A Company LSTs had mishaps. These two ships were grounded on the hidden coral reefs and were stuck in the surf before reaching the beach. But H&S and B Company came to their rescue. They built a jetty and made a road from the beach to the ship. This enabled the troops to disembark and unload on Dec. 22.

The following day the exact same thing happened to A Company and a jetty had to be built to unload *their* LST.

Because of these landing mishaps, actual road construction was not started until Dec. 22. But a 50-foot coral ridge hampered the construction, so it had to be blasted away with explosives. I imagine it was quite an exciting experience for my father, farm boy, to watch the engineers blast away the coral.

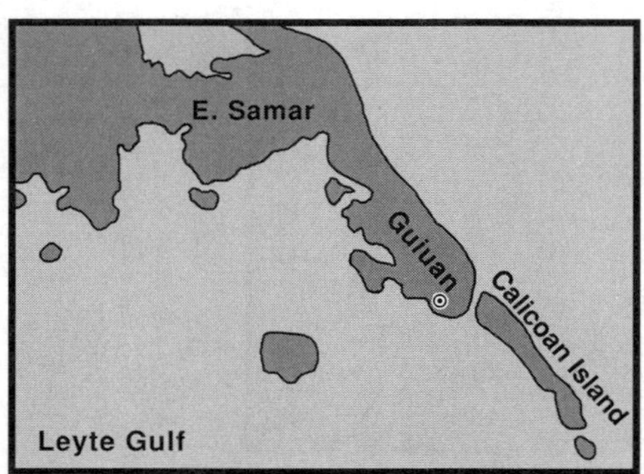

The 863rd Engineer Aviation Battalion's first stop in the Philippines – Calicoan Island.

Christmas Day, Dec. 25, arrived, but there is no turkey for the boys, not yet. They were told to get all the work done and celebration time would come later.

Once all four companies were up to ramming speed, they accomplished a lot, such as noted in the following report.

Historical Work Report

December 1944

- Established and maintaining a water point.
- Assisted in placing of loading jetties for LSTs, constructed from Navy Cubes. Maintaining 7000 feet of existing roads in the Calicoan area.
- Cleared 1 1/4 miles of 30-foot-wide road right of way for the 75th Naval Construction Battalion.
- 3400 feet of all-weather road, 30 feet wide was completed during this period. This project required the removal of 8200 cubic yards of earth, 400 yards of which was in the form of coral composite hill, requiring demolition. One thousand pounds of dynamite was used in this operation.

All work stopped at the close of this period for the continuance of our journey to our original destination.

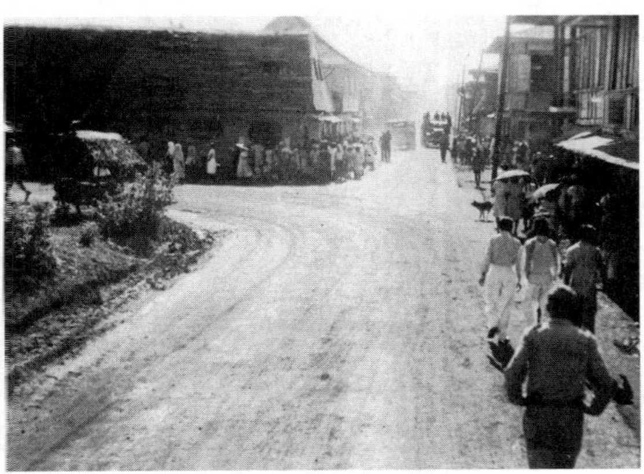

Dad wrote: "We have just arrived in the Philippine Islands after leaving Biak Island. This is the first street I've seen in Guiuan, Eastern Samar."

The name of the town of Guiuan is pronounced "Ghi-wan."

JANUARY 1945

ELSEWHERE IN THE WAR

Jan. 1: The Luftwaffe launches its last major air offensive of the war in the West.

Jan. 4: U.S. Navy air attacks on Taiwan.

Jan. 9: U.S. Seventh Fleet Invasion of Lingayen Gulf, Luzon, Philippines.

Jan. 16: United States First and Third Armies link up following Battle of the Bulge.

Jan. 16: Soviet troops lay siege to Budapest, Hungary.

Jan. 17: The Battle of the Bulge has ended.

Jan. 17: U.S. B-25s bomb Japanese planes on Clark Field, 50 miles north of Manila.

Jan. 18: Americans drive on Manila.

Jan. 20: Franklin D. Roosevelt is sworn in as president (his fourth term); Harry Truman sworn in as vice president.

Jan. 25: American Navy bombards Iwo Jima in preparation for invasion.

Jan. 27: Auschwitz concentration camp in Poland is liberated by Soviet troops.

Jan. 31: Battle for the Recapture of Bataan, Philippines.

<> <> <> <> <>

Goodbye Calicoan Island

On Jan. 1, 1945, the battalion finished their job for the navy, loaded the cargo on the LSTs, and set their course for San Pedro Bay, Leyte, where they arrived six and one-half hours later. While anchored, the captain sent a small boat to get the battalion's mail. Receiving mail from home after a long time proved to be a great morale booster. After being anchored for eight days, the remainder of the convoy arrived on Jan. 8 and set sail to the Battle of the Lingayen Gulf in northern Luzon.

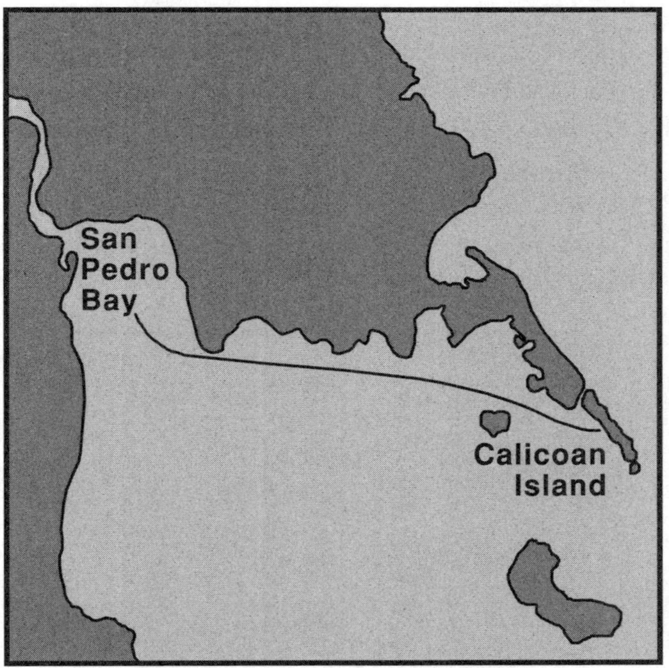

From Calicoan Island to San Pedro Bay, then north up the channel to Lingayen Gulf in Luzon.

Welcome to the Lingayen Gulf

While my father's engineer battalion was sailing to Leyte, a battle ensued at their new destination. A heavy air and naval bombardment of Japanese defenses on the Lingayen coast began the previous week on Jan. 4, 1945. A total of 203,608 soldiers were eventually landed over the next few days, establishing a 20-mile-wide (32 km) beachhead. The military had success in driving out the Japanese forces stationed there. However, the naval convoys sustained heavy losses due to kamikaze attacks: a total of 24 ships were sunk and another 67 were damaged by the Japanese crashing their planes into the ships.

As they approached their next location, out in the distance the battleship U.S.S. Pennsylvania and her sister ships could be seen. Of all the sights seen in the war, the most majestic were those of huge battleships shooting their guns, blasting planes out of the sky, and destroying tanks on shore. They hooped and hollered and cheered the ships as they witnessed the enemy getting hit. This feeling of protection was very reassuring to my father and his friends. However, danger still lurked nearby.

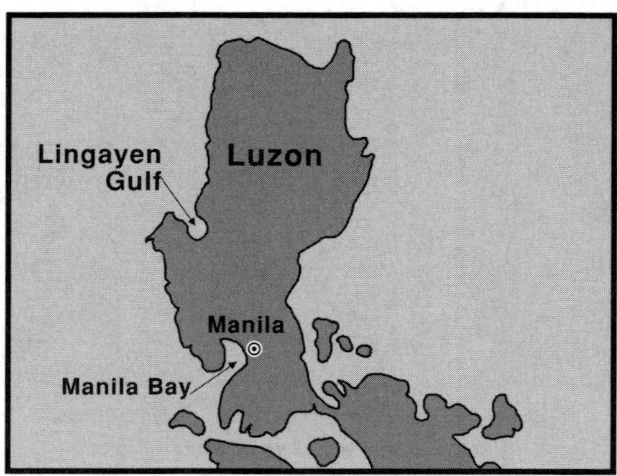

They sailed from San Pedro Bay to Lingayen Gulf where they witnessed a battle while aboard their LST.

We're Under Attack

It was 1 pm on Jan. 12. The convoy was approaching their anchorage point in the Lingayen Gulf. A Liberty ship nearby seemed to explode as a torpedo hit it. A destroyer launched two depth charges to fight back. My dad's ship, LST #623, went to help. The mechanics were able to repair the port (left) engine in 35 minutes. Five enemy planes, or bogies, were sighted at 2:20 pm, all boats commenced with anti-aircraft fire. One plane was shot down as a result. At 6:30 pm the Liberty ship on our starboard (right) side was hit by a diving plane, which crashed into the ship causing many explosions. Another diving plane missed the Liberty ship off our port side and crashed in the sea. A few minutes later another bogie came in on our starboard side and was driven off with anti-aircraft fire. Both the Liberty ship that was torpedoed and the one hit by the diving plane were able to continue in the convoy. It was now 7:45 pm.

Jap Saboteurs

The convoy arrived at noon on Jan. 13, and anchored in the Lingayen Gulf. The next day, the LST captain received information regarding attempts by Japs to approach the ships in small boats or swim under floating debris and toss hand grenades aboard. Armed guards were posted at strategic spots throughout the hours of darkness and fired at any objects that approached ships. This made for an uneasy night. It was not ascertained whether any of the enemy were killed.

It wasn't until high tide on the following night, at 10 pm Jan. 15, that my father's LST reached the floating dock. Unloading of equipment began immediately and continued throughout the night. All heavy equipment was removed by 8 am on the 16th. Personnel and remaining equipment were unloaded and moved to the new camp area. The kitchen was set up and the noon meal was served. By nightfall the entire camp was completely set up.

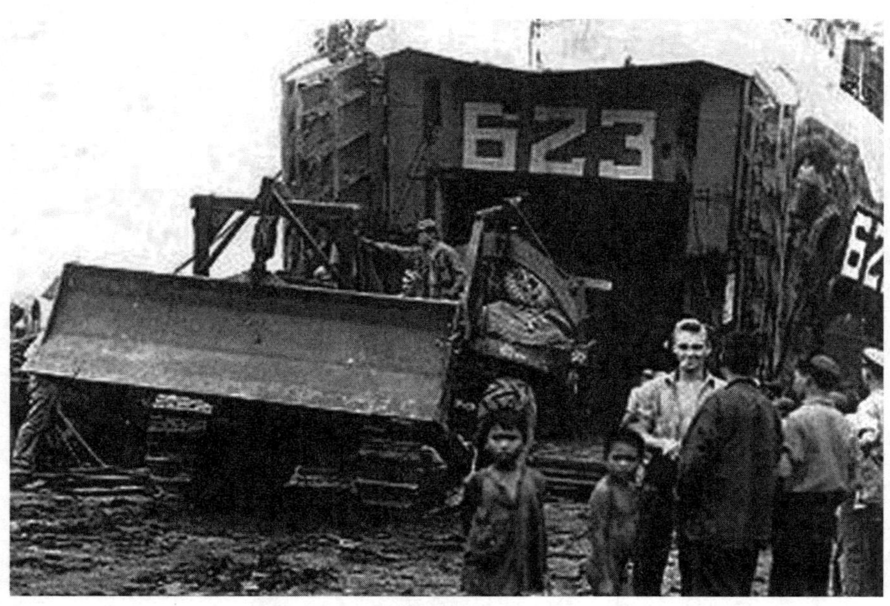

The ship my father was on, LST #623, is unloading equipment on the beach at Lingayen, in northern Luzon, Philippines, Jan. 15, 1945.

The next morning, the officers of the 863rd met with the brass of the 5202nd Engineer Construction Brigade 12 miles away. Instructions were received on what the priorities were. They delivered official mail, and they picked up mail for the battalion.

The Neighborhood Is on Fire

A few days later, on Jan. 20, enemy planes flew in and attacked their area, starting a fire which set four native houses ablaze. The conflagration was prevented from consuming a large group of highly flammable homes by quick work on the part of the battalion's equipment operators in conjunction with the 594th Amphibious Engineers. The operators bulldozed a firebreak completely around the stricken area and brought the fire under control. A bucket brigade was formed using helmets, which worked effectively in putting out the fire.

Introduction to January 1945

My father's battalion arrived in northern Luzon on LSTs by coming through the Lingayen Gulf. They disembarked and got to work on rebuilding the infrastructure – roads, bridges, and railroads.

The U.S. Army Infantry preceded them by a few weeks and did their job of fighting and eliminating the enemy threats. There were as many as 350,000 Japanese soldiers in the Philippine Archipelago, and only an estimated 50,000 were left when Japan surrendered.

The infantry went ahead of my father's battalion all the way to Manila, clearing the enemy out of the way, making it safe for the engineers to do their job, as well as enabling the civilians to return to a peaceful life.

Civilian life in Manila, however, was a different story. At this time horrendous atrocities were being committed by the Japanese on the innocent Filipino population.

As my father's H&S Company went about their daily work repairing the streets, they were frequently approached by the locals who were friendly to them. One family and their children in particular made friends with my father: a sister and brother named Conchita and Gregorio David.

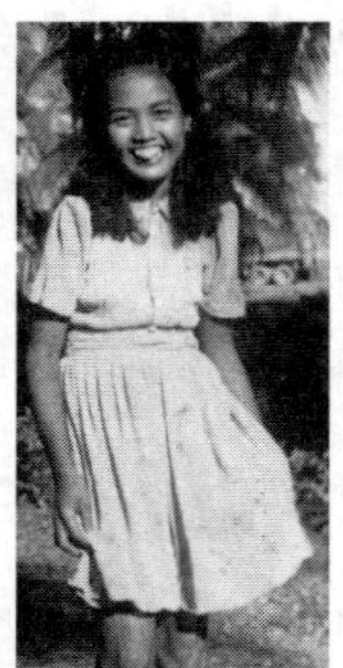

Dad wrote on the back of this picture, "Pretty little Conchita David makes a face sticking her tongue out at me. " In Camiling.

Gregorio, brother of Conchita David.

Historical Work Report
January 1945

Started work on the north and south approaches to the Calmay River Bridge. Demolition work by our unit in Lingayen was carried on, and debris used for fill on this bridge.

- Built a Navy pontoon bridge crossing the Agno River, Lingayen.
- Road maintenance.
- Constructed a Navy cube bridge.
- Repaired the bridge across the Camiling River.
- Established a water point at the town of Camiling.

The cathedral in the photo below is in the town of Lingayen, near the coastline of the Lingayen Gulf. The town was established in 1614 by the Spaniards. The construction of this church was started in 1710 and completed in 1714. It became the seat of the Diocese of Lingayen in 1928. Part of the church was destroyed during WWII, and the bishop's residence and the convent was badly damaged. It was rebuilt after the war and is now called the Cathedral of Epiphany of the Lord Parish.

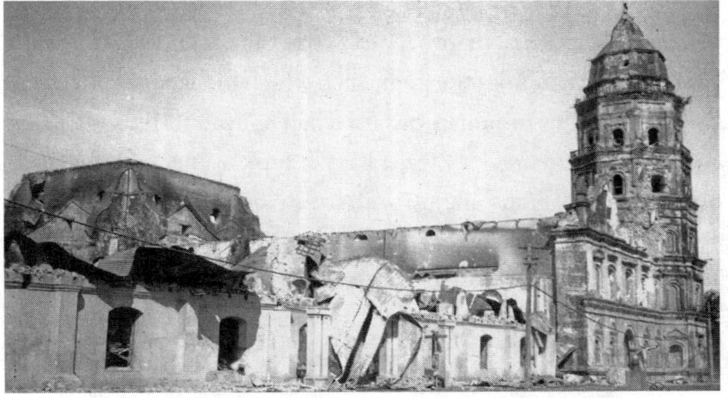

This church in Lingayen got bombed. Near Lingayen Gulf.

Zigzag Pass

In Jan. 1945, General MacArthur ordered the capture of the Bataan Peninsula and the island fortress of Corregidor, which guarded the entrance to Manila Bay. Once the bay was seized and cleared of enemy resistance, shipping could resume into the Port of Manila, bringing in needed supplies and equipment.

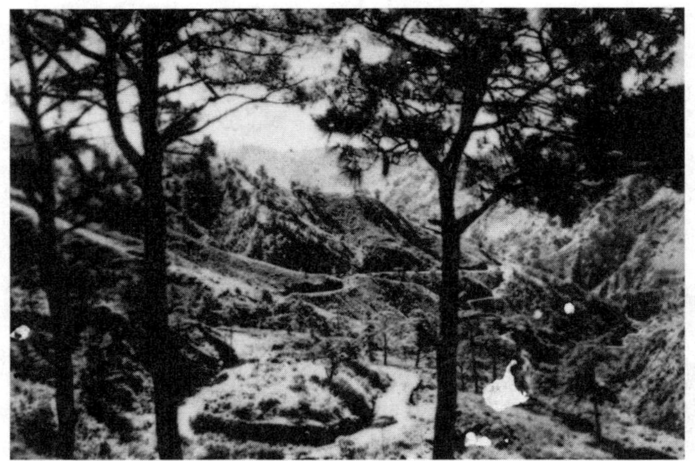

Zigzag Pass, Philippines.

In the dense jungle of Bataan, the Japanese seized a high ridge over a mile long and turned it into a series of reinforced pillboxes and foxholes. This was along Route 7, the main road across the peninsula, which blocked the forward progress of the U.S. infantry. This mountainous road had hairpin turns and horseshoe curves, so the soldiers named it Zigzag Pass. It took over a week for the infantry to root out and eliminate the enemy, with much loss of life on both sides. Having accomplished this, the Bataan Peninsula was soon cleared of enemy troops and Corregidor was liberated shortly thereafter. This enabled the Americans full use of Manila Bay and its world-class deep water port. This development subsequently allowed the easy resupply of U.S. forces retaking Manila.

FEBRUARY 1945

ELSEWHERE IN THE WAR

Feb. 3: U.S. forces enter Manila, the capital of the Philippines, to help the Allied Philippine Commonwealth troops and recognized guerillas. Japanese massacre 100,000 Filipino civilians and devastate the city. A vicious urban battle ensues lasting for weeks.

Feb. 4: Yalta Conference begins.

Feb. 4: Manila prison camps at Santo Thomas University and Bilibid Prison are captured and over 1,500 prisoners freed.

Feb. 5: U.S. troops storm Manila from assault boats on Pasig River. The next day, the 11th Airborne Division enters Manila from the south, and the 37th Infantry went in from the north.

Feb. 13/14: Dresden, Germany, is firebombed by Allied Air Forces.

Feb. 16: American naval vessels bombard Tokyo and Yokohama.

Feb. 16: Allied troops assault Corregidor, the island fortress in Manila Bay.

Feb. 19: U.S. Marines invade Iwo Jima.

Feb. 23: Old Glory goes up over Iwo Jima.

Feb. 24: Massive bombing of Germany by approximately 9,000 bombers.

Feb. 25: After ten days of fighting, American and Filipino troops recapture Corregidor Island in Manila Bay.

Feb. 28: The U.S. Sixth Army captures Manila.

<> <> <> <> <>

Historical Work Report

February 1945

Feb. 3 – Captured five Japs; two killed while trying to escape.

Feb. 7 – One half of Clark Field #4 Strip has been cleared and repaired and is ready for traffic.

Feb. 10 – Moved battalion headquarters to Santo Domingo just south of San Fernando on Hwy 3. A mile of high line wiring was run from hospital to hydroelectric plant. Built the twin tank water point at Stotsenburg Hospital with 20,000 gallon/day output. Working on repairing Tarlac streets. Rebuilt Railroad Bridge across Labangan River. Graders working on both overruns on Clark Field.

Feb. 17 – Constructing loading ramp at drum filling station south of Tarlac with roads to this area under construction.

Feb. 21 – Repaired railroad water station tank at Tarlac.

Feb. 26 – Drum filling plant at Dau completed. Repair Railroad Bridge near Longos.

Feb. 28 – Battalion headquarters moved to Queson City, Manila.

Clark Field Under Attack

Just after noon on Dec. 8, 1941, Japan's 11th Air Fleet achieved complete tactical surprise when they attacked Clark Field and the nearby fighter base at Iba Field. They destroyed or disabled 18 B-17s, 53 P-40s, three P-35s and more than 25 other aircraft. Substantial damage was done to the bases, 80 casualties were reported, and 150 soldiers were left wounded.

What was left of the Far East Air Force was all but destroyed over the following days. The enemy held the high ground in the hills next to the airport and placed artillery and mortars there to control the area. Even though the outlook wasn't promising, the one thing the Japanese severely underestimated was the spirit of the Allied forces. And that would come back to haunt them.

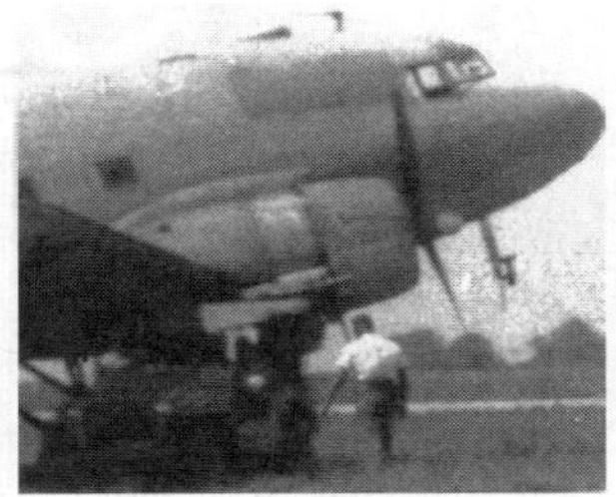

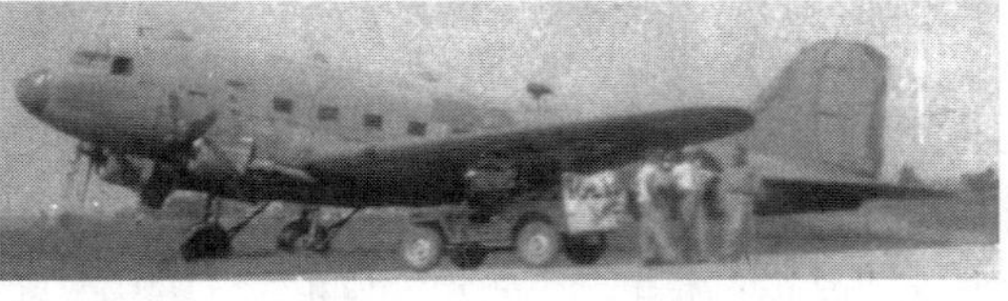

Above are two C-47 cargo transports that landed on Strip #4 at Clark Field airport, 50 miles north of Manila, on Feb. 8, 1945. The engineers and crew spent many weeks repairing the runways, often under attack by Japanese snipers and artillery. They were finally able to get these planes in to bring needed supplies.

My father was awarded the ribbon shown below:

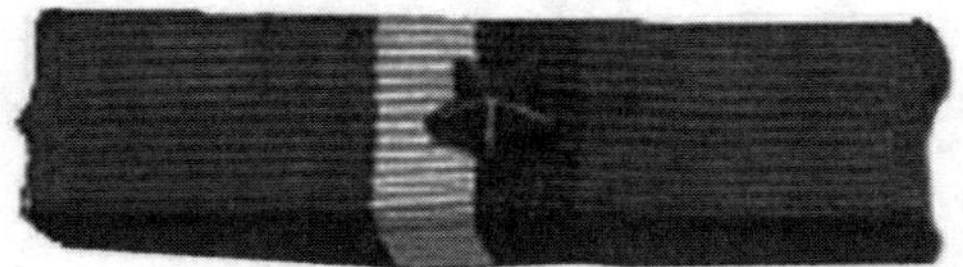

Philippines Liberation ribbon with bronze star.

The Philippine Liberation Ribbon with Bronze Star was awarded by the Philippine Commonwealth for service in the liberation of the Philippine Islands from Oct. 17, 1944 to Sept. 3, 1945. In order to qualify, one of the following provisions must be met:

- Participation in the initial landing operation on Leyte and adjoining islands from Oct. 17-20, 1944.
- Participation in any engagement against the enemy during the Philippine Liberation Campaign.
- Service in the Philippine Islands or in ships in Philippine Waters for not less than 30 days during the period from Oct. 17, 1944 to Sept. 2, 1945.

Individuals were eligible under any two of the foregoing provisions and were authorized to wear one bronze star on the ribbon bar. Personnel eligible under all three provisions were authorized to wear two bronze stars on the ribbon bar. It was an honor for my father to receive this ribbon, and he was proud to serve his country.

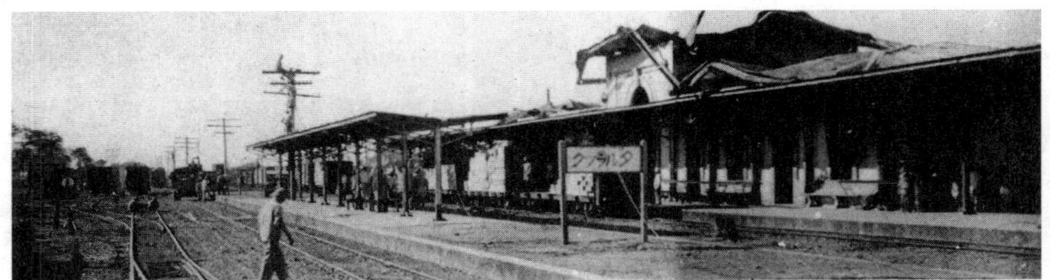

Railroad station being repaired.

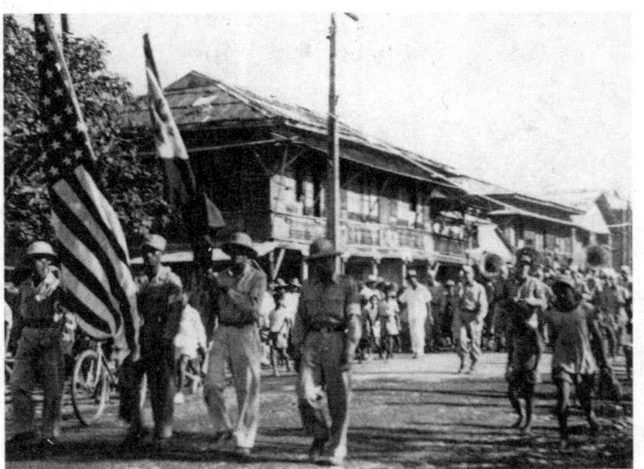

Victory parade in Tarlac on Feb. 12, 1945.

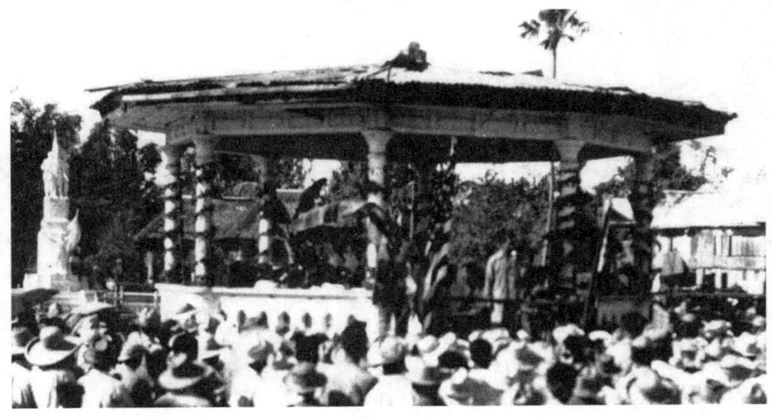

A victory speech being given in the plaza in front of the Tarlac Municipal Building on Feb. 12., 1945.

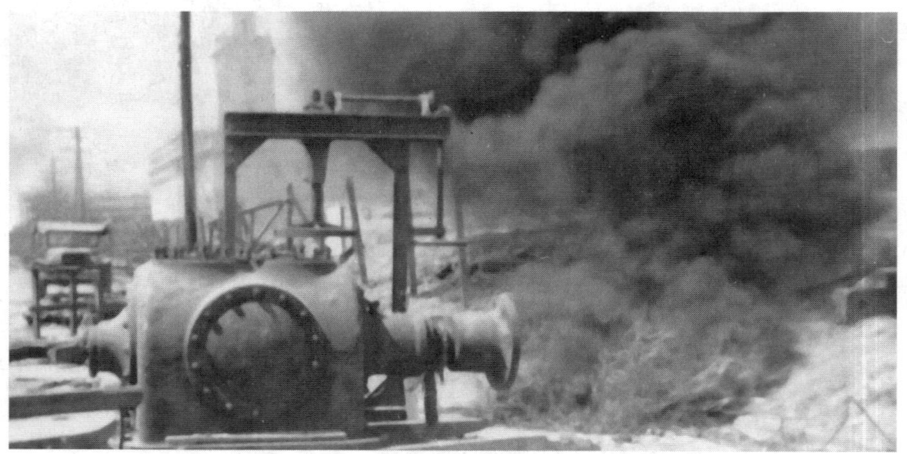

Burning an enemy corpse. Bureau of Customs building in background.

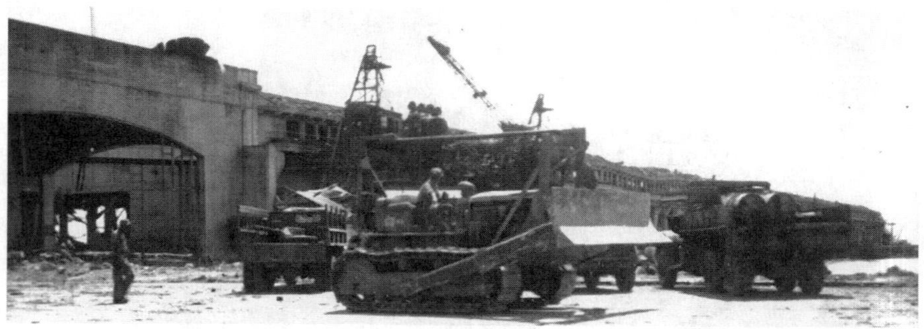

Picture showing World's Longest Covered Pier.

Bridges Destroyed

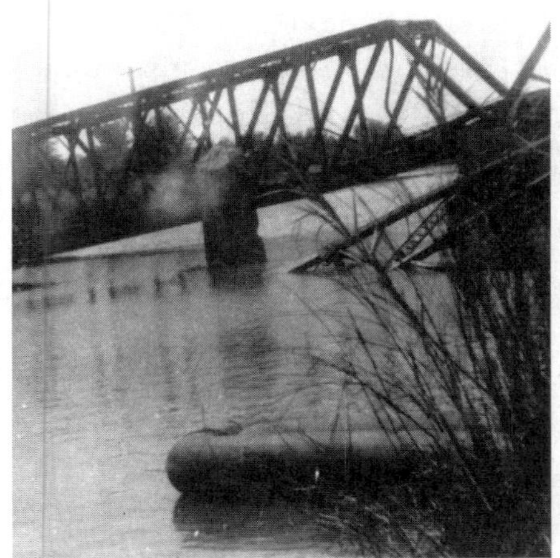

One of the destroyed bridges. The first pontoon hits the water.

All of the bridges across the Pasig River between North Manila and the Intramuros and Ermita districts in central Manila were blown up by Feb. 7, 1945. This forced U.S. troops to make amphibious landings to attack the main fortifications of the Japanese.

Once the Japanese forces had been pushed back, the first thing the battalion engineers did was construct a pontoon bridge. It was built adjacent to the destroyed bridge west of the general post office, which was the main access for the military to move from North Manila to Central Manila.

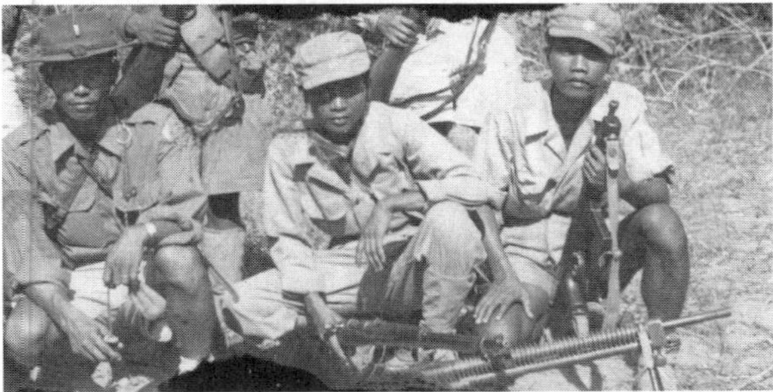

A rugged bunch of Filipino guerillas with their machine guns and rifles. These heroic men fought the Japanese for years before MacArthur returned as he had promised.

Manila Port Terminal was one of the many locations where the enemy made a stand and fought. In the photo below, notice the sandbag wall with two peepholes to shoot from.

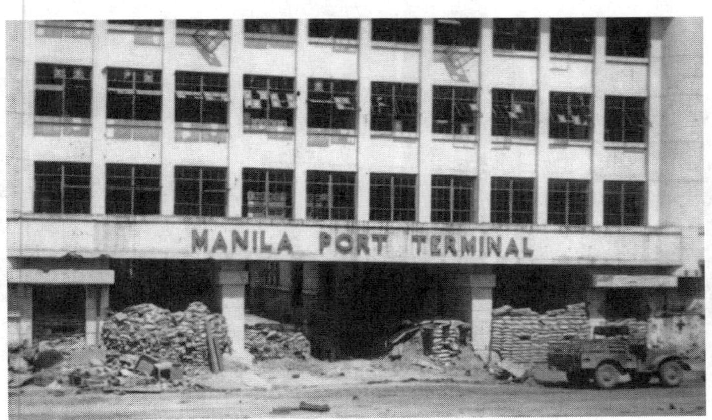

How Manilia Port Terminal looked after being shelled. This building is located just across the street from the docks.

HISTORY OF INTRAMUROS

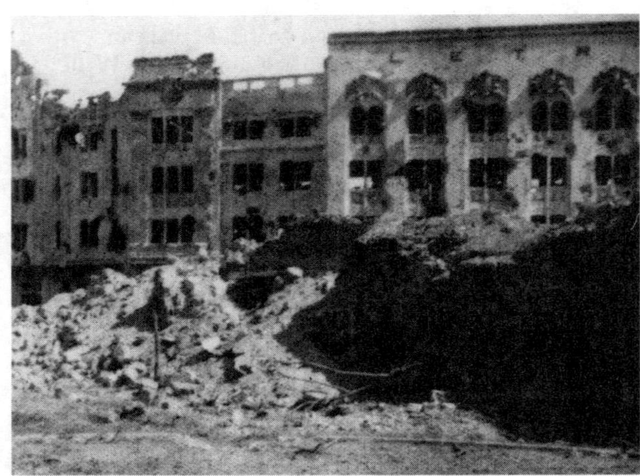

The walls of Intramuros were 16 feet high, 40 feet thick at the base, tapering to 20 feet thick at the top.

Intramuros is the original city of Manila built by the Spaniards. It is surrounded by massive walls that are over 400 years old.

It became the main Japanese defensive position and was subject to three weeks of heavy artillery bombardment by U.S. forces. The Japanese held many Filipinos within their defensive perimeter, using them as human shields, and thousands died in the battle at Intramuros.

On Feb. 23, 1945, troops from the 37th Infantry breached the walls and started building-to-building fighting to dig out the defenders who fought to the death. Virtually no building was left standing within the Intramuros, and the ancient walls were reduced to rubble.

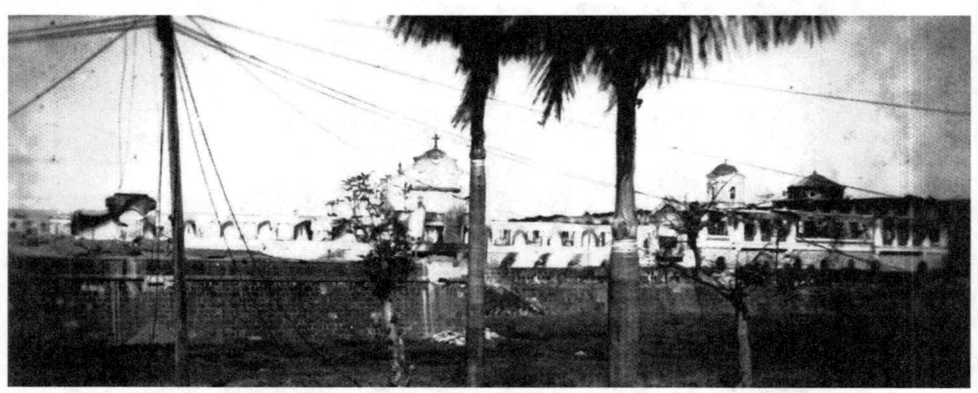

Another view of the Walled City of Manila, or Intramuros. This is where Dad found the Japanese rifle he brought back with him.

Japanese Rifle and Bayonet

My father found this Japanese rifle and bayonet in Manila within the Walled City. The gun has a bullet hole through the wooden forestock, preventing the bayonet from attaching to it. You can see a piece of the metal protruding at the far right of photo. On the far left you can see a seam in the stock. It was made with two pieces of wood stuck together to save on wood.

The rifle is an Arisaka Type 38 made by the Koishikawa arsenal in Tokyo before 1935. It has the chrysanthemum emblem with 16 petals (the symbol of the Japanese Emperor) stamped on the receiver. This was placed on rifles manufactured for the Imperial Japanese Army, indicating that the rifle belonged to the Emperor.

Years ago when I was about 21 years old, my dad and I went to his farm and shot this rifle. We didn't know if it was safe to shoot since he had never fired it. We rigged it up with a long string around the trigger, placed a heavy sandbag over the gun to keep exploding parts from hitting us, and pulled the string. It fired perfectly. So we each took turns firing it. I remember it has quite a kick to it.

After my father died in Sept. 2000, I inherited this rifle.

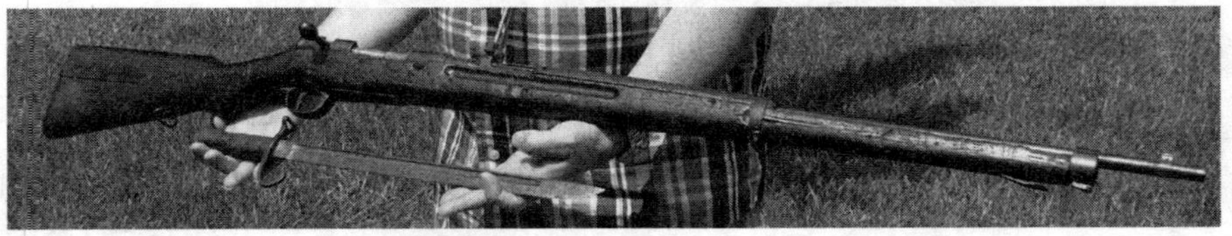

Japanese Arisaka rifle and bayonet my father found inside the Walled City.

After the Battle of Manila, the streets were full of bomb craters from the artillery bombardment. The roads needed to be repaired so the Allied troops could get themselves and much needed supplies to key strategic points.

U.S. solders and local laborers repaired this road called España Avenue, and now it is being graded.

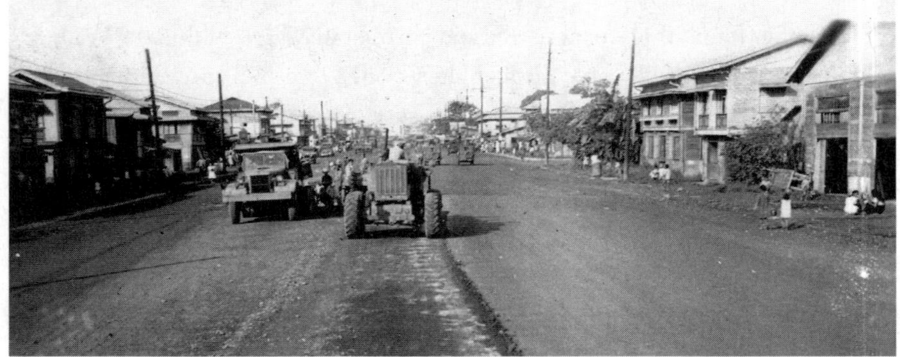

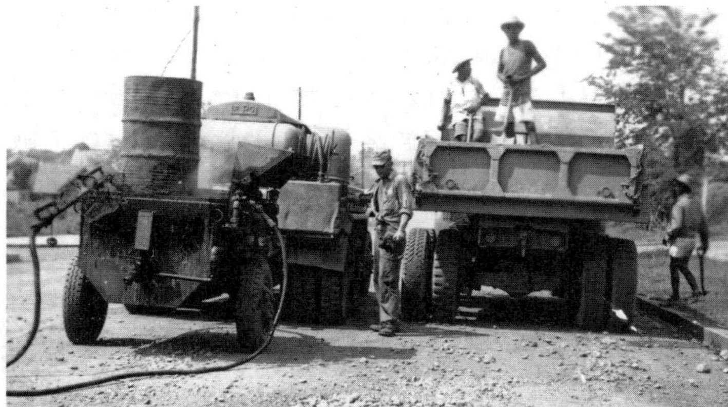

Asphalting the roads in Manila.

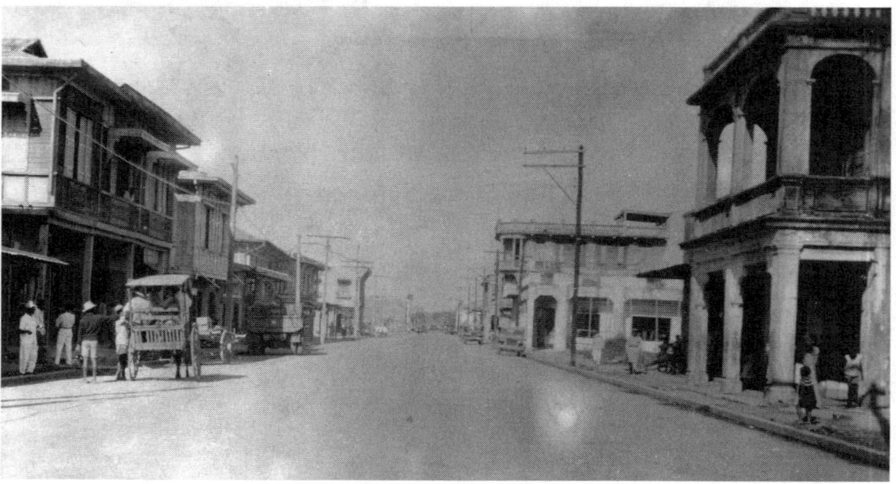

More road work completed.

MARCH 1945

ELSEWHERE IN THE WAR

Mar. 7: German troops fail to dynamite the Remagen Bridge; Americans begin crossing the Rhine into Germany.

Mar. 10: Mindanao, Philippines, invaded by U.S. troops.

Mar. 16: Iwo Jima finally secured after a month of fighting.

Mar. 18: The Japanese bastion of Panay Island, Philippines, falls to U.S.

Mar. 27: The Western Allies slow their advance and allow the Red army to take Berlin.

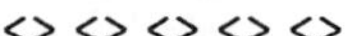

Historical Work Report
March 1945

- Started clearing debris from Manila streets and dock area.
- Repair Calumpit-Plaridel Road.
- Start clearing and repairing of Pier #7.
- Grading of an air strip for Piper Cubs at Grace Park.
- Repair of the Marpayo Railroad Bridge south of Caloacan. Constructed 5 LST slots between Pier #1 and #3.
- All damaged and bent steel removed from Highway Bridge across Labangan River.
- Demolished and cleared ruined buildings in the LST Dock area. Heavy scrap machinery and scrap iron being removed in the clearing of Pier #7 project. Started clearing area in North Harbor Section. Reconstruct main post office.
- Battalion received Letter of Commendation from superior officers. The letter stated:

"Your battalion has repaired, with great credit, the railroad bridge across the Labangan River just south of Calumpit, railroad bridge on the main line near Longos south of the Labangan River, and Marpayo railroad bridge just south of Caloacon. All of these have been done under difficult conditions and in the immediate proximity of the enemy. Their rapid accomplishment under these conditions is worthy of the highest praise."

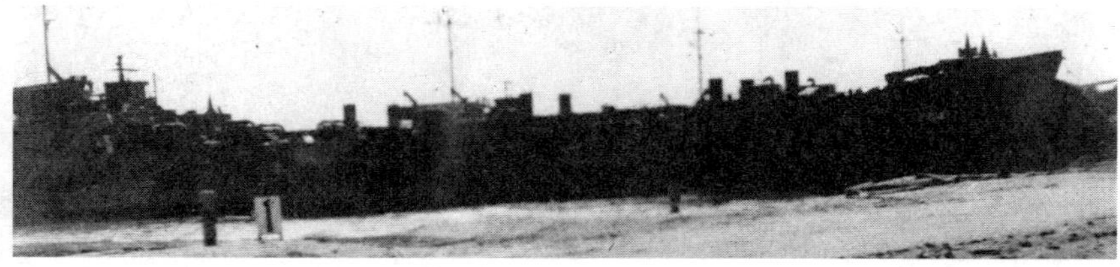

Five LST slots were constructed between Pier No. 1 and No. 3. Here LST No. 204 is in one of them.

To date, this organization has removed over 1400 tons of debris from Pier #7. In addition, have installed two 50-foot Single Single Bailey Bridges, one 70-foot Double Single Bailey Bridge, three 80-foot Double Single Bailey Bridges and two 40-foot timber bridges on this pier which is now being used to unload Liberty ships. The fourth Liberty is now unloading, with one-way traffic plan in operation all the way around this 1400-foot long by 400-foot wide concrete pier. The 863rd Engineer Aviation Battalion was the first Engineer Aviation Battalion to work south of the Pasig River and commenced work on Pier #7 and other assignments in the South Harbor area while this area was still under enemy sniper fire. LST slots constructed between Pier #1 and #3, South Harbor, has received over 50 LST loads and hundreds of LCM (Landing Craft, Mechanized), LCT (Landing Craft, Tanks) and small craft loads, and in addition, a few units have shipped out through these LST (Landing Ship, Tank) slots.

One of the guns that liberated Manila:
The 240 mm Howitzer M1.

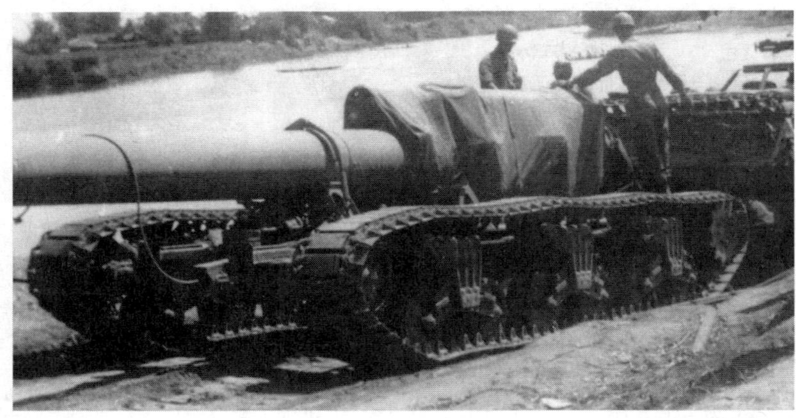

The Japanese made their last stand inside the Intramuros. They had settled in with their artillery and mortars and fired at the Allied troops. The only way to eliminate this threat was to return fire and kill the enemy, because they were not going to surrender. Several 240-mm Howitzer M1's were transported to Manila to fire on Intramuros, the Walled City, where the walls were sixteen feet high, forty feet thick at the base, tapering to twenty feet at the top.

Under the cover of darkness on Feb. 22, all available artillery and personnel were moved into key strategic positions and at 0730 (7:30 am) the following morning, the assault on Intramuros began.

The powerful Howitzer M1s, weighing in at 28 tons, could shoot a 360-pound shell 14 miles. These huge guns were instrumental in blasting 50-foot-wide holes in the wall. This allowed equipment and troops to enter unhindered, as well as destroy enemy strongholds in buildings.

Once the walls were breached and the attacking troops had entered, savage fighting ensued. Not a single building escaped damage. On Feb. 25, the entire area of the Walled City was in U.S. hands.

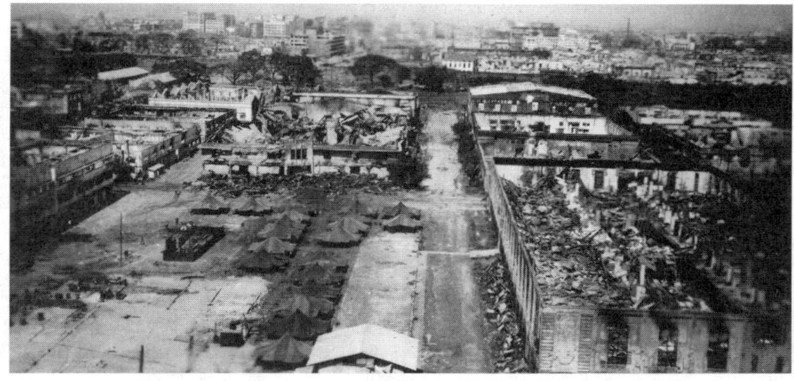

View of destruction in Manila from atop the Bureau of Customs.

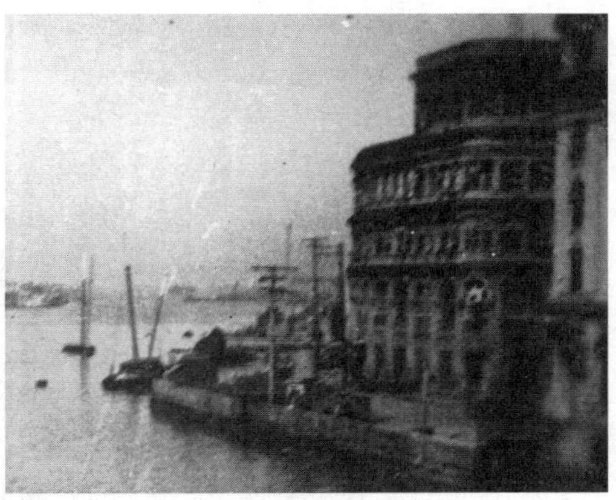

The south bank of the Pasig River.

The south bank of the Pasig River. This photo was taken from a Bailey Bridge the troops constructed. The original bridge was destroyed by the enemy as they left Manila. These buildings are near the general post office and other civic buildings. It was the site of heavy fighting during mid-February 1945. On the right is the rear of the General Post Office, showing damage from the heavy fighting to control the building. Manila, March 1945.

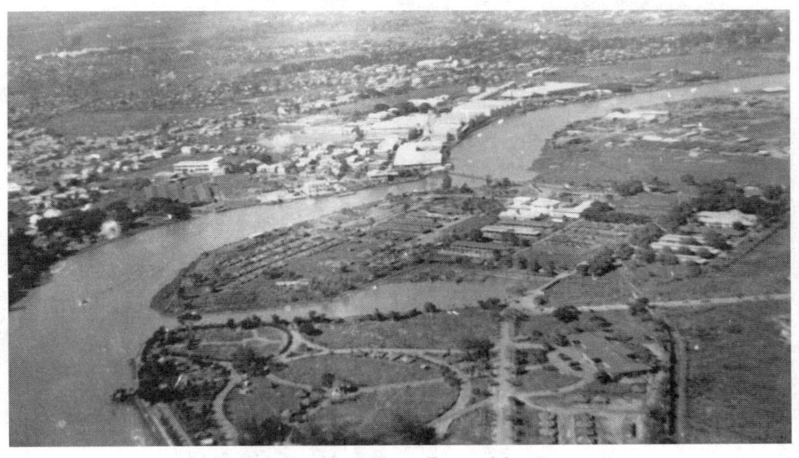

Aerial view of Pasig River, Manila.

Salvage of Ships

Manila had a large, well-developed port facility and harbor. Throughout the war, its infrastructure, piers, docks, warehouses, Manila harbor, and the bay itself suffered greatly.

When the Japanese retreated from Manila, they did a successful job of blocking the harbor entrance with four large ships, rendering the port useless. They did this by blowing up the ship's magazines with the crews still on board, allowing the ships to sink immediately.

According to www.history.navy.mil/pubs/MudMuscleMiracles.pdf, all Japanese had not been driven away by the assault forces. Suicide squads hid in the wrecks until the salvors came aboard and then attacked them with machine guns and hand grenades.

Before salvage work or survey work could begin, the remaining Japanese had to be cleared out. U.S. Army troops with flame throwers, supported by PT boats and light aircraft, began sweeping the wrecks to clear them of suicide squads. The sweeps had to be repeated several times over because as soon as soldiers cleared the wrecks more Japanese would swim out and form new suicide squads.

The salvors removed 750 ships, barges, and assorted craft from Manila Bay. Of these, 100 were wooden hull Japanese cargo ships that were easily raised. Considering the number of wrecks, the Port of Manila was opened reasonably fast.

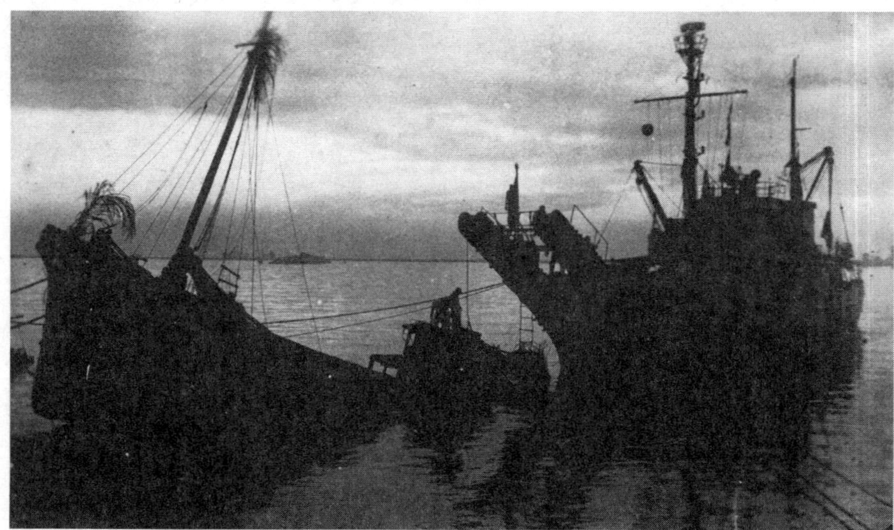

U.S. Navy salvage crews at work. March 1945, Manila.

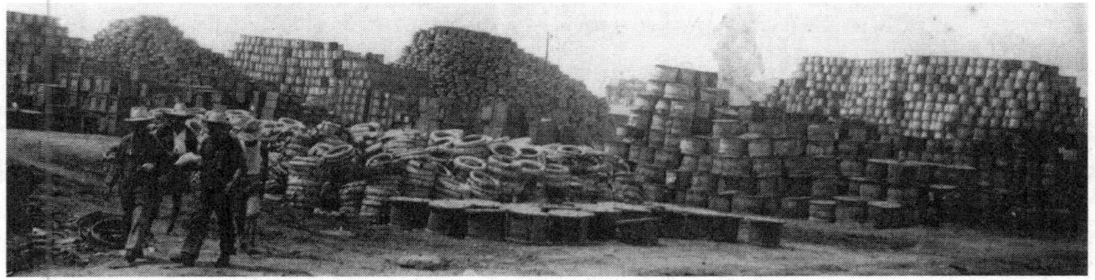

Battalion supply depot located at the North Harbor, Manila.

After the Battle of Manila, the harbor area became a huge depot for supplies for the continued fighting in the Philippines and in preparation for the invasion of the Japanese Home Islands. This area is the supply dump. The earth was first leveled and smoothed with a grader, and a tall chain link fence was built around it. My father made regular trips here to get supplies.

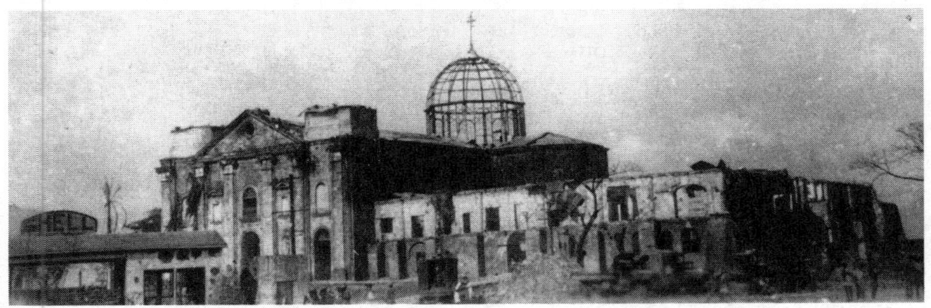

Tondo Church, Manila. Notice the Shell gas station sign in bottom left corner.

This is the north, or rear face of the main building on the campus of the University of Santo Tomas, which was designated Santo Tomas Internment Camp by the Japanese. When liberated, the camp held 3,876 American and Allied Alien civilians, and 480 had died during their internment as a result of torture and execution, disease and starvation, and enemy action.

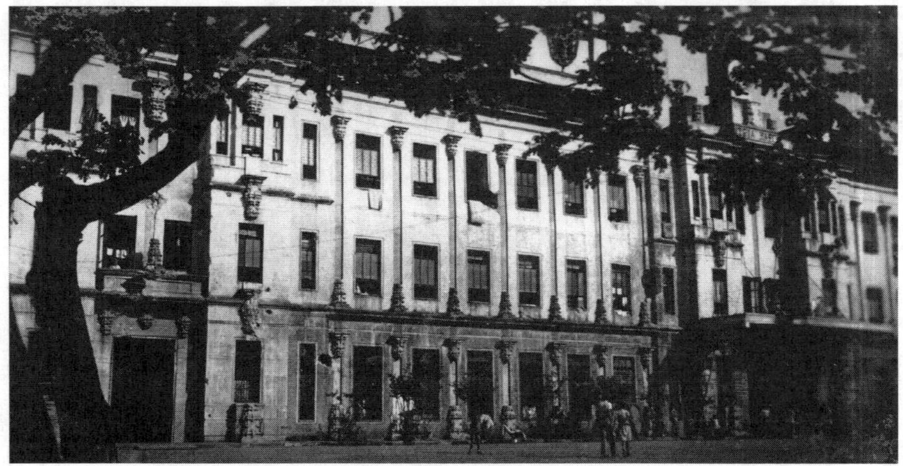

Santo Tomas University.

In this photo below, you can see many of the sunken ships in the harbor. The ship at the dock appears to be the SS John Lykes. It was the first repatriation ship to carry civilian ex-prisoners directly from the Port of Manila and departed April 2, 1945, on a 31-day voyage to Los Angeles Harbor, carrying approximately 500 civilians and 500 U.S. soldiers.

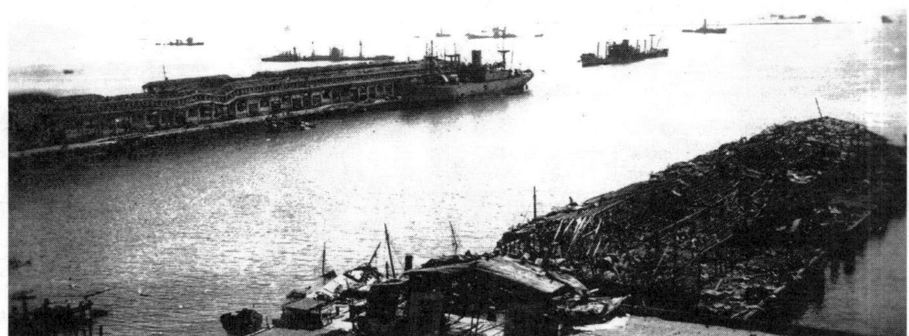

Pier #7, the longest covered pier in the world, bombed. Manila.

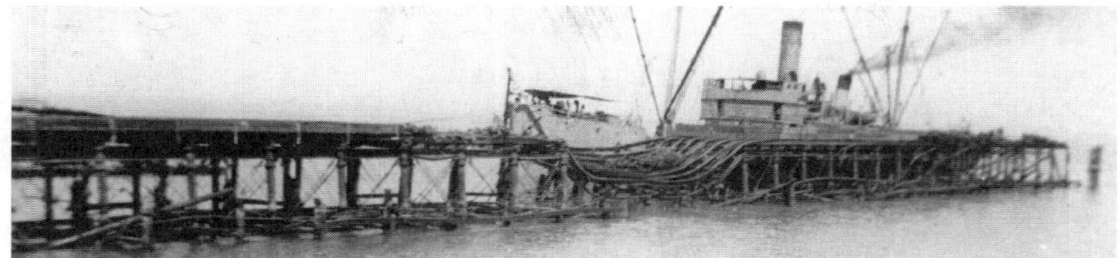

Bombed pier.

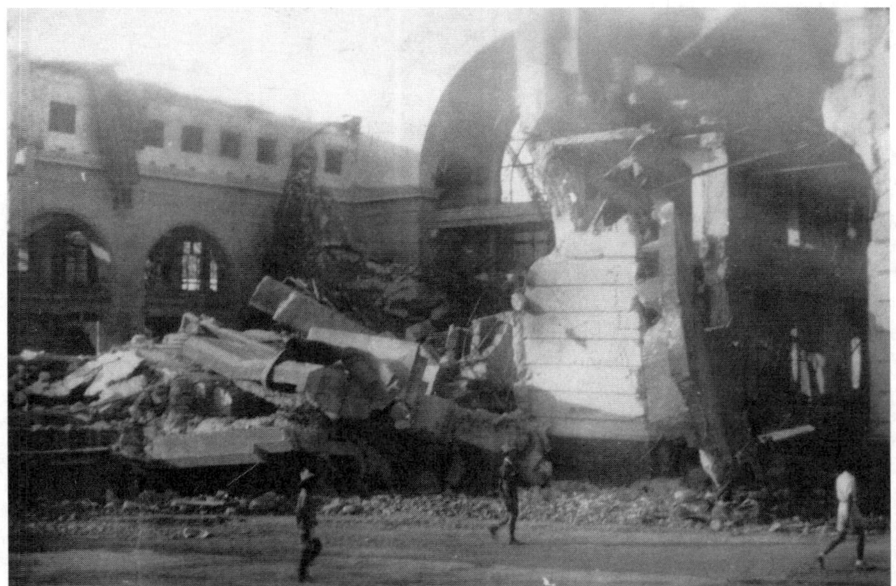

Front view of Pier 7.

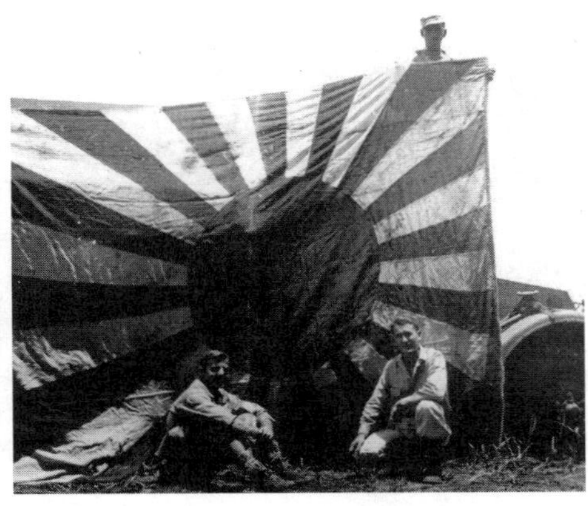

Captured Japanese flag.

APRIL 1945

ELSEWHERE IN THE WAR

Apr. 1: Okinawa, Japan, invaded.

Apr. 7: Operation Ten-Go, South of Kyushu Island, Japan.

Apr. 10: Buchenwald concentration camp in Germany liberated by American forces.

Apr. 11: Japanese kamikaze attacks on American ships continue at Okinawa; the carrier Enterprise and the battleship Missouri are heavily damaged.

Apr. 12: President Roosevelt dies; Harry Truman sworn in.

Apr. 17: Allied troops make a second landing on Mindanao, Philippines.

Apr. 28: Italian Fascist dictator Mussolini captured and killed.

Apr. 29: War ends in Italy.

Apr. 29: Dachau concentration camp in Germany, is liberated by the U.S. 7th Army.

Apr. 29: All forces in Italy officially surrender and a cease-fire is declared.

Apr. 30: Soviet troops declared final victory over Germany.

<> <> <> <> <>

Historical Work Report
April 1945

Repaired seven Railroad Bridges on Mainline south of Manila.

Rehabilitation of Rizal Stadium starts.

Construct La Loma Play House.

Start working on the Marsman building.

At Fort McKinley hospital site, started work clearing out area. Removed old cars, iron, tin, logs, and other debris from hospital site. Bulldozers started filling in Jap defense positions and leveling off area.

Repaired 10 railroad bridges and 40 kilometers of railroad track.

Built a 1000-bed hospital at Fort McKinley.

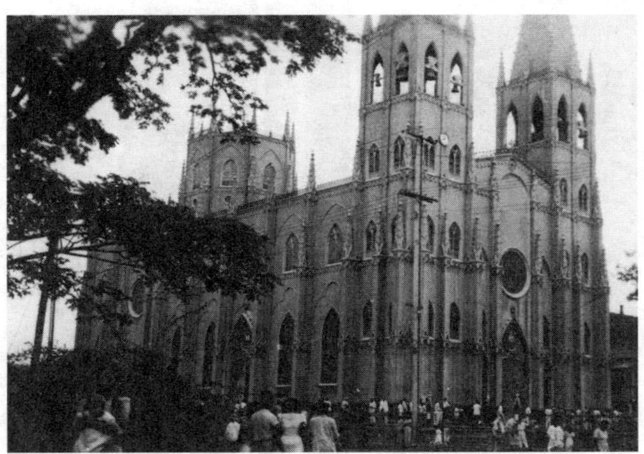

The San Sebastian Church in Manila.

The San Sebastian Church in Manila was designed in 1883 to be earthquake proof. It is the only all-steel Gothic church in Asia. The church, weighing almost 50,000 tons, was pre-fabricated in Belgium and transported to the Philippines in six separate ships.

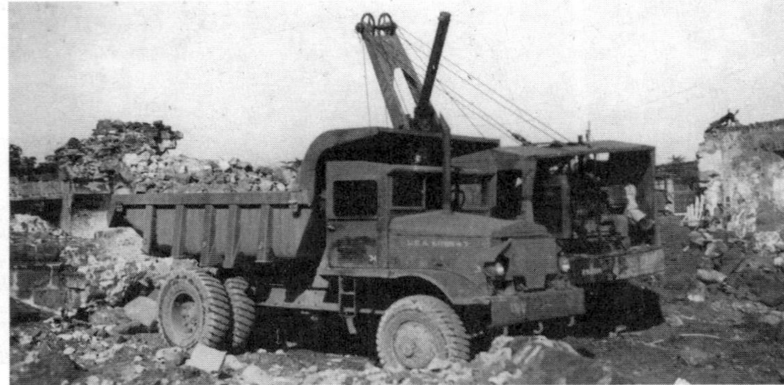

Fort Santiago in rubble.

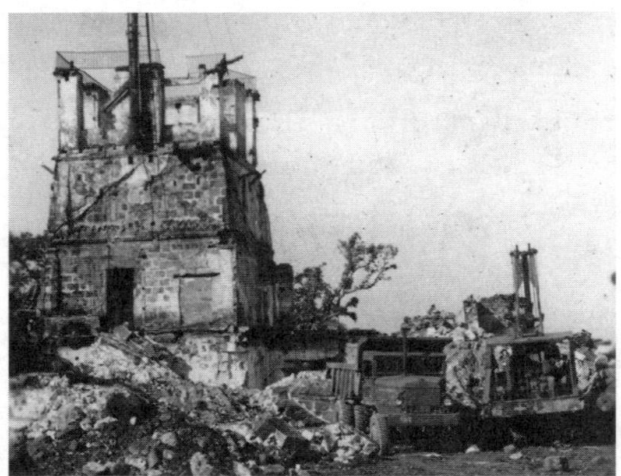

Fort Santiago after the battle.

Fort Santiago, located on the northern side of the ancient walled Spanish city was the headquarters of the Kempetai, the Japanese secret police. During the Battle of Manila, the Intramuros was used as a major fortified defensive position by the Japanese and was subjected to days of aerial and artillery bombardment by the invading U.S. Forces. The Japanese held about 500 prisoners in Fort Santiago during the battle, most of whom died of thirst while locked in cells or were drowned after being herded into an underground bunker that was then flooded when the tide rose. During the Battle of Manila in February 1945, Fort Santiago was captured by the Japanese Imperial Army who used its prisons and dungeons for hundreds of prisoners who were killed near the end of the war (search Manila massacre on the Internet for more information.). The fort sustained heavy damage from American and Filipino mortar shells.

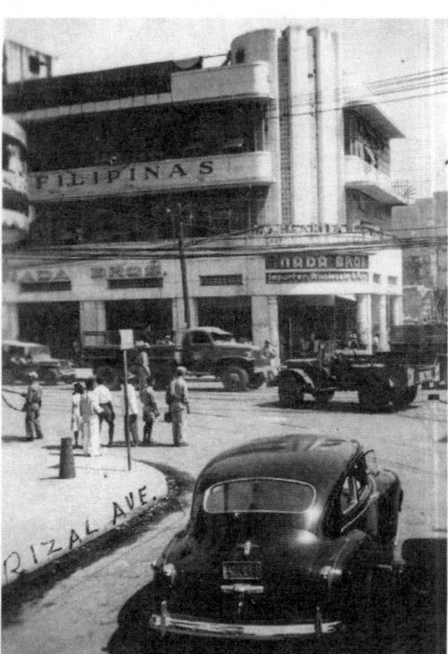

Rizal Avenue in Manila.

The building with the tower is the main building of the Santo Tomas Internment Camp. It is in the center of a 65-acre walled campus. The building to its left is the Dominican Seminary, and it was isolated from the internment camp. This picture was taken from España Boulevard, which runs in front of the campus. The main gate of the campus was breached on the evening of February 3, 1945, by members of the 1st Cavalry Flying Column, an 800-man force that had raced 100 miles to enter Manila and liberate the prisoners before they could be executed by the Japanese. The main building came under artillery fire for three days starting on Feb. 7, killing 22 people and wounding 100.

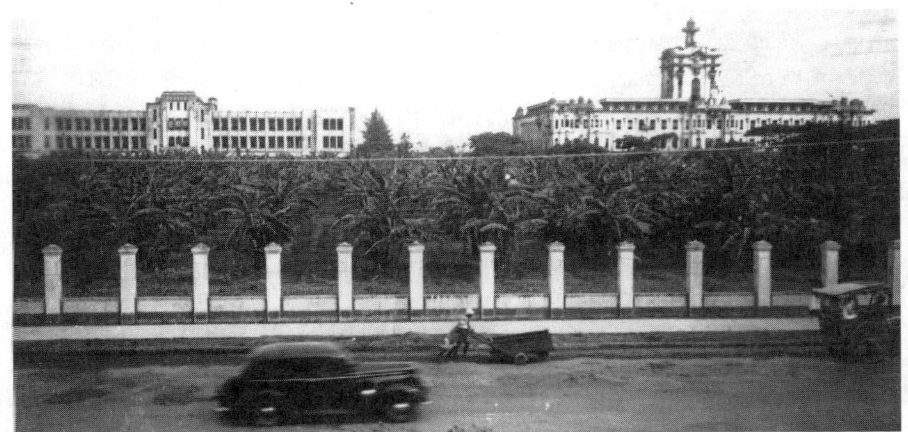

Santo Tomas University on España Boulevard.

The General Post Office is located on the south bank of the Pasig River, and on the maps provided to invading U.S. troops, was marked as the central point in Manila from which distances were measured to other buildings. It was exactly one mile from the corner of the Santo Tomas Internment Camp. The Japanese fortified the building, and in mid-February the U.S. troops fought a tough battle for control of the building.

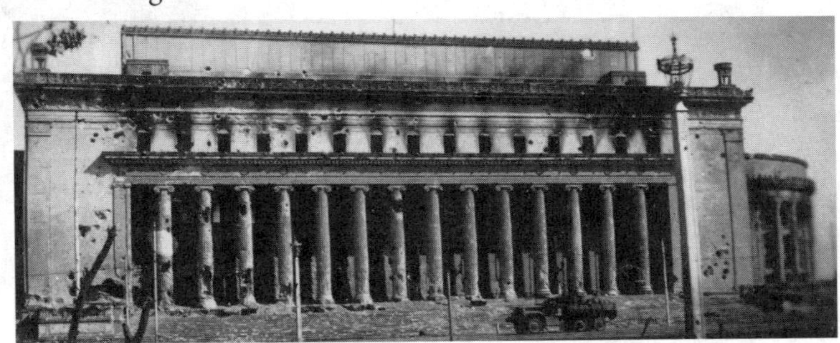

Manila Post Office after the battle.

OFFICIAL MILITARY RECORD ENTRY:

Apr. 9 – "In seven days the men of this battalion have completed their new theater. It is 58 feet wide with a 40-foot stage, 33 feet deep and 33 feet high. All materials were salvaged. All work was done in off-shift hours, with no time being lost from their regular duties. The first production was Irving Berlin's "This is the Army." Mrs. Douglas MacArthur attended the first performance on April 9, 1945. For the first five nights 50,000 people were in attendance. Located to the northwest of the Espana traffic circle in Quezon City, it is easily accessible from all directions. A clear view from any angle or distance is possible, as the stage sits at the base of several tiers of rice paddies. In spite of it being their first venture of this sort, the men of this battalion were paid high tribute when members of the cast pronounced La Loma Play House the finest that had housed them on their entire tour."

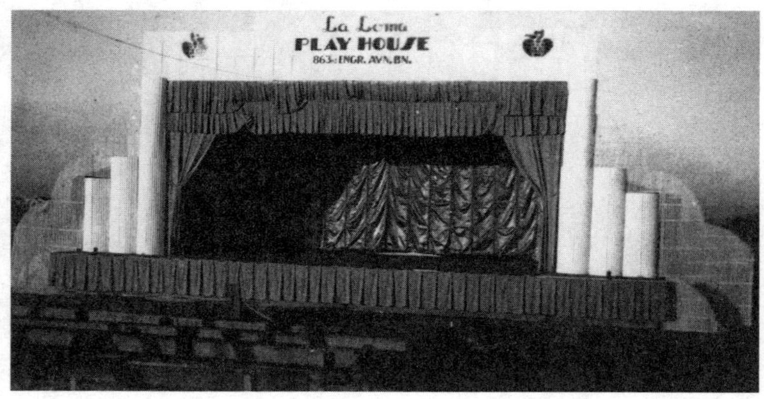

La Loma Play House. Outdoor theater constructed in seven days by the 863rd Engineer Aviation Battalion.

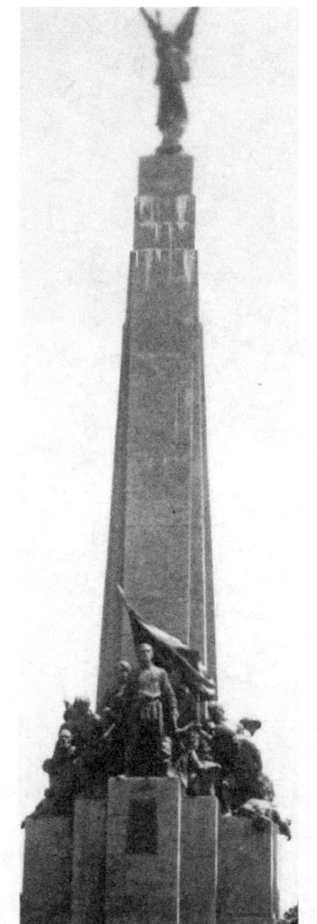

The Bonifacio monument at the entrance of Manila.

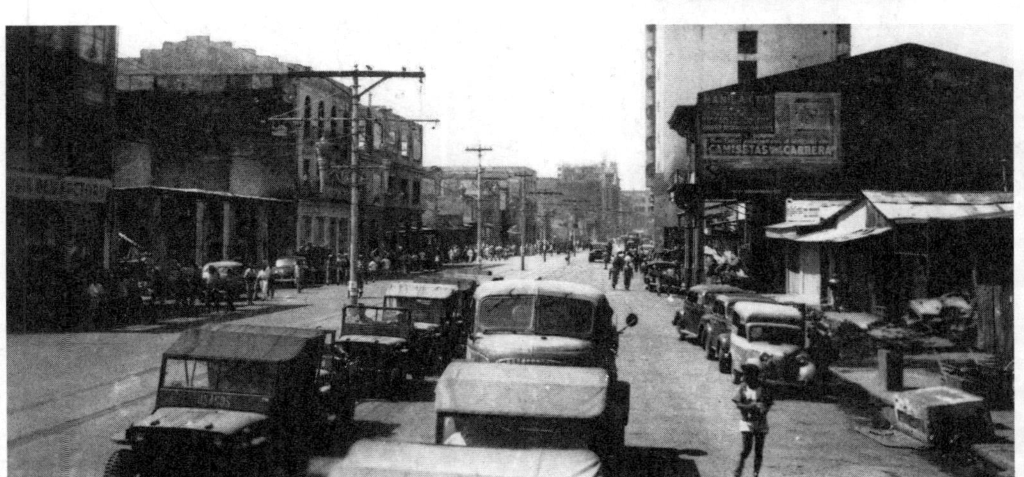

Rizal Avenue, Manila.

MAY 1945

ELSEWHERE IN THE WAR

May 1: Adolph Hitler reported dead, body not found.

May 1: Battle of Tarakan, Borneo.

May 2: Berlin falls to the Russians.

May 4: Admiral Karl Dönitz orders all U-boats to cease operations.

May 6: The last day of fighting for American troops in Europe.

May 7: Germany surrenders unconditionally at Reims, France.

May 8: Allied leaders proclaim Victory over Europe Day (V-E Day).

May 15: Battle of the Malacca Strait, off Sumatra Island.

May 23: Heinrich Himmler, head of the notorious SS, commits suicide.

<> <> <> <> <>

Dump Truck Explodes

While working at the Ft. McKinley hospital site at 11 a.m. on May 14th, a loud explosion rocked the area. T/5 Audry McDonald was delivering a load of lumber in his four-ton dump truck. As he was backing up, the inside left rear tire rolled over a land mine. The rear end of the truck was blown up and the lumber was scattered in all directions. McDonald walked away without a scratch.

Up to this time it had been assumed that the area was free of mines. Captain Betson, the Company A Commander and one Sergeant decided to look over the area for any further mines. Mine detectors were used at first, but this proved impractical due to the large amount of shell fragments and partially buried pieces of metal.

After the first mine was discovered it was found to be an Anti-Vehicular Yardstick Mine rather than personnel. It was three feet long, four inches wide, two inches deep, and had 12 pounds of standard Japanese explosives. Pressure detonators were used, requiring 300 pounds of weight on it before it would be set off. This made the removal of the mines a comparatively easy procedure. The probing method was employed. This proved to be very successful. A total of 35 mines were removed.

Several booby traps intended as anti-personnel mines were encountered in the form of a pipe filled with explosive and pull-type detonator attached to crude trip wires.

Historical Work Report

May 1945

– Cutting steel superstructure at Pier #7 continues. Maintenance and traffic control on Bailey Bridges over Jones Bridge continues 24 hours daily. Hauling scrap iron and tin from Engineer Island to Walled City Dump. Removal of earth, policing, erection of water tank, stripping with burlap, and screening at Rizal Stadium. Work on Marsman Building, consisting of five floors and penthouse, continues. Continuous maintenance of Walled City Dump. Pouring cement and repairing girders at Medical Depot Building.

– Cleared area thought to be a mine field at Ft. McKinley Hospital site; numerous duds were removed, none exploding and no casualties. Hauling gravel, clearing and grading area, and repairing buildings at GHQ Motor Pool. Unloading Liberty ships and stockpiling of building materials and hospital supplies for Fort McKinley Hospital.

– Building "K" completed at GHQ Motor Pool project. Celebrated our 2nd anniversary overseas. All work at Rizal Stadium completed. Pouring of concrete on roof of Medical Depot completed. Stock piling gravel at Mariquina Pit. Completed grease rack at GHQ Motor Pool. Patched Medical Depot roof with three layers of tar and tar paper.

– Additional work of building mess tables and lavatories at Rizal Stadium started. Completed septic tank at Ft. McKinley Hospital. Started work on five-story Samanillo Building. Building road and cutting ditches at GHQ Rest Camp. Erecting prefab for garage at GHQ Motor Pool. Area graded and leveled and drainage system completed at GHQ Rest Camp. Four-ton dump truck went over a mine at Ft. McKinley Hospital site and rear end of truck was blown up. Driver unhurt. A further search of area disclosed 35 more anti-tank mines.

– Started assembling Bailey Bridges for Pier #8. Men taken from GHQ Motor Pool job and Samanillo Building job and put to work on GHQ Rest Camp, which had a higher priority. Completed erection of first Bailey Bridge (70-foot) at Pier #8. Trucking of gravel to GHQ Rest Camp completed. Completed latrines at GHQ Motor Pool. Clearing and grading area for erection of warehouse at Ft. Santiago.

- Dock #8 completed. Roads maintained and ditches completed at GHQ Rest Camp, with wiring of area 50 percent complete. Started maintenance and repair of Santa Cruz and Jones Bridges across Pasig River. Relieved from GHQ Rest Camp job. Two wards completed and work continues at Ft. McKinley Hospital.

- Started work on Philippine Racing Club, taking over job from 841st Engineer Aviation Battalion. Another ward and two utility buildings completed at Ft. McKinley Hospital. Completed roof at Medical Depot Building. Gutter and roofing completed at GHQ Motor Pool. Roughing in of plumbing completed at Marsman Building. Completed pouring concrete floors at GHQ Motor Pool, and also completed patching of tire shop.

- Blasted sealed vault at Ft. Santiago warehouse so that Chemical Warfare could get at dead bodies entombed within and burn them. Started new work at Rizal Stadium.

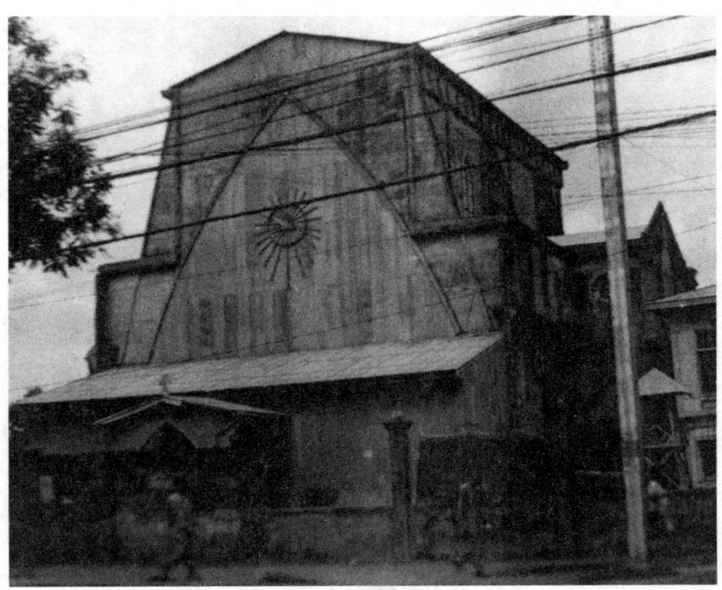

Church in Rizal, Manila.

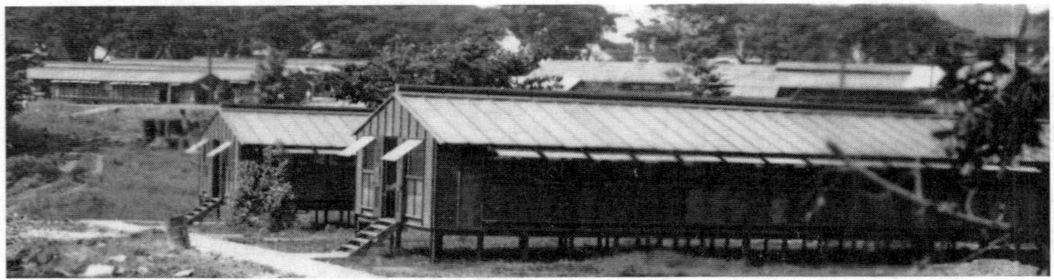

Fort McKinley, 51st General Hospital, seven miles south of Manila. Built by my father's group, the 863rd Engineers. During the World War II era, it was where United States Armed Forces in the Far East (USAFFE) had its headquarters for the Philippine Department and the Philippine Division. This was where specialized artillery training was conducted.

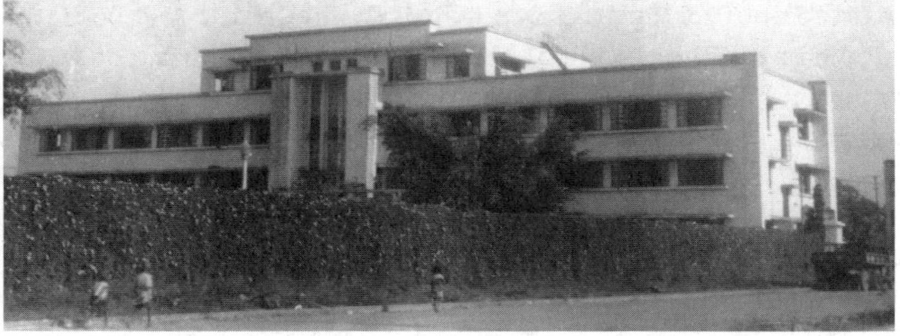

Marsman Building.

The Marsman Building in Manila was Asiatic Fleet headquarters and is located near the waterfront. It was designed in the Moderne style that was to be known later as Art Deco.

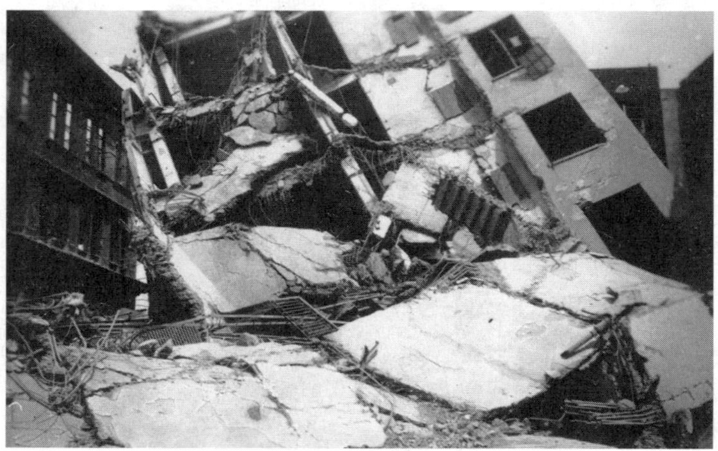

A destroyed building in Manila.

JUNE 1945

ELSEWHERE IN THE WAR

June 10: Operation Oboe Six, North Borneo.

June 16: Battle of North Borneo.

June 18: Nearing end of Okinawa campaign.

June 21: The defeat of the Japanese on Okinawa is now complete.

June 26: The United Nations Charter is signed in San Francisco.

<> <> <> <> <>

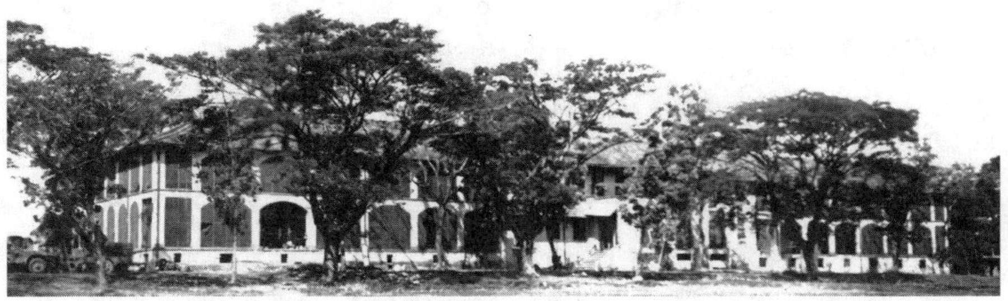

Hall Circle at Fort McKinley.

Historical Work Report
June 1945

– Ft. McKinley Hospital: Rehabilitation of original building, construction of eight new buildings and 42 wards, including water lines, sewage systems, electrical, etc.

– Philippine Racing Club (race horse track): ammunition removed; constructed new buildings, kitchen, mess hall, showers, latrines, installed electric and water, including a 5000-gallon tank. Built a prisoner of war compound; mess hall, showers, latrines, for Women's Army Corps (WACs); part of building renovated to be used as an orderly room, PX, dispensary, and supply room.

– Marsman Building: This building was Pacific Fleet headquarters, and received a direct hit from a bomb dropped by a Jap plane at the time of the initial invasion. The entire building had to be renovated.

– Fort Santiago had to be completely renovated and new buildings added.

– Rizal Sports Stadium had an excess amount of damage and had to be completely renovated inside and out.

– Certain bridges require continuous maintenance, using three shifts daily.

– Walled City Dump consists of continuous maintenance of dump control.

– Mariquina Pit consists of continuous stockpiling of gravel on adjacent high ground to permit loading of trucks during rainy season. 50,000 square yards have been stockpiled to date.

– By far, the most beneficial event with relation to the entertainment and morale of the personnel of this battalion was the presentation of the show "Oklahoma." Total attendance figures for the 15-day run are an estimated 127,000. The May 11 issue of Yank magazine clearly portrayed the trials, tribulations and accomplishments of the 863rd Engineer

Aviation Battalion in an article describing their work in the rehabilitation of Pier #7. While there has been frequent notice stressing the value of the repairs to Manila pier and dock installations, as seen through the eyes of the press, this is the first known instance of recognition being shown by direct identification of this unit. This has had a remarkable effect on morale.

Ipo Dam and hydroelectric plant in Norzagaray, Philippines, about 49 km from Manila. At top of tower it reads M.W.D. – 1938, meaning built by the Manila Water District that year. By mid-April 1945 an acute water shortage had developed within Manila. Sewage disposal throughout the city was becoming increasingly difficult because water pressure was insufficient to carry off refuse. Flush toilets were clogged. There was very real danger that severe epidemics might break out within the city at any moment, but Ipo Dam was still in Japanese hands. On April 22, General MacArthur ordered that Ipo Dam must be captured and would solve Manila's water supply problems. On May 17, Ipo Dam was captured intact. The Japanese had prepared demolitions at both the dam and powerhouse but had failed to set them off. Read the story at: www.ibiblio.org/hyperwar/USA/USA-P-Triumph/USA-P-Triumph-22.html

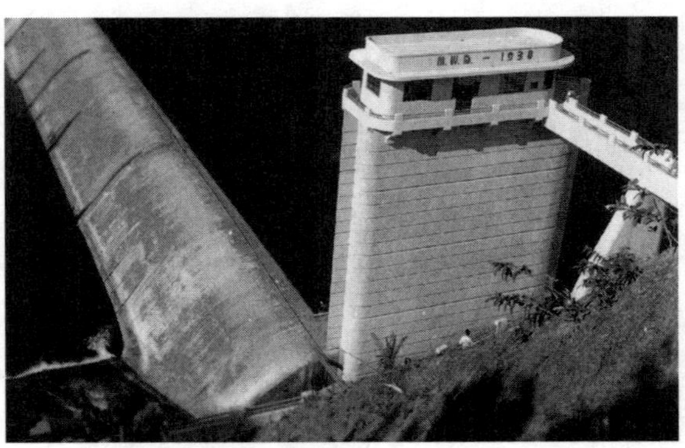

Ipo Dam (photo by Roxas).

JULY 1945

ELSEWHERE IN THE WAR

July 1: Battle of Balikpapan, Borneo.

July 4: General MacArthur announces that the Philippines have been liberated.

July 16: U.S. conducts the Trinity test at Alamogordo, New Mexico, the first test of a nuclear weapon.

July 17: The Potsdam (Germany) Conference begins.

July 30: The USS Indianapolis sunk by Japanese submarine after having delivered atomic bomb material to Tinian.

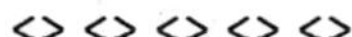

Historical Work Report

July 1945

- The food and supply situation is good. Morale is good, considering the length of time this unit has served overseas. A football team is being formed. Discipline is excellent.

- The adequate supervision of the 800-odd Filipinos has presented a problem. This has been solved by pressing into use as foremen, increasing numbers of qualified personnel familiar with the various projects. Considerable time is expended in gathering the widespread groups of civilian employees and transporting them to assigned jobs

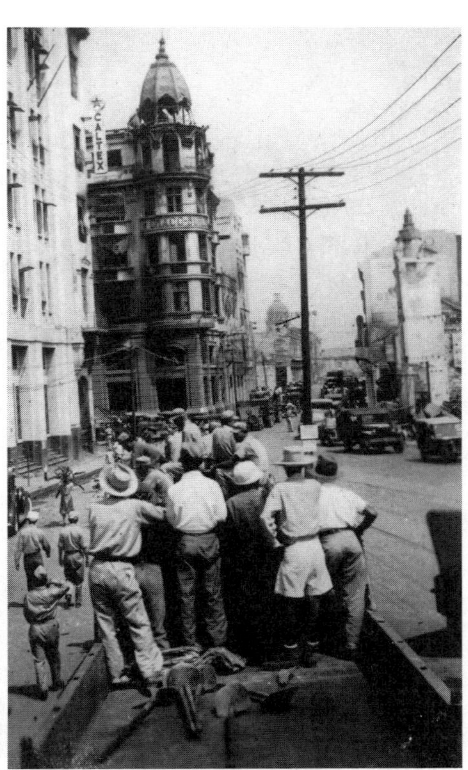

Escolta Street. Every morning local laborers had to be transported by truck to help the efforts to pick up rubble and repair the city.

- Accomplishments on the Fort McKinley project consist of the completion of: all clearing and grading, all roads in the area, four Medical and Administrative buildings, 40 wards, 20 latrines and showers, six buildings constructed as quarters complete with latrines and showers, Nurses' lounge completed, Patient's Mess with 20-foot x 90-foot general building, Pharmacy building, refrigeration building. 4600 feet of steel pipe laid at Ft. McKinley pipeline project.

- Adobe brick prisoner of war compound constructed at Philippine Racing Club. Rehabilitation of several buildings nearing completion and six miles of barbed wire fence placed around enclosure.

- There have been no combat operations or service functions performed in areas subject to enemy fire during the month.

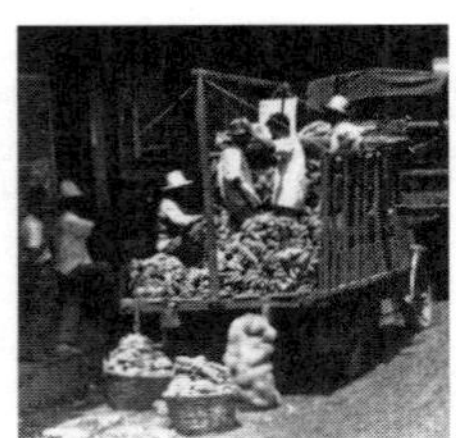

Selling bananas in Chinatown, Manila.

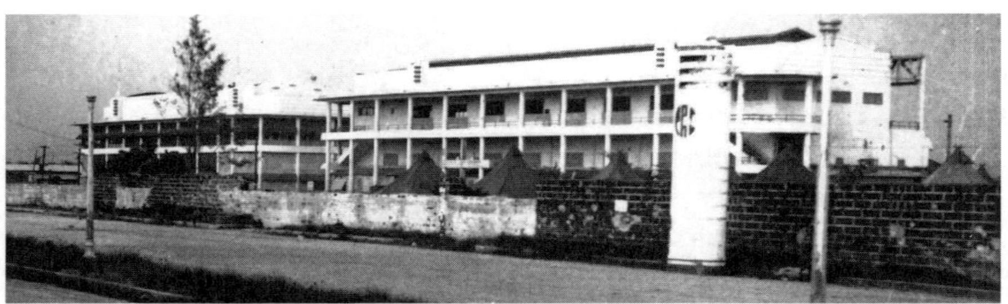

Philippines Racing Club, another horse racetrack. A prisoner of war compound was constructed here.

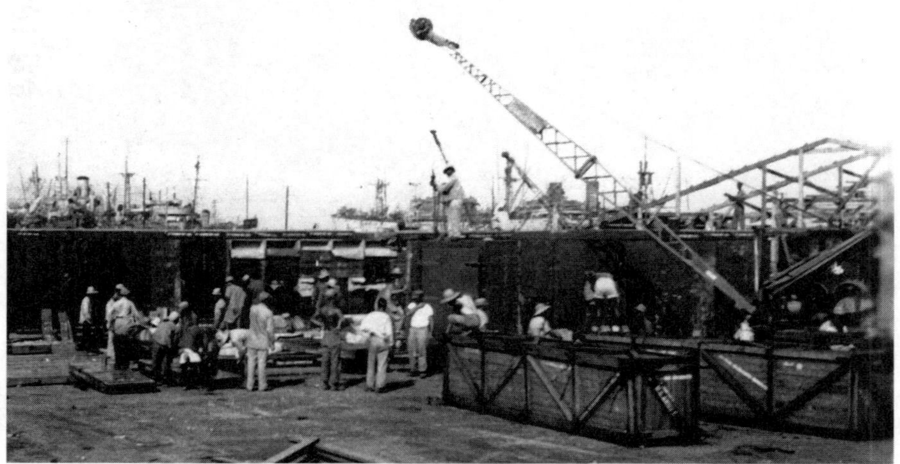

Installing refrigeration units. Manila.

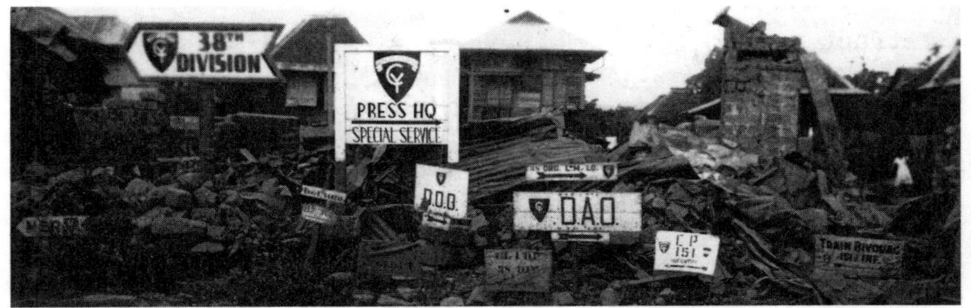

Signs pointing the way to various military services.

Old Bilibid was a prison built by the Spaniards in the early 18th Century and was condemned by the U.S. Bureau of Prisons. After New Bilibid was built at Muntinglupa in the late 1930s, the demolition of Old Bilibid was started in 1941. When the Japanese invaded, they took it over and used it as a prisoner of war camp and a way station for prisoners of war being shipped to slave labor camps. It was discovered by a patrol from the 37th Infantry as it entered North Manila on the evening of Feb. 5, and when liberated, they discovered 800 military and 500 American and Allied Alien civilian prisoners, all in terrible shape. The prison had to be evacuated the next day as Japanese set fire to the city, and the prison was threatened by a nearby ammunition dump and fuel depot. The prison was designed in the shape of a wagon wheel with the buildings going out from the central hub as spokes.

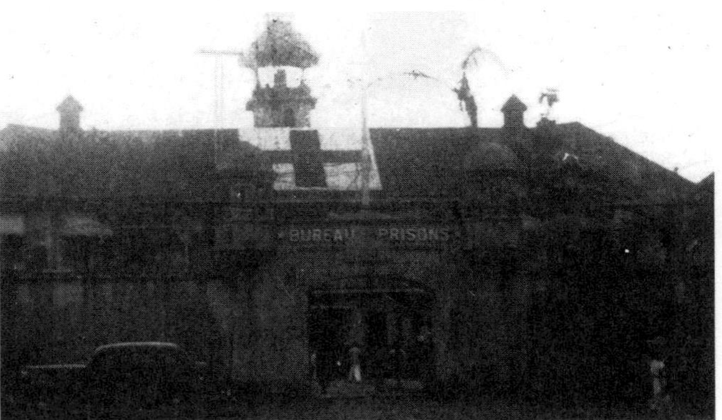

Exterior of Bilibid Prison, Ascarraga Street, Manila.

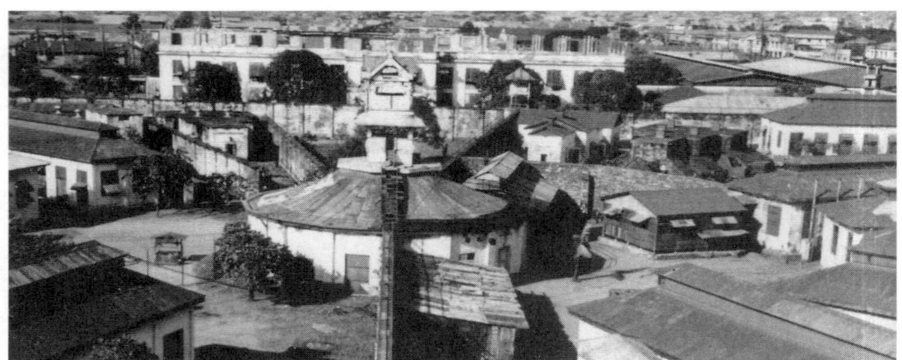

Behind the walls of Bilibid Prison.

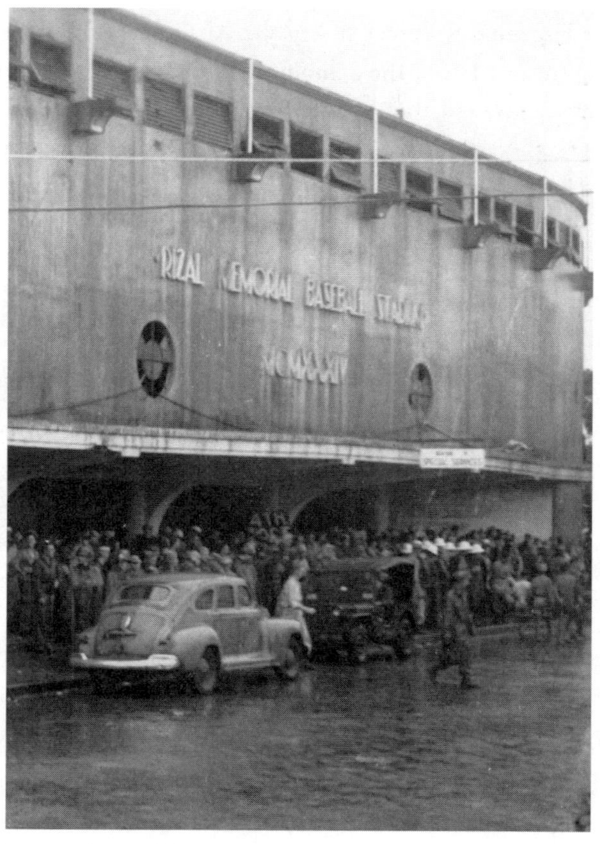

The Rizal Memorial Baseball Stadium was built in 1934. Photo taken on July 4, 1945.

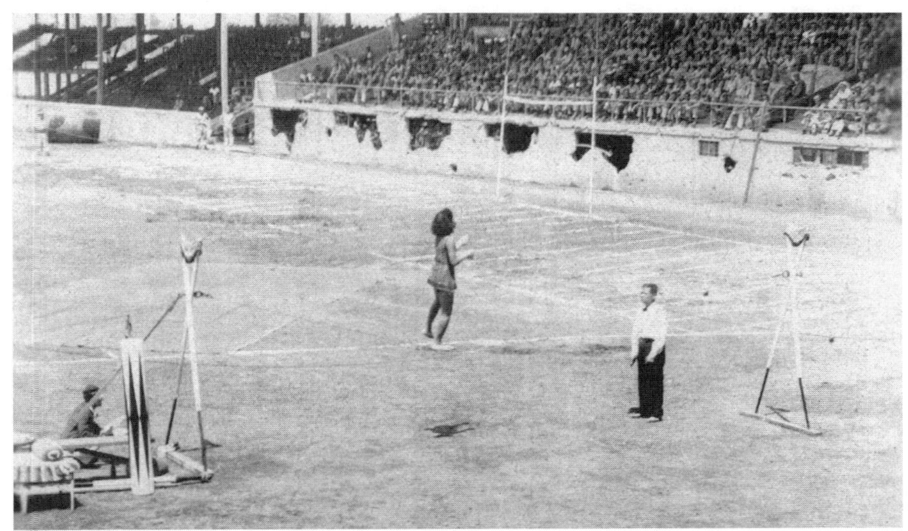

A woman walking on a tightrope in Rizal Stadium. A spotter is standing nearby. Major reconstruction work was done here due to battle damage.

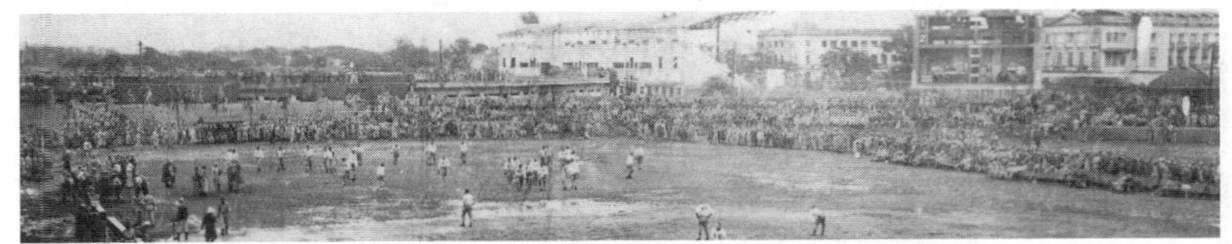

Dad wrote on the back of the picture: "The Manila Bowl, Army vs. Navy, score 0-0. De La Salle College in back."

AUGUST 1945

ELSEWHERE IN THE WAR

Aug. 6: B-29 Superfortress Enola Gay drops the first atomic bomb, "Little Boy," on Hiroshima.

Aug. 9: B-29 Superfortress Bockscar drops the second atomic bomb, "Fat Man," on Nagasaki.

Aug. 9: Soviet Invasion of Manchuria.

Aug. 14: Japan surrenders unconditionally; WWII is over.

Aug. 15: Worldwide celebration of Victory over Japan (VJ) Day.

<> <> <> <> <>

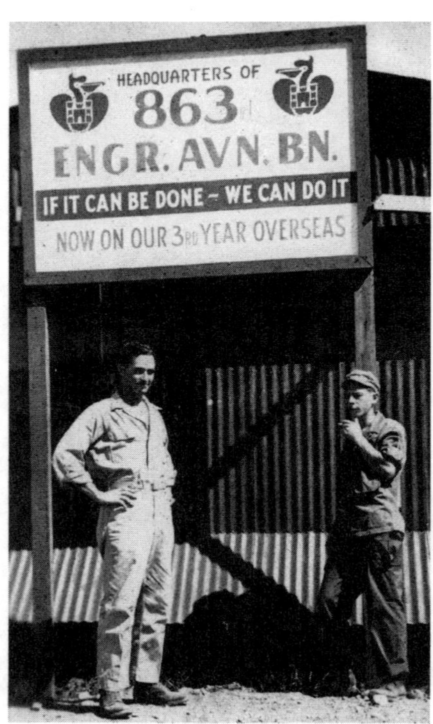

Dad and his good friend Mally Bass from Texas standing in front of their headquarters building in Manila.

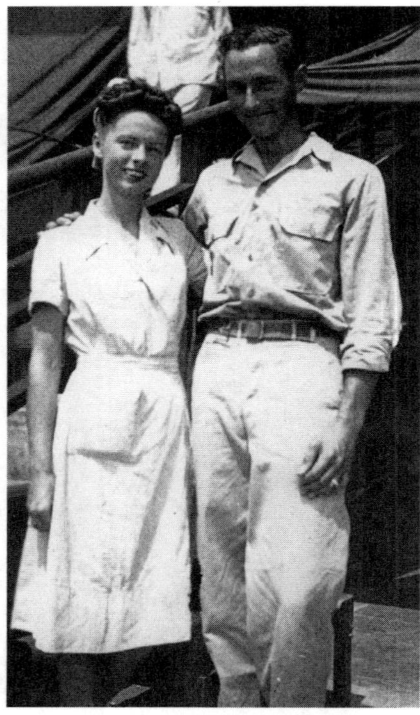

My father with Rowena, a nurse, at the Jockey Club Racetrack, now the 49th General Hospital.

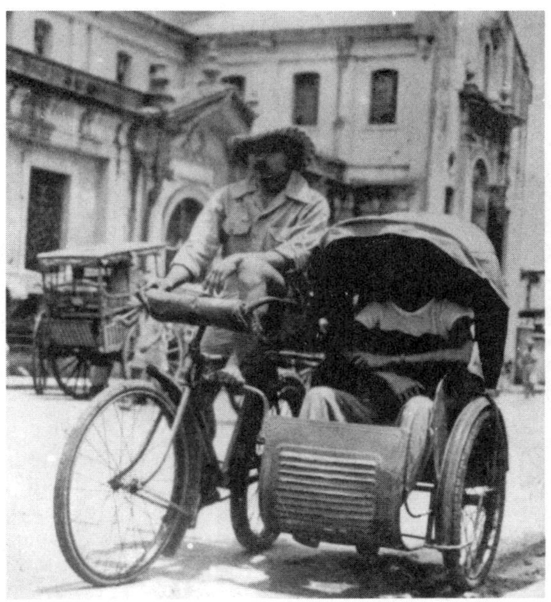

Tricycle, or pedi cab, in the Philippines.

After working non-stop for months cleaning up debris and rebuilding Manila, permission was given to start their own football team for recreation. The sign below reads,

"863 ENGR AVN BN –
If it can be done, we can do it."
Manila, 1945.

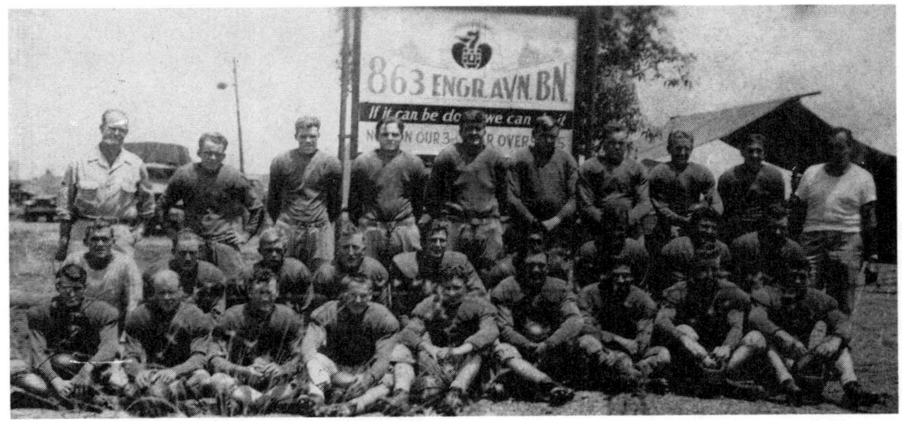

Our football team.

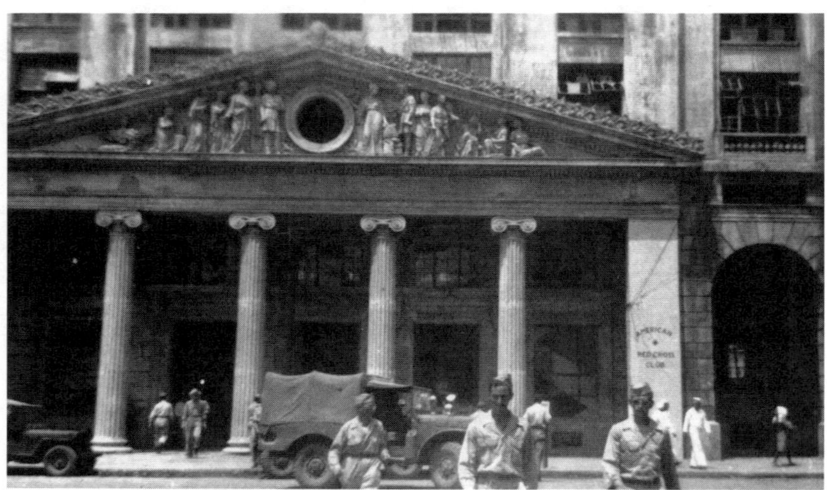

In front of Monte de Piedad Building, used as the American Red Cross Club.

In the Philippine Islands, enemy pockets of resistance were cleared out and by August 15, 1945, when hostilities officially ended, the U.S. forces had reported 40,565 casualties including 7,933 killed. The Japanese lost over 192,000 killed and approximately 9,700 captured. Of the more than 350,000 enemy troops in the entire Philippine Archipelago only an estimated 50,000 were left when Japan capitulated.

This information was taken from *U.S. Army in World War II, Pictorial Record – The War Against Japan,* pages 379 and 385.

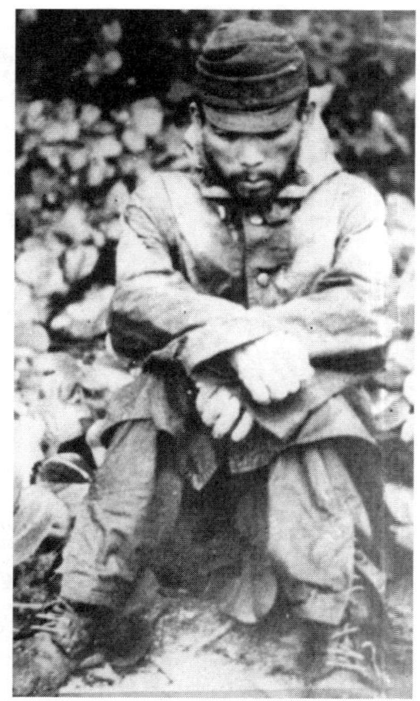

Captured Japanese soldier.

SEPTEMBER 1945

ELSEWHERE IN THE WAR

Sept. 2: The Japanese Instrument of Surrender signed aboard the USS Missouri in Tokyo Bay. This day is officially recognized in the U.S. as Victory over Japan Day (V-J Day).

Sept. 2: The commander of the Imperial Japanese Army, General Tomoyuki Yamashita, surrenders to Philippine and American troops at Kiangan, Ifugao, in Northern Philippines.

Sept. 5: Singapore is officially liberated by British and Indian troops.

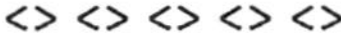

Historical Work Report
September 1945

- The transfer this month of 212 enlisted men and four officers from this organization as replacements for other units has directly affected the accomplishments of this unit for the month of September.

- Lt. Colonel John H. Hamilton is now Battalion Commander.

- The large number of projects, the reduced size of the battalion, and a critical shortage of transportation posed a difficult problem. The 1275th Engineer Combat Battalion, with almost no equipment, was assigned to this unit for operational control. By furnishing equipment and two 4-ton dump trucks to the 1275th, progress was maintained on projects that would otherwise have come to a standstill.

- At the Insular Life Building vault, the vault doors and six of the eight walls were constructed. The 30 refrigerators were completed but the access road was not finished due to lack of dump trucks. All roads assigned this unit were maintained and traffic was kept flowing without interruption.

- Company A of this battalion received a letter of commendation for the superior work accomplished on the 51st General Hospital, at Fort William McKinley by Colonel E.L. Steger, Commanding officer. Captain Jack C. Betson, Commanding Officer of Company A, has been recommended by Colonel E.L. Steger for Bronze Star Medal for this superior accomplishment.

- There have been no combat operations or service functions performed in areas subject to enemy fire during the month.

OCTOBER 1945

The war has been over for a month. This was a time of rest, relaxation, and sightseeing.

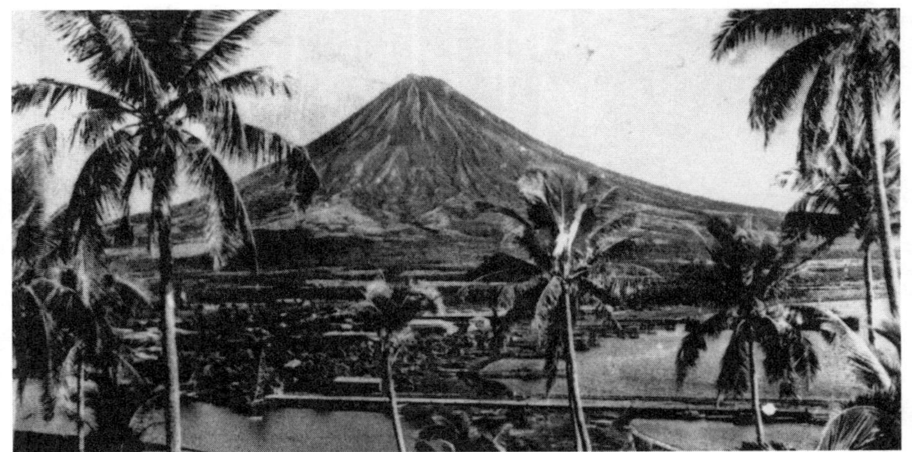

The Mayon volcano, an active volcano in the Philippines.

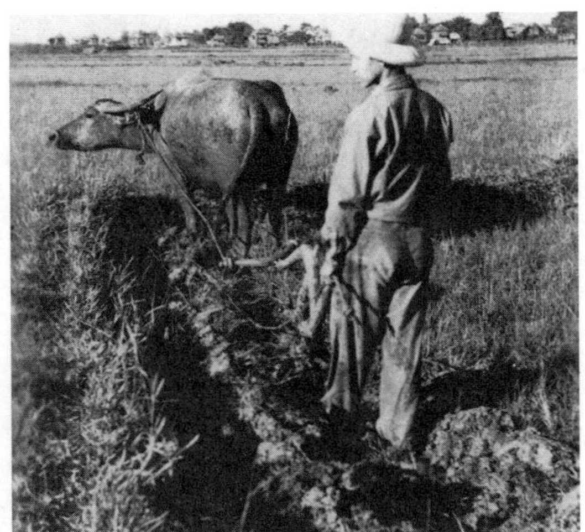

Farmer and carabao.

Since my dad was a farmer, he wanted to experience how rice farming was done in Southeast Asia. As he traveled through the area, he took pictures of the various farming operations and procedures. Something he had never seen before were people planting rice to the rhythm of a guitar. Back home on the farm a tractor was used, or a farmer would use a mule to pull a plow. But here, farmers used carabao instead of a mule. The carabao is a subspecies of the domesticated water buffalo. They are associated with farmers, being the farm animal of choice for pulling both a plow and the cart used to haul produce to the market. This was a different farming practice that he captured in photos.

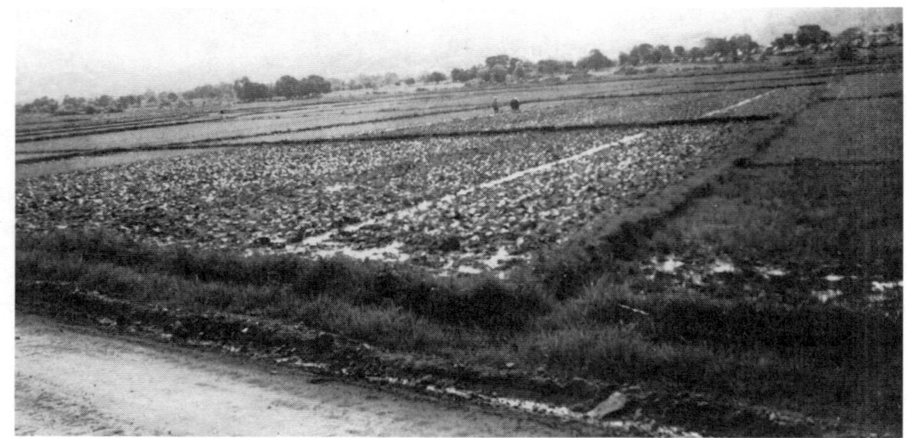

Rice fields near Marikino.

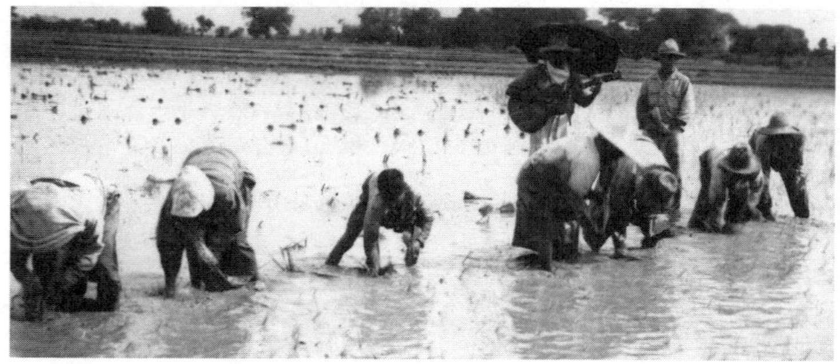

Planting rice near San Mateo, Rizal. Notice the guitar player providing the rhythm for planting the rice.

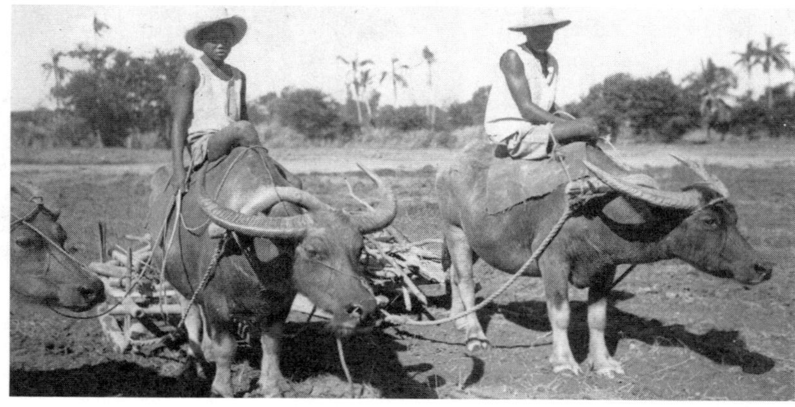

Caraboa and farmers working.

Souvenirs from the Philippines

Japanese currency used in the Philippines.
The actual size is a 4 3/16 inches long by 2 inches wide.

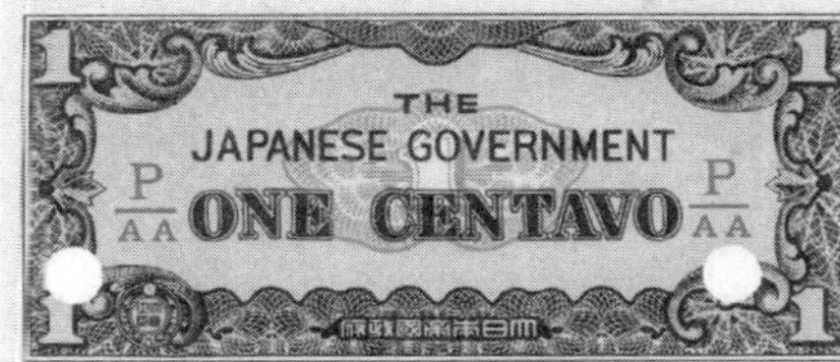

front

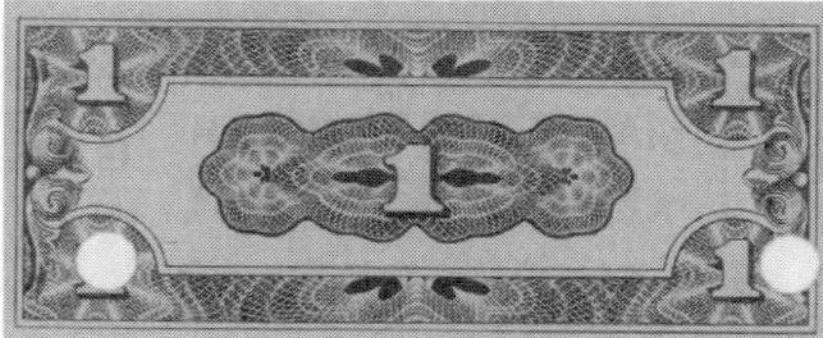

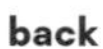

back

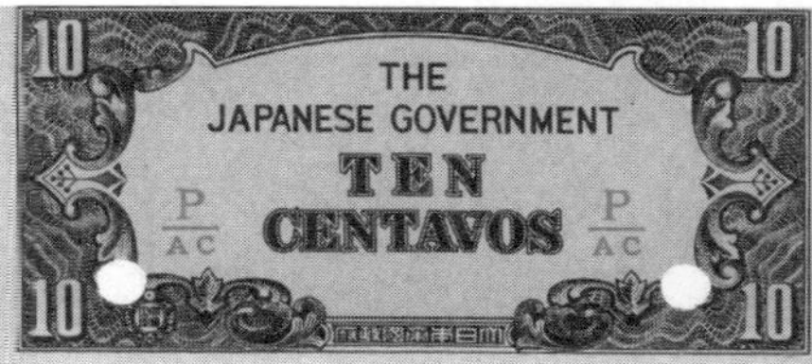

front

back

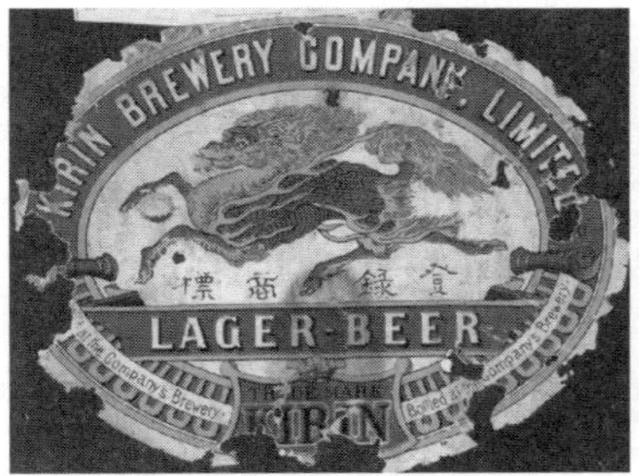

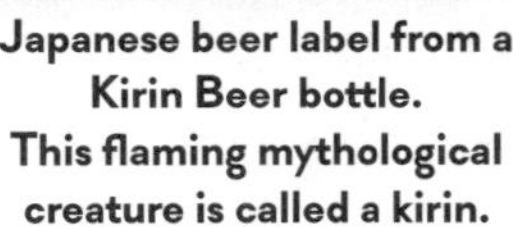

Japanese beer label from a Kirin Beer bottle. This flaming mythological creature is called a kirin.

Japanese matchbox, opened up.

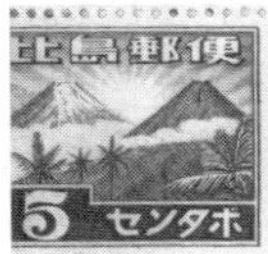

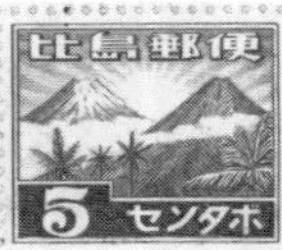

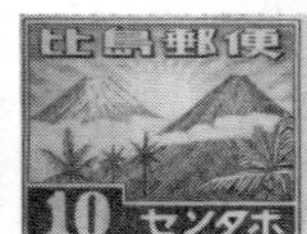

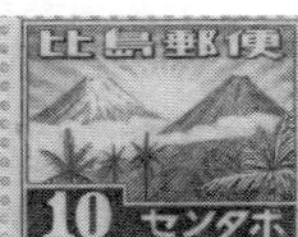

Japanese stamps.

CHAPTER 9

Returning Home

NOVEMBER 1945

OFFICIAL MILITARY RECORD ENTRY:

"On 1 November 1945 six Officers and 354 enlisted men of this organization were transferred to the 1879th Engineer Aviation Battalion for return to the United States."

Dad and his friends were notified by officers on Nov. 1, 1945, that they were going home. You can just imagine the rush of emotions upon hearing this good news! Undoubtedly there was a whole lot of whooping and hollering going on.

Dad could finally relax and breathe a big sigh of relief. I imagine he was thinking: "The war is finally over. I made it out alive. God answered our prayers. Not only did I not die, I didn't even get hurt. God protected me. My mother and my brothers, Yoy, Nig, and Vernon, and their families will be rejoicing that I'm coming home safe, and sound. Now I can get back to my life on the farm. I'm sure Mom will have a coming home celebration and gather all of the aunts, uncles, and cousins to celebrate with a big barbecue. When I get home, I'm going to buy a new tractor with my earnings from the Army."

When he left home for boot camp 35 months earlier he was skin and bones. However, three years of hard labor will put some muscle on you. Plus, constantly being in the South Pacific sun gave him a dark tan. I'm sure his brothers ragged on him a bit for that.

Yet, the joy of returning home to loved ones will always be tempered with the reality of those who were left behind. Nobody should forget that.

Some of my father's friends were wounded and some gave their lives for their country. McGee and Cothan received the Purple Heart medal for shrapnel injuries. Wynne died because a bomb exploded while the crew was unloading ammunition. World War II was traumatic and stressful. The war was hell. Those who served in the war cannot forget that.

Dad was gone 35 months without a furlough, from Jan. 1943 until he got home at the beginning of Dec. 1945. In the years to come, he tried hard to put the bad memories in the back of his mind. He would focus on work and on his family and friends.

There were times when he would open up and let us into his journey across the Pacific. His pictures were the easiest way in. When my father revealed details about the images he took you could see the spark in his eyes – like the flash of a camera. I loved to see it. I loved him. What was there not to love? He helped saved the world after all.

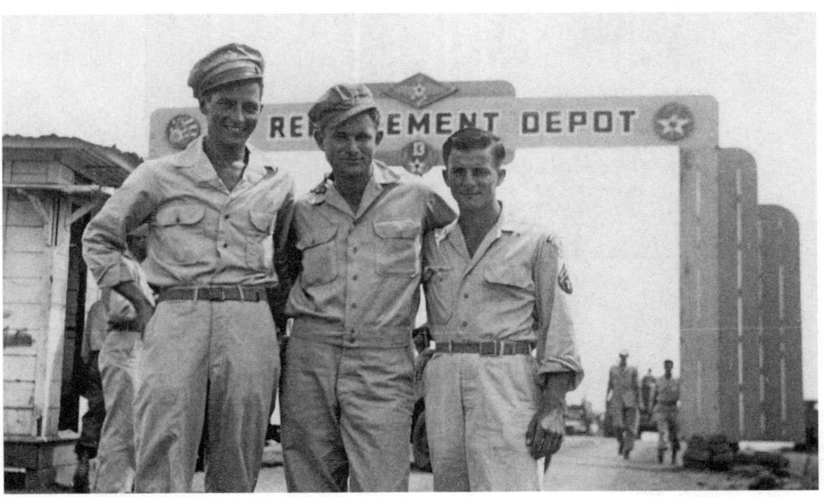

My dad and two friends are at the Replacement Depot being processed to go back home.

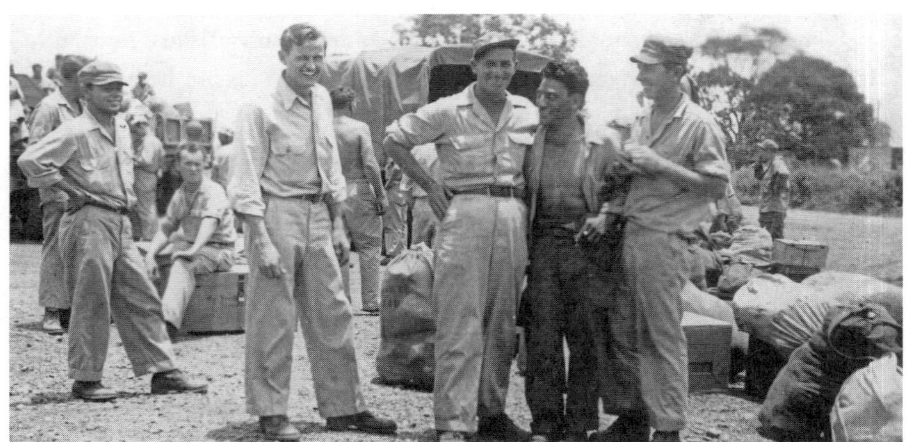

The war is over. Big smiles on the faces of these men who are ready to go home.

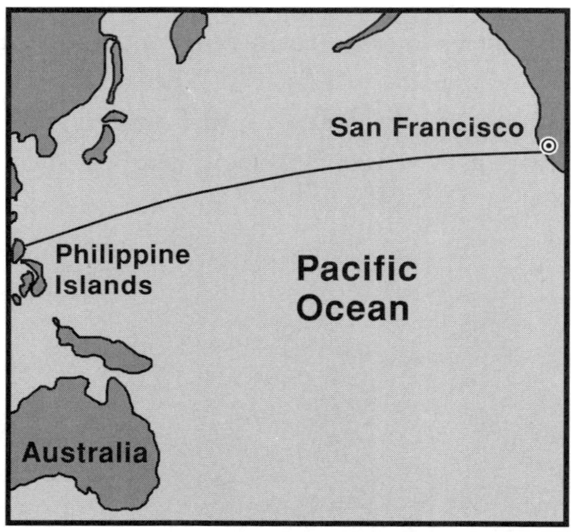

From the Philippine Islands to San Francisco, California.

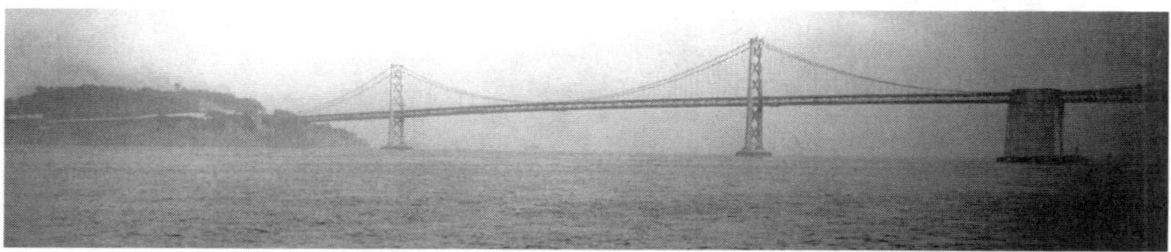

Dad is arriving at the Golden Gate Bridge in San Francisco, California.

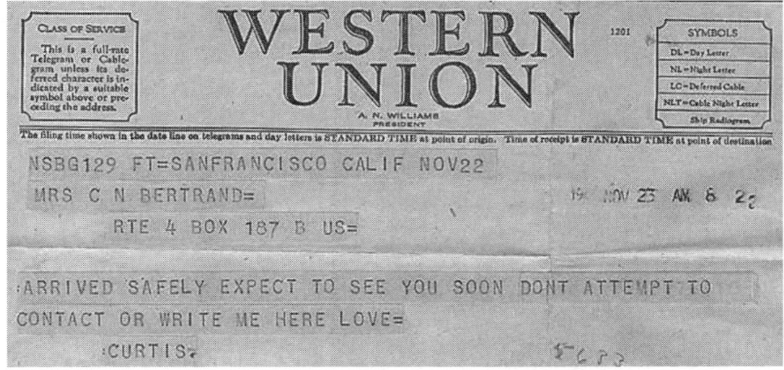

CLASS OF SERVICE

This is a full-rate Telegram or Cablegram unless its deferred character is indicated by a suitable symbol above or preceding the address.

WESTERN UNION

A. N. WILLIAMS
PRESIDENT

1201

SYMBOLS
DL=Day Letter
NL=Night Letter
LC=Deferred Cable
NLT=Cable Night Letter
Ship Radiogram

The filing time shown in the date line on telegrams and day letters is STANDARD TIME at point of origin. Time of receipt is STANDARD TIME at point of destination

NSBG129 FT=SANFRANCISCO CALIF NOV22
MRS C N BERTRAND= 19 NOV 23 AM 8 2
RTE 4 BOX 187 B US=

ARRIVED SAFELY EXPECT TO SEE YOU SOON DONT ATTEMPT TO
CONTACT OR WRITE ME HERE LOVE=
CURTIS.

Telegram my dad sent to his mother upon arrival in San Francisco, Nov 22, 1945.

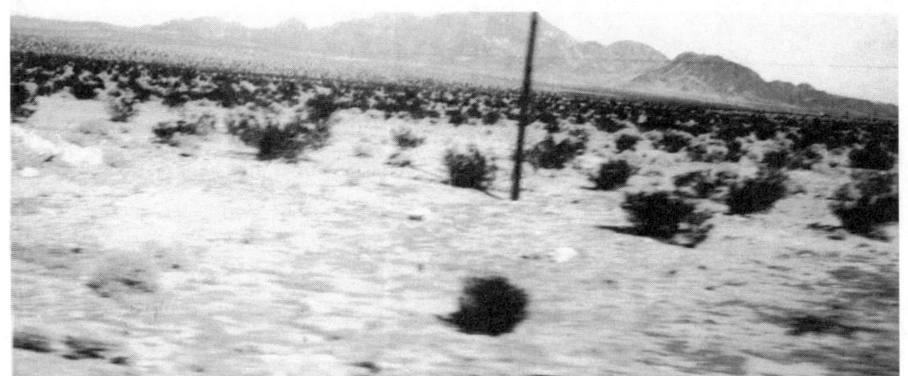

Passing through the Arizona desert on the train ride home, Dec 2, 1945.

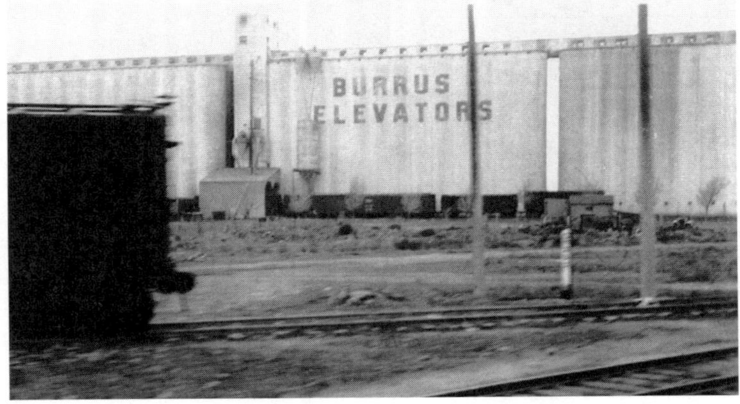

Photo taken on the train while passing through Lubbock, Texas, on his way back home. The skyline of the Burrus Grain Elevators in the background.

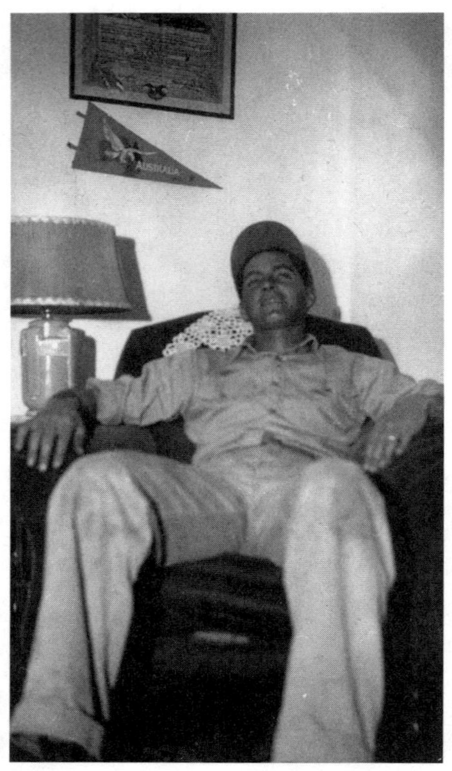

In the words of my father, "Ahh, it's good to be home." Mallet, LA, December 1945.

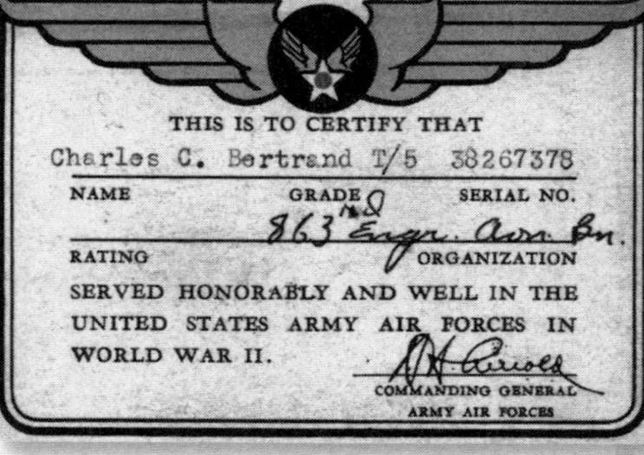

THIS IS TO CERTIFY THAT

Charles C. Bertrand T/5 38267378

NAME GRADE SERIAL NO.

863rd Engr. Avn. Bn.

RATING ORGANIZATION

SERVED HONORABLY AND WELL IN THE UNITED STATES ARMY AIR FORCES IN WORLD WAR II.

H.H. Arnold

COMMANDING GENERAL
ARMY AIR FORCES

Dad's honorable discharge card.

THIS CARD WILL SERVE TO INTRODUCE YOU WHEN YOU VISIT AIR FORCE STATIONS

MAR 10 1946

DATE ISSUED

ISSUING OFFICER

GPO O—667957

CHAPTER 10

Postwar Life

After he returned home, my dad spent a lot of time with his mom catching up on things that happened in his absence. One day, soon after he returned, my dad and his cousins went to a local photography studio and had a group picture taken.

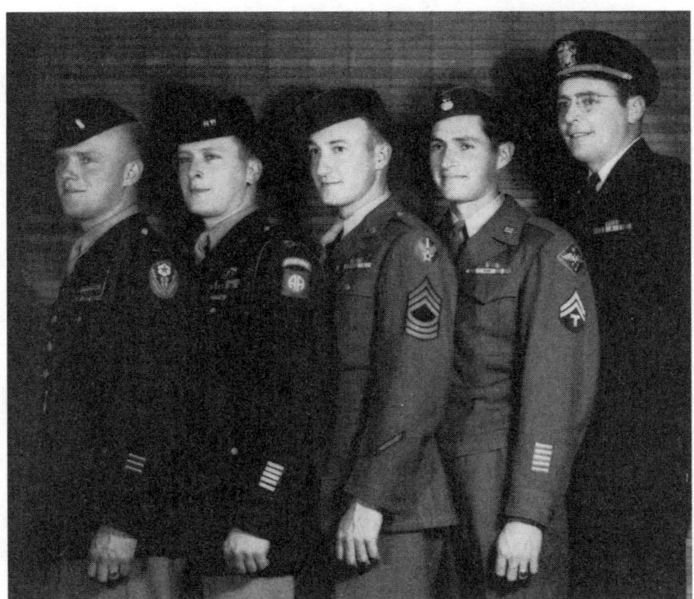

From left to right are five war hero cousins: Jevese (J.M.) Lafleur, Wilfred Joubert, J.C. Lafleur, Curtis Bertrand, and Floyd Andrepont.

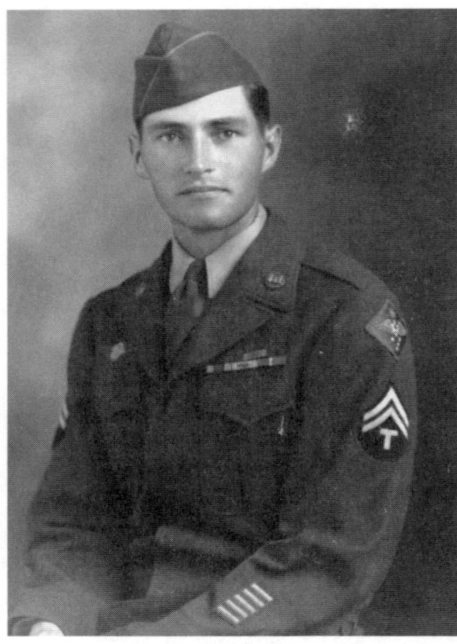

Dad attained the rank of Technician Fifth Grade (T/5). He is wearing the patch of the Far East Air Force (FEAF) on his left shoulder, his ribbons he earned above his left pocket, and the ruptured duck emblem above his right breast pocket.

How My Parents Met

Shortly after returning home from the war, my father's family put on a homecoming celebration complete with barbecue to welcome him back. They invited family and friends to join in the festivities, including a new neighbor who had just moved into the area a few farms over.

This pretty young lady was introduced to my father, a charismatic world traveler. She was starstruck at how tall, dark, and handsome he was (after all, the south Pacific sun had given him a dark tan). He thought she was beautiful, and they started seeing each other on a regular basis. They were married on June 20, 1948. The rest is nothing more than happily ever after.

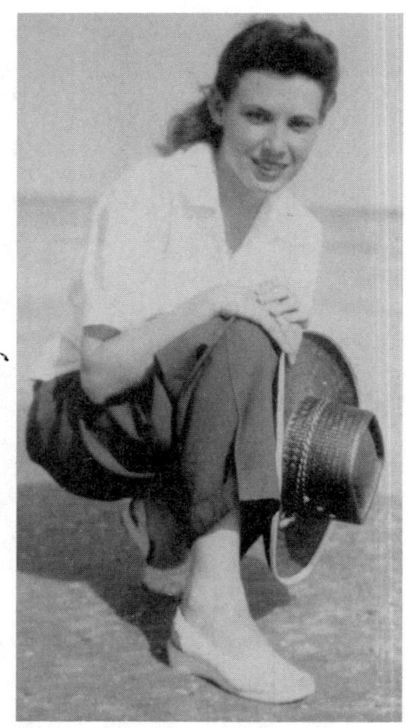

Dad took this picture of my mother, Edmay Stelly Bertrand, at the beach in Cameron, Louisiana, 1948.

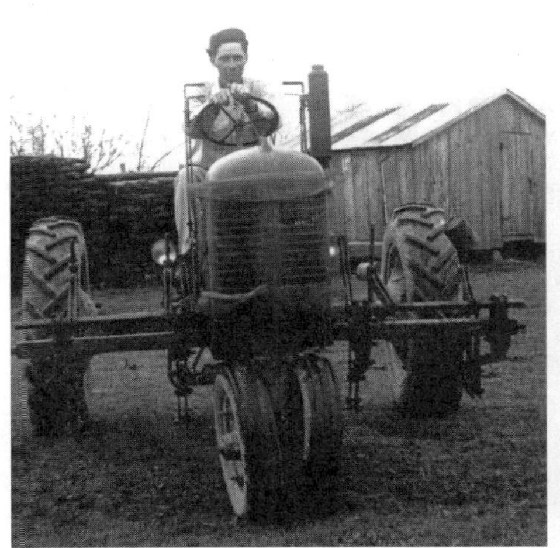

Dad is back home at work on his tractor.

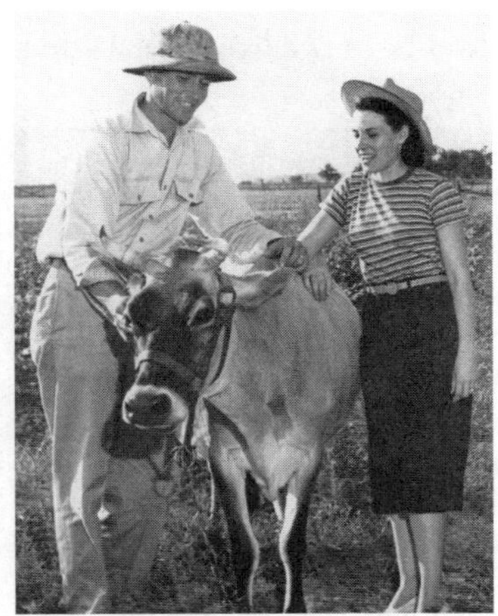

Dad and Mom with one of their cows. (Reprinted with permission from the Daily World newspaper.)

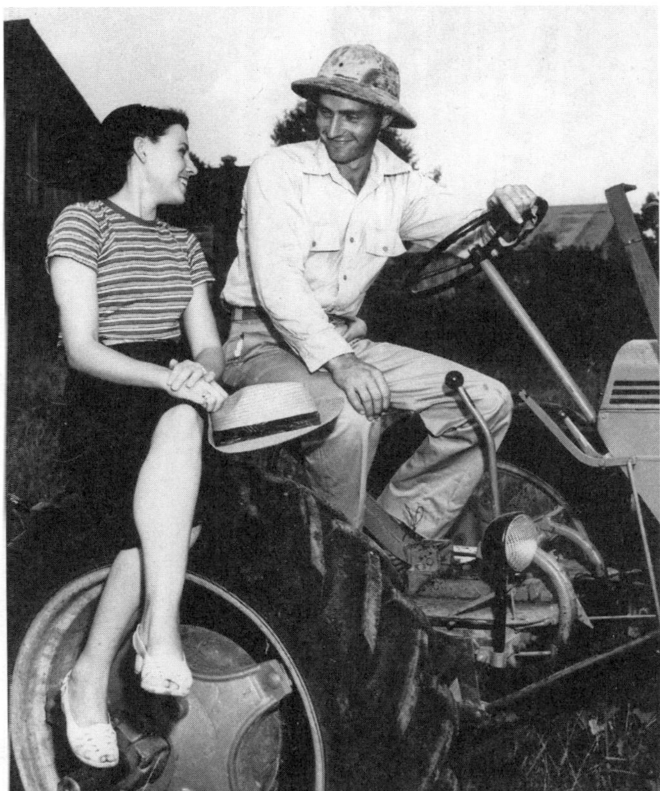

Mom and Dad on his new tractor. (Reprinted with permission from the Daily World newspaper.)

I was born and lived in the same home as my dad until I was three years old.

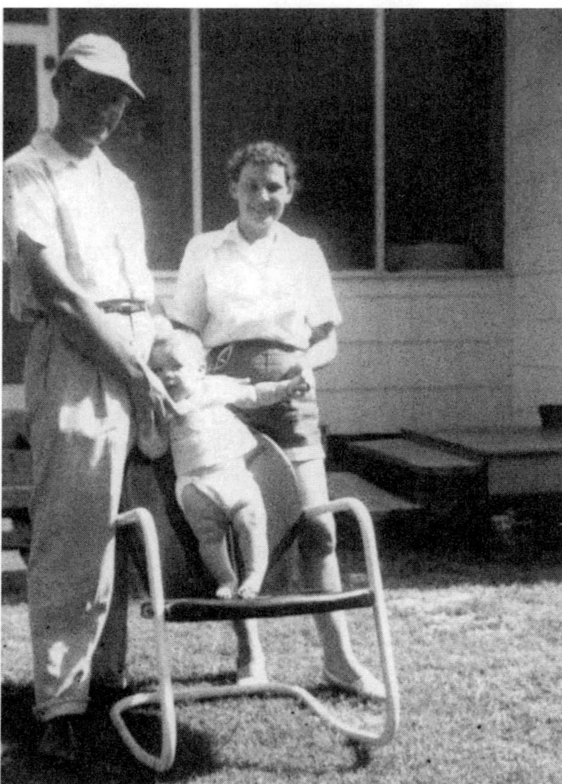

Dad, Mom, and me.

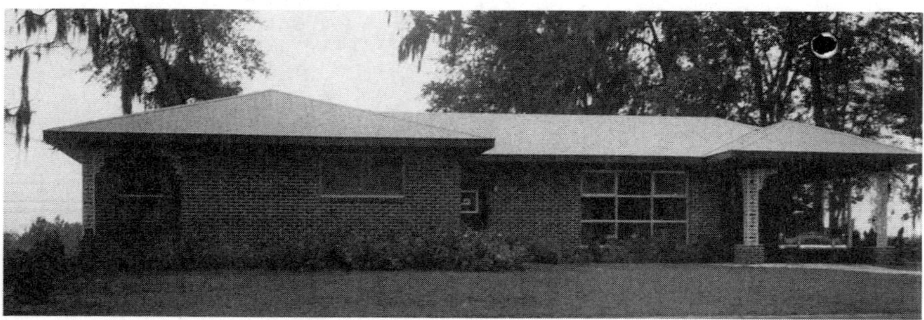

In 1955 we moved from the country to Opelousas where Dad had this house built. A 1952 Chevy Fleetline is under the carport.

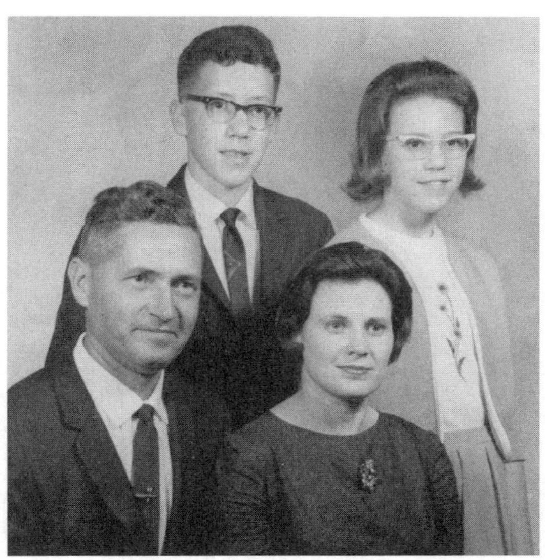

Family photo with my sister Karen and me, circa 1963.

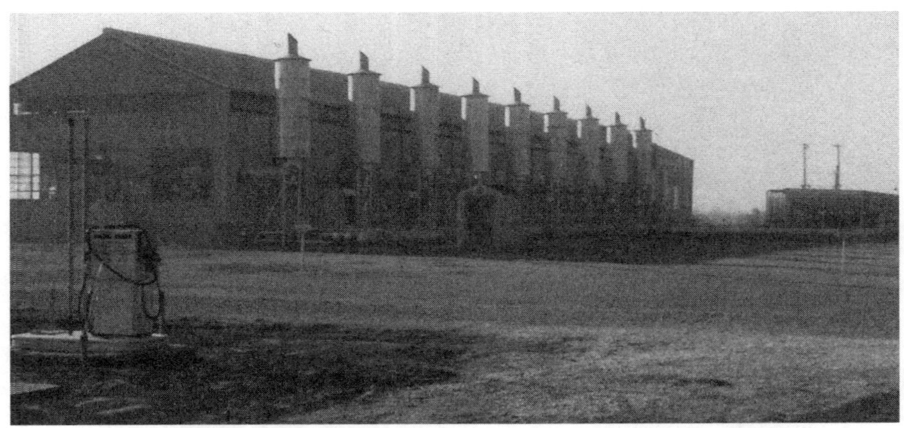

The Texas Eastern natural gas booster station near Opelousas. This is where Dad worked until he retired.

My father also worked on his farm, raised cattle, and planted and harvested crops on a share basis with other local farmers. After he retired, he took art classes and became a talented oil painter.

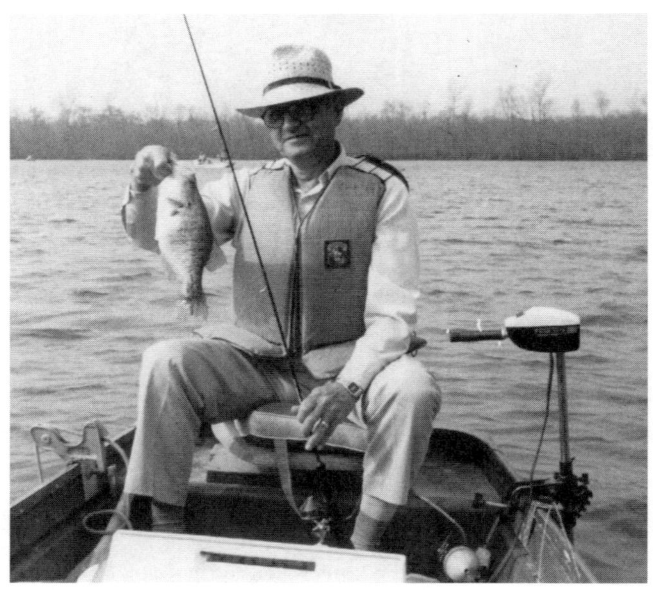

Dad just caught what is called a crappie or white perch, known in Cajun Country as a *sac-a-lait*.

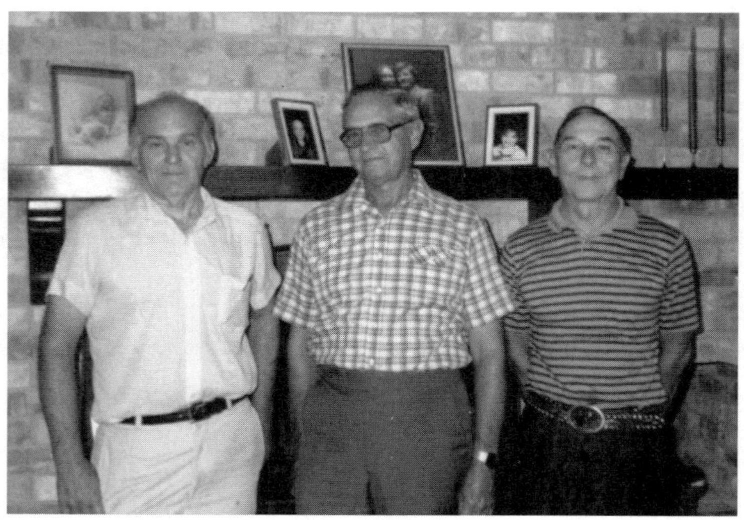

On occasion, he visited with his war buddies.
(Left to right): Phillip Sandras, Cut Off, La;
Curtis Bertrand, Opelousas, La; Mally Bass, Lone Star, Texas.

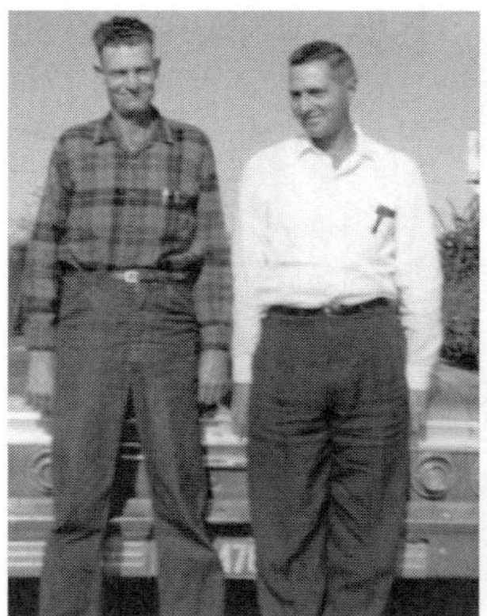

Homer Fleming and dad visited in 1960.

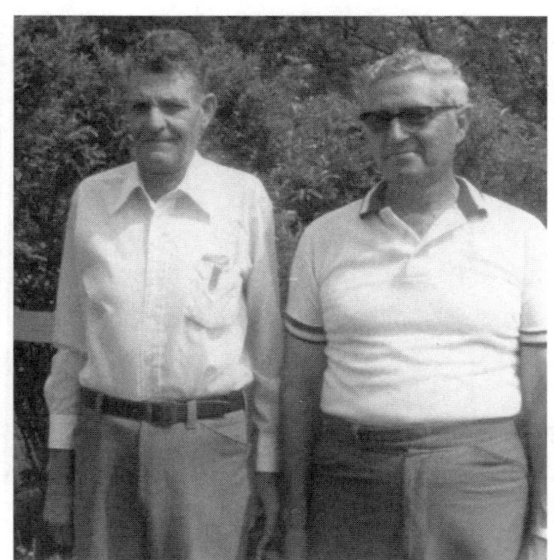

Our family went to Summersville, Missouri, in 1966 so my dad could visit with war buddy Homer Fleming.

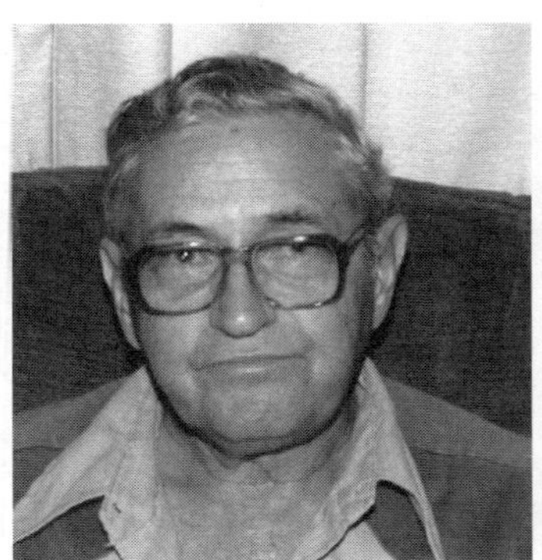

A close-up of Dad.

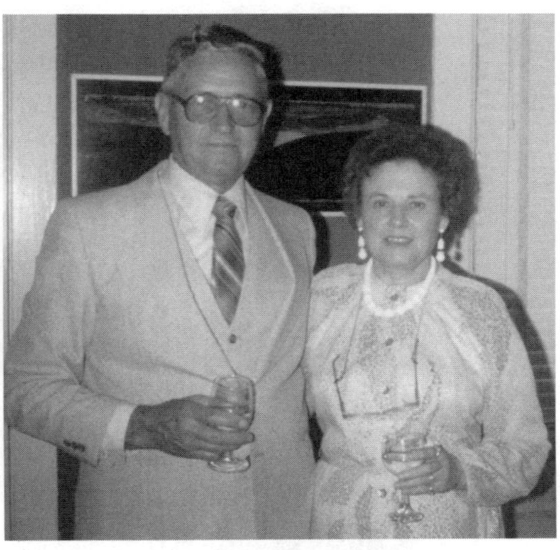

Dad and Mom at a party.

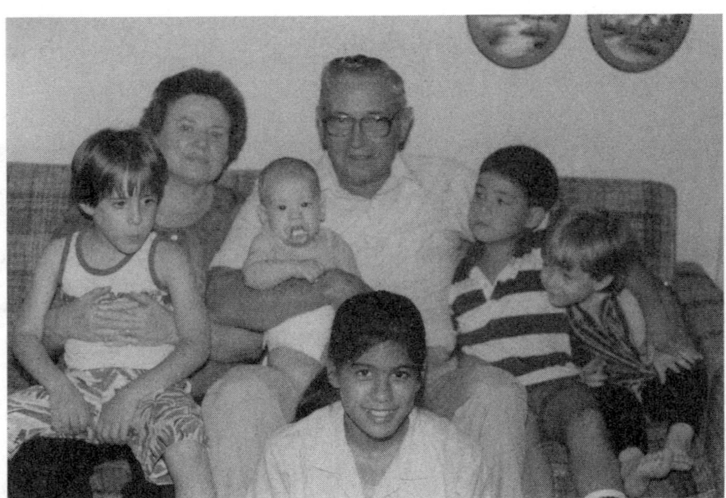

MawMaw and PawPaw Bertrand posing with their five grandkids in 1987.

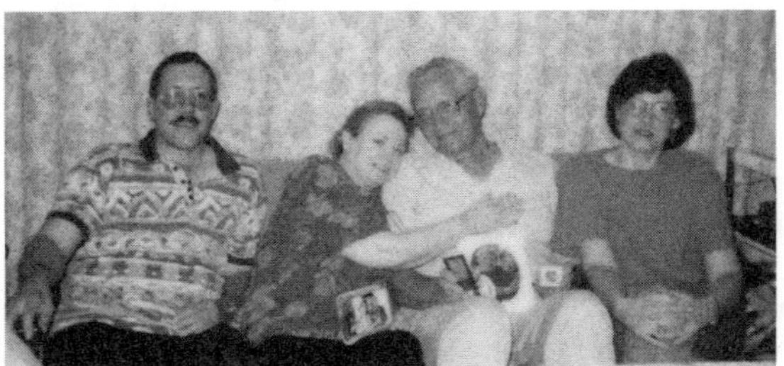

My sister Karen and me with our parents on their 50th wedding anniversary, June 20, 1998.

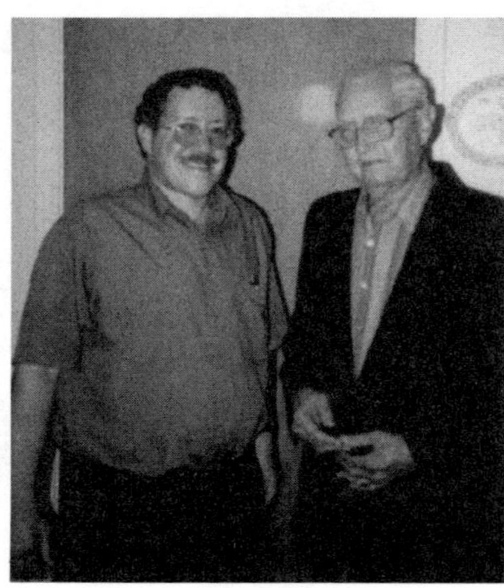

Me and my dad one week before he passed away on Sept. 27, 2000, exactly one month before his 80th birthday.

ACKNOWLEDGMENTS

I would like to thank the following people and associations for their help with this book. The information provided by correspondence and/or their websites was extremely valuable.

Lt. Colonel Robert A. Lynn, Florida Guard, a military history writer who helped to identify dad's uniform emblems, patches and medals.

Mr. Ray J. Bowden, Dorset, England www.usaaf-noseart.co.uk

Steve Lucas at http://www.nose-art.net

Scott Van Aken, Owner, Publisher, and Editor, www.modelingmadness.com

The folks at www.warbirdregistry.org and www.pacificwrecks.com

Kelly B. Kalcheim, P-38 National Association, http://p38assn.org

L-5 Sentinel experts Norm Goyer and Jim Gray, Sentinel Owners and Pilots Association at www.sentinelclub.org

Daniel Stockton, www.b24bestweb.com

Scott Rose, www.warbirdsresourcegroup.org

The people at http://aerothentic.com

http://8thattacksqdnassoc.tripod.com/WWIIa.html#Dobodura

www.daveswarbirds.com

Many thanks to Angus Lorenzen, John Ream and Sascha Jansen of The Bay Area Civilian Ex-Prisoners of War (BACEPOW) for contributing priceless information for the captions for many of the photos in the Philippines chapter. Thanks to John Ream for contributing photos. This organization is dedicated to supporting and telling the story of all of the people who were captives of the Japanese. Though the organization was founded in the San Francisco area, its membership is now nationwide, with members in several countries. They welcome those who were civilian and military prisoners, their families and friends, and those who are interested in the history of the prison camps in East Asia. See their website at www.bacepow.net.

Many thanks to the people who supplied the official "Military Record" of the 863rd Engineer Aviation Battalion. Without this daily diary this project would not have been complete. To get a military record, they can be reached at this address:

Air Force Historical Research Agency
600 Chennault Circle
Maxwell AFB, AL 36112
(334) 953-5834
www.afhra.af.mil

APPENDIX 1

World War II Airplanes and Their Erotic Nose Art
Bombers, Fighters and More

When I began working on this project, I had no idea how to identify the 14 different types of airplanes my father had photographed. Nor did I know how I was going to match the nose art with the type of plane it was painted on. It took over two months of research to figure it all out, with the help of experts in the field as well as WWII plane and nose art websites. To learn more about these planes, and to see more photos, search online or visit your local library.

Section 1

Consolidated B-24 Liberator Bomber

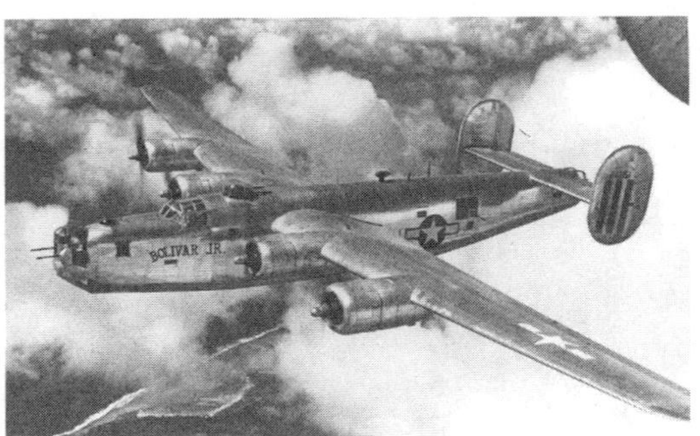

The Consolidated B-24 Liberator was an American heavy bomber, designed by Consolidated-Vultee Aircraft of San Diego, California. The B-24 was used in World War II by several Allied Air Forces and Navies and by every branch of the American armed forces during the war, attaining a distinguished war record with its operations in the Western European, Pacific, Mediterranean, and China-Burma-India (CBI) Theaters.

Mass production was brought into full force by 1943 with the aid of the Ford Motor Company through its newly constructed Willow Run facility in Michigan, where peak production had reached one B-24 per hour and 650 per month in 1944. Other factories soon followed. The B-24 ended World War II as the most produced Allied heavy bomber in history and the most produced American military aircraft at over 18,400 units, due largely to Henry Ford and the harnessing of American industry.

Often compared with the better-known B-17 Flying Fortress, the B-24 was a more modern design with a higher top speed, greater range, and a heavier bomb load. Popular opinion among aircrews and general staffs tended to favor the B-17's rugged qualities above all other considerations in the European Theater.

The placement of the B-24's fuel tanks throughout the upper fuselage and its lightweight construction, designed to increase range and optimize assembly line production, made the aircraft vulnerable to battle damage. The B-24 was notorious among American aircrews for its tendency to catch fire. Moreover, its high fuselage-mounted "Davis wing" also meant it was dangerous to ditch or belly land, since the fuselage tended to break apart. Nevertheless, the B-24 provided excellent service in a variety of roles thanks to its large payload and long range.

Although primarily a heavy bomber, the Liberator was also a very effective fighter in that it shot down approximately 2,600 enemy aircraft, it was the leading Allied oceanic patrol and anti-submarine aircraft, and the leading Allied long-range cargo transport.

This plane went through 15 major variants. Under the mid/high-mounted wing were two bomb bays, each as large as that of a B-17. The next model was drastically altered to have a conventional nose with the navigator and bombardier in the front and a side-by-side cockpit further back with a stepped windscreen. Each of the bomb bays could carry 4,000 lb (1814 kg) of bombs.

The B-24D saw service in every theatre and in 1942-43 was by far the most important long-range bomber in the Pacific area. By late 1942 it equipped 15 anti-submarine squadrons using radar-equipped aircraft all around the North Atlantic.

TECHNICAL NOTES:

Name: Consolidated-Vultee B-24D-85-CO Liberator

Type: Heavy bomber

Crew: 10

Armament: One (usually three) 50-cal. (12.7-mm) nose gun, two in dorsal turret, two in tail turret, two in retractable ball turret underneath and two in waist (side) positions; plus a maximum internal bomb load of 8,000 lb (3,629 kg)

Powerplant: Four 1,200-hp (895-kW) Pratt & Whitney R-1830-43 turbo-supercharged Twin Wasp radial piston engines

Propeller: Three-bladed

Performance:

Maximum speed: 303 mph (488 km/h);

Cruising speed: 175 mph

Initial climb rate: 1,100 ft (335 m) per minute

Range: 1,080 miles (1,730 km) with 5,000-lb (2,268 kg) bomb load

Service ceiling: 28,000 ft.

Dimensions:

Wingspan: 110 ft. (33.52 m)
Length: 66 ft. 4 in. (20.22 m)
Height: 17 ft. 11 in. (5.46 m)

Weight: Empty 33,980 lb (15413 kg); maximum take-off 60,000 lb (27216 kg)

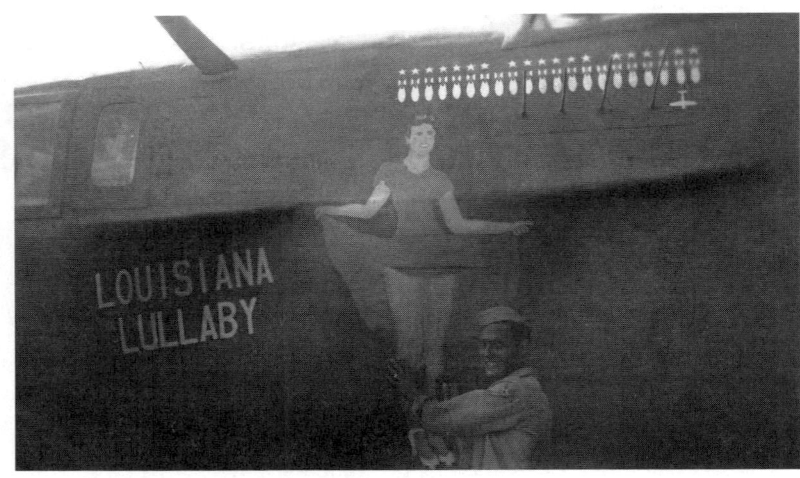

My dad admires the B-24 named "Louisiana Lullaby."
Note the number of bombing missions with one enemy plane shot down. New Guinea, 1943.

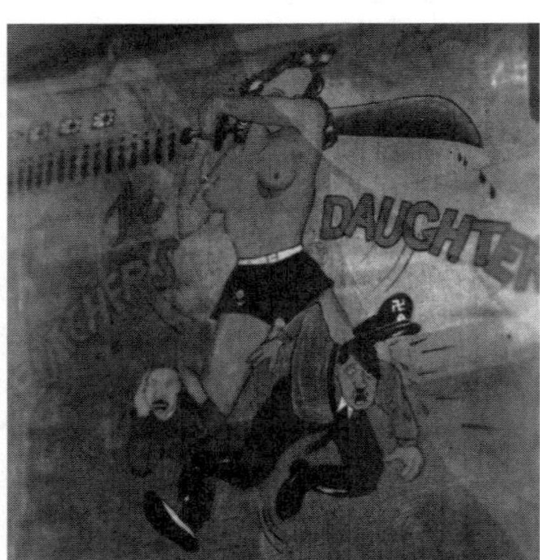

B-24 named "Butcher's Daughter." She's positioned on top of Tojo and Hitler, swinging her long blade at them. Mokmer Drome, Biak, 1944.

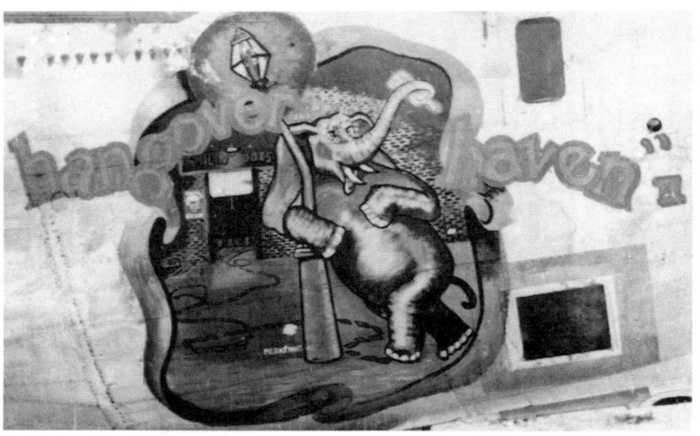

"Hangover Haven II."
B-24J-1-CF (F-7A)
Serial# 42-64053;
20th Combat Mapping Squadron, Biak, 1944.
B-24 Photo Recon.

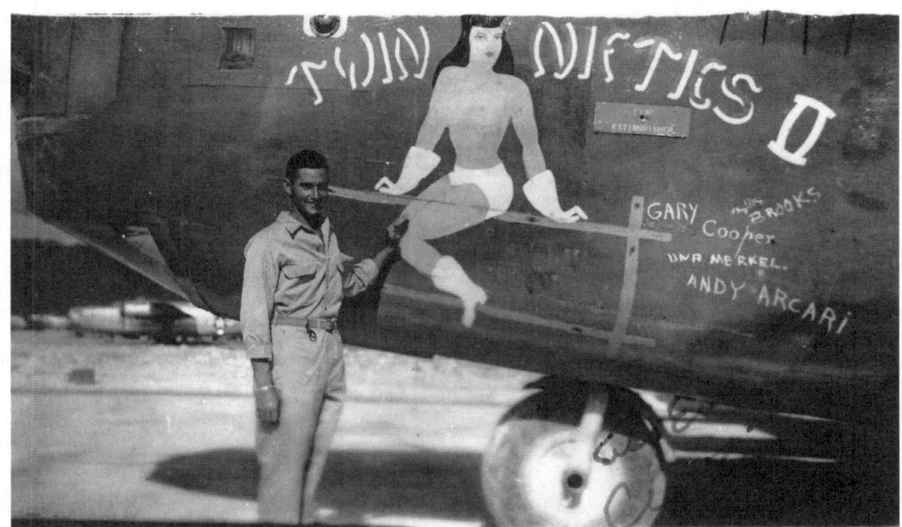

Dad admires "Twin Nifties II." Aug. 1944, Biak.

Twin Nifties II is a B-24D-115-CO, Serial# 42-40928. It was part of the USAAF, 5th Air Force, 90th Bomb Group, 400th Bomb Squadron. It was scrapped on Dec. 13, 1944, four months after this photo was taken. This bomber was autographed by USO Show performers Gary Cooper, Phyliss Brooks, Una Merkel, and accordionist Andy Arcari.

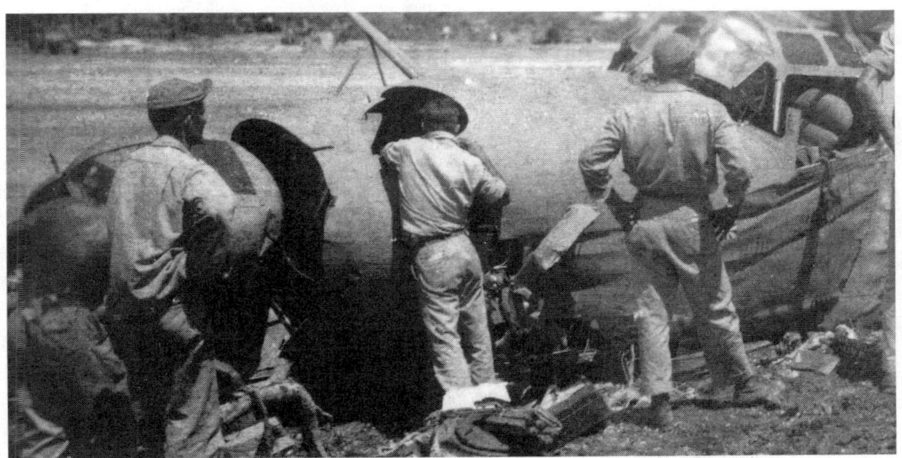

This B-24 came in on a flat tire and crashed. No one was hurt. Aug. 1944, Biak.

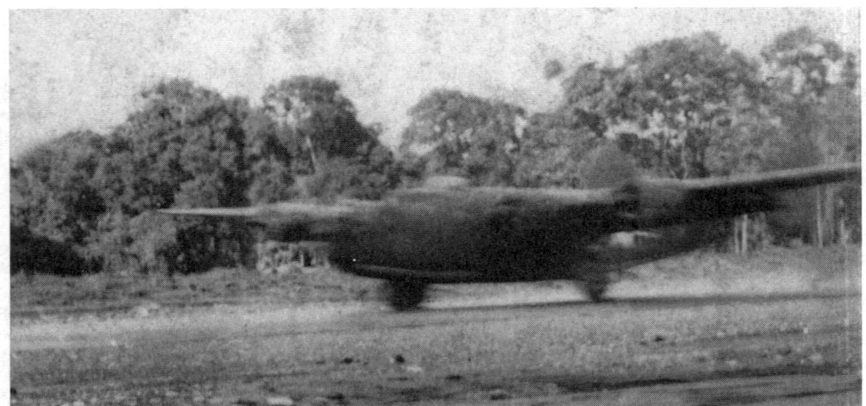

A B-24 taking off from Mokmer Drome, Biak, in 1944.

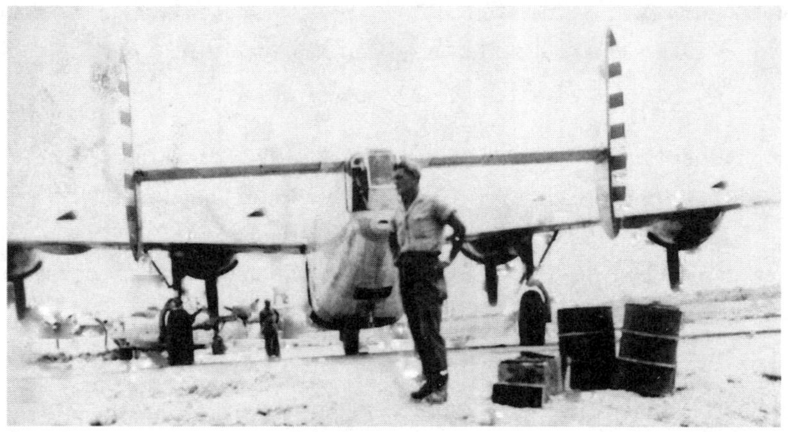

Two B-24 bombers. This is my dad's friend Philip Sandras from south Louisiana. The photo was taken on Biak Island, 1944.

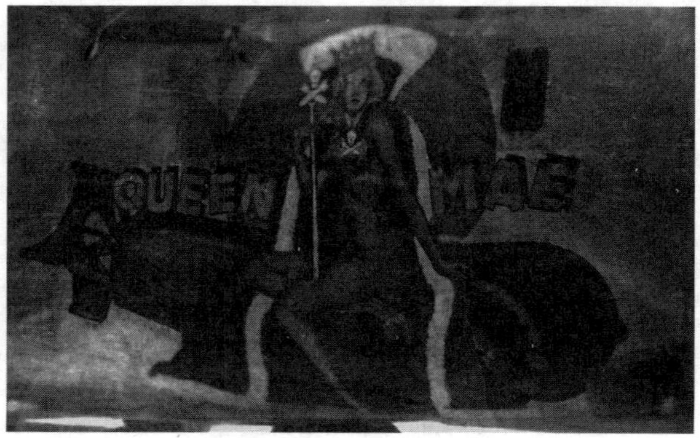

"Queen Mae" is enthroned on a bomb; B-24D; 90th Bomb Group; 319th Squadron; Serial #44-40337.

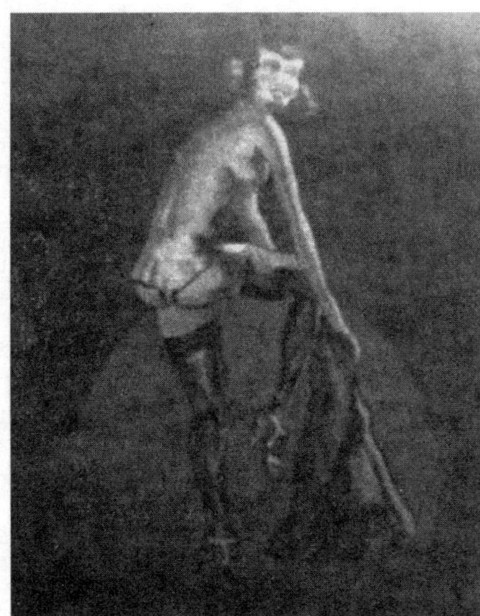

The artwork is based on artist Gil Elvgren's pin-up girl titled "FRENCH DRESSING." There were over a dozen planes that used this theme.

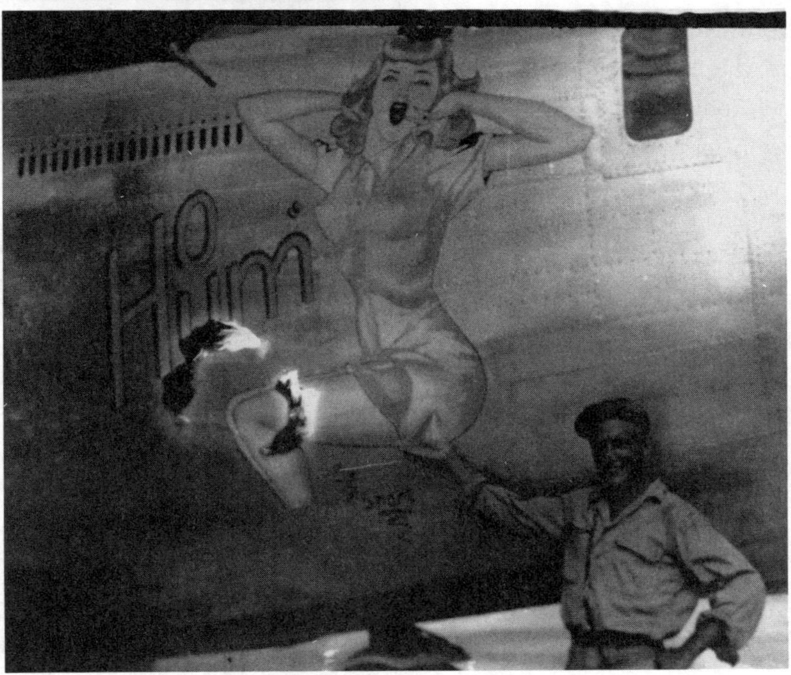

Darel Gipe admired a B-24 named "Ho Hum," painted by an artist named Short.

Patched Up Piece

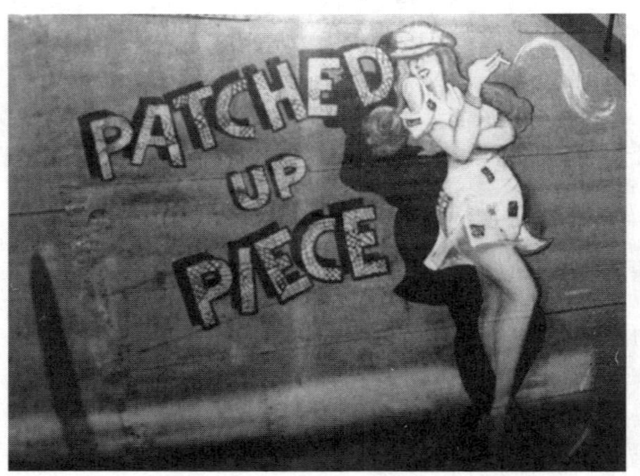

BEFORE

"Patched Up Piece" had to be repainted after stripping off the camouflage paint. A machine gun is sticking out the side. B-24. F-7A-CO. Serial #42-64047 from the 20th Combat Mapping Squadron; 6th Photo Reconnaissance Group; Fifth Air Force. It was a converted Consolidated Liberator, and the first aircraft of the 20th Combat Mapping Squadron air echelon to depart the U.S. for the Pacific, which it did on Feb. 23, 1944, at 2300 hours. It was also the first aircraft to land at Middleburg Aug. 14, 1944, due to engine troubles. This aircraft began life as the first B-24J-1-CF manufactured at Fort Worth, and made its inaugural flight from the Texas factory on Sept. 14, 1943. The noseart was painted by Al Merkling, the most famous of all Fifth Air Force artists.

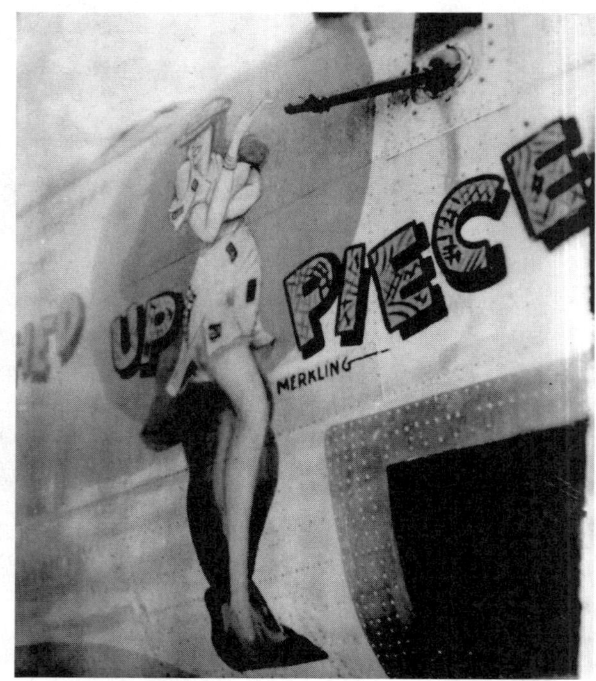

AFTER

Pappy's Passion

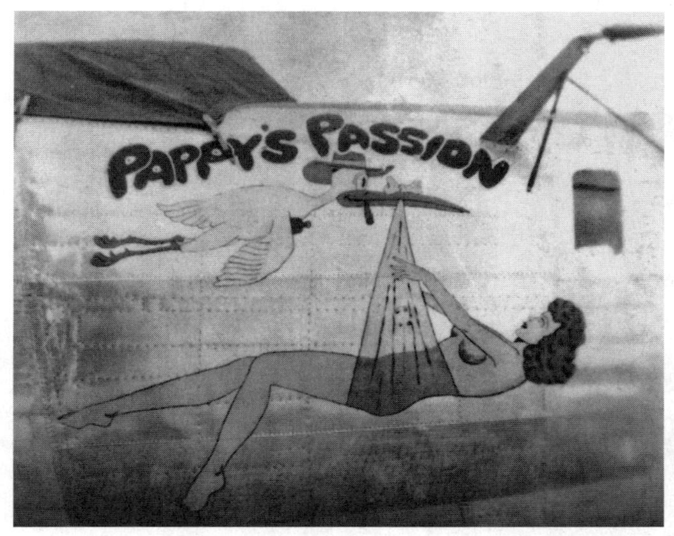

B-24J, 90th Bomb Group, 319th Squadron, Serial #42-100222.

Road to Tokyo

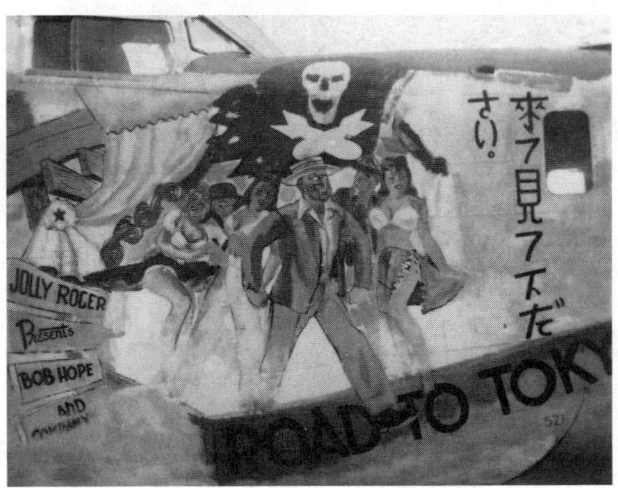

B-24, J-165-CO of the 319th Bomb Squadron,
90th Brigade "The Jolly Rogers," 5th Air Force.

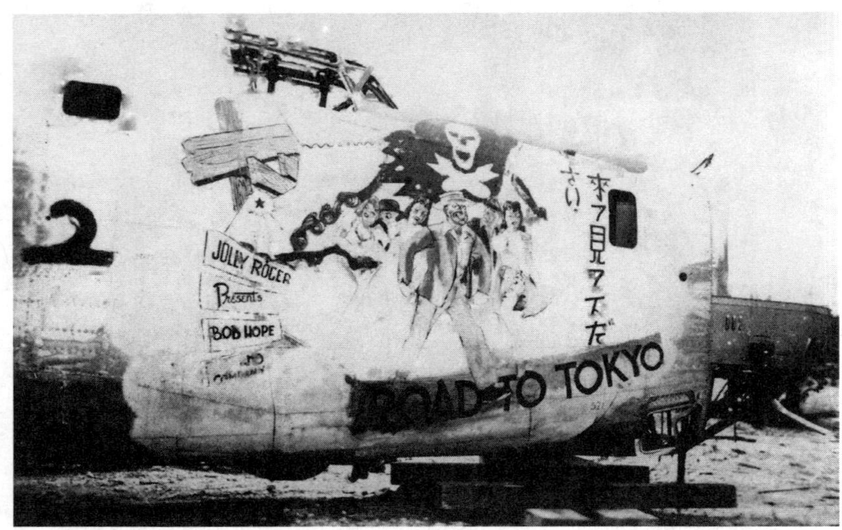

Road to Tokyo crashed later and is shown resting on blocks.

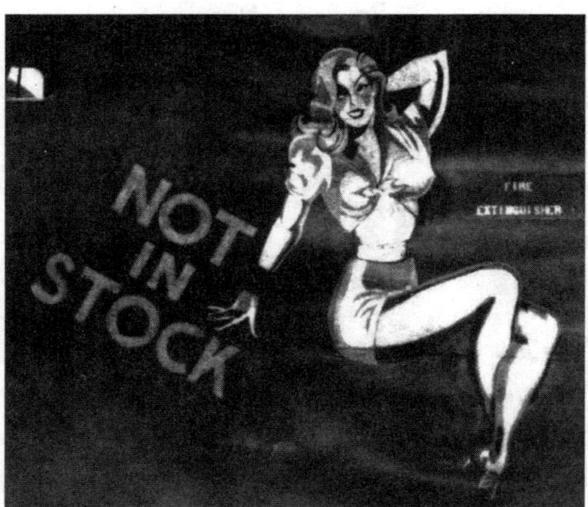

This B-24 is named “Not in Stock” and is a B-24D-130-CO, serial #42-41077. It was assigned to the 5th Air Force, 90th Bomb Group “The Jolly Rogers,” 400th Bomber Squadron called the Black Pirates. It was salvaged in the USA.

Photo Queen

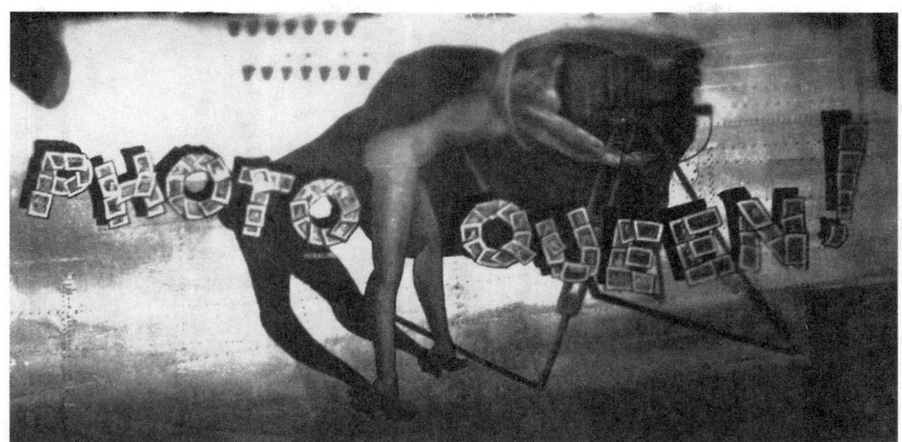

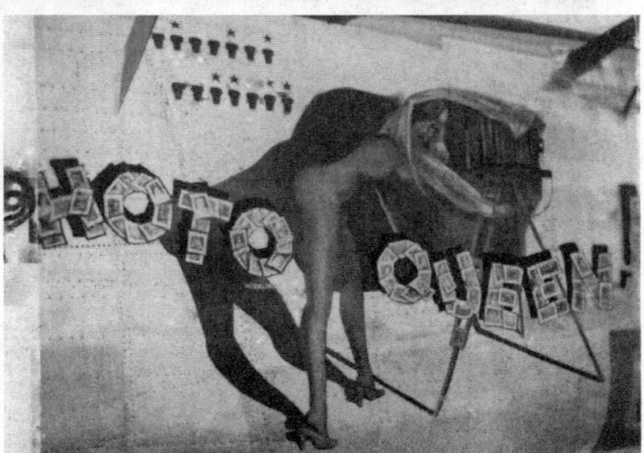

Photo Queen was a photo-taking reconnaissance aircraft.

"Photo Queen!" B-24 F-7A 42-73049 20th Combat Mapping Squadron (CMS). Another stunning creation by Al Merkling. "Photo Queen!" portrayed the mission of the 20th CMS in a new and very appealing light to men incarcerated on remote Pacific islands. His work on the titling style alone would have been a fine embellishment to any aircraft but his figure work was simply magnificent. It is hard to appreciate the extreme conditions under which he worked. Burning temperatures instantly dried the paint, which was a mixture of shellac lacquers, house paint, and USAAF official airplane paint, thinned with high-octane fuel and applied with a rough and ready collection of available brushes. In spite of all this, Merkling's skill reigned supreme, and he produced some of the finest examples of nose art to be seen in the Pacific region. Its first combat photo mission was on April 16, 1944, and completed a further 13 sorties before being retired due to combat damage. Notice the 14 emblems or decals designating missions flown. There would be no further missions after this photo was taken.

Yankee Doodle Dandy

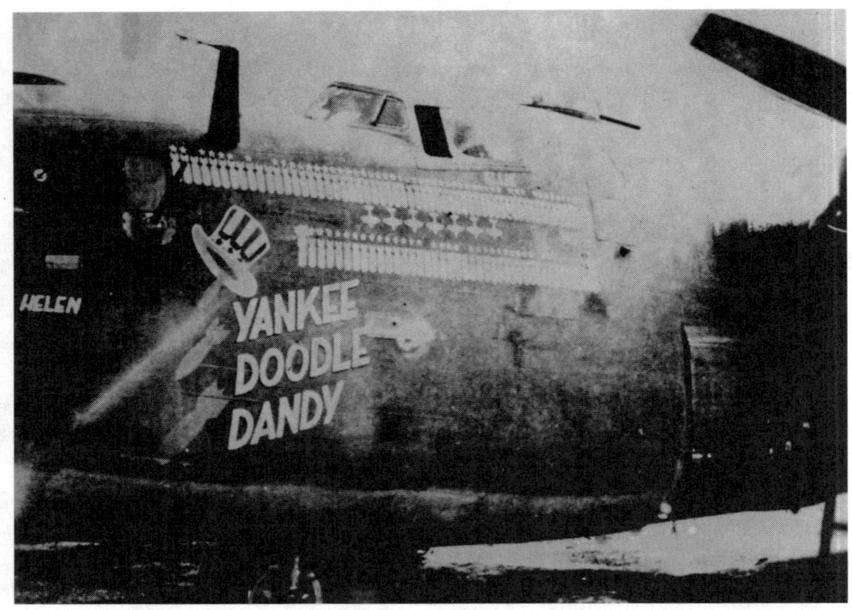

B-24. "Yankee Doodle Dandy." Notice the missions flown and the kills. According to the Missing Air Crew Report (MACR 4926), the plane was lost April 12, 1944, on a bombing mission to Hollandia, Dutch New Guinea.

Double Trouble (unfinished artwork)

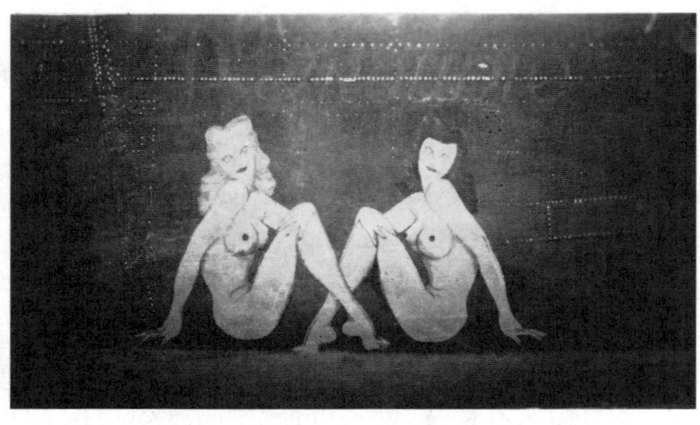

"Double Trouble" B-24D; 43rd Bomb Group, 64th Squadron; Serial #42-41226. Dad wrote on the back of the photo that it is "a blonde & redhead." Dad took this photo while art was in progress. You can barely see the stencil outline of the name "Double Trouble" before the artist painted it. Photo taken in New Guinea in 1943 or 1944.

The Wango Wango Bird

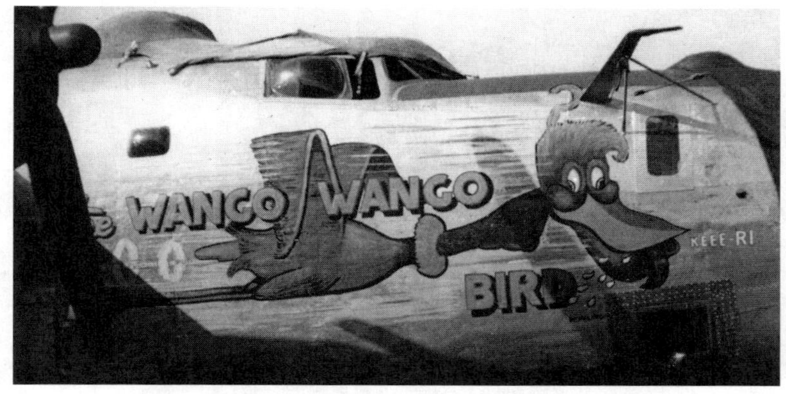

B-24 F-7A, #42-64048, 20th Combat Mapping Squadron. Clearly a product of Al Merkling's vivid imagination, this camera-equipped F-7A version of the B-24 was assigned to 1Lt Roy Hunt and flew overseas from Hunter Field, Georgia, on February 10, 1944.

About Average

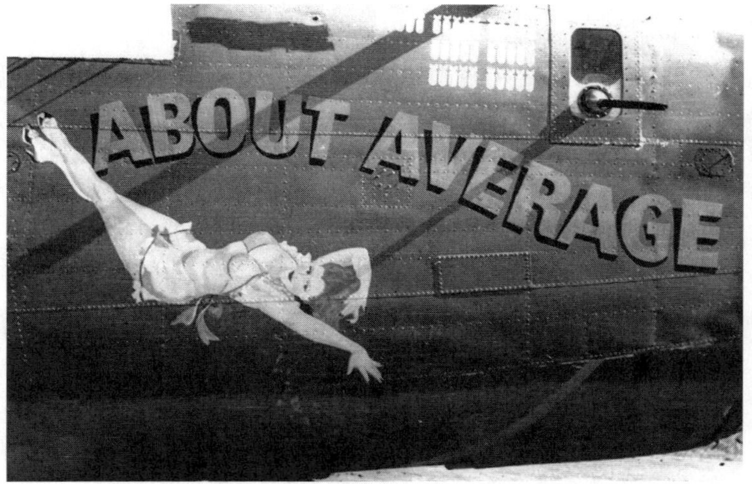

B-24 bomber. Notice the number of bombing missions and the machine gun barrel sticking out of the gun port.

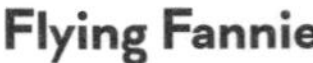

Flying Fannie

Sweet Racket

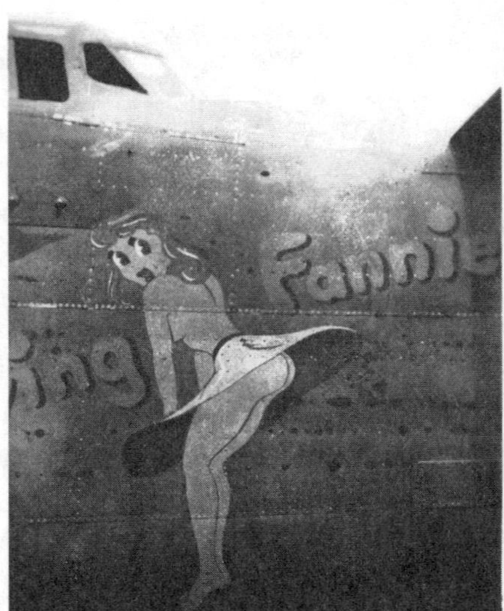

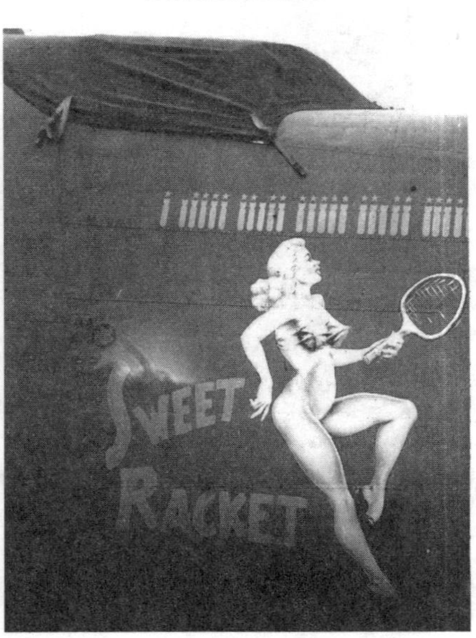

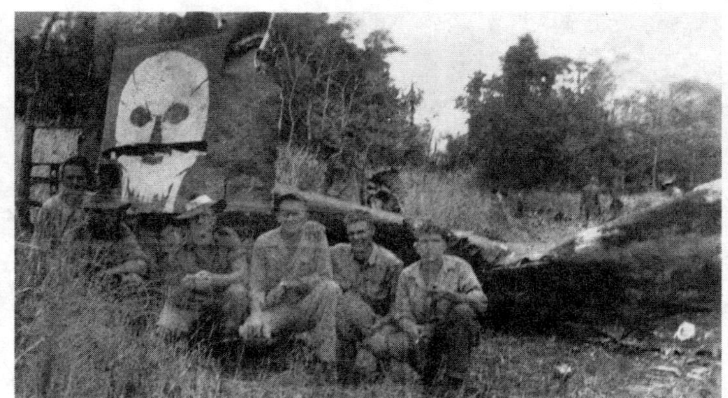

B-24 of the Jolly Roger 90th Bomber Group crashed.
Australian and U.S. soldiers pictured here.

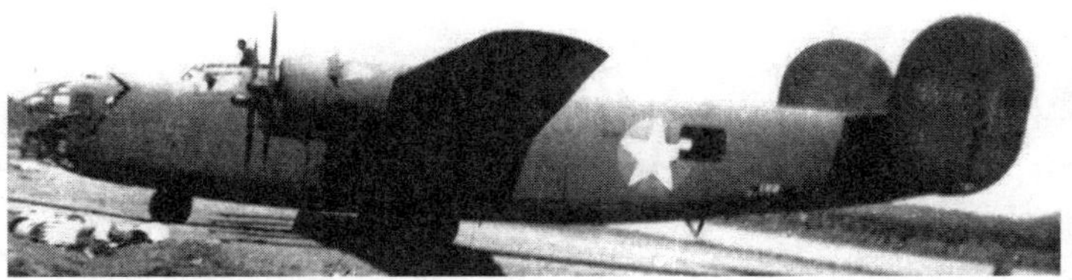

Side view of a B-24 bomber.

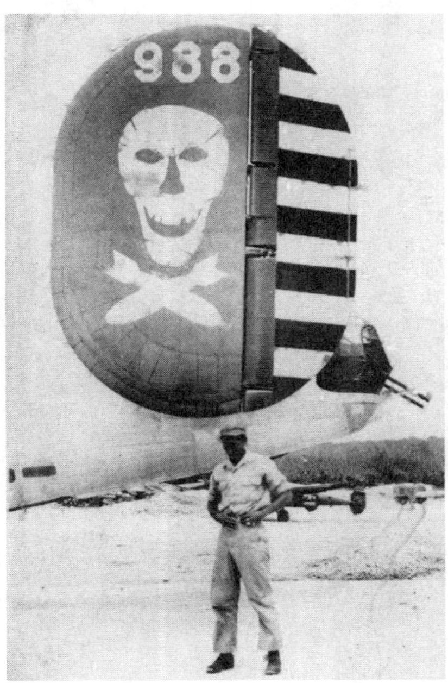

Tail guns on the PHYLLIS T. OF WORCESTER.

Curtis Bertrand beneath the tail fin of Jolly Roger bomber, the "PHYLLIS T. OF WORCESTER", B-24J-120-CO, #42-109988; Mokmer Drome, Biak, 1944.

How'm -I-Doin'

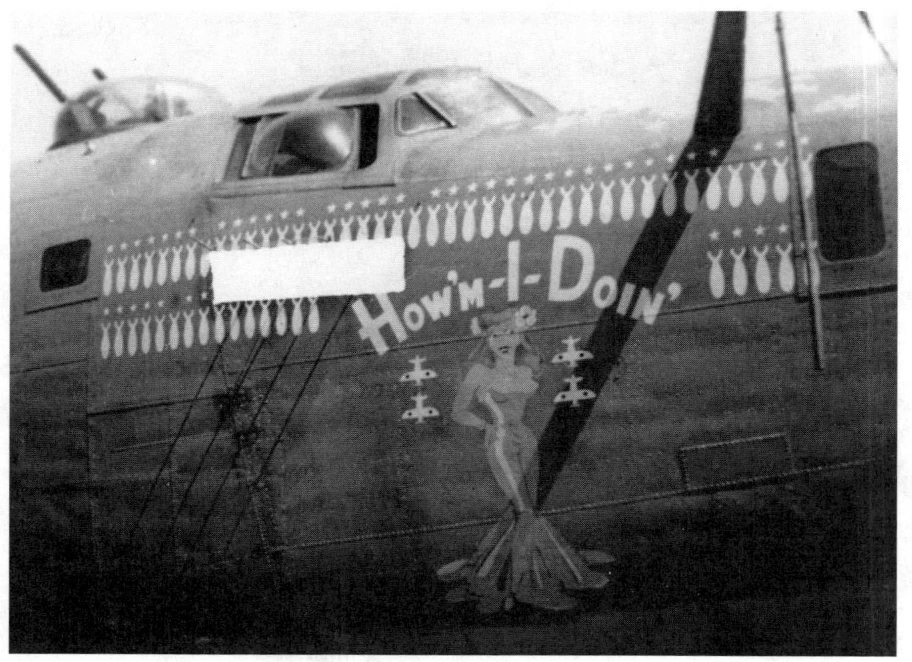

B-24D bomber; 90th Bomb Group; 319th Squadron;
Serial #42-41223. Notice the number of missions and kills.

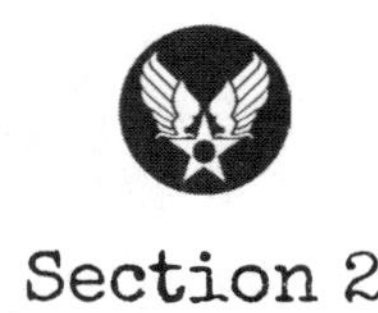

Section 2

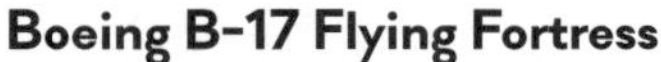

Boeing B-17 Flying Fortress

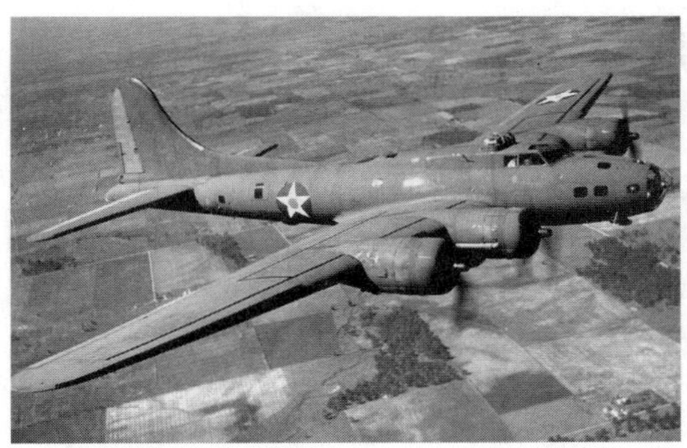

The Boeing B-17 Flying Fortress is a four-engine, heavy bomber aircraft developed in the 1930s for the then United States Army Air Corps (USAAC). The B-17 was primarily employed by the United States Army Air Forces (USAAF) in the daylight precision strategic bombing campaign of World War II against German industrial and military targets. The B-17 also participated to a lesser extent in the War in the Pacific where it conducted raids against Japanese shipping and airfields. The B-17G was the final version of the B-17, and in total 8,680 were built.

B-17s were used in early battles of the Pacific with little success, notably the Battle of Coral Sea and Battle of Midway. While there, the Fifth Air Force B-17s were tasked with disrupting the Japanese sea lanes. Air Corps doctrine dictated bombing runs from high altitude, but it was soon discovered that only 1 percent of their bombs hit targets. However, B-17s were operating at heights too great for most A6M Zero fighters to reach, and the B-17s heavy gun armament was easily more than a match for lightly protected Japanese planes.

In mid-1942 General Arnold decided that the B-17 was inadequate for the kind of operations required in the Pacific and made plans to replace all of the B-17s in the theater with B-24s as soon as they became available. Although the conversion was not complete until mid-1943, B-17 combat operations in the

Pacific theater came to an end after a little over a year.

In the Pacific, the planes earned a deadly reputation with the Japanese, who dubbed them "four-engine fighters." The Fortresses were also legendary for their ability to stay in the air after taking brutal poundings. They sometimes limped back to their bases with large chunks of the fuselage shot off.

See www.boeing.com/history/boeing/b17.html

TECHNICAL NOTES:

Name: Boeing B17 Flying Fortress

Type: Heavy Bomber

Crew: 10: Pilot, co-pilot, navigator, bombardier/nose gunner, flight engineer, top turret gunner, radio operator, waist gunners (2), ball turret gunner, tail gunner

Armament:

Guns: 13 × .50 in (12.7 mm) M2 Browning machine guns in 8 turrets in dorsal, ventral, nose and tail, 2 in waist positions, 2 beside cockpit and 1 in the lower dorsal position

Bombs:
Short range missions (<400 mi): 8,000 lb (3,600 kg)
Long range missions (˜800 mi): 4,500 lb (2,000 kg)

Powerplant: Four 1,200-horsepower Wright R-1820-97 "Cyclone" turbo-supercharged radial engines

Propeller: Three-bladed

Performance:
Maximum speed: 287 mph (249 kn, 462 km/h)
Cruising speed: 182 mph (158 kn, 293 km/h)
Range: 2,000 mi (1,738 nmi, 3,219 km) with 2,700 kg (6,000 lb) bomb load
Service ceiling: 35,600 ft (10,850 m)

Dimensions:
Wingspan: 103 ft. 9 in.
Length: 74 ft. 9 in.
Height: 19 ft. 1 in.
Weight: 65,000 pounds gross

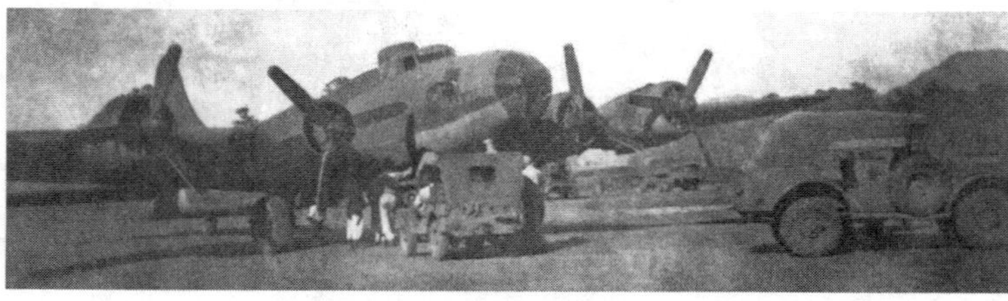

The crew is examining this B-17.

Section 3

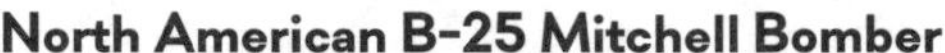

North American B-25 Mitchell Bomber

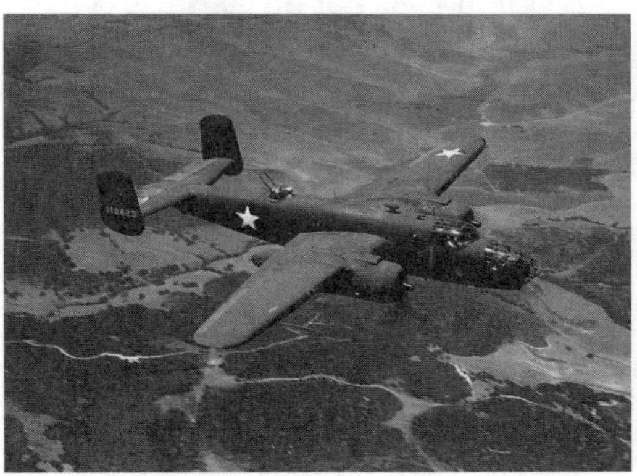

The North American B-25 Mitchell twin-engine, medium attack bomber was one of America's most famous airplanes of World War II. It was the type used by General Jimmy Doolittle for the Tokyo Raid April 18, 1942.

Although the airplane was originally intended for level bombing from medium altitudes, it was used extensively in the Pacific Theater for bombing Japanese airfields and beach emplacements from treetop level and for strafing and skip bombing enemy shipping.

No doubt, part of its heroic stature derives from its namesake, the outspoken General Billy Mitchell. He proved once and for all that bombers could destroy targets and that wars would nevermore be decided only on land or sea.

Under the leadership of Lieutenant General George C. Kenney, B-25s of the Fifth and Thirteenth Air Forces devastated Japanese targets in the Southwest Pacific Theater (SWPA) from 1942 to 1945 and played a significant role in pushing the Japanese back to their home islands.

By the end of the war, North American Aviation had built a total of 9,816 B-25s at its California and Kansas plants.

TECHNICAL NOTES:

Name: North American B-25 Mitchell

Role: Medium bomber

Crew: 6

Armament: 12 to 18 .50-cal. machine guns; 3,000 lbs of bombs; 4,000 lbs on short missions

Powerplant: Two Wright R-2600s "Cyclone" engines with 1,700 hp each

Propeller: Three-bladed

Performance:
Maximum speed: 328 mph
Cruising speed: 233 mph
Range: 1,350; 2,500 miles (with auxiliary tanks)
Service Ceiling: 21,200 ft

Dimensions:
Wingspan: 68 ft
Length: 53 ft
Height: 16 ft 9 in
Weight: 29,300 lbs maximum

Reference: www.nationalmuseum.af.mil/factsheets/factsheet.asp?id=476

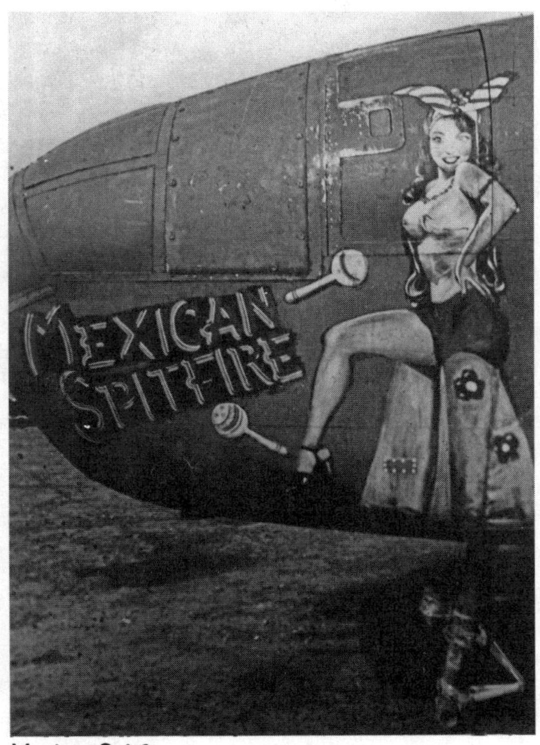

Mexican Spitfire

A Mitchell B-25D bomber, (strafer conversion), B-25D-20-NC, #41-30592, 345th Bomb Group, 500th Bomb Squadron (Rough Raiders) as flown by Lieutenant Merwyn Bruce. When it was shot down it was being flown by 2/Lt. Lloyd B. Bardwell Jr. His aircraft was hit by anti-aircraft fire on a mission to Lambeh Strait, Celebes, and ditched in the sea seven miles northeast of Lambeh Island. It made a good water landing, nosed under, then came back up minus the tail assembly and right wing. A Japanese "Zeke" fighter strafed the wreckage as the crew was getting out, but was driven off by U.S. planes that circled overhead and attacked the fighter with their nose guns. Five crewmen were seen in the water with Mae West life vests inflated, but the life raft appeared damaged. As their fuel became exhausted, the escort planes left the area and subsequent searches for the crew were unsuccessful. This action took place on Sept. 2, 1944. Lloyd was twenty-four years old. He was from Arkadelphia, Arkansas.

This information was taken from www.nose-art.net/kenwilson.htm which has a photo of the plane and pilot.

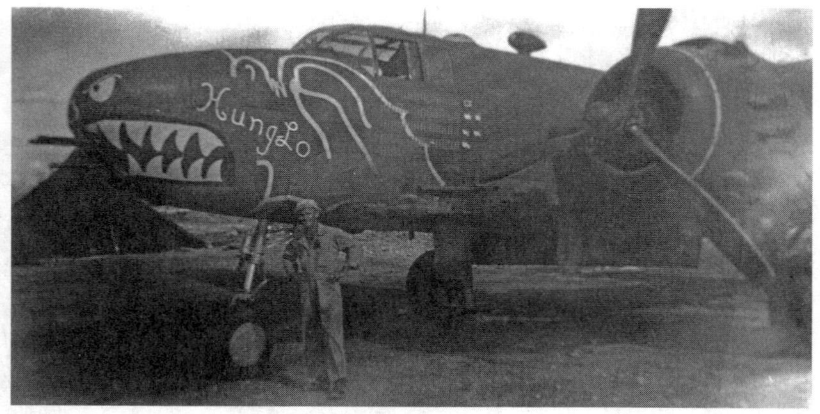

Hung Lo

My dad had a personal connection with the pilot of this next plane, a B-25D-5 Mitchell bomber named "Hung Lo," with the "Bats Out of Hell" artwork on it. The plane was flown by 2nd Lieutenant George P. "Jack" Voitier of Opelousas, Louisiana, and crew . It was shot down by the Japanese at Halmehera Island on the equator, SW Pacific, 1944. My dad took this loss very personally as both families were good friends.

Jack Voitier

"Hung Lo" was assigned to the 345th Bombardment Group, 499th Medium Bombardment Squadron, the "Bats Out of Hell," Serial Number 41-30084, on May 17, 1944. (from http://bathead.com/noseart1.html) (Unidentified man standing in front.)

Former Assignment: 501st BS
Crashed: August 13, 1944

The following information was adapted from the book, *Warpath Across the Pacific,* by Lawrence J. Hickey, pages 178, 179, 371, 388.

"Hung Lo" was one of six bombers that took off from Mokmer Drome on Biak for a strike against Lolobata village west of the Loelie River on Halmahera Island. After strafing the target and a lugger, the formation passed over an anti-aircraft gun position and this B-25 was hit in the left engine at low altitude. Damaged, the left wing struck the sea and snapped off, then the right wing hit and the tail broke off as it crashed into the shallow water of Wasile Bay, roughly 90 yards off shore.

The remaining B-25s circled for 90 minutes to protect the crew. At least three crewman survived the ditching. Two were on the wing and waved to the other B-25s, and a third was wounded getting first aid.

Low on fuel, the B-25s departed and the crew were never seen again. Presumably, all were captured by the Japanese and otherwise killed or died. Reportedly, one was buried on the beach.

Additional references were taken from

www.pacificwrecks.com/aircraft/b-25/41-30084.html

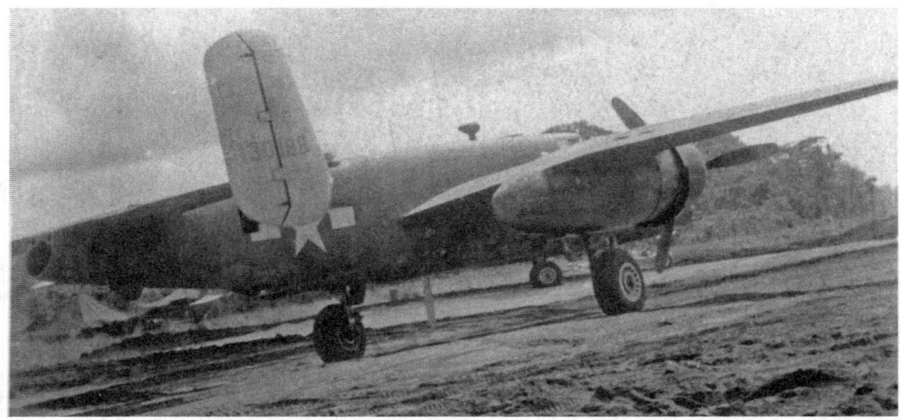

B-25 Mitchell bomber.

Section 4

Douglas A-20 Havoc

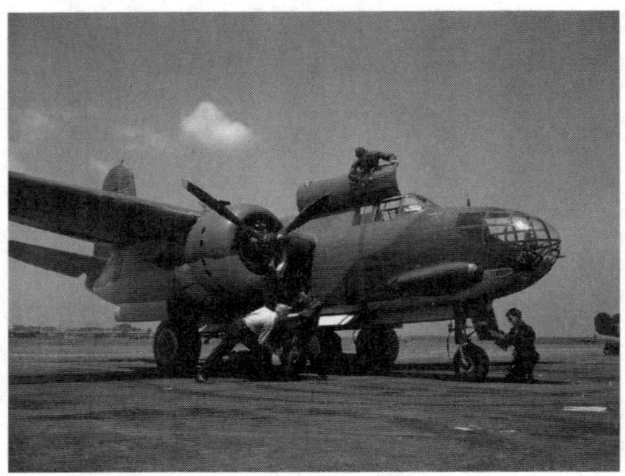

The Douglas A-20 Havoc was a family of American attack, light bomber and night fighter aircraft of World War II. Attacking with forward-firing .50-cal. machine guns and bombs, the A-20G lived up to its name by creating havoc and destruction on low-level strafing attacks, especially against Japanese shipping and airfields across the Southwest Pacific.

In August 1942 the A-20 attacked the Japanese Air base at Lae. This was the first of a long series of low-level strafing attacks on the Japanese that would become the specialty of the A-20 in the Pacific and would lead to the development of the solid nosed A-20G. This aircraft was also used in dropping "parafrags" – small fragmentation bombs with time delay fuses dropped by parachute. These small bombs were very effective against Japanese bases and against flat bottomed barges.

Originally trained to fly P-40s, the men of the 312th Bombardment Group transitioned to the A-20G in the field. Calling themselves the "Roarin' 20s," the men of the 312th fought their way across the Southwest Pacific from New Guinea to the Philippines.

Flown by the Allies in the Pacific, the Middle East, North Africa, Europe, and Russia, the versatile A-20 went through many variants. The A-20G, which reached combat in 1943, was produced in larger numbers than any other model. By the time production ended in September 1944, American factories had built a total of 7,098, of which 2,850 were solid nose A-20G models.

TECHNICAL NOTES:

Name: Douglas A-20 Havoc

Role: light attack bomber

Crew: 3

Armament: 12 50-cal. machine guns; 4,000 lbs. of bombs (2000# internal, 2000# external)

Powerplant: Two Wright R-2600-23 Cyclone supercharged radials of 1,600 hp each

Propeller: Three-bladed

Performance:
Maximum speed: 317 mph
Cruising speed: 256 mph
Range: 1,240 miles; 950 miles (combat)
Service Ceiling: 28,175 ft

Dimensions:
Wingspan: 61 ft. 4 in
Length: 48 ft
Height: 17 ft 7 in
Weight: 26,580 lbs loaded

Reference: www.nationalmuseum.af.mil/factsheets/factsheet.asp?id=2957
http://8thattacksqdnassoc.tripod.com/WWIIa.html

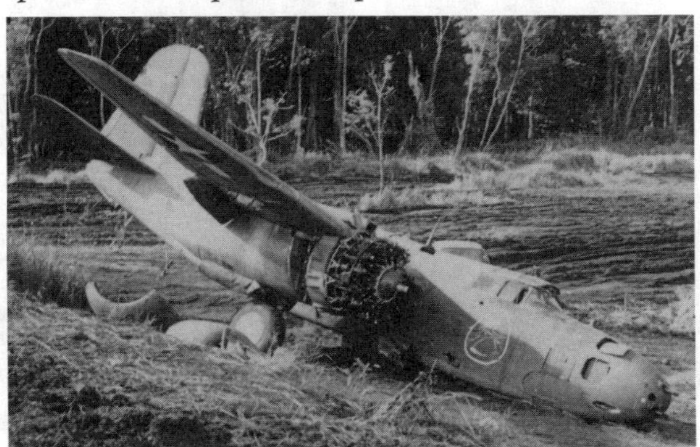

A damaged A-20. Saidor, New Guinea, 1944.

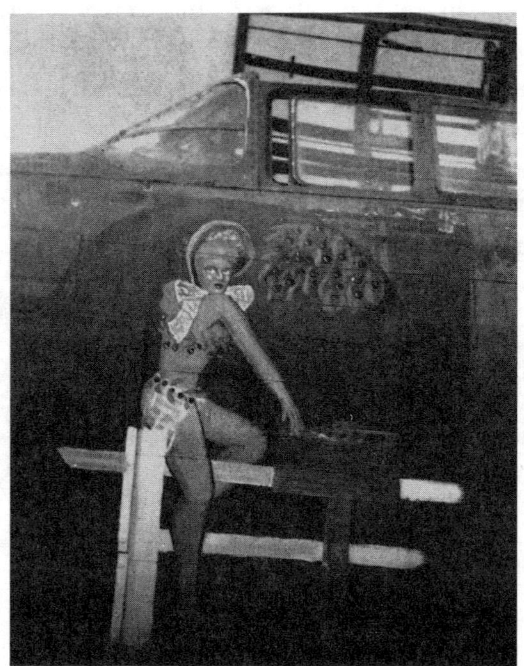

Hard to Get (unfinished artwork)

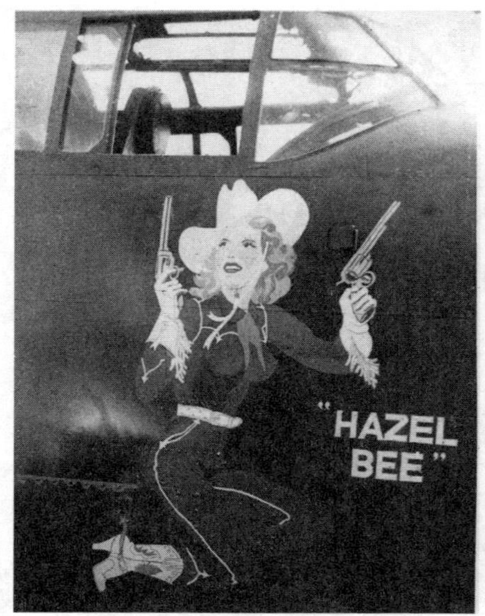

Hazel Bee

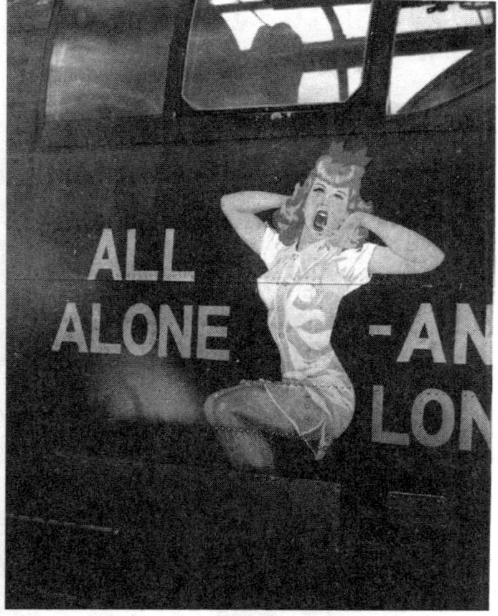

All Alone - And Lonely

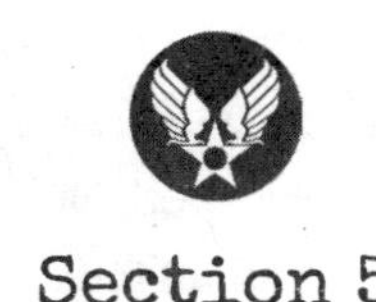

Section 5

Lockheed P-38 Lightning

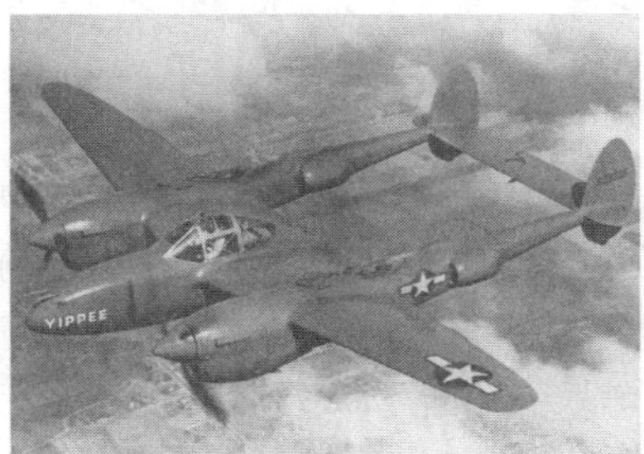

The Lockheed P-38 Lightning was a World War II American twin-engine fighter designed as a high-altitude interceptor. The "P" stands for "Pursuit." It was designed to fly at 413 mph, about 100 mph faster than any other aircraft of the period. It had twice the power and almost twice the size of its predecessors.

The multi-engine configuration reduced its loss-rate to anti-aircraft gunfire during ground attack missions, enabling the pilot to return if one engine was damaged. It had distinctive twin booms and a single, central nacelle containing the cockpit and armament, earning it the nick-name "fork-tailed devil" by the Luftwaffe and "two planes, one pilot" by the Japanese.

It was unusually quiet for a fighter, the exhaust being muffled by the turbo-superchargers. It was the first fighter with the so-called "tricycle" undercarriage, instead of the two wheels in front and a small wheel under the tail.

This technological marvel was the fighter of choice for pilots and was used in a number of roles, including dive bombing, skip bombing, high- and low-altitude bomber escort, and air-to-air combat. It was also used for high-altitude level bombing, ground-support bombing and strafing, day and night reconnaissance (photographic and visual), and extensively as a long-range escort fighter when equipped with drop tanks under its wings. The plane carried high explosive and incendiary bomb loads of up to 4,000 pounds, competing with the early WWII bomber aircraft. It operated in every imaginable weather condition.

The P-38 could not out-turn the A6M Zero and most other Japanese fighters but had superior speed coupled with a good rate of climb. Its focused firepower was concentrated in the central fuselage pod, eliminating the need for a propeller synchronizer. It shot a parallel stream of four .50-cal. machine guns and one 20mm cannon, which allowed aerial victory at much longer distances than fighters carrying wing guns.

It had enough firepower to sink a ship, and sometimes did. It helped win the Battle of the Bismarck Sea, a crushing defeat for the Japanese, and was responsible for killing Admiral Isoroku Yamamoto, the architect of Japan's naval strategy in the Pacific, including the attack on Pearl Harbor.

In the Pacific theater, the P-38 downed over 1,800 Japanese aircraft, more than any other USAAF fighter. More than 100 P-38 pilots became aces by downing five or more enemy aircraft. America's top aces, Richard Bong (40 victories) and Thomas McGuire (38 victories) flew the P-38.

As a World War II fighter, the Lightning's legacy is unmatched. Approximately 10,000 P-38s were built during the war – including 18 distinct models – flying more than 130,000 missions in theaters around the world. P-38 pilots shot down more Japanese aircraft than any other fighter and, as a reconnaissance aircraft, obtained 90 percent of the aerial film captured over Europe.

See www.lockheedmartin.com/us/100years/stories/p-38.html
and www.p38assn.org

TECHNICAL NOTES (P-38L):

Name: Lockheed P-38 Lightning

Crew: 1

Armament

Guns:
 1 x Hispano M2(C) 20 mm cannon,
 4 x Colt-Browning 50-cal. machine guns

Bombs/Rockets:
 10 x 5 in High Velocity Aircraft Rockets, or 4 x M10 three-tube 4.5 in, or up to 4,000 lbs in bombs

Powerplant: 2 x Allison V-1710-111/113 liquid-cooled turbo-supercharged V-12, 1,725 hp

Propeller: Three-bladed

Performance:
 Maximum speed: 443 mph
 Cruising speed: 275 mph

Range: 1,300 miles (combat)
Service ceiling: 44,000 ft

Dimensions:
Wingspan: 52 ft
Length: 37 ft 10 in
Height: 9 ft 10 in
Weight: 12,780 lbs empty; 17,500 lbs loaded

Reference: www.nationalmuseum.af.mil/factsheets/factsheet.asp?id=495

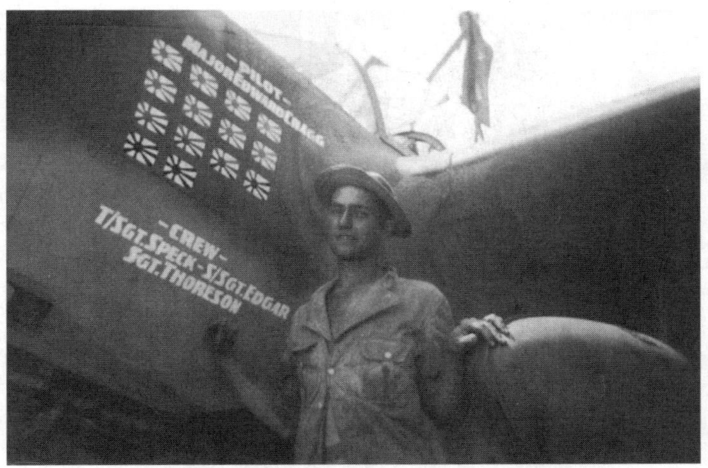

Dad with Major Edward Cragg's P-38 named "Porky II" 11 days before it was shot down.

Curtis Bertrand standing by Major Edward Cragg's P-38 named "Porky II." His left hand is on one of the belly tanks, otherwise known as a drop tank or external fuel tank. He has a nice score of 14 Jap planes shot down so far as of the date this photo was taken on Dec. 15, 1943, which was 11 days before he got shot down.

Edward "Porky" Cragg (Sept. 8, 1919 – missing in action Dec. 26, 1943 – finding of death Jan. 16, 1946) was a triple ace (15 kills) and a major in the United States Army Air Forces.

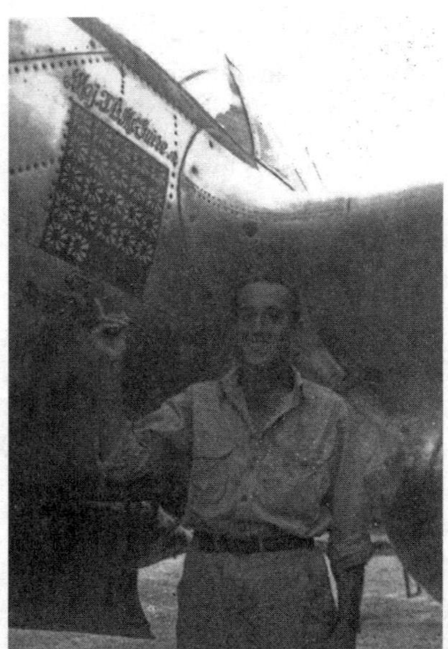

A co-worker is standing proudly next to "Pudgy III," Major McGuire's plane.

"Pudgy III" is a P-38 Lightning; squadron plane number is 131. The plane was flown by WWII Ace Major Thomas B. McGuire, who was assigned to the 431st Fighter Squadron of the 475th Fighter Group known as Satan's Angels. There are 22 Japanese flags on the plane saying how many planes he shot down when this photo was taken in August 1944. 'Mac' was the USA's top scoring ace behind Dick Bong. 'Mac' was killed when his drop tank-laden P-38 Lightning plowed into the ground during a dogfight over the Philippines, on January 7th, 1945. His last P-38, 'Pudgy V', had 38 'kills' painted on it, 2 less than Dick Bong.

For more information visit

www.warbirdregistry.org/p38registry/p38-4453015.html

www.pacificwrecks.com/aircraft/p-38/44-24155.html

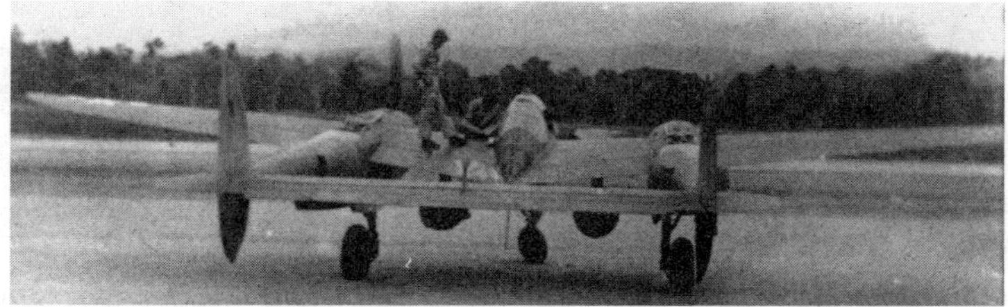

P-38 being serviced.

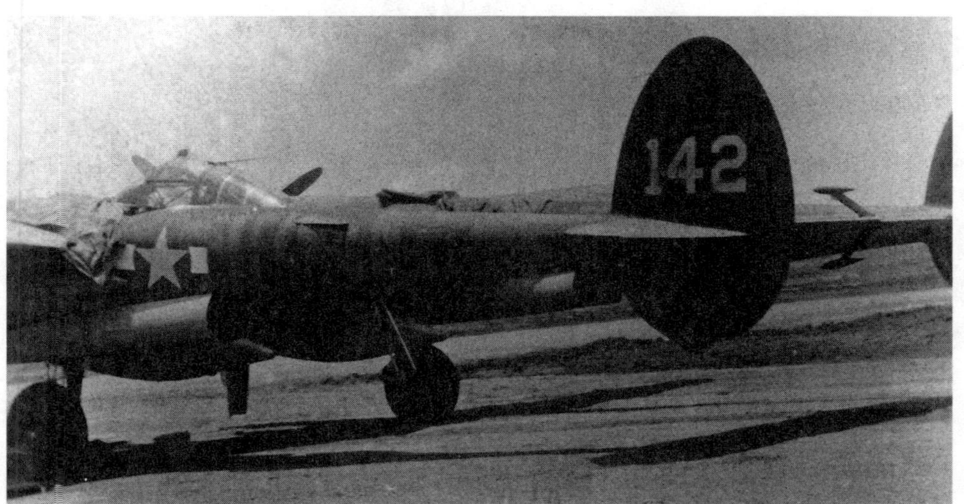

Plane #142 being serviced.

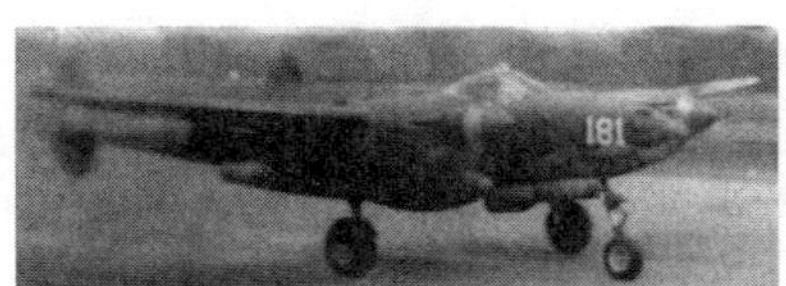

A zoomed-in photo of a P-38 taking off to hit the enemy. Plane #181.

Section 6

Bell P-39 Airacobra

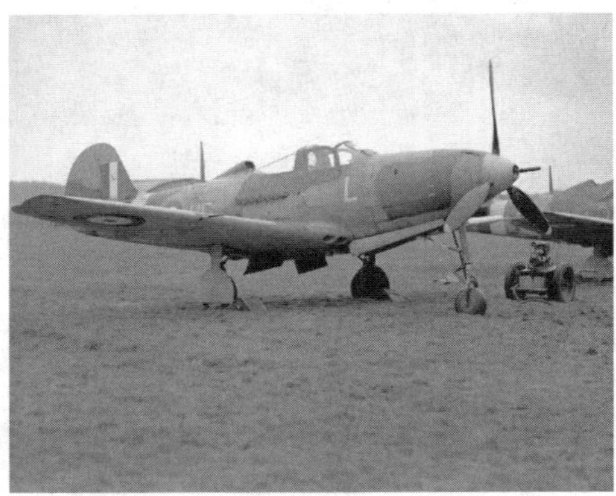

The Bell P-39 Airacobra was an all-metal, low-wing, single-engine fighter with a tricycle undercarriage. It was equipped with an Allison V-1710 liquid-cooled V-12 engine that produced 1,150 hp. The P-39 was the first to have the engine installed in the center fuselage, behind the cockpit.

It was handicapped by the absence of an efficient turbo-supercharger, limiting it to low-altitude work. It was one of the principal American fighter aircraft in service when the United States entered World War II.

In both Western Europe and the Pacific, the Airacobra found itself outclassed as an interceptor, its earliest proposed role, and the type was gradually relegated to other duties. The P-39 performed best below 17,000 feet (5,200 m) altitude.

Though outclassed by Japanese fighter planes, it performed well at altitudes below 17,000 feet (5,200 m). It excelled at missions such as ground strafing and bombing runs, often proving deadly in ground attacks on Japanese forces trying to retake Henderson Field on Guadalcanal. P-39s did not score more aerial victories in the Solomons due to the aircraft's limited range and poor high-altitude performance.

Airacobras fought Japanese Zeros over New Guinea from May to August 1942 on a regular basis. The P-39 was phased out in New Guinea in 1943 because there were too many design flaws, such as the guns jamming, and did not attain air superiority over the Japanese Zero.

It was the least well-regarded fighter aircraft to serve in large numbers with the USAAF during the Second World War. Despite this, it did perform some useful services on New Guinea and Guadalcanal early in the war in the Pacific, as well as serving as a training aircraft used by the majority of American fighter pilots.

The unusual layout of the Airacobra was dictated by the choice of the American Armament Corporation T-9 37mm cannon as its main weapon, firing through the propeller spinner. This large gun left no room in the nose for the engine, so it was placed behind the pilot. This then required the use of a long propeller drive shaft running under the pilot's seat.

The Airacobra was never outstanding in combat. Ironically, it was extremely difficult to service because of the engine placement. The final model, the P-63 Kingcobra, was considerably improved.

See www.aviation-history.com/bell/p39.html

TECHNICAL NOTES:

Name: Bell P-39 Airacobra

Role: Fighter

Crew: 1

Armament:
- 1 x 37 mm M4 cannon
- 2 x 50-cal. machine guns
- 4 x 30-cal. machine guns
- Up to 500 lbs. of bombs

Powerplant: 1 × Allison V-1710-85 liquid-cooled V-12, 1,200 hp

Propeller: Three-bladed

Performance:
- Maximum speed: 376 mph
- Cruising speed: 330 mph at 5000 ft
- Range: 300 miles typical, 975 miles max
- Service ceiling: 35,000 ft

Dimensions:
- Wingspan: 34 ft
- Length: 30 ft 2 in
- Height: 12 ft 5 in
- Weight: 5,347 lbs empty, 7,379 lbs loaded,
- Maximum Takeoff Weight: 8,400 lbs

Reference: www.nationalmuseum.af.mil/factsheets/factsheet.asp?id=2207

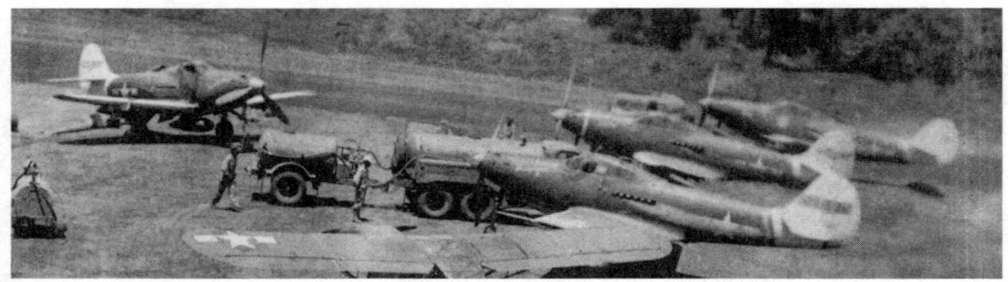

P-39 Airacobras being serviced at the airdrome.

The four single-wing fighter aircraft are P-39 Airacobras. The P-39 had the engine behind the pilot. Notice the fuel trucks refueling the planes.

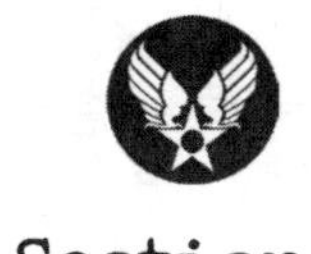

Section 7

Curtiss P-40 Warhawk

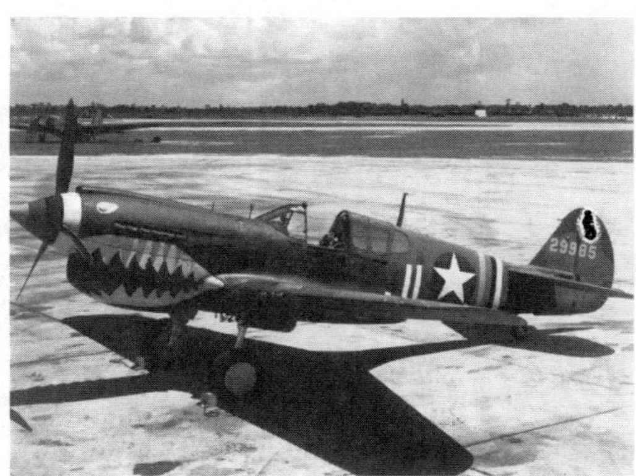

The Curtiss P-40 Warhawk was an American single-engine, single-seat, all-metal fighter and ground attack aircraft that first flew in 1938. It had good agility, especially at high speed and medium to low altitude. It was one of the tightest-turning monoplane fighters of the war. However, poor ground visibility and the relatively narrow landing gear track led to many losses upon landing.

The P-40 was America's foremost fighter in service when World War II began. It engaged Japanese aircraft during the attack on Pearl Harbor and the invasion of the Philippines in December 1941.

Though often outclassed by its adversaries in speed, maneuverability and rate of climb, the P-40 earned a reputation in battle for extreme ruggedness. Other positive attributes were good armor, firepower, roll rate, and dive speed, making it one of the best low-altitude fighters of the war. Japanese pilots rated the Warhawk their most dangerous foe at low altitude.

They also were flown in China early in 1942 by the famed Flying Tigers. After only six months of combat the Flying Tigers had shot down 297 enemy aircraft confirmed, (and another 153 probable), for only 12 planes lost in combat. The P-40 was the main USAAF fighter aircraft in the southwest Pacific and Pacific Ocean theaters during 1941-42. They were flown in North Africa in 1943 by the first AAF all-black unit, the 99th Fighter Squadron.

In order for the U.S. to win the war, air superiority had to be taken from the Japanese. Otherwise, the enemy bombers would be able to fly unopposed over Allied ships and territory. The P-40s of the 49th Fighter Group reached New Guinea in time to take part in the allied counterattack. They played an important role in stopping Japanese reinforcements reaching New Guinea by attacking shipping in the Bismarck Sea. It also helped to win air superiority over Guadalcanal.

However, the bulk of the fighter operations by the USAAF in 1942-43 were borne by the P-40 and the P-39 Airacobra. In the Pacific, these two fighters, along with the U.S. Navy's Grumman F4F Wildcat, contributed more than any other U.S. types to breaking Japanese air power during this critical period. However, their role in New Guinea was short-lived. Their last aerial victory came in May 1943.

In 1945, the 71st Reconnaissance Group employed them as armed forward air controllers during ground operations in the Philippines until it received delivery of P-51s. They claimed 655 aerial victories. The P-40 pilots, with their superior observation, began directing artillery fire onto the Japanese from the air via radio, as well as carrying out their own strafing and bombing.

It was the third most produced American fighter after the P-51 Mustang and P-47 Thunderbolt. At the end of the P-40's brilliant career, more than 14,000 had been produced for service in the air forces of 28 nations. Fifty-two hundred P-40Ns were built, more than any other version.

TECHNICAL NOTES:

Name: Curtiss P-40 Warhawk

Role: Fighter

Crew: 1

Armament:
- 6 × 50-cal M2 Browning machine guns
- 250 to 1,000 lb bombs to a total of 2,000 lb

Powerplant: 1 × Allison V-1710-39 liquid-cooled V12 engine, 1,150 hp

Propeller: Three-bladed

Performance:
- Maximum speed: 360 mph
- Cruising speed: 235
- Range: 850 miles
- Service ceiling: 29,000 ft

Dimensions:
Wingspan: 37.33 ft
Length: 31.67 ft
Height: 12.33 ft
Weight: 6,350 lbs empty, 8,280 lbs loaded;
Maximum Takeoff Weight: 8,810 lbs

Reference: www.nationalmuseum.af.mil/factsheets/factsheet.asp?id=2208
www.chuckhawks.com/p40.htm

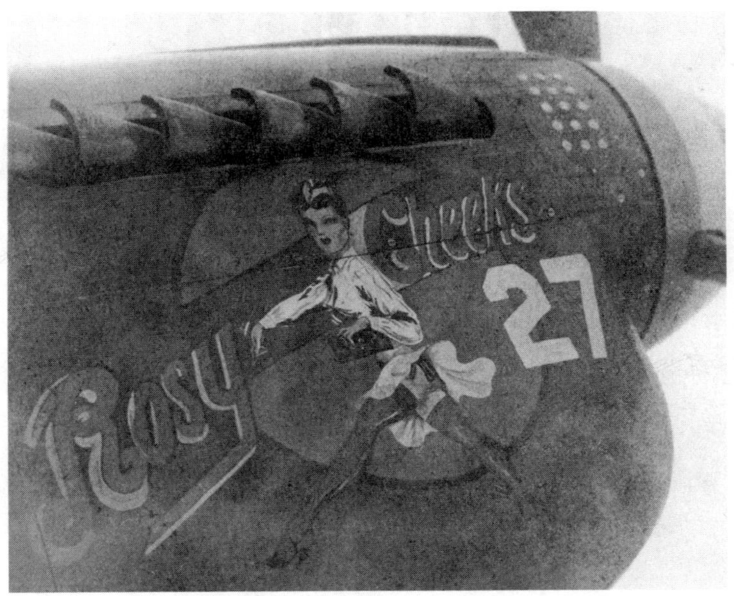

Rosy Cheeks. Biak 1944.

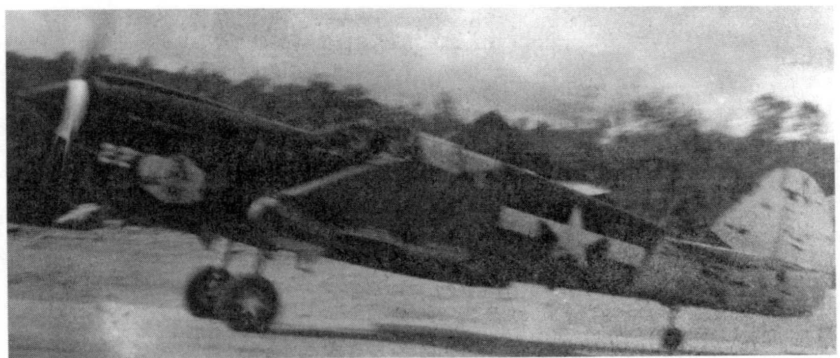

P-40 is taking off. Biak 1944.

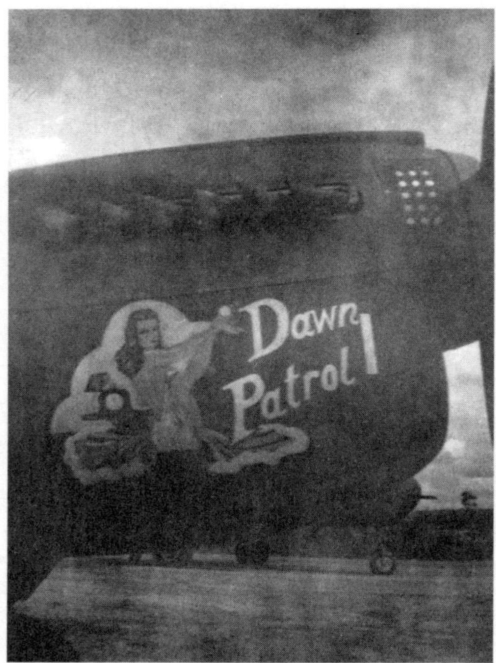

Dawn Patrol. Biak 1944.

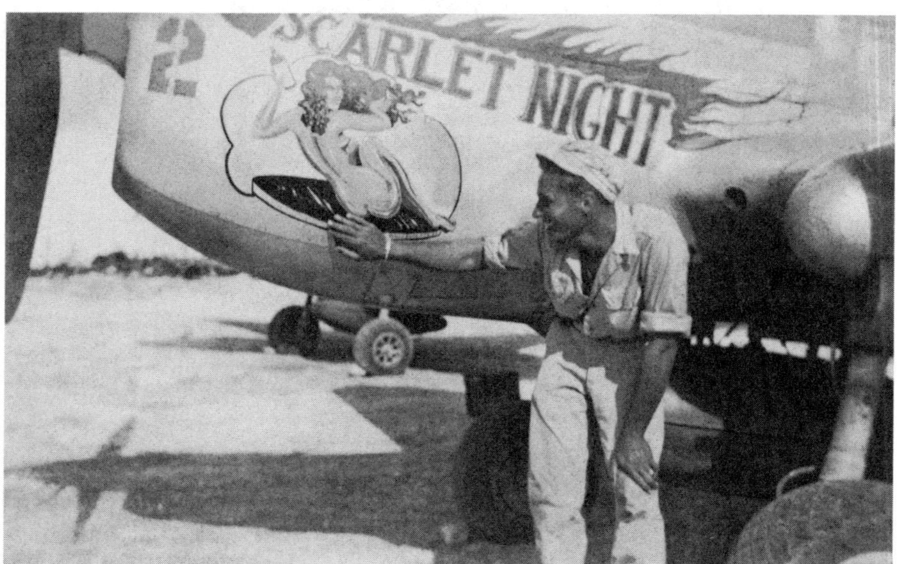

Dad admires the artwork on Scarlet Night. Biak, August 1944.

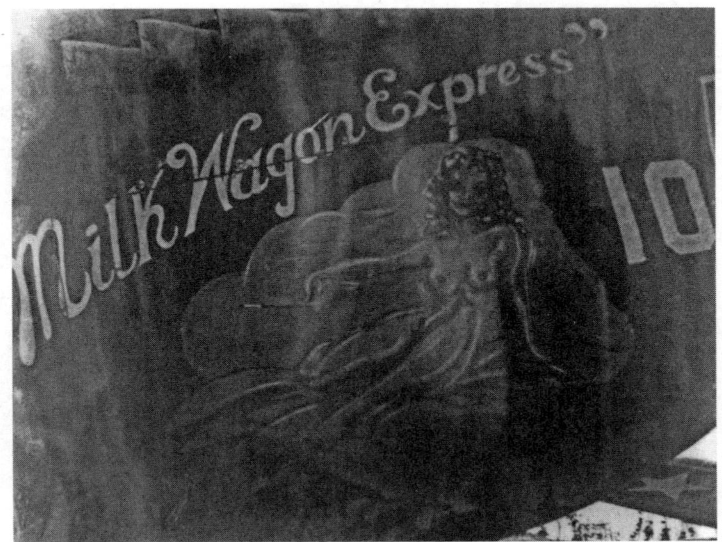

Milk Wagon Express

Curtiss P-40N Warhawk, 49th Fighter Group, 7th Flight Squadron, Dobodura, New Guinea, 1943. It later had its number changed from 10 to 00 and the artwork was changed to "Daddy Please."

See www.replicainscale.blogspot.com/

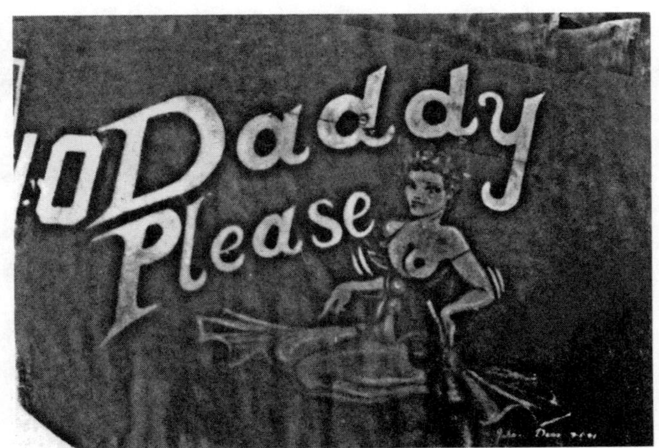

Daddy Please was assigned to 49th Fighter Group's 7th Squadron.

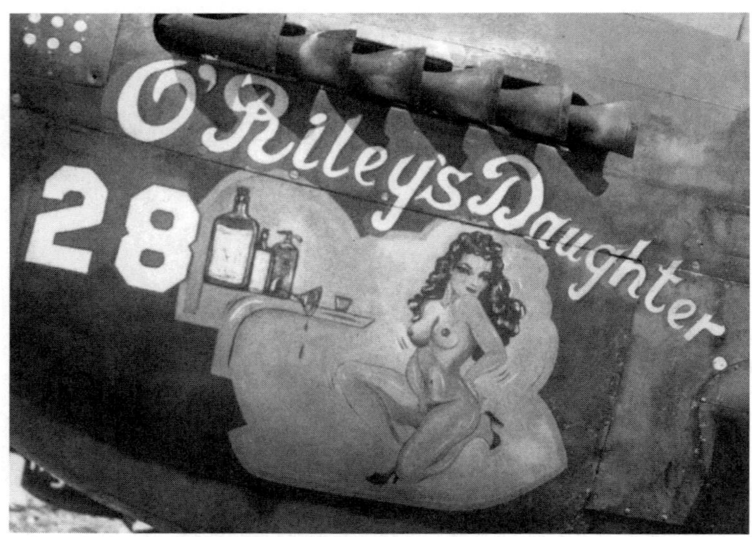

O'Riley's Daughter
This artwork is based on the popular wartime drinking song by the same name.

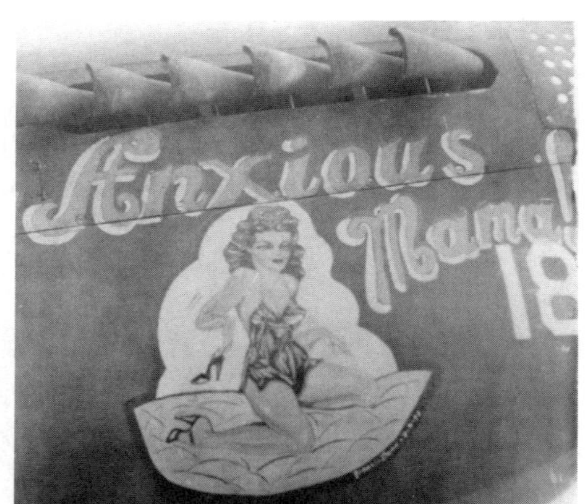

Closeup of My Anxious Mama! Aug. 1944.

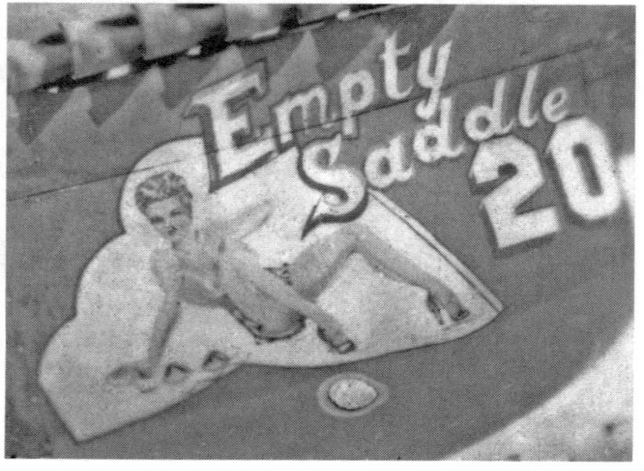

Empty Saddle

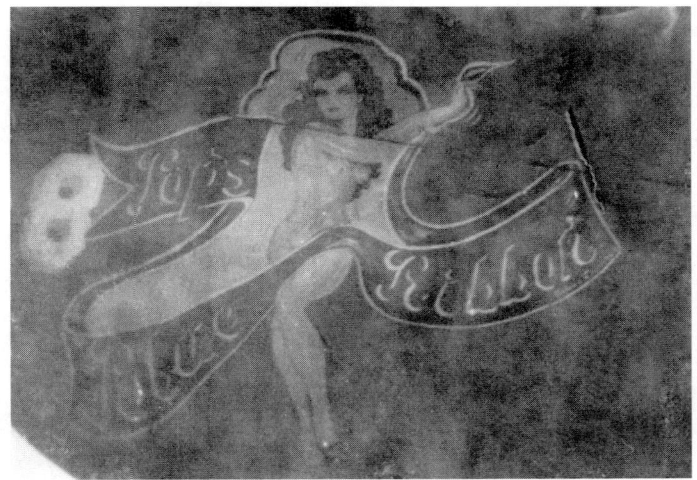

Pop's Blue Ribbon

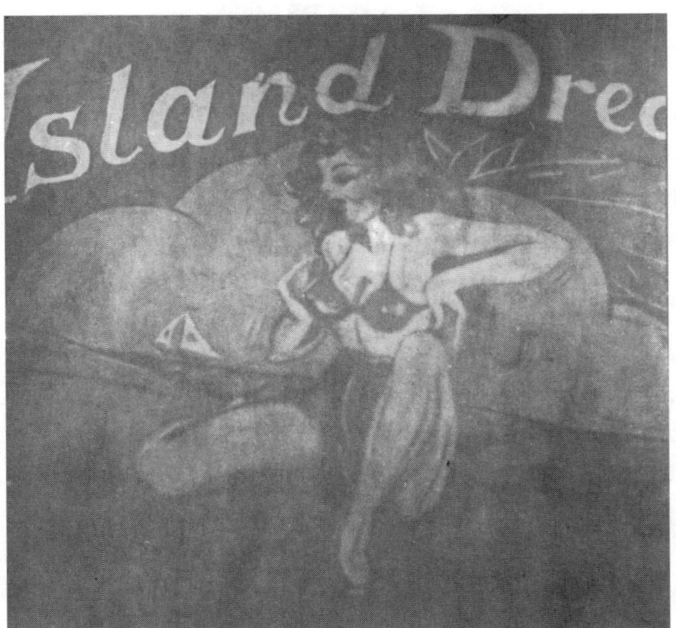

Island Dream

"Island Dream" was a P-40 Warhawk assigned to 49th Fighter Group's 7th Squadron, #15. Most pictures of it on the Internet show a different version with the word "Island" missing as well as the sailboat. This is perhaps due to damage that occurred to this side of the plane and then having been repaired.

Section 8

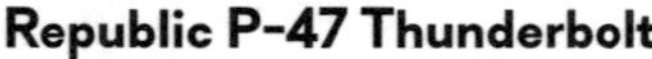

Republic P-47 Thunderbolt

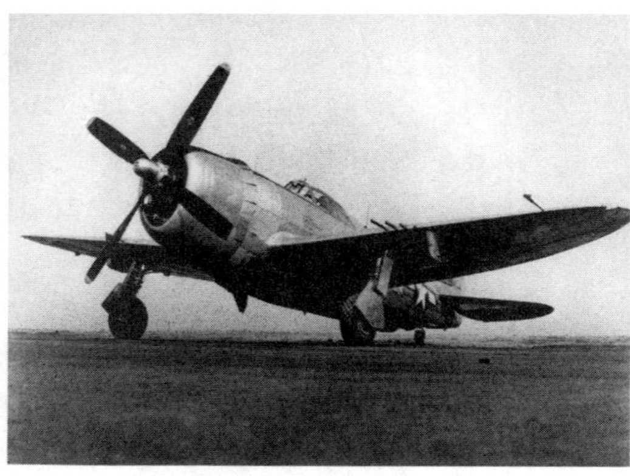

Affectionately nicknamed "The Jug," (because it was shaped like a milk jug, or it was short for "juggernaut"), the Republic P-47 Thunderbolt was one of the most famous Army Air Forces (AAF) fighter planes of WWII. Although originally conceived as a lightweight interceptor, the P-47 developed as a heavyweight fighter.

The P-47 Thunderbolt was the largest, heaviest, and most expensive fighter aircraft in history to be powered by a single reciprocating engine. It had a super-turbocharger and a four-blade propeller.

It was heavily armed with eight .50-caliber machine guns, four per wing. When fully loaded, the P-47 weighed up to eight tons, and in the fighter-bomber ground attack roles could carry five-inch rockets and/or a significant bomb load of 2,500 pounds. The armored cockpit was roomy inside, comfortable for the pilot, and offered good visibility.

The Thunderbolt ended the war with 3,752 air-to-air kills claimed in over 746,000 sorties of all types. Thunderbolt units claimed destroyed: 11,874 enemy aircraft (in the air and on the ground), 86,000 railroad cars, 9,000 locomotives, 6,000 armored fighting vehicles, and 68,000 trucks at the cost of 3,499 P-47s lost to all causes in combat. It broke the back of Germany's Luftwaffe in the critical period of January – May 1944.

Used as both a high-altitude escort fighter and a low-level fighter-bomber, the P-47 quickly gained a reputation for ruggedness. M and N series production aircraft were given clear "bubble" canopies, which gave the pilot improved rearward vision.

The P-47 Thunderbolt was not generally welcomed in the Pacific theatre. It was seen as too clumsy to compete with the very agile Japanese fighters and it did not have the range for operations over the vast expanses of the Pacific.

Worse, the P-47 was best at the high altitudes at which American bombers operated over Europe. However, in Japan most combat occurred below 20,000 feet, where the P-47 was at its least maneuverable. P-47 squadrons later saw heavy action in the Philippines campaign, and longer-range P-47Ns flew escort and fighter sweep missions over the Japanese mainland from bases in Okinawa.

In the Pacific, Colonel Neel E. Kearby of the Fifth Air Force destroyed 22 Japanese aircraft and was awarded the Medal of Honor for an action in which he downed six enemy fighters on a single mission. He was shot down and killed over Wewak, New Guinea, in March 1944.

See www.nationalmuseum.af.mil/factsheets/factsheet.asp?id=2213
and www.historyofwar.org/articles/weapons_P-47_pacific.html

TECHNICAL NOTES:

Name: Republic P-47 Thunderbolt; Nickname: The Jug

Role: Fighter, bomber escort, dive bomber, ground attack

Crew: 1

Armament

8 × 50-cal. (12.7 mm) M2 Browning machine guns
Up to 2,500 lb of bombs
10 x 5-inch unguided rockets

Powerplant: 1 × Pratt & Whitney R-2800-59 twin-row radial engine, 2,535 hp

Propeller: Four-bladed

Performance:

Maximum speed: 433 mph
Cruising speed: 350 mph
Range: 800 miles (combat)
Service ceiling: 43,000 ft

Dimensions:

Wingspan: 40 ft 9 in
Length: 36 ft 1 in
Height: 14 ft 8 in
Weight: 10,000 lbs empty; 17,500 lbs loaded

Reference: www.warbirdalley.com/p47.htm

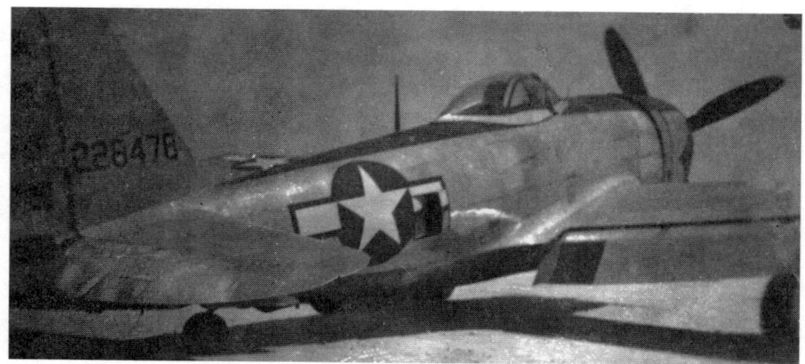

With bubble canopy.
At Mokmer Drome on Biak, 1944.

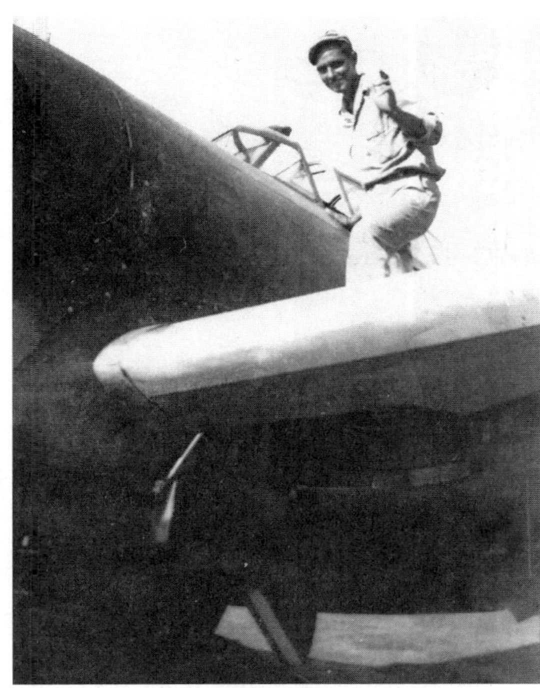

**On plane wing of P-47.
New Guinea, May 1944.**

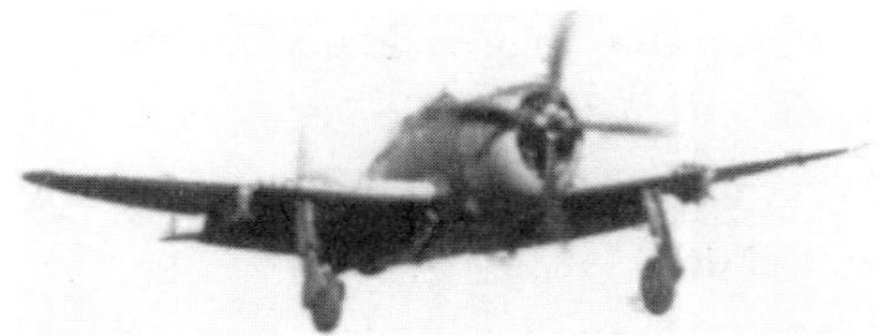

**Coming in
for a landing.
New Guinea, 1944.**

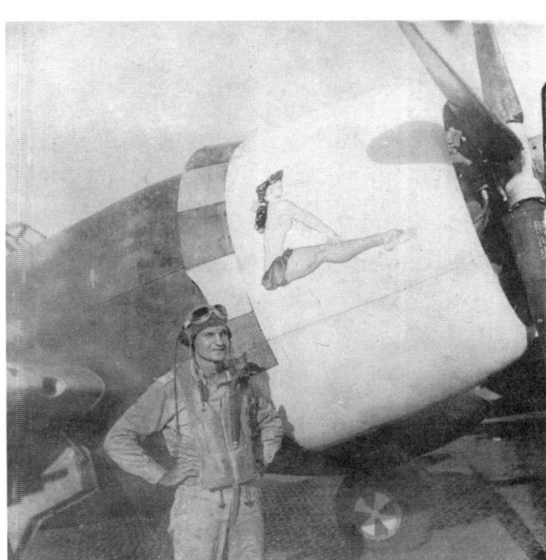

**P-47 and pilot.
New Guinea, 1943.**

Section 9

Douglas C-47 Skytrain

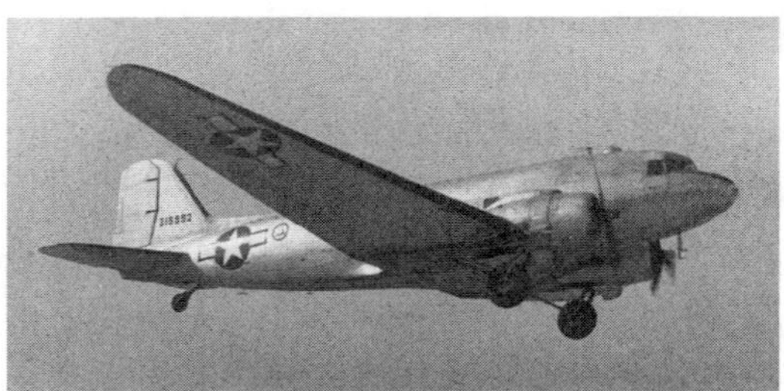

The Army Air Forces selected a modified version of the DC-3, the C-47 Skytrain, to become its standard transport aircraft. It had two 1,200-hp Pratt & Whitney R-1830-S1C3G Twin Wasp radial piston engines. Major modifications to the aircraft included a reinforced fuselage floor, the addition of a large cargo door, fitting of cargo hooks beneath the center wing section, and the removal of the tail cone to mount a hook for towing gliders.

As a supply plane, the C-47 could carry up to 6,000 pounds of cargo. It could also hold a fully assembled jeep or a 37 mm cannon. As a troop transport, it carried 28 soldiers in full combat gear. As a medical airlift plane, it could accommodate 14 stretcher patients and three nurses.

Every branch of the U.S. military and the entire major Allied powers flew it. It came to be known universally as the "Gooney Bird."

The C-47s carried personnel and cargo around the globe. They also towed troop-carrying gliders, dropped paratroops into enemy territory, and air evacuated sick or wounded patients.

If a glider landed in a combat zone undamaged, a C-47 could tow it back to base to be reused for more flights. Gliders landing in small fields where C-47s could not land had to be disassembled and hauled out, which took time and manpower. Therefore, the U.S. Army Air Forces developed a way for a C-47 to fly low across the field with a hook and "snatch" a glider into the air.

It was also used as a fighting machine as the AC-47D gunship ("Puff, the Magic Dragon") of the Vietnam war, where the plane was equipped with three modernized Gatling guns (General Electric Co. 7.62 mm "Miniguns," each mounted and firing from the left side) for use as a target suppressor, circling a target, and laying down massive fire to eliminate or at least subdue the enemy position.

The 6th Airlift Squadron made airlift history during World War II when, in October 1942, it was transferred to Port Moresby, New Guinea. Then flying C-47s, the 6th became the first personnel transport squadron to fly in the Pacific. It was during this assignment that the squadron earned the nickname Bully Beef Express, as it carried tons of boiled beef to Allied combat troops in Australia and New Guinea. The French term for boiled beef is *bouilli boeuf*, and the Americanization of the term has continued to this day to be the squadron's emblem.

TECHNICAL NOTES

Name: Douglas C-47 Skytrain; Nickname: Gooney Bird, Biscuit Bomber

Role: transport up to 6000 lbs of cargo or 28 troops

Crew: 4

Armament: None

Powerplant: 2 × Pratt & Whitney R-1830-90C Twin Wasp 14-cylinder radial engines, 1,200 hp (895 kW) each

Propeller: Three-bladed

Performance:
Maximum speed: 224 mph (195 kn, 360 km/h)
Cruising speed: 160 mph (139 kn, 257 km/h)
Range: max 3800 miles, normal 1600 miles (1,391 nmi, 2,575 km)
Service ceiling: 24,000 ft

Dimensions:
Wingspan: 95 ft 6 in
Length: 63 ft 9 in
Height: 17 ft
Weight: 31,000 lbs

Reference: www.boeing.com/boeing/history/mdc/skytrain.page
www.warbirdalley.com/c47.htm

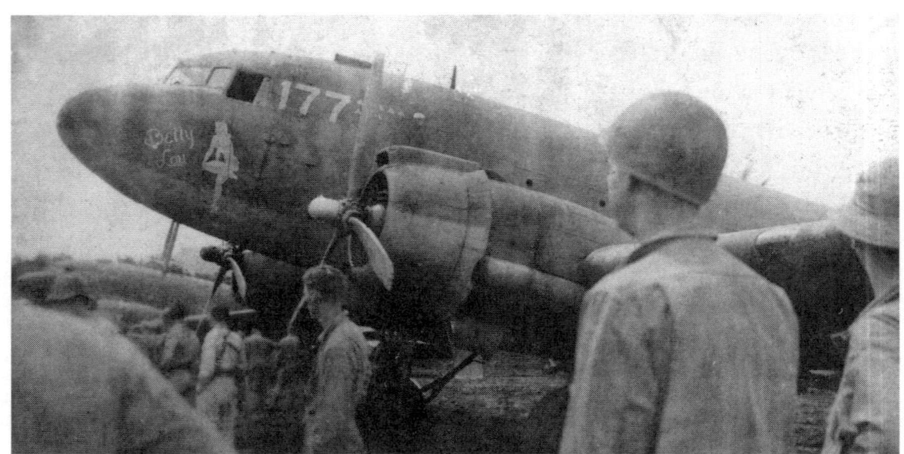

Betty Lou. New Guinea, 1944.

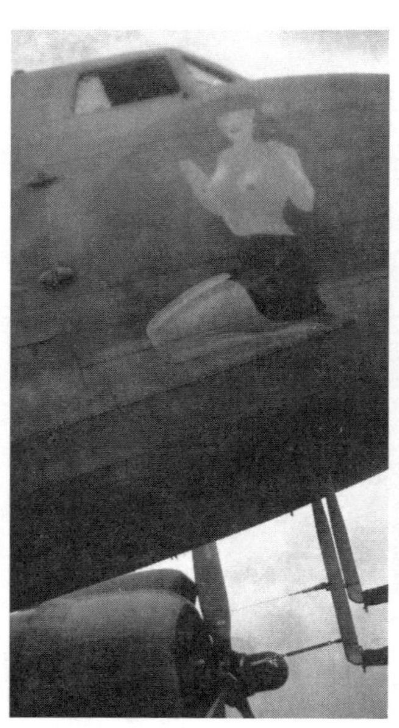

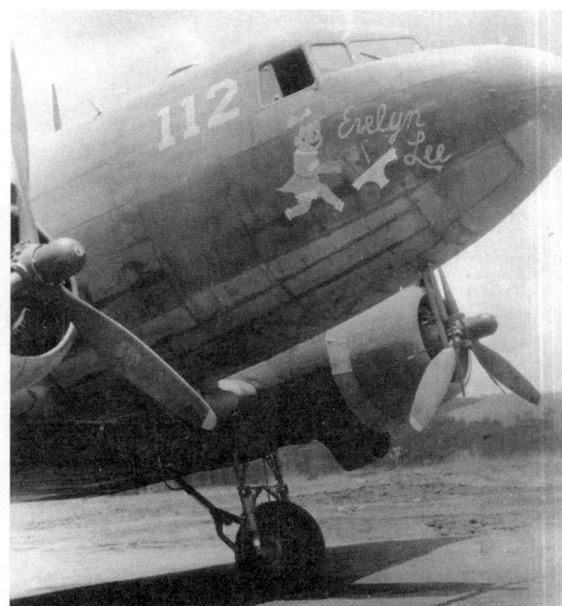

Evelyn Lee

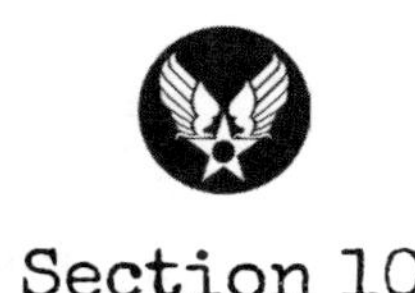

Section 10

Douglas C-54 SkyMaster

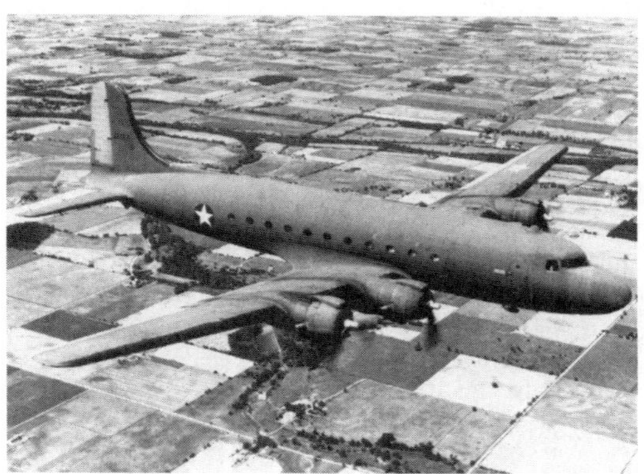

The Douglas C-54 Skymaster was a four-engine transport aircraft used by the United States Army Air Forces and British forces in World War II and the Korean War. Besides transport of cargo, it also carried presidents, British heads of government, and military staff.

Dozens of variants of the C-54 were employed in a wide variety of noncombat roles such as air-sea rescue, scientific and military research, and missile tracking and recovery. During the Berlin Airlift it hauled coal and food supplies to West Berlin.

After the Korean War it continued to be used for military and civilian uses by more than thirty countries. This was one of the first aircraft to carry the president of the United States and to assume the call sign Air Force One. Dubbed "The Sacred Cow," this was the plane that took the president to Tehran, Casablanca, and Hawaii.

The Douglas C-54 Skymaster was the military version of the DC-4 airliner and was the first truly effective four-engine transport aircraft to enter USAAF service.

It had a circular fuselage and used a tricycle undercarriage. It could carry 40 passengers in ten rows of four seats or 28 passengers in a sleeper version.

The first C-54 Skymaster entered USAAF service on March 20, 1942, and by the end of the year enough had been delivered to begin to make a real impact on the war effort. It was used on the long-range routes that linked the continental United States with the various theatres of war, while the shorter ranged C-47s did much of the work in-theatre.

TECHNICAL NOTES

Name: Douglas C-54 Skymaster

Role: Transport of cargo and passengers

Crew: 6 plus 2 relief members

Armament: None

Powerplant: Four 1,450-hp Pratt & Whitney R-2000-2SD-13G Twin Wasp radial piston engines

Propeller: Three-bladed

Performance:
Maximum speed: 274 mph
Cruising speed: 190 mph
Range: 3,900 miles
Service ceiling: 22,300

Dimensions:
Wingspan: 117 ft 6 in
Length: 93 ft
Height: 27 ft 6 in
Weight: Empty 43,300 lbs, Max Takeoff 73,000 lbs

Reference:
www.historyofwar.org/articles/weapons_douglas_C-54_skymaster.html
www.warbirdalley.com/c54.htm

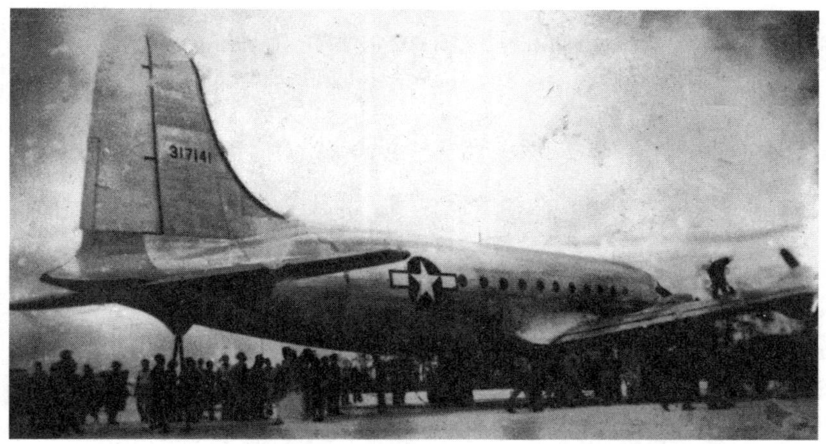

Bob Hope's tourist ship at Mokmer airdrome on Biak.

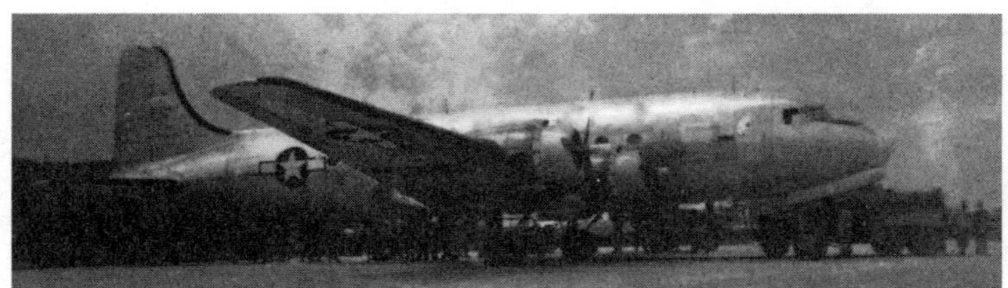

Above is Bob Hope's tourist ship, a Douglas C-54 SkyMaster, after landing at Mokmer Airdrome on Biak. He and his fellow USO show entertainers came in 1944 and put on two performances in Biak. For more information on this plane see: www.warbirdsresourcegroup.org/URG/c54skymaster.html

Section 11

Consolidated OA-10 or PBY Catalina

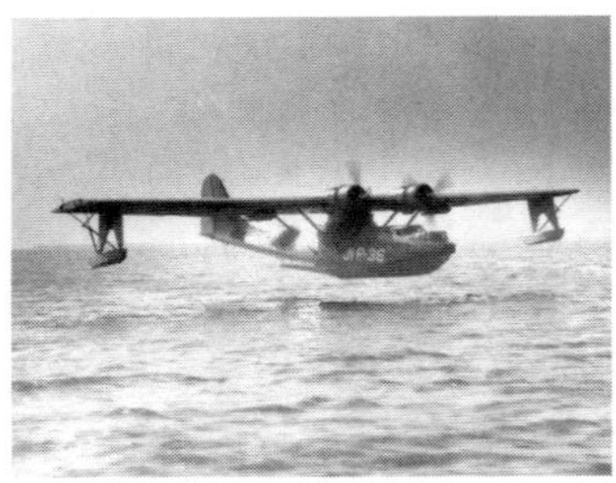

The OA-10 was quite a large aircraft. It was equipped with a flying boat hull, retractable tricycle landing gear, and retractable wing-tip floats. To keep the engines and propellers away from the water spray, the wing was put on top of a sturdy pylon and braced with two struts on each side.

The OA-10 flying boat was the U.S. Army Air Force version of the PBY series flown extensively by the U.S. Navy during World War II. The Navy designation for it was PBY Catalina, whereas in the U.S. Army Air Force, its designation was OA-10 Catalina. The initials PB represent "Patrol Bomber" and Y being the code used for the aircraft's manufacturer, Consolidated Vultee Aircraft Corporation.

During World War II, PBYs were used in anti-submarine warfare, patrol bombing, convoy escorts, and cargo transport. It was a Catalina that first located the advancing Japanese forces during the decisive Battle of Midway.

The Catalina also proved effective in air-sea search and rescue missions, code-named "Dumbo," taken from the unofficial nickname for any air-sea rescue aircraft, including flying boats. Small detachments, normally of three PBYs, routinely orbited on standby near targeted combat areas. One detachment based in the Solomon Islands rescued 161 airmen between Jan. 1 and Aug. 15, 1943, and successes increased steadily as equipment and tactics improved.

The development of effective radar, and Japanese reliance on night transport, led to the development of the "Black Cat Squadrons." These crews performed nighttime search and attack missions in their black-painted PBYs. The tactics were spectacularly successful and seriously disrupted the flow of supplies and personnel to Japanese island bases.

TECHNICAL NOTES

Name: Consolidated OA-10 or PBY Catalina; Nickname: Cat, Dumbo

Role: Maritime flying boat, patrol bomber

Crew: 7 to 9

Armament:
3 × .30 cal (7.62 mm) machine guns
(two in nose turret, one in ventral hatch at tail)
2 × .50 cal (12.7 mm) machine guns (one in each waist blister)
4,000 lb (1,814 kg) of bombs, mines or depth charges;
torpedo racks were also available

Powerplant: 2 Pratt & Whitney R-1830-92 14-cylinder Twin Wasp air-cooled radial engines generating 1,200 hp each.

Propeller: Three-bladed

Performance:
Maximum speed: 179 mph (288 kmh; 156 kts)
Cruising speed: 155 mph (250 km/h)
Range: 2,545 miles (4,095 km)
Service ceiling: 14,698 ft (4,480 m; 2.8 miles)

Dimensions:
Wingspan: 104 ft (31.72 m)
Length: 63 (19.46 m)
Height: 22 ft 5 in (5.65 m)
Empty Weight: 20,911 lbs (9,485 kg); Loaded: 36,400 lbs

Reference: www.warbirdalley.com/cat.htm and
www.nationalmuseum.af.mil/factsheets/factsheet.asp?id=522

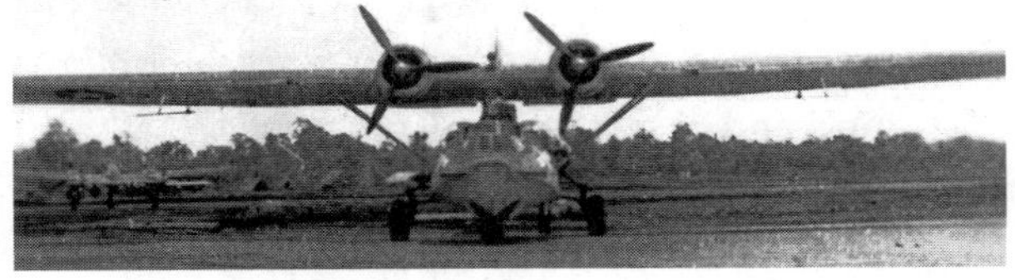

Consolidated PBY Catalina twin-engine Navy patrol boat.

Section 12

Martin M-130 China Clipper

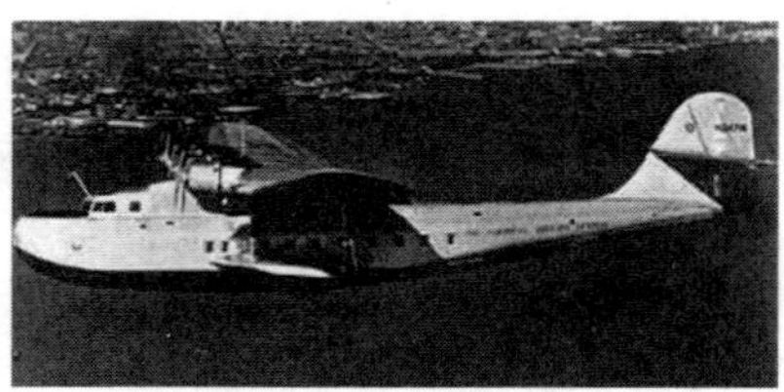

The Martin M-130 was a commercial flying boat designed and built in 1935 by the Glenn L. Martin Company in Baltimore, Maryland, for Pan American Airways. They were the first successful transoceanic intercontinental airliners. They were designed to Pan Am's specifications for long haul, over-water service with payload capacity, and cabins outfitted for passenger comfort.

Only three Martin M-130s were built: the China Clipper, the Philippine Clipper, and the Hawaii Clipper. Martin designated them as the Martin Ocean Transports, but to the public they were all referred to as the China Clipper, a name that evolved into a generic term for Pan Am's entire fleet of large flying boats.

The China Clipper flew numerous scheduled flights as well as military missions in both the Pacific and the Atlantic. It was instrumental in delivering a shipment of uranium ore from Africa for the Manhattan Project.

The Martin M-130 was the first airliner that could fly nonstop the 2,400-mile (3,840-kilometer) distance between San Francisco and Honolulu, Hawaii, the longest major route in the world without an emergency intermediate landing field. The China Clipper and its sister ships demonstrated that there were no technological barriers to transoceanic travel.

Its sister ships, the Hawaii Clipper and the Philippine Clipper both crashed, the former into the ocean in 1938 and the latter into a mountain in 1943. After more than three million miles of service, the final Martin M-130, the China Clipper, broke up and sank during landing at Port of Spain, Trinidad and Tobago, on Jan. 8, 1945, killing 23 of the 30 aboard.

TECHNICAL NOTES

Name: Martin M-130; Nickname: China Clipper

Crew: 5 and then eventually 8

Armament: None

Powerplant: 4x Pratt & Whitney R-1830-S2A5G Twin Wasp 14-cylinder Radial Engines (830 horsepower each – later 950 hp with hydromatic propellers)

Propeller: Triple blade

Performance:
- Maximum speed: 180 mph
- Cruising speed: 163 mph
- Range: 3,200 miles / 5150 km
- Service ceiling: 17,000 feet / 5,182 m

Payload: 36 passengers

Dimensions:
- Wingspan: 130 ft
- Length: 91 ft
- Weight: 52,850 pounds

Reference: www.flyingclippers.com/M130.html

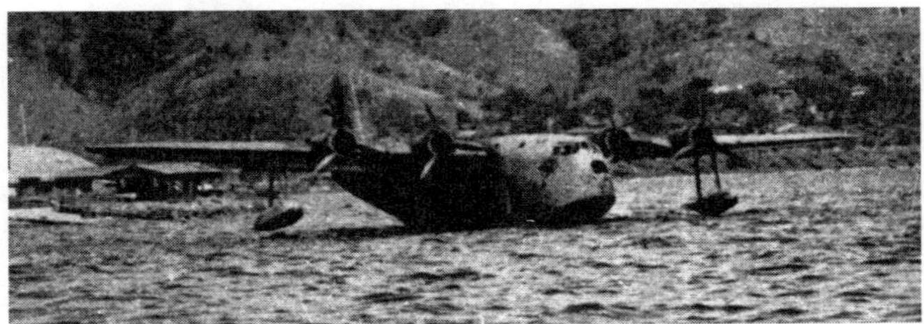

Martin M-130 China Clipper, known as a flying boat.

Section 13

Stinson L-5 Sentinel

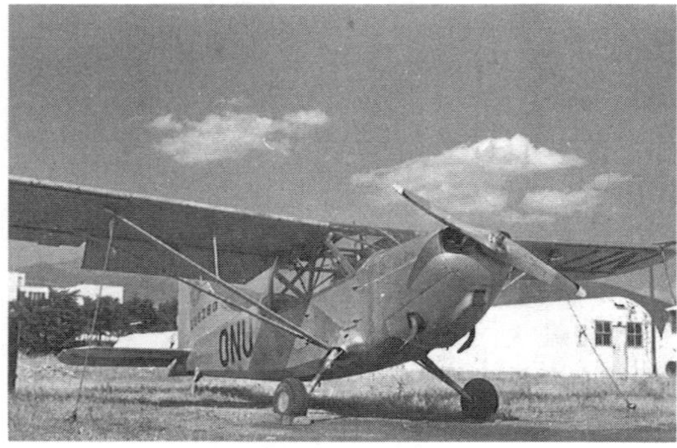

Capable of operating from short unimproved airstrips, the L-5 Sentinel delivered personnel, critical intelligence, and needed supplies to the front-line troops. On return flights, wounded soldiers were often evacuated to rear area field hospitals for medical treatment, providing a huge boost to the morale of combat troops fighting in remote areas.

L-5s were used for many other important activities, such as aerial photography, controlling vehicle convoys, and para-dropping food, medical supplies, and ammunition. It was also a valued asset in laying communication wire, distributing propaganda leaflets, spraying pesticide, transporting prisoners, and directing fighter-bombers to ground targets.

The L-5 was also popular with generals and other high-ranking officers for fast, efficient short-range transportation. It featured two side-by-side seats in the front and a third "jumpseat" in the rear, in which a small passenger could sit sideways. The design was easy to fly, and it was difficult to stall or spin.

The primary purpose as a liaison airplane was courier and communication work with the Army Air Forces and artillery spotting with Army Ground Forces. The later models were redesigned with a wider and deeper rear fuselage section and a rear door that allowed a patient on a stretcher to be loaded.

Nicknamed "The Flying Jeep," the L-5 demonstrated amazing versatility.

It was known to land and take off from tree-top platforms constructed above a thick Burmese jungle, which could not be cleared for more conventional airstrips. It also earned the nickname "Grasshopper." This term started with the Piper L-4 and the name spread to all light liaison aircraft.

Stinson Aircraft Company became a subsidiary of the Vultee Aircraft Corporation in 1940. Over 3,000 L-5s were constructed and served with distinction in Europe and in the Pacific.

Capable of operating from forward unimproved airstrips, the L-5 Sentinel delivered information and needed supplies to the front-line troops. On the return trip, it would evacuate the badly wounded soldiers to rear area field hospitals for medical attention.

TECHNICAL NOTES

Name: Stinson L-5 Sentinel; Nickname: Grasshopper, Flying Jeep

Role: Liaison / Observation / Light plane

Crew: 2, a pilot and observer

Armament: None

Powerplant: One Lycoming O-435-1 engine

Propeller: Two-bladed

Performance: Produced 185 hp
- Maximum speed: 130 mph
- Cruising speed: 90 mph
- Range: 360 miles
- Service ceiling: 15,600 feet

Dimensions:
- Wingspan: 34 ft (10.36 m)
- Length: 24 ft (7.34 m)
- Height: 7 ft 11 in (2.41 m)
- Weight: 2,050 lbs

Reference: www.warbirdalley.com/l5.htm
www.sentinelclub.org

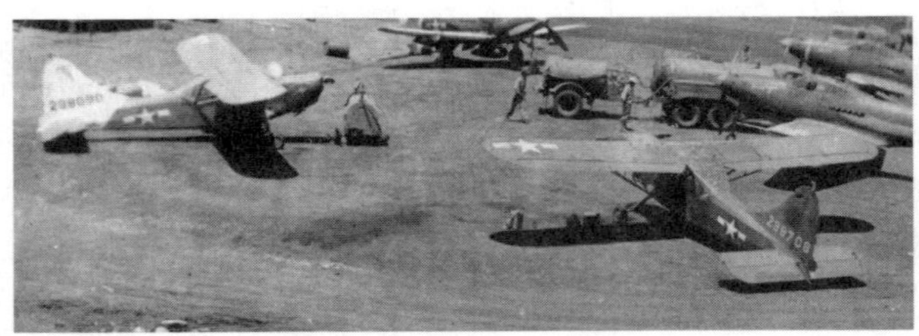

Stinson L-5 Sentinel.

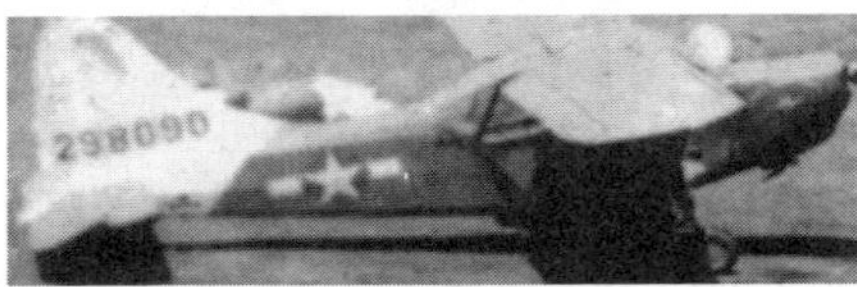

The Guinea Short Lines kangaroo logo is barely visible behind the propeller in this zoomed-in shot.

In the top photo, the two light planes in the front are the L-5 Sentinels, being re-fueled and having their batteries charged. The planes in the background are P-39 Airacobras. The L-5s are from the 25th Liaison Squadron ("Guinea Short Lines") and the P-39s are from the 71st Tactical Reconnaissance Group to which the 25th belonged. Photo taken in Saidor, New Guinea, near the ocean.

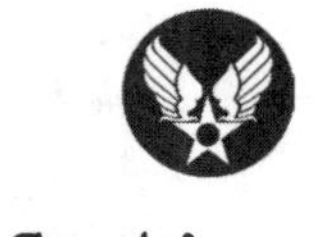

Section 14

WACO CG-4 Glider

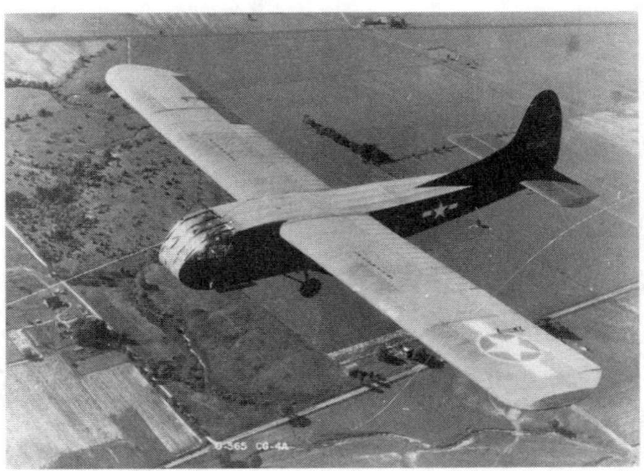

The WACO CG-4 became the first and most widely used U.S. troop glider of World War II. Of rugged steel tube, wood and fabric construction, the glider carried a crew of two and accommodated up to 15 fully equipped troops or two U.S. tons (1,814 kg) of cargo. The cockpit section was hinged so it could be lifted up over the top of the aircraft allowing cargo, usually troops, vehicles, artillery, or supplies, to enter or exit the open nose.

The WACO Aircraft Company initially started under the name Weaver Aircraft Company of Ohio but changed its name in 1928. Between the wars, the WACO name was well represented in the U.S. civil aircraft registry with more WACOs registered than the aircraft of any other company.

The films *A Bridge Too Far* and *The Longest Day* show gliders being towed by C-47 Gooney Birds. In *Operation Burma*, a glider is snatched from the ground by a low-flying C-47 and towed back to base.

In June 1945, in Mission Appari, American glider pilots delivered 11th Airborne Division troops to northern Luzon in the Philippines. This was the first and last glider mission in the Pacific and the last glider mission of WWII.

Most gliders did not arrive at their landing zones intact. They were usually heavily damaged or destroyed since they landed in fields, not runways.

The gliders of WWII and the sacrifices of the brave men who flew them earned their place in military history. These aircraft proved the high value of quickly transporting troops to distant locations and bringing them to the ground in cohesive units.

TECHNICAL NOTES

Name: WACO CG-4 Glider; Nicknames: Silent Wings, Flying Coffins, and Two Targets

Crew: 2

Armament: None

Powerplant: None

Number of propeller blades: None

Performance: Towed behind a C-47
Maximum speed: 130 mph behind tow plane

Gliding speed: 72 mph once released

Range: N/A

Service ceiling: N/A

Dimensions:
Wingspan: 83.5 ft
Length: 48 ft
Height: 15 ft 4 in
Weight: 3,440 lbs empty

Payload: 15 troops or 4,000 lbs (1,814 kg) of cargo.

Reference: www.fiddlersgreen.net/models/aircraft/WACO-CG-4.html
www.combatreform.org/gliders.htm

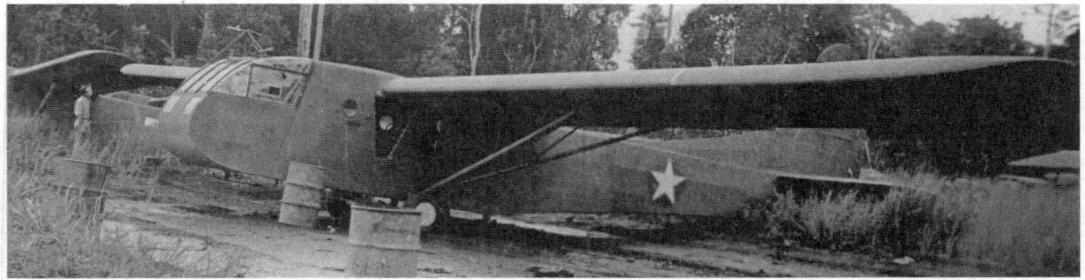

WACO CG-4 Glider.
Although not totally visible, there are three gliders on the field in the above photo.

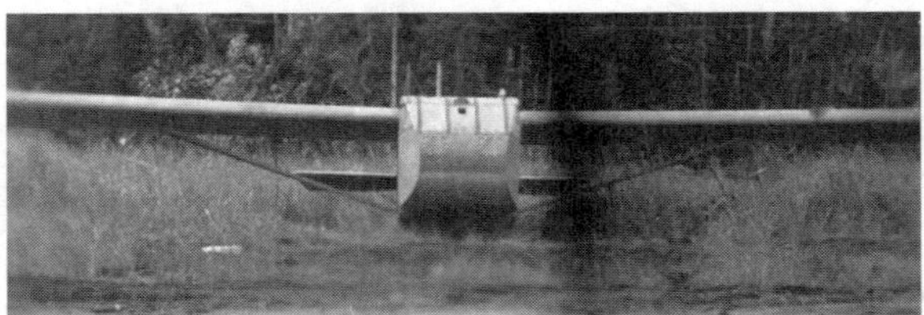

The cockpit section was hinged so it could be lifted up over the top of the aircraft, allowing troops or vehicles to enter or exit the open nose.

WEBSITES LISTED IN THE PLANES APPENDIX

All of these websites were in working order at press time. If the site is not found, use a search engine or or video site such as Youtube to to find what you are looking for.

www.b24bestweb.com/butchersdaughter2.htm
www.usaaf-noseart.co.uk/misslist-64053.htm
www.pacificwrecks.com/aircraft/b-24/42-40348.html
www.b24bestweb.com/hohum2.htm
www.b24bestweb.com/pappyspassion2.htm
www.b24bestweb.com/yankeedoodledandy-v1-2.htm
www.usaaf-noseart.co.uk/merk-wango.htm
www.b24bestweb.com/flyingfannie1.htm
www.b24bestweb.com/sweetracket2.htm
www.ozatwar.com/90thbg.htm
www.boeing.com/boeing/history/boeing/b17.page
www.nationalmuseum.af.mil/factsheets/factsheet.asp?id=476
www.nose-art.net/kenwilson.htm
www.fineartofdecals.com/goodies/148-treasures-allied/
bathead.com/noseart1.html
www.pacificwrecks.com/aircraft/b-25/41-30084.html
www.nationalmuseum.af.mil/factsheets/factsheet.asp?id=2957
8thattacksqdnassoc.tripod.com/WWIIa.html
www.lockheedmartin.com/us/100years/stories/p-38.html
p38assn.org
www.nationalmuseum.af.mil/factsheets/factsheet.asp?id=495
secure.wikimedia.org/wikipedia/en/wiki/Edward_%22Porky%22_Cragg
www.warbirdregistry.org/p38registry/p38-4453015.html

www.pacificwrecks.com/aircraft/p-38/44-24155.html

www.aviation-history.com/bell/p39.html

historyofwar.org

www.nationalmuseum.af.mil/factsheets/factsheet.asp?id=2207

www.nationalmuseum.af.mil/factsheets/factsheet.asp?id=2208

www.chuckhawks.com/p40.htm

replicainscale.blogspot.com/2010_09_01_archive.html

www.nationalmuseum.af.mil/factsheets/factsheet.asp?id=2213

www.historyofwar.org/articles/weapons_P-47_pacific.html

www.warbirdalley.com/p47.htm

www.boeing.com/boeing/history/mdc/skytrain.page

www.warbirdalley.com/c47.htm

www.historyofwar.org/articles/weapons_douglas_C-54_skymaster.html

www.warbirdalley.com/c54.htm

www.warbirdsresourcegroup.org/URG/c54skymaster.html

www.warbirdalley.com/cat.htm

www.nationalmuseum.af.mil/factsheets/factsheet.asp?id=522

www.hq.nasa.gov/office/pao/History/SP-468/ch8-7.htm

www.flyingclippers.com/M130.html

www.warbirdalley.com/l5.htm

www.sentinelclub.org

www.fiddlersgreen.net/models/aircraft/WACO-CG-4.html

www.combatreform.org/gliders.htm

APPENDIX 2

South Pacific Natives in Daily Life

The wonderful thing about a series of pictures is that it allows you to be an eyewitness to what is in the scene. No matter what it is or where it is, you are transported alongside the photographer.

My father had uncles who fought in World War I and brought back pictures to show their families. His uncles may have encouraged him to do the same. He took many incredible photos of what he was seeing in these foreign lands to show his family back home on the farm.

He had no desire to be in the spotlight. He had no intentions of being a photojournalist, but as it turns out, that is what happened. Thankfully, he wrote the date on the back of most of the pictures. This, in conjunction with the daily Military Record entries, enabled me, 70 years later, to trace my father's steps from boot camp to war and home again.

The following section shows the New Guinea natives going about life as usual. It turned out they liked having their picture taken. They were happy to stop what they were doing and pose for the camera.

Some men wore more clothes than others. The women usually went topless and wore either a grass or cloth skirt while the little children usually wore nothing. Please be forewarned that the following contains indigenous nudity. If you are intrigued by a true representation of what my dad saw and photographed along his journey abroad, please continue on and enjoy a glimpse into the daily life of the South Pacific natives.

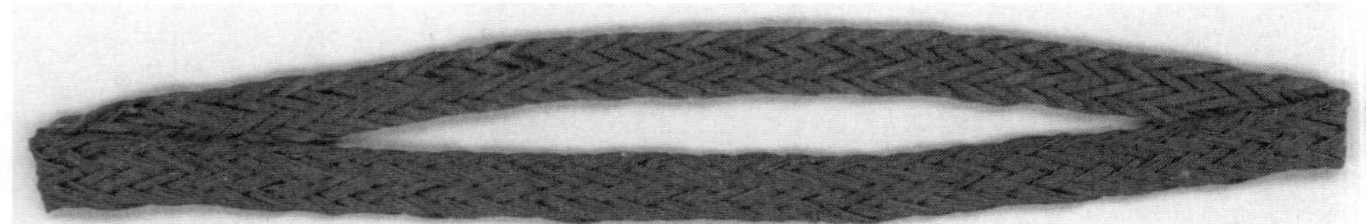

A New Guinea armband Dad brought back as a souvenir.

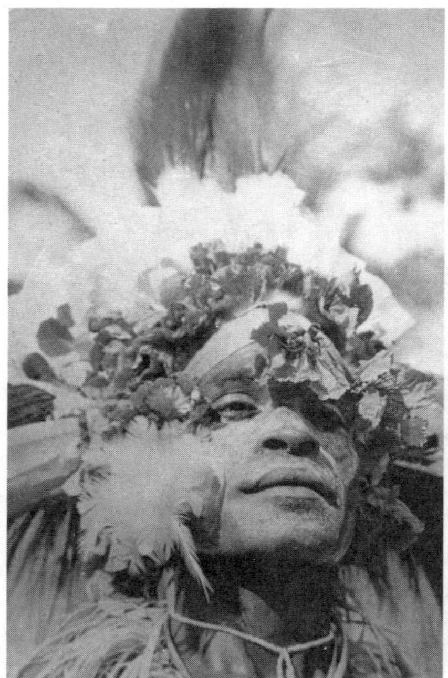

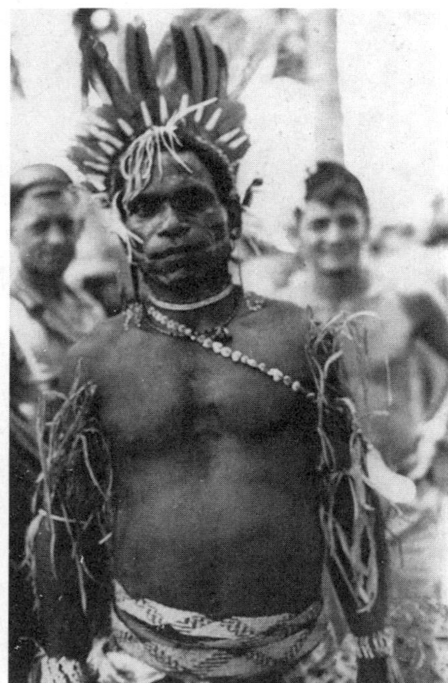

Native New Guinea dancers.

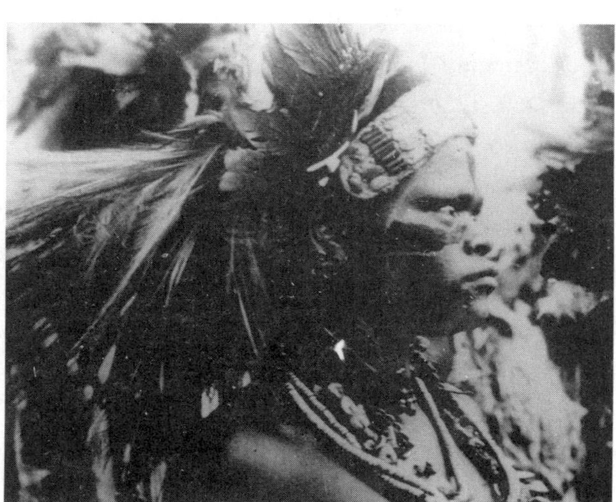

Native dancer. Dobodura, New Guinea, 1943.

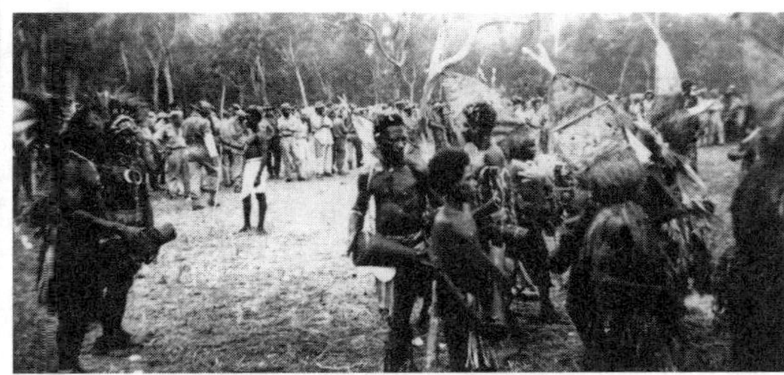

Dancing and playing their kundu drums in Dobodura, New Guinea, 1943.

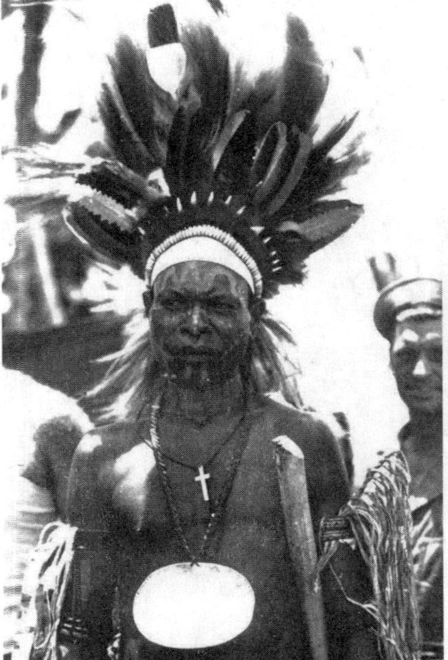

Dobodura, New Guinea, 1943.

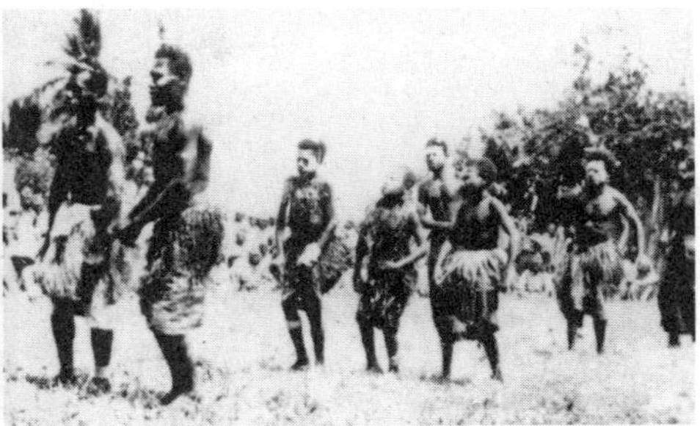

Warrior dancers. Saidor, New Guinea 1944.

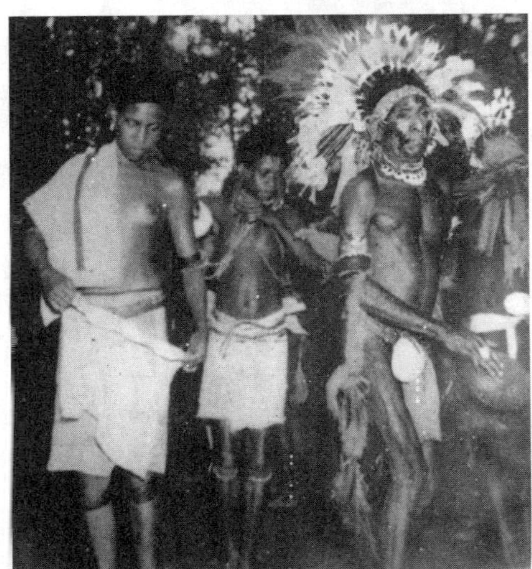

Saidor, New Guinea 1944.

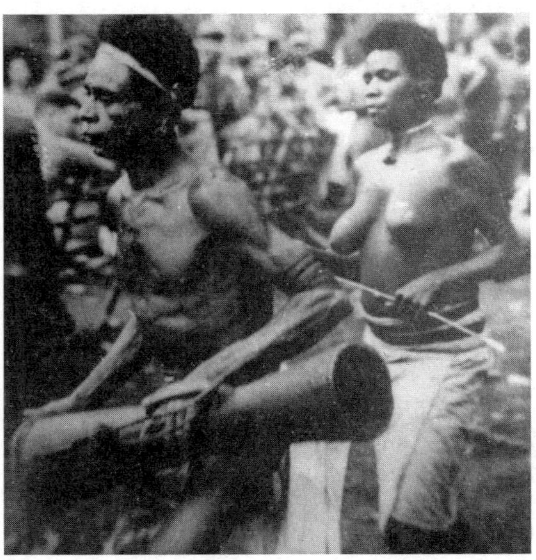

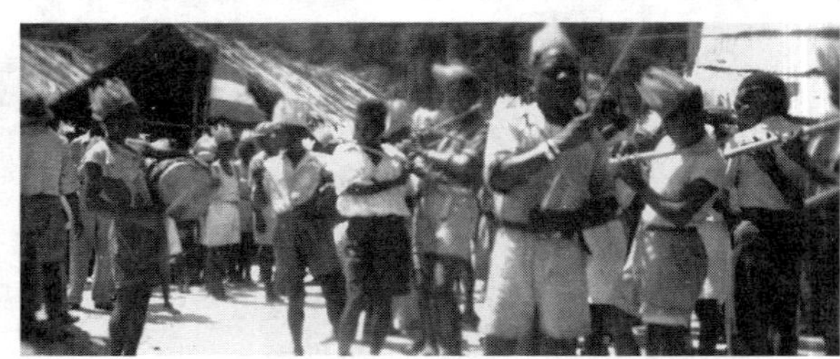

Native celebration given in honor of Queen Wilhelmina's birthday. This is the parade band, consisting of drums and bamboo flutes. Biak, Aug. 31, 1944.

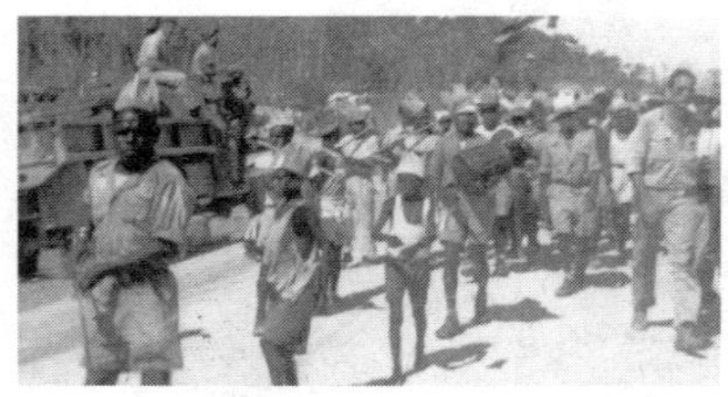

The beginning of the celebration, as the marching band comes along. Aug. 31, 1944. Biak.

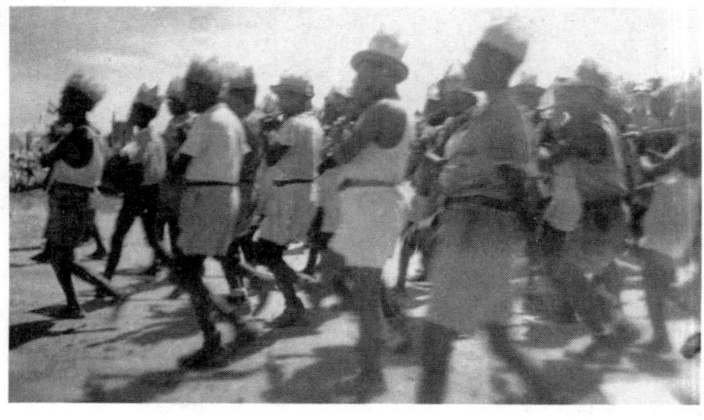

Parade is passing by while the band is playing their bamboo flutes.

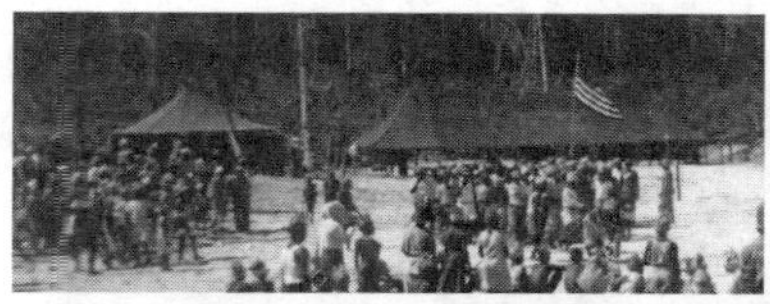

The dance on Queen Wilhelmina's birthday. Aug. 31, 1944.

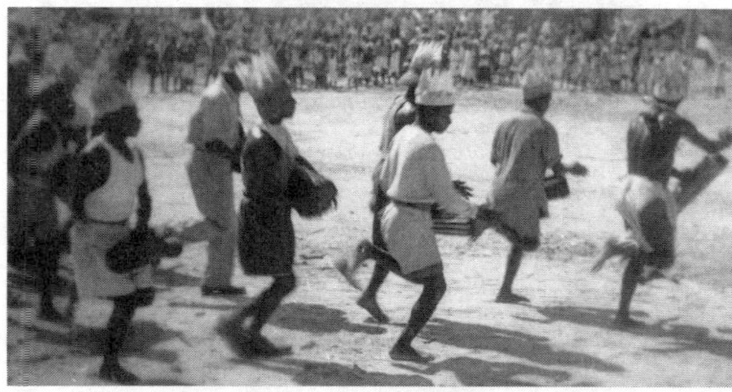

Dad wrote "Boogie Woogie" on the back of this photo. Biak, Aug. 31, 1944.

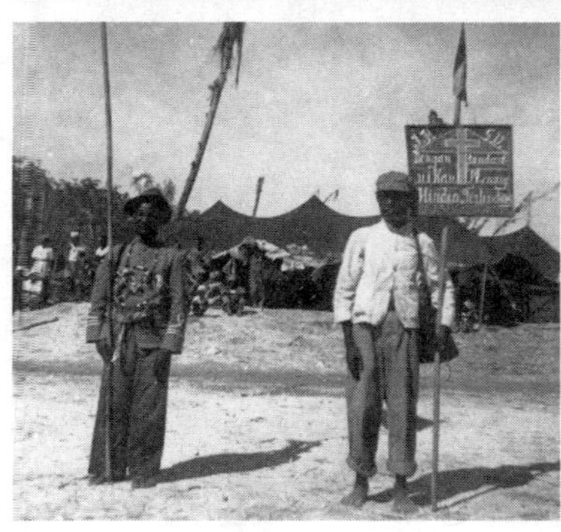

The "Boss" (left) holding the Dutch flag and the other fellow is holding the sign board of their religion.

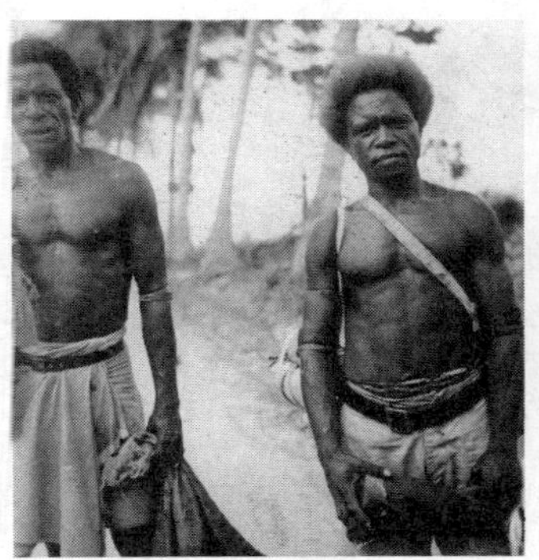

Drummer holding his kundu drum. Biak, Aug. 1944.

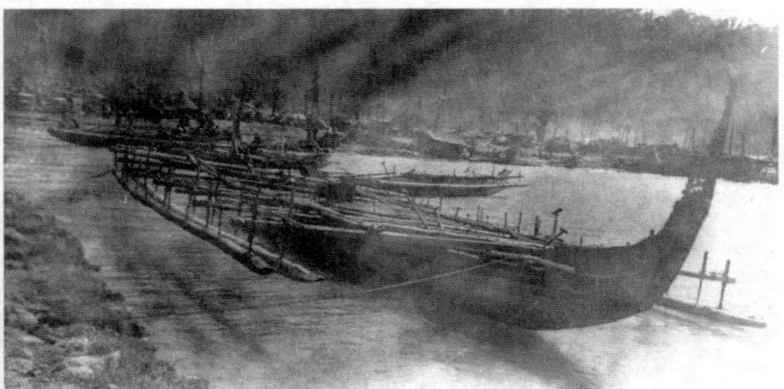

Long outrigger canoe ready for the canoe race.

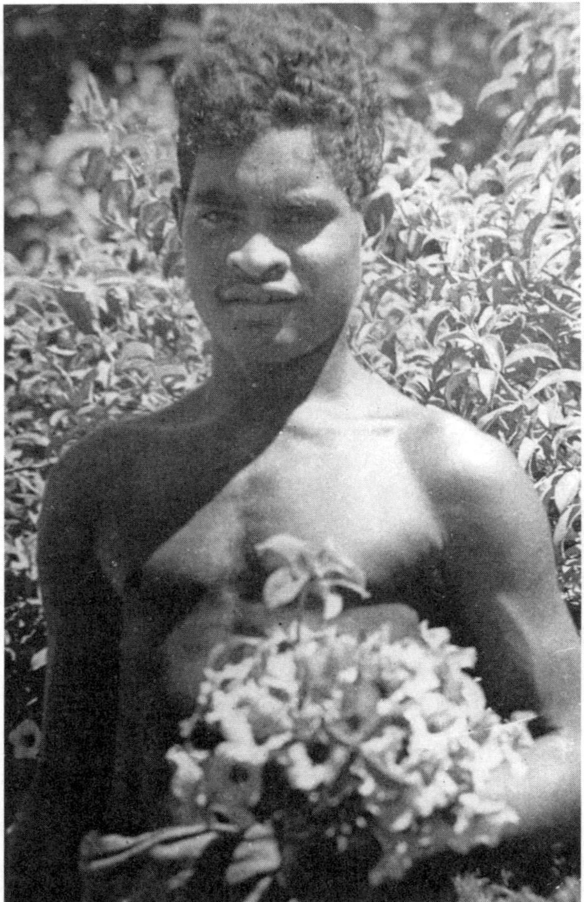

Natives of Saidor, New Guinea, May 1944.

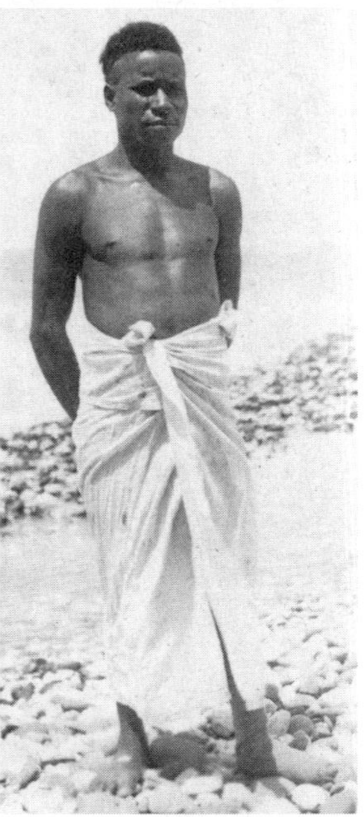

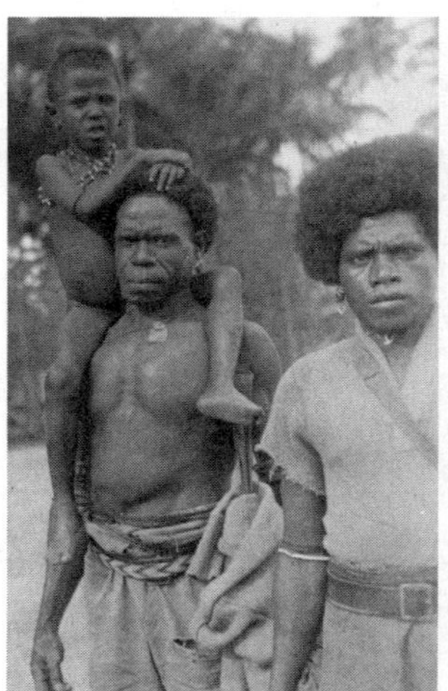

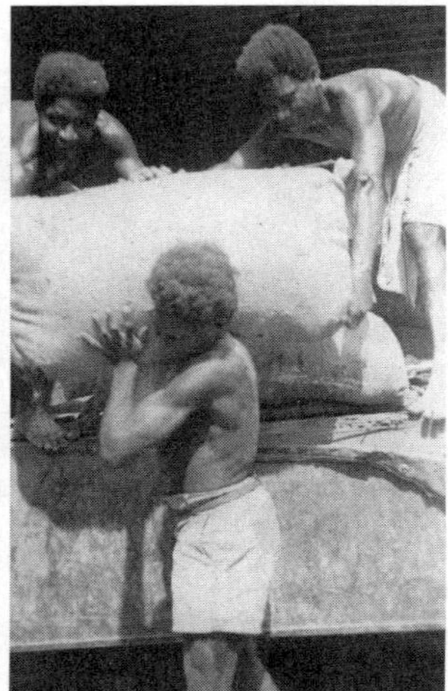

Hauling supplies.

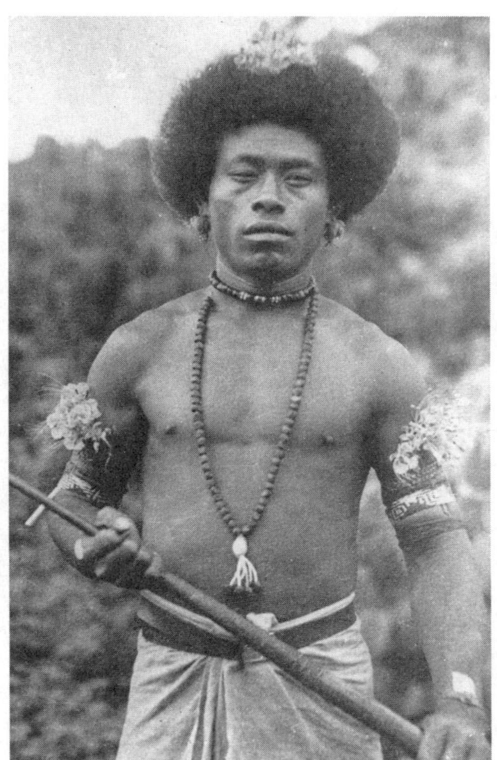

New Guinea warrior.

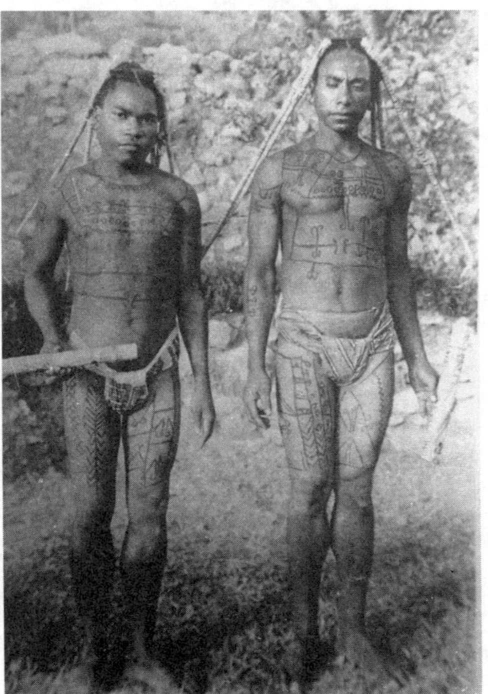

Tattooed warriors of New Guinea.

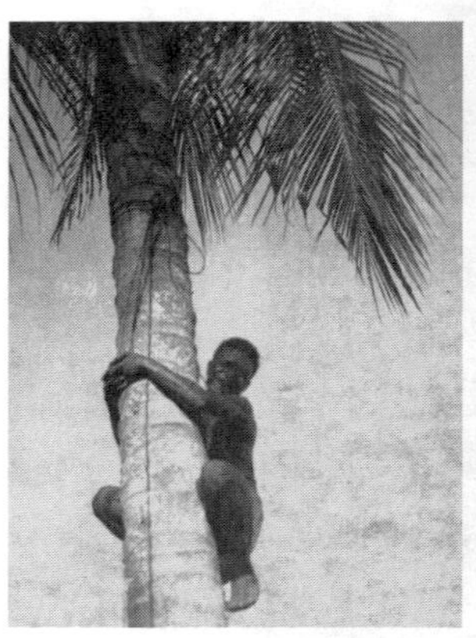

Climbing to get coconuts. Saidor, New Guinea, May 1944.

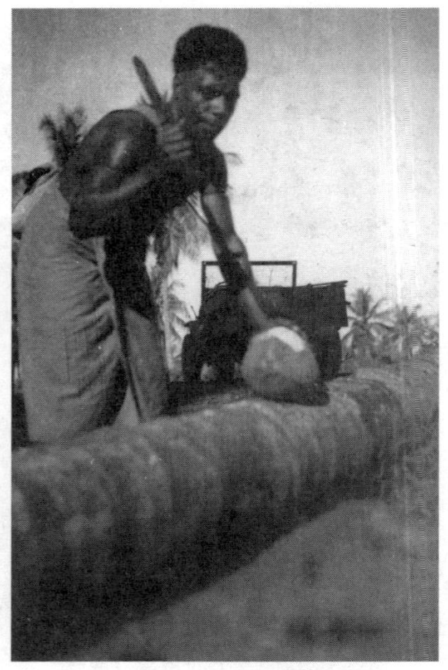

Opening a coconut. Saidor, New Guinea, May 1944.

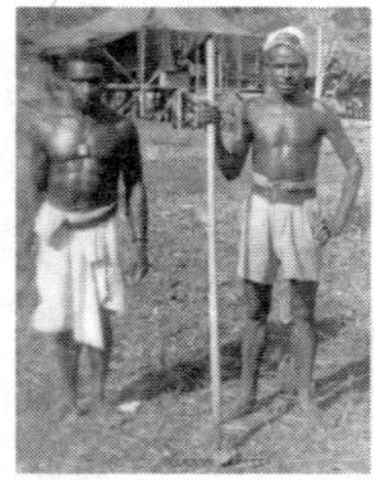

Garden helpers.

Dad created a makeshift grass skirt with string and glued it on this photo to hide his privates. Saidor, New Guinea, 1944.

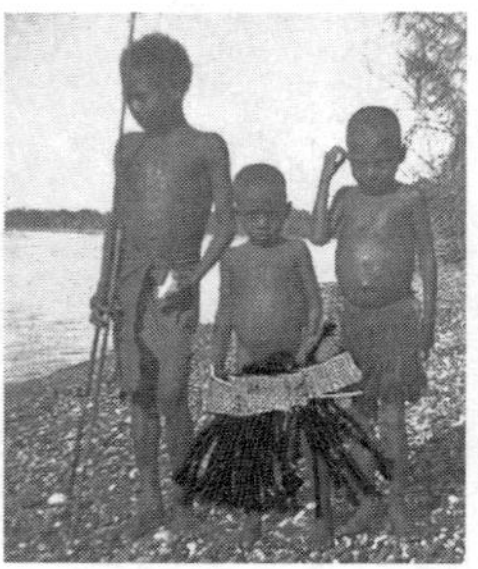

Mother feeding her baby.

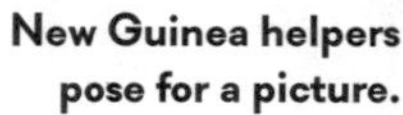

New Guinea helpers pose for a picture.

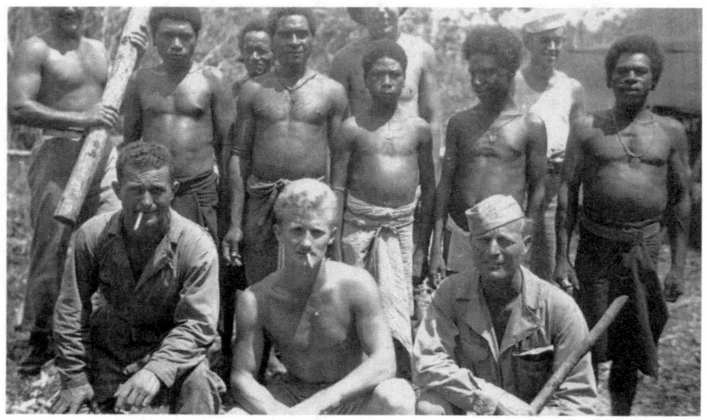

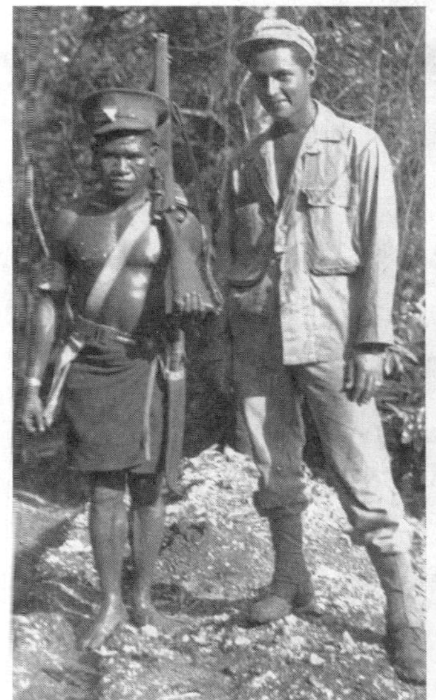

Native Sgt. of Aussie Army played a big part in training the local militia. He is with my father. Saidor, New Guinea, April 1944.

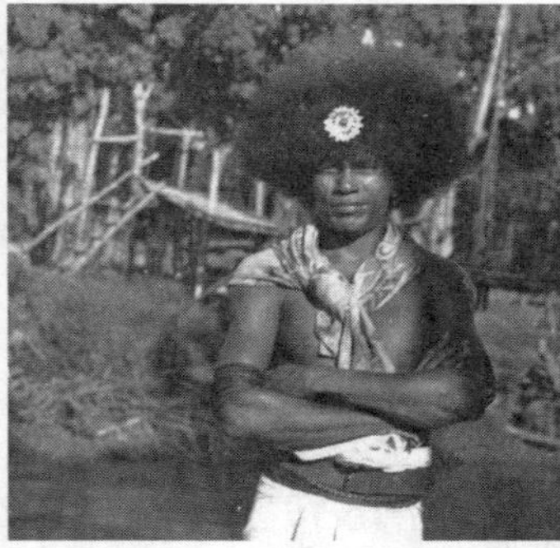

One of the "Fuzzy Wuzzy Angels" who was instrumental in helping carry wounded allied soldiers to safety and to hospital tents for treatment of their injuries.

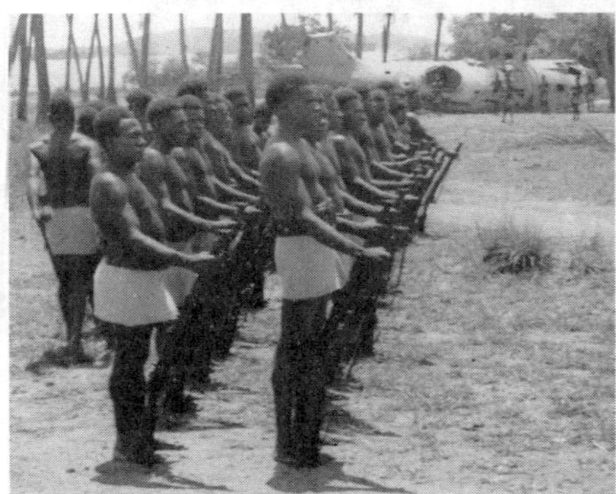

Training the local militia at Saidor. The fuselage of a PBY Catalina is in the background.

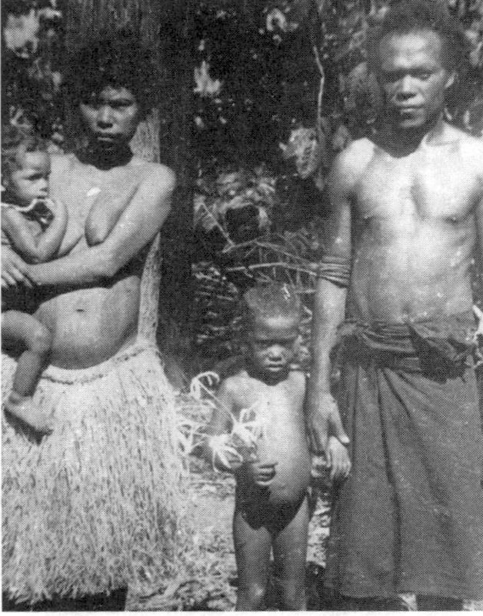

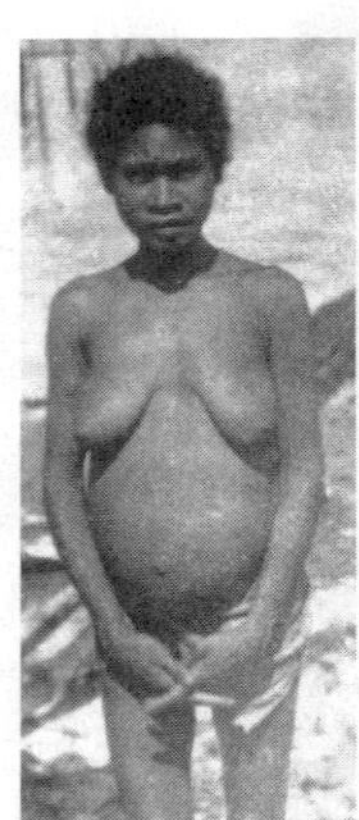

On Biak Island, 1944.

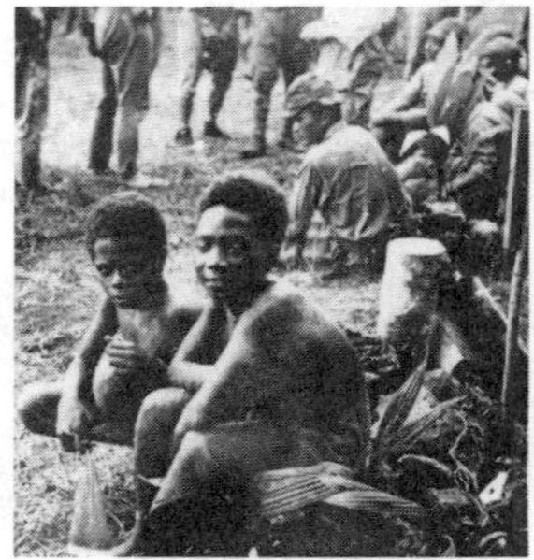

New Guinea natives with Japanese soldiers, 1944. Photo is from a captured Japanese camera.

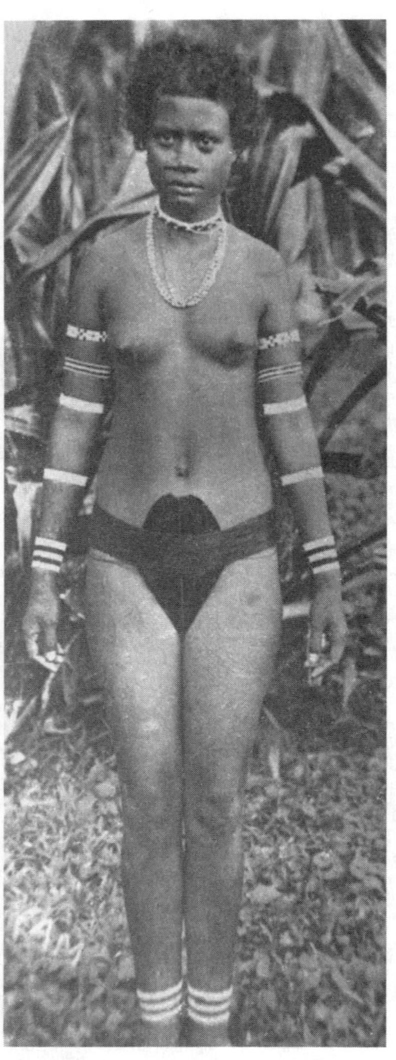

A stylish girl sporting a New Guinea bikini and arm and leg bracelets.

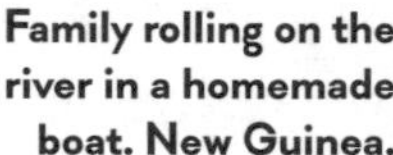

Family rolling on the river in a homemade boat. New Guinea.

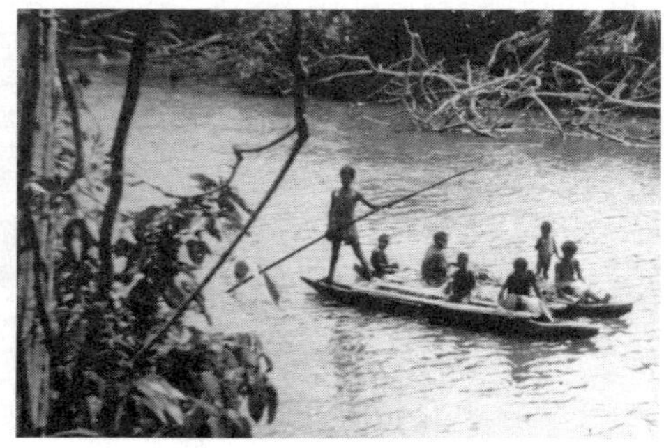

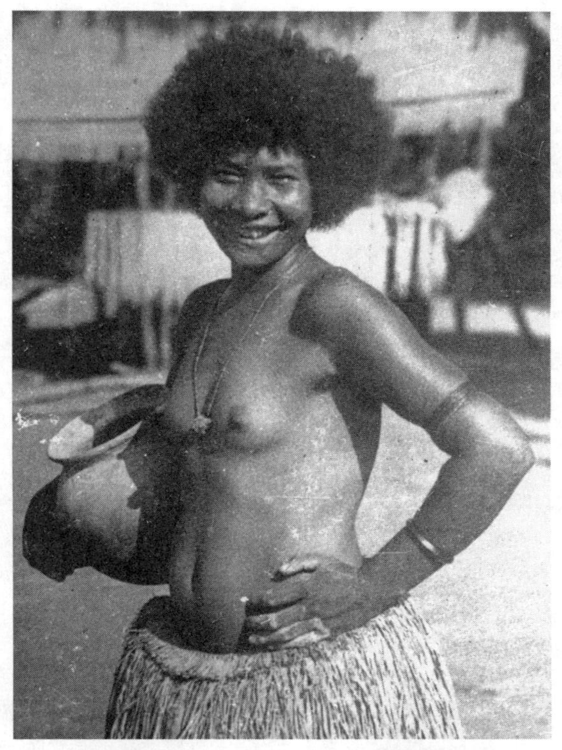

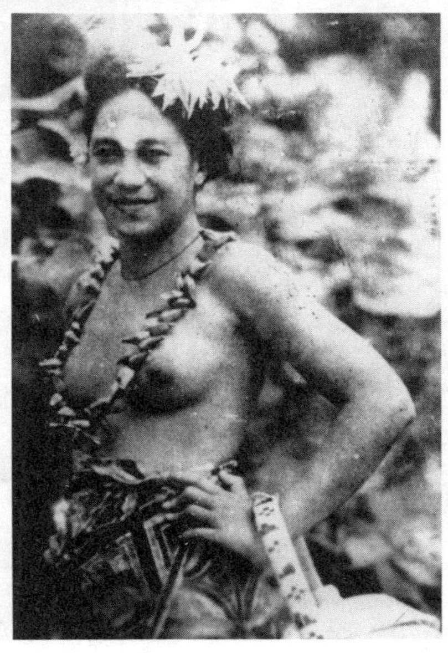

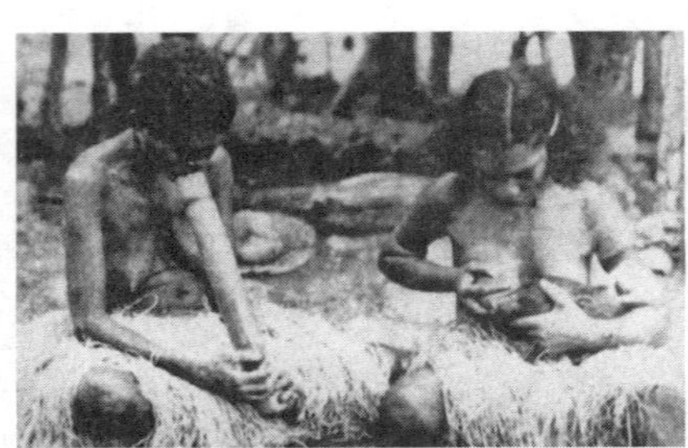

Nursing a small pig.
Her friend is playing the flute.

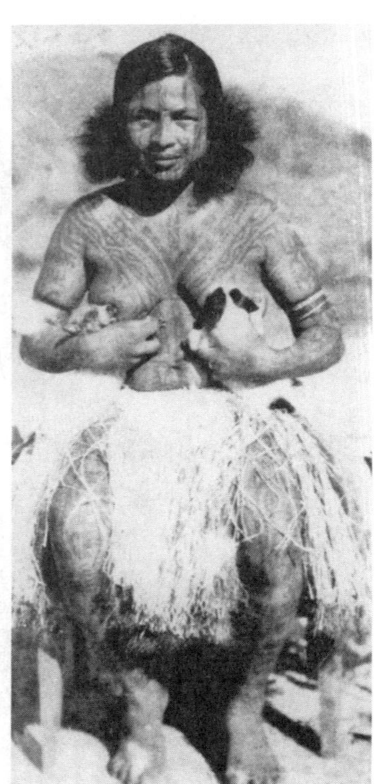

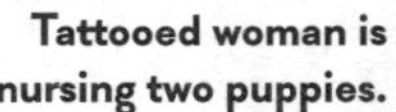

Tattooed woman is nursing two puppies.

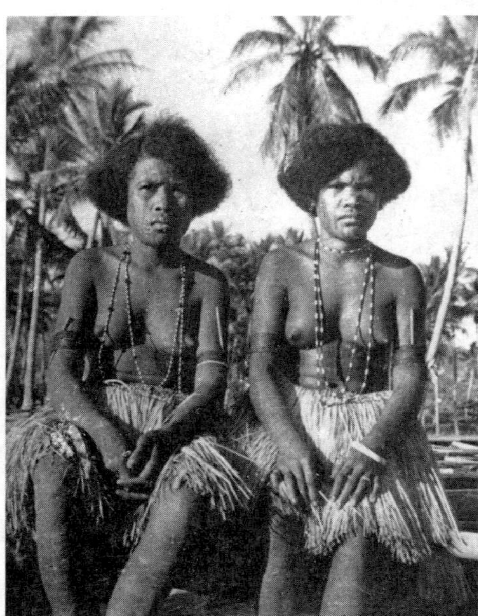

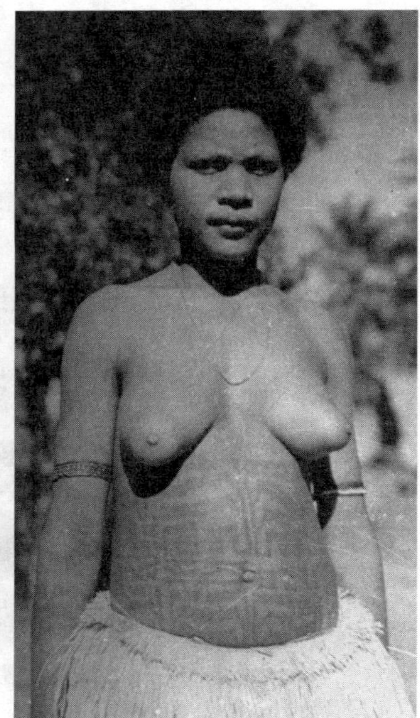

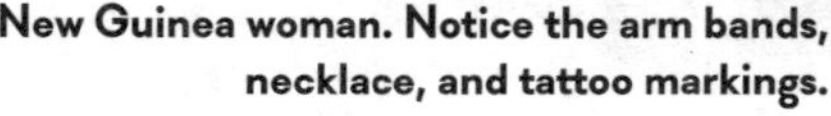

New Guinea woman. Notice the arm bands, necklace, and tattoo markings.

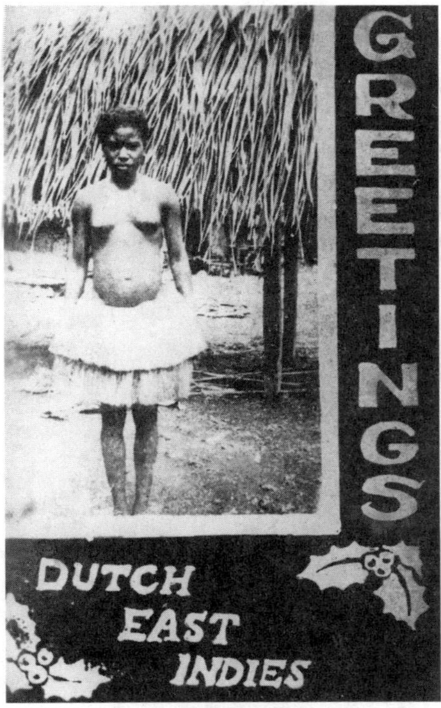

Christmas card.

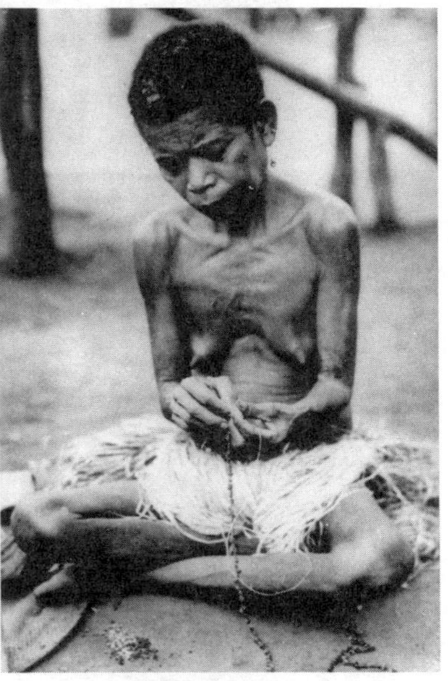

Native woman working her craft.

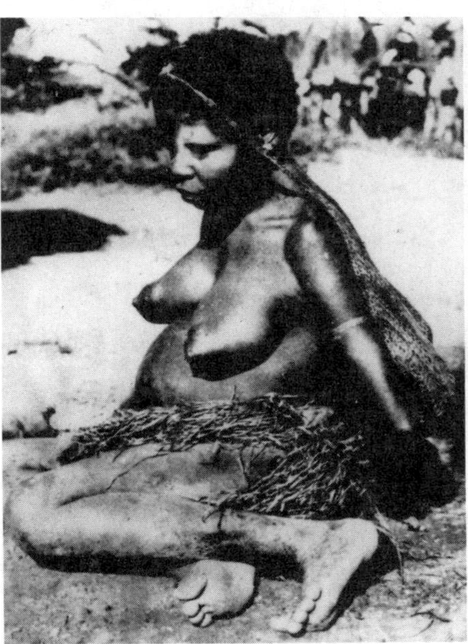

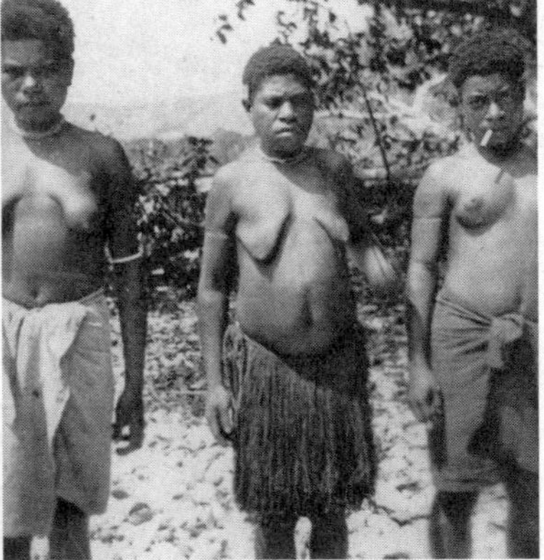

According to Dad, this native woman was in labor and about to deliver her baby where she was seated.

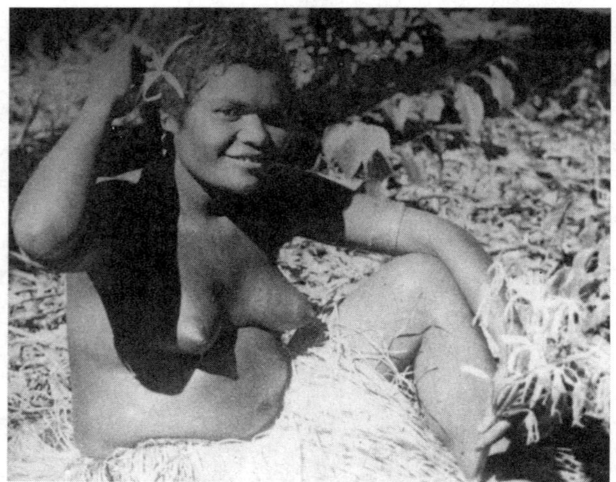

Showing off the pretty flower in her hair.

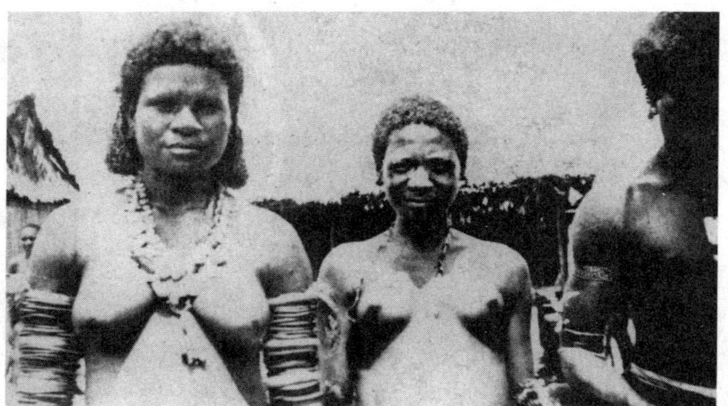

Native woman wearing many armbands.

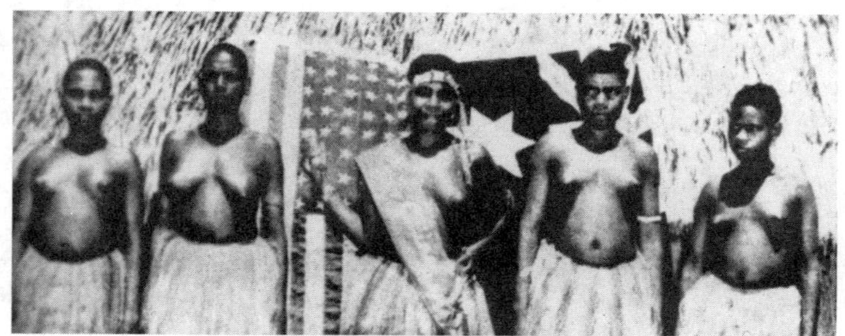

Miss New Guinea 1943. In Dobodura.

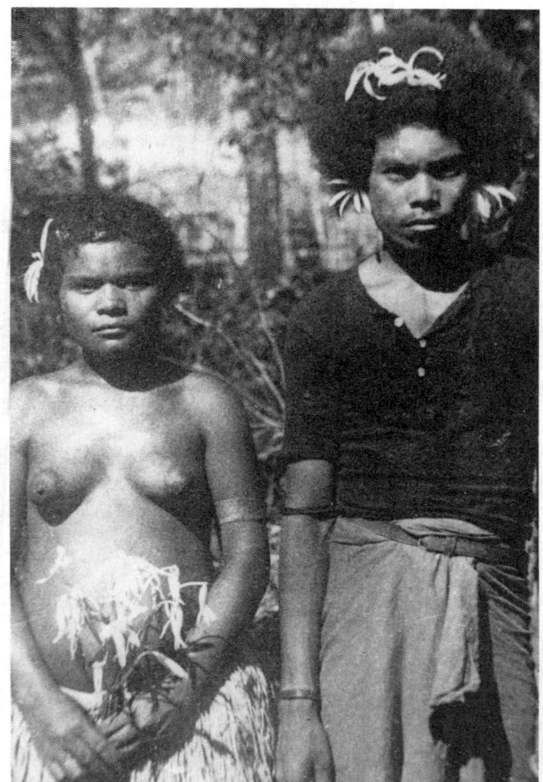

Her man has some flowers too.

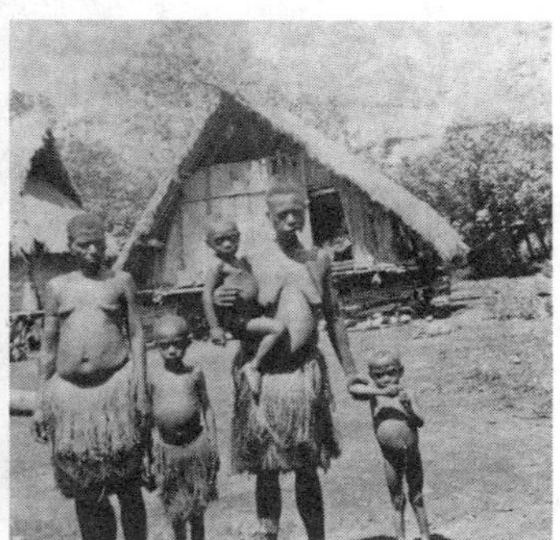

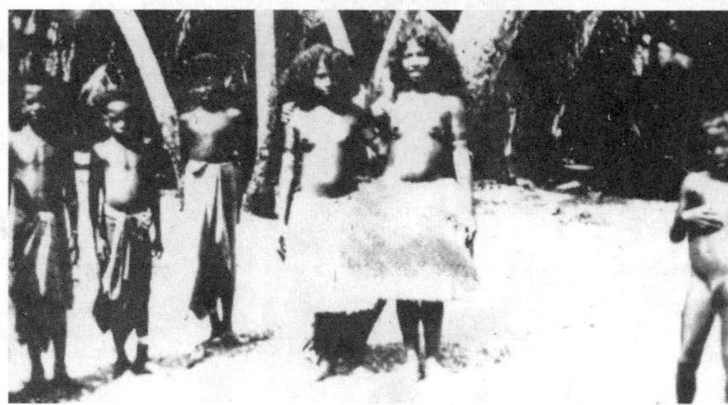

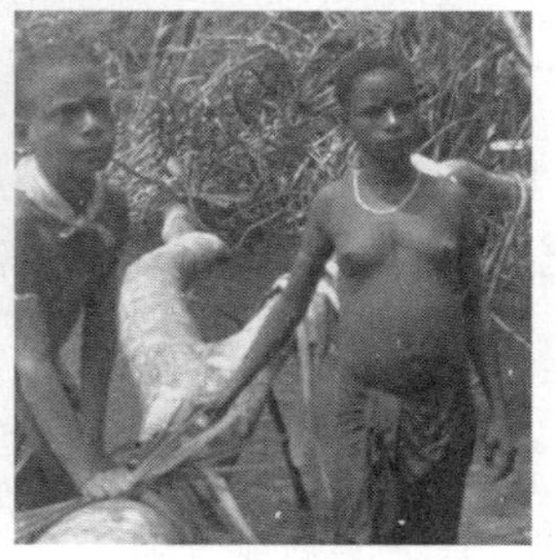

Young New Guinea natives in the river.

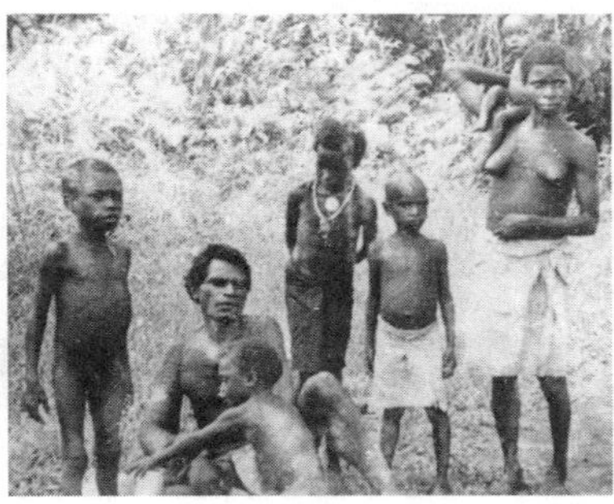

A father and mother with five children.

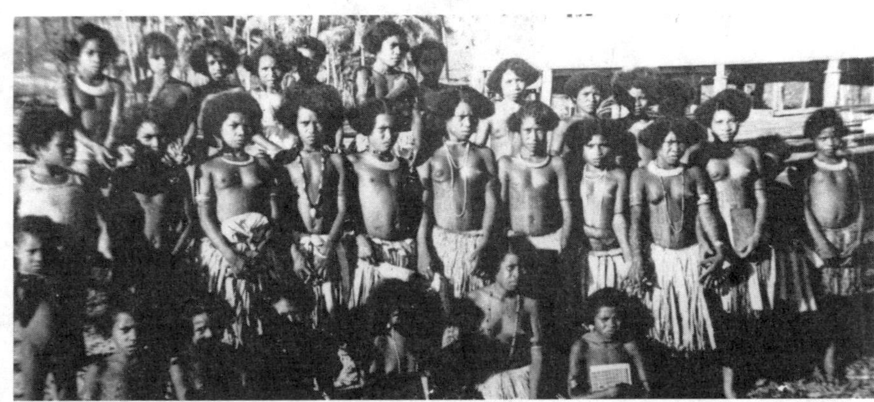

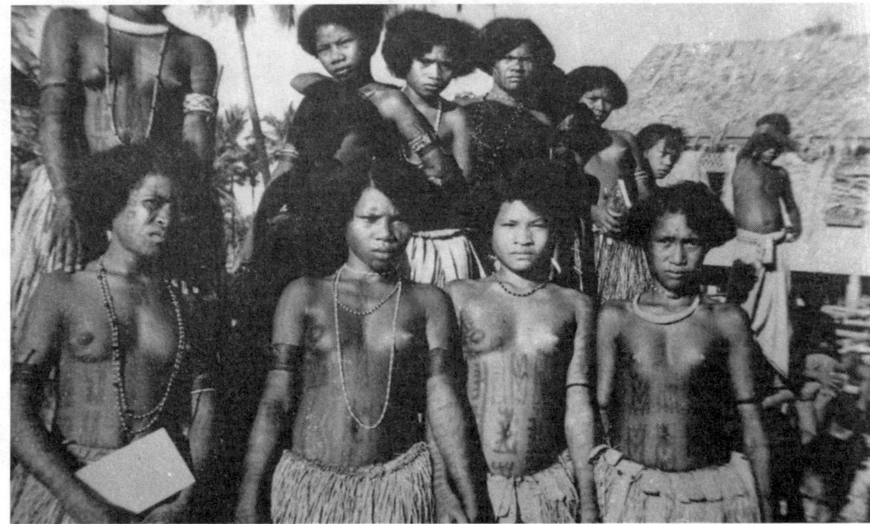

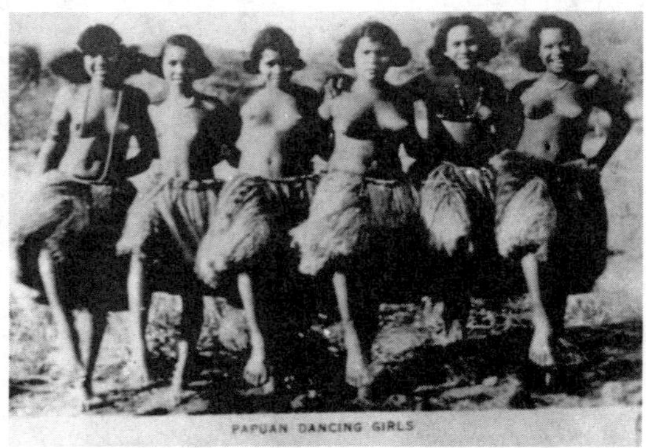

Papuan Dancing Girls, New Guinea.

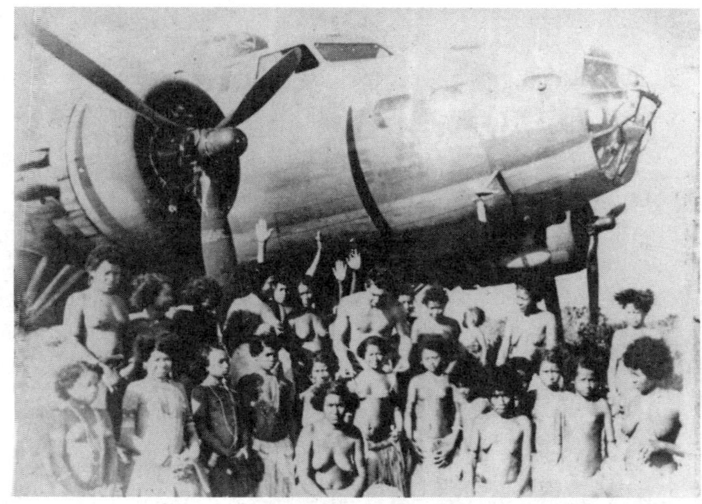

New Guinea natives beneath a Boeing B-17 bomber, 1944.

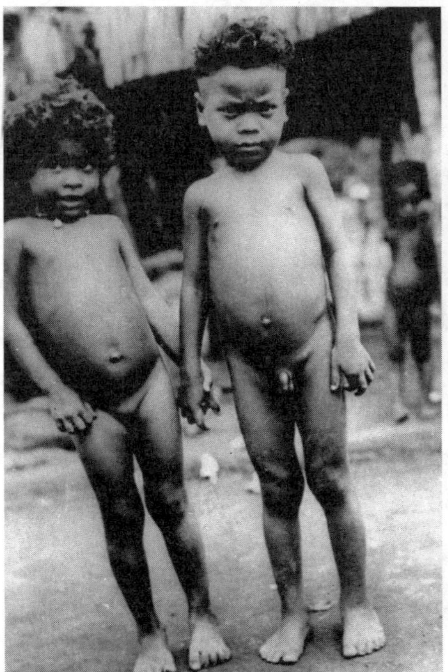

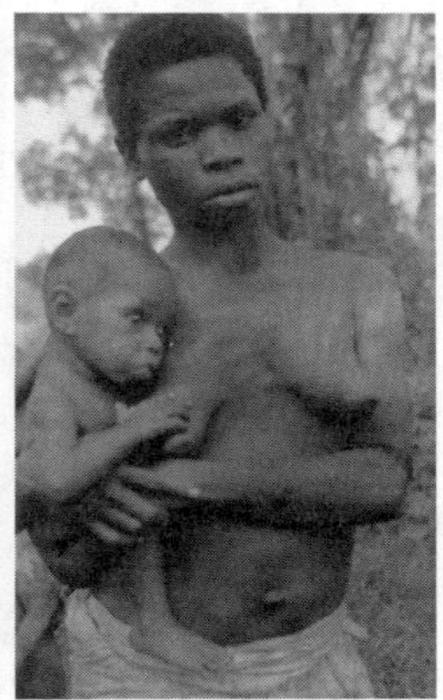

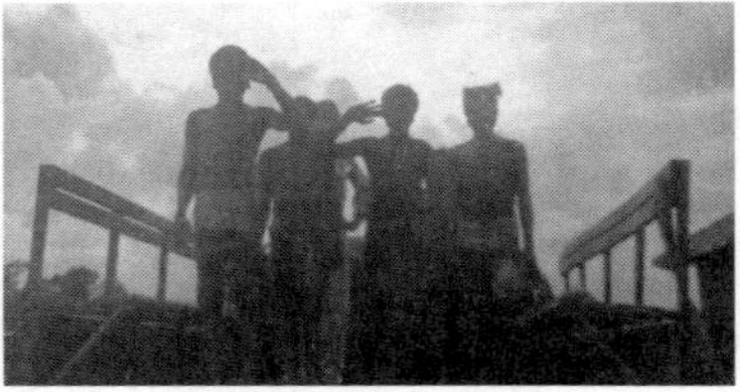

Saluting natives.

Glossary

AA, or Ack-Ack – Anti-aircraft guns.

airdrome – Air strip runway, usually with a control tower; airport. It was also spelled aerodrome.

alert area – A site adjacent to a runway where fighter aircraft, fueled, armed, and ready to take off, would be parked.

alert hut – A hut or building in the alert area where pilots would be on duty, ready to man their aircraft should enemy aircraft be detected in the area.

Arisaka rifle – The official rifle of the Imperial Japanese Army.

Aussie – Nickname for Australian.

BACEPOW – The Bay Area Civilian Ex-Prisoners of War organization is dedicated to supporting and telling the story of all of the people who were captives of the Japanese.

Bailey bridge – A prefabricated steel bridge that was assembled in the field; it came in a variety of sizes.

battalion – My father's battalion was the 863rd Engineer Aviation Battalion and was comprised of 777 enlisted men and 29 officers.

Biscuit Bombers – Nickname for the DouglasC-47 Skytrain, which delivered food and supplies to the troops.

bore sighting range – Firing range targets that pilots could shoot at while sitting in their plane cockpits to determine the accuracy of their guns.

corduroy road – An impromptu road made of split logs.

corvette – A small ship.

dispersal area – A parking lot for airplanes, designed in such a way so planes would be scattered, as opposed to being parked wingtip to wingtip, to lessen the damage done by enemy planes dropping bombs or strafing.

disrupted – A piece of war machinery that has been damaged and is no longer working.

eight-yard pan – A heavy road machine that scraped up excess dirt.

EM – Enlisted Men.

H&S Company – Headquarters and Service Company, the company my father was in. There were four companies in the 863rd Engineer Aviation Battalion: A, B, C and H & S.

hardstanding – A plane parking spot that has been packed and leveled by heavy equipment. Also called hardstand.

Japs – Nickname for Japanese.

Liberty ships - Cargo ships built in the United States during World War II. They were cheap and quick to build and came to symbolize U.S. wartime industrial output. Eighteen American shipyards built 2,710 Liberty ships between 1941 and 1945.

LST – Landing Ship, Tank. This ship carried troops and equipment to their destination.

mess hall – Place for the soldiers to eat; lunchroom.

Nips – Nickname for Japanese, from the name Nippon or Nipponese.

PX – Post Exchange; a military convenience store.

revetment – A high, earthen horseshoe-shaped barrier or wall built by heavy, road building machinery to protect parked airplanes. It was a barricade from bombs exploding nearby or from enemy planes strafing the area. Each hardstanding had its own protective revetment.

steel mat – Also called Marston Matting, Pierced Steel Plank (PSP), or PSP Mat. These steel mats covered the packed and leveled airstrip runways.

Victory ships - The Victory ship was a type of cargo ship produced in large numbers by North American shipyards during World War II to replace losses caused by German submarines. Based on the earlier Liberty ship, but with more powerful engines, 531 Victory ships were built.

VOCO – Verbal Order of Commanding Officer.

ABOUT THE AUTHOR

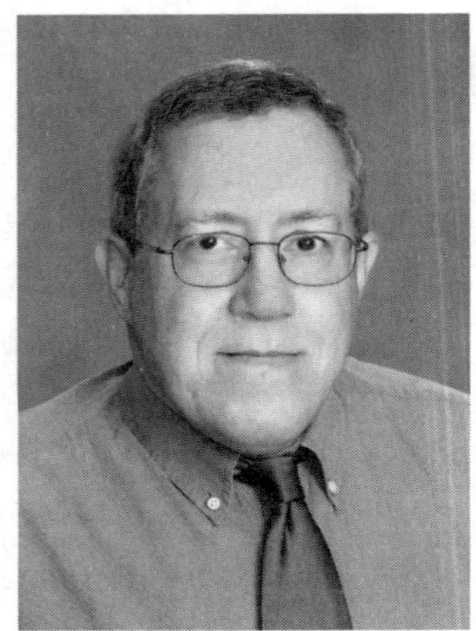

Neal Bertrand was born and raised in Opelousas, Louisiana, in the heart of Cajun Country. Cajun and Cooking are synonymous to those familiar with the culture, so it's no coincidence that Neal started his company, Cypress Cove Publishing, putting out cookbooks. It's also no coincidence that his moniker since 2005 has been The Cookbook Dude. He is quick to recall that family holidays always revolved around food, no matter where he was. Whether it was barbecued steak from the cattle his family raised, or gumbo, Neal grew up with food and fun.

The cookbooks he has written and published have sold over 100,000 copies, and they are available both as print and e-book on Amazon, BN.com and through his website at www.cypresscovepublishing.com

In 2009, Neal and his son Jeremy began scanning and photo-editing the war pictures of Neal's dad. Neither had ever seen the backs of the photos until then because they had been attached to the pages of three photo albums kept in a cedar chest in the hallway of Neal's childhood home. The photos were put in the albums in no particular order. But once he figured out the timeline, Neal was able to organize them by country, month, and year. After six months of researching battalion diary entries and culling the photos, Neal was able to trace his father's steps from boot camp to war and back home and he began compiling his findings into *Dad's War Photos*.

Prior to starting the war book, Neal was involved in charting his genealogy. He joined two genealogy societies and charted his ancestry back ten generations. Genealogy is one of Neal's favorite pastimes, as is starting a major creative project and watching it come to life, which he has done admirably with *Dad's War Photos*.

Visit our website at www.DadsWarPhotos.com

ORDER FORM

To order additional copies of *Dad's War Photos: Adventures in the South Pacific*, please make a copy of this Order Form, fill in the blanks, and mail your check, money order, or credit card authorization to address below.
Make payable to Cypress Cove Publishing.

Cypress Cove Publishing
ATTN: Order Dept.
PO Box 91195
Lafayette, LA 70509-1195

THIS BOOK MAKES A GREAT GIFT!

Do you know a WWII veteran? Or a descendant of a WWII veteran?
Or perhaps you would like to donate copies to a school or library.

❑ **YES, this is a gift:** *If you are buying for someone beside yourself, or in addition to yourself, please check the box and write the name and address of the recipients on a separate sheet of paper. We will ship the books to them on your behalf!*

❑ **YES! Please rush:**

_____ copies of softcover version x $19.95 each = $________

_____ copies of hardcover version x $29.95 each = $________

subtotal = $________

Louisiana residents please add 4% sales tax = $________

Shipping: $5.00 for 1st book, $1 each additional book = $________

Total $________

❑ Charge $___________ to my ❑ Visa ❑ MasterCard ❑ Discover ❑ AmEx

Card # ______________________________ Exp. Date ___/___ CVN#______

Signature ____

RUSH TO THIS ADDRESS:

Name ____

Address ____

City ____ State _______ ZIP ____________

Telephone __________________________ email _____________________________________

FOR MORE INFORMATION

EMAIL neal@CypressCovePublishing.com WEBSITE Dad'sWarPhotos.com

QUESTIONS? Want to order by phone? Call toll-free (888) 606-3257.